THE MEASURE OF AMERICA

THE MEASURE OF AMERICA

AMERICAN HUMAN DEVELOPMENT REPORT 2008–2009

,

WRITTEN, COMPILED, AND EDITED BY
Sarah Burd-Sharps, Kristen Lewis, and Eduardo Borges Martins

WITH FOREWORDS BY
Amartya Sen and William H. Draper III

A joint publication of the **Social Science Research Council**
and **Columbia University Press**

COLUMBIA UNIVERSITY PRESS

Publishers Since 1893
New York   Chichester, West Sussex

Library of Congress Cataloging-in-Publication Data

Burd-Sharps, Sarah.
    The Measure of America : American human development report, 2008–2009 / written, compiled,
and edited by Sarah Burd-Sharps, Kristen Lewis, and Eduardo Borges Martins ; with forewords by
Amartya Sen and William H. Draper.
        p. cm.
    ISBN 978-0-231-15494-9 (cloth : alk. paper) — ISBN 978-0-231-15495-6 (pbk. : alk. paper) —
ISBN 978-0-231-51090-5 (e-book)
    1. United States—Social conditions—1980—Statistics 2. Quality of life—United States—Statistics.
    3. Social indicators—United States—Statistics.
I. Lewis, Kristen. II. Martins, Eduardo Borges. III. Title.

HN59.2.B865 2008
306.0973'090511—dc22

                                                                                        2008020177

Printed in the United States of America

Designed by Humantific | UnderstandingLab, Inc.

c 10 9 8 7 6 5 4 3 2 1
p 10 9 8 7 6 5 4 3 2 1

Team for the preparation of American Human Development Report 2008–2009

AMERICAN HUMAN DEVELOPMENT PROJECT CODIRECTORS
Sarah Burd-Sharps and Kristen Lewis

AUTHORS
Sarah Burd-Sharps, Kristen Lewis, and Eduardo Borges Martins (Statistics Director)

RESEARCHERS/CONTRIBUTORS
William Rodgers III, Namrita Khandelwal, Theodore Murphy, Elizabeth Nisbet, Caroline Repko, Elizabeth Stanton

INDICATOR TABLES
Charles Jennings, Tristi Nichols, Caroline Repko, Alejandro Reuss, Elizabeth Stanton

RESEARCH ASSISTANCE
Benjamin DeMarzo, Sarah Lynn Geiger

ADVISORY PANEL
Craig Calhoun, Ellen Chelser, Dalton Conley, Sheldon H. Danziger, Sherry Glied, Neva Goodwin, Carla Javits, Jeff Madrick, Marque Miringoff, Raymond C. Offenheiser, Oliver Quinn, the Right Reverend Mark Sisk, William E. Spriggs, Adela de la Torre

SUBSTANTIVE EDITING
Francis Wilkinson

COPYEDITING
Bob Land

DESIGN
Humantific | Understanding Lab, Inc.

Contents

Boxes, Figures, Maps, and Tables

ACCESS TO KNOWLEDGE 80

A DECENT STANDARD OF LIVING 120

Foreword

by Amartya Sen

When as a young man, Prince Gautama, later known as Buddha, left his royal home in the foothills of the Himalayas in search of enlightenment, he was moved by the physical sight of mortality, morbidity, and disability, and was distressed by the ignorance he saw around him. Buddha did not lack wealth or status or authority, but his focus was on the priority of life and death, of health and illness, of education and illiteracy. He felt overwhelmed by the deprivations that human beings suffered across the world. This was some twenty-five hundred years ago. Buddha searched for his own way of dealing with these general problems, but those problems are central also to the focus of the "human development approach" (pioneered by Mahbub ul Haq two decades ago), which is now in much use in the evaluation of social change and progress.

The similarity is not, in fact, just a coincidence. Mortality, morbidity, ignorance, and other restraints on human lives are matters of universal concern for people all over the world, and have been so for thousands of years. Seen this way, the remarkable thing is not so much that the human development approach emerged when it did, but rather why it took so long for social evaluators and statisticians to take direct note of what interests people most. Why has there been such a long tradition of insisting on seeing human progress in terms of alienated variables distant from human lives, like the GNP (gross national product), which at best relate indirectly and imperfectly to human lives and freedoms?

There is, in fact, something of a gap here between the traditions of evaluative statistics, on the one hand, and views of progress, on the other, advanced by visionary social scientists. The basic importance of enriching the lives and freedoms of ordinary human beings has been a central concern in the social sciences for a very long time. This applies not only to insightful economists such as Adam Smith, but also to earlier writings, even to Aristotle, who argued in *Nicomachean Ethics* that "wealth is evidently not the good we are seeking; for it is merely useful and for the sake of something else." We have to judge the success of a society, including its economy, not just in terms of national wealth or the ubiquitous GNP, but in terms of the freedoms and capabilities that people enjoy to live as they would value living.

If the human development approach has done a great deal across the world to reduce the artificial gap between what people really worry about and how their lives are assessed in national statistics, the approach has been remarkably neglected in the United States in particular. This is especially striking since this country has an arrestingly sharp—and contrary—record of a major discrepancy between opulence and social achievement. The United States is, in most ways of counting, the wealthiest nation in the world, and yet its accomplishments in longevity, secure health, fine education, and other such basic features of good living are considerably below those of many other—often much poorer—countries. What is no less extra-ordinary is that the relative position of the United States has been steadily falling over the years as the powerful growth of the U.S. economy fails to be adequately translated into better lives for Americans, especially those from disadvantaged backgrounds. The human development approach can be put to excellent use in America, both because that perspective is so important for the problems of this country and because the approach has been so widely neglected here.

This book makes a big contribution to meeting this neglect, and one hopes that it will be followed by further explorations of different aspects of American human de-velopment. It is, in fact, the first comprehensive study of the basic features of human development in the United States seen in a global context. As someone who has been involved, right from the start, in working with Mahbub ul Haq to develop the human development approach, it gives me the greatest of pleasure to write this foreword. Mahbub—a close lifelong friend whom I miss greatly since his untimely death in 1998—would have been delighted to see the fruits of his work being used with such dexterity and reach for assessing what is going on in the country with the highest economic opulence in the world without corresponding achievements in human development. He would have been pleased also by what William Draper III, the former administrator of the United Nations Development Programme (whose support to Mahbub was crucial for the beginning of his project), says in his own piece here, parti-cularly his point about making "governments more accountable to the citizens."

We get in this report not only an evaluation of what the limitations of human development are in the United States, but also how the relative place of America has been slipping in comparison with other countries over recent years. Also, in the skilled hands of Sarah Burd-Sharps, Kristen Lewis, and Eduardo Borges Martins, the contrasts within the country—related to region, race, class, and other important distinctions—receive powerful investigation and exposure. In these growing gaps we can also see one of the most important aspects of the souring of the American Dream, which is so much under discussion today.

I feel privileged to play a small part in placing this pioneering and powerful report before the American public and the increasingly vocal civil society—here and abroad. I do not doubt that the book will receive the huge attention that it richly deserves.

Amartya Sen
Harvard University
Nobel Laureate in Economics, 1998

Foreword

by William H. Draper III

In America, when we hear the word "development," we are likely to think either of fund-raising in the nonprofit arena or of bulldozers, cranes, and other heavy construction equipment. Yet from Africa to Asia, and from Latin America to parts of Europe, development is not fund-raising or construction, but strategies and action to fight poverty and create dynamic, growing economies.

For many decades, development focused exclusively on economic growth, trade, and investment. Over the last three decades, a new concept has gained traction, positing that while growth is absolutely necessary for development, it is not sufficient. The human development approach is based on the premise that people must be at the center of development. The aim is to offer people more choices and opportunities to make their own decisions for long, healthy, and creative lives. One variable is to have a sustainable livelihood and earn money, but there are other crucial variables, including the ability to live a long and healthy life, to have access to decent schooling, to participate in decisions that affect you, to live in a safe, clean environment and a stable community, and more.

From 1986 to 1993, I served as administrator of the United Nations Development Programme. A visionary economist, Mahbub ul Haq, who had served at the World Bank in Washington and as Pakistan's minister of finance, came to me with an idea. He was very disappointed that the dominant strands of development thought were not translating into tangible improvements in people's lives, and he wanted to research and write an annual report on the "state of the human condition." By giving Mahbub sufficient financial resources, editorial independence, and intellectual freedom, I enabled him to work with a distinguished team of consultants, including his Cambridge University friend, Amartya Sen, who later received a Nobel Prize. In 1990, UNDP published the first *Human Development Report*, "Concept and Measurement of Human Development." The report broke new ground with its controversial Human Development Index showing that some societies had achieved high levels of human development at modest income levels, and that others had not been able to translate their high income levels into commensurate levels of human progress. What were the policies that led to these results? This line of enquiry opened up an exciting, endless investigation that had ground-shaking implications for governments, the private sector, civil society organizations, and individuals. The report helped to make governments more accountable to their citizens. Coinciding with the end of the Cold War, when a shift from military spending was possible, the report had an impact on the allocation of funds available for sustainable human development.

Several years after the first annual global *Human Development Reports*, a number of countries adopted this approach nationally. Now, seventeen years later, there are more than five hundred national and regional reports, using this well-honed tool to shed new light on factors inhibiting human development, and to explore realistic solutions.

The *American Human Development Report 2008–2009* is the first such report for the United States. It couldn't come at a better time. America is a country of unparalleled opportunity. We have vast natural resources, world-class institutions, and creative, compassionate, generous people. Yet we face mounting challenges in making ours a society that allows all of us to invest in ourselves and our families, and lead healthy, productive lives. Human development means more than the intrinsic value of personal fulfillment. An economy that hopes to stay competitive amid rapid globalization must draw on everyone's talents. The skills needed to compete tomorrow require concerted national investment in children and adults alike today. As this report documents, some entrenched problems are not going away, and some new trends can result in large numbers of Americans falling behind. We can, and indeed must, do better.

The good news is that progress is possible. History shows that Americans have been tremendously resourceful in developing practical policies in the public, private, and nonprofit arena to increase the likelihood that every person can live up to his or her full potential. New approaches to challenges in health care and the environment seem imminent. At the same time, corporate social responsibility is quickly becoming much more than window dressing, as American businesses, large and small, take action to protect our natural resources and invest in improving the lives of our people. Social entrepreneurs, moreover, are pursuing impressive, innovative approaches to social problems every day. This report provides a rich analysis that will help us forge ahead in creating more economic dynamism, more effective social policies, and an expansion of everyone's freedom and opportunities.

William H. Draper III
Draper Richards L.P.

Acknowledgments

Words cannot express our profound gratitude to the many individuals and institutions who supported this project. First and foremost, we are grateful to our funders for believing in this initiative and for their steadfast support and encouragement. They include: the Conrad N. Hilton Foundation—Ed Cain; Oxfam America—Ray Offenheiser and Ellen Seidensticker; the Social Science Research Council—Craig Calhoun and Mary McDonnell; the Rockefeller Foundation—Darren Walker and Margot Brandenburg; and the Annenberg Foundation—Sylia Obagi.

We are deeply indebted to our Advisory Panel, an engaged group that, acting in their personal capacities, provided invaluable guidance at every stage of the project.

The report also benefited considerably from the inputs of a group of reviewers, who read and commented on drafts along the way: Leanne Burney, Peter Dixon, Geoffrey Hewings, Kim Hopper, June Junn, George Kaplan, Roberto Lenton, Peter Levine, Karen Manship, Marielza Oliveira, Richard Ponzio, Khalil Shahyd, Walter Stafford, and Pamela Walters.

We owe tremendous thanks to the following people, who offered extensive expertise in critical areas: Keith Woodman and Edwards Angell Palmer & Dodge LLP (legal), Becky Castle and Pam Wuichet of Project Resource Group (fundraising), and Bianca DeLille (communications).

The report benefited from the background papers of the following sectoral or thematic experts and researchers: Richard Alba, Proochista Ariana, Deepayan Basu Ray, Blaire Benavides, John Bouman, Louise Cainkar, Louis DeSipio, Josh DeWind, Jennifer Hajj, Marcia Henry, Charles Hirschman, Namrita Khandelwal, Jeffrey Lowe, Melissa Mahoney, Karen Manship, Elizabeth Nisbet, Wendy Pollack, Alejandro Portes, Jyotsna Puri, Ruben Rumbaut, Todd Shaw, Elizabeth Stanton, and Clyde Woods.

We deeply appreciate the written contributions of Phil Buchanan, John J. Dilulio, William Draper III, Ellen Bassuk, Carla Javits, Thomas Koulopoulos, and Amartya Sen.

We wish to thank the following people for their contributions to the project through providing information or administrative support, taking part in consultations, and sharing their knowledge: Sara Acosta, Sabina Alkire, Lisa Anderson,

Robert Anderson, Aidee Arjona, Gerald Barney and Our Task, Neil Bennett, Asa Blomstrom, John Bouman, Martha Bowers, Henry M. Brickell, Carolyn Brown, Carrie Brunk, Anne Buffardi, Eric Burd, Sandy Burd, Sam Carter, Carlos Centeno-Lairet, Mary-Lea Cox, Ana Cutter, Bowman and Abigail Cutter and The Cedars Foundation, Inc., Debbie Czegledy, Josh DeWind, Mari Denby, Séverine Deneulin, Thomas Dunn, Mike Ettlinger, Sakiko Fukuda-Parr, Amie Gaye, Jessica Gordon Nembhard, Robert Gronski, Gina Guillemette, Gerald Harris, Ilze Hirsh, Susan Holcombe, Julia Holmes, Kim Hopper, Jane Huber, Eve Jespersen, Velika Kabakchieva, Eliana Katsiaouni, Ruth Katz, Alison Kennedy, David Kirby, Thomas Koulopoulos, David Krauskopf, Kay Lapeyre, Paul Lapeyre, Michele Learner, Ellen Levy, Jim Lyons, Andrew Lewinter, Eugene Linden, Deirdre Martinez, Rita McLennon, Judy Miller, Sonia Mistry, Dawn Moses, Roger Munns, Austin Nichols, Chris Patusky, Ken Prewitt, Jaycee Pribulsky, Mattia Romani, Judith Ross, Diana Salas, Zarana Sanghani, Marisol Sanjines, Doug Schenkelberg, Papa Seck, Michael Sisk, Daniel A. Smith, Adrienne Smith, Leena Soman, Cynthia Spence, Dorothy Thomas, Ashley Tsongas, Cássio Turra, Kevin Watkins, and Veronica White.

Special thanks to Ekaterina and friends in Brighton Beach, Brooklyn, and high school students in Crown Point, New Mexico, for sharing their stories with us.

To the talented professionals who turned the manuscript into an actual book, we owe a huge debt of gratitude; a thousand thanks to Frank Wilkinson, Bob Land, and the Humantific | UnderstandingLab team of Elizabeth Pastor, Garry K. VanPatter, Michael Babwahsingh, and Evan Dody, who designed the book and introduced us to visual sense-making. Paul Price of the Social Science Research Council was a great ally throughout the process. Columbia University Press was amazingly flexible and supportive; special thanks to Peter Dimock for being such a champion of the book, and to his colleagues Kabir Dandona, Brad Hebel, Clare Wellnitz, Meredith Howard, Lisa Hamm, and Vin Dang for making everything come together.

We are tremendously grateful for the enthusiastic, generous support of our dear parents, siblings, in-laws, extended families, and friends, who no doubt grew weary of hearing about the results of the American Human Development Index, but kindly didn't let on.

And last, but certainly not least, we must thank our husbands, wives, daughters and sons: David, Dalia, and Sophie Sharps; Paul, Zoë, Sophie, and Benjamin Lewis Ewing: and Ana, Helena, and Lúcia Martins. They believed in us from the start, helped in untold ways large and small, and buoyed us in our moments of quiet (and unquiet) despair with patient good humor. Their support made this book possible; their love makes life worth living.

thank you!

THE MEASURE OF AMERICA

Executive Summary

American history is in part a story of expanding opportunity to ever-greater numbers of citizens.

Practical policies such as the GI Bill and Medicare have allowed more Americans to realize their potential for a good life.

This report introduces a new framework for measuring and analyzing well-being and human progress that can be used to build upon these past policy successes and to create an infrastructure of opportunity that serves a new generation of Americans.

Executive Summary

Economists, politicians, journalists, and ordinary citizens have many ways to track how America is doing. Monitoring the stock market, watching real estate prices, keeping an eye on interest rates—to follow these figures is to see how the country is progressing in one way or another. But we all have a harder time when trying to look at the big picture: on the whole, are things getting better or worse, and for whom? To answer these questions and to gauge how they stack up compared to their neighbors, countries worldwide have embraced an idea that captures key dimensions of national well-being in one framework: human development.

It has been eighteen years since the UN Development Programme published the first Human Development Report. In the nearly two decades since then, journalists, policy makers, governments, and the global development community have made important use of these studies—more than five hundred in all—on nations and regions around the world. What is new, however, and perhaps somewhat unexpected, is a Human Development Report on the United States.

Yet as the American Human Development Report itself confirms, the human development concept is as relevant and applicable to the home of the world's largest economy as it is to the home of the smallest. The indicators most frequently deployed in evaluating public welfare in the United States—GDP, the Dow Jones and NASDAQ, consumer spending, and the like—only address one aspect of the American experience. The human development model emphasizes the broader, everyday experience of ordinary people, including the economic, social, legal, psychological, cultural, environmental, and political processes that shape the range of options available to us. This approach has gained support around the world as a valuable tool in analyzing the well-being of large population groups.

The report and its American Human Development Index contain a host of useful data on economic, social, political, military, and environmental issues. However, both the report and the index emphasize three core areas of well-being: living a long and healthy life, having access to knowledge, and enjoying a decent standard of living. All data come from official U.S. government sources. (The most recent year for which all data needed to calculate the index are available is 2005.)

The American Human Development Index (page 162) provides a single measure of well-being for all Americans, disaggregated by state and congressional district, as well as by gender, race, and ethnicity. Overall, for example, Connecticut ranks first among states on the index, and Mississippi ranks last. The American HD Index registers a thirty-year gap in human development between the two states. Among the nation's 436 congressional districts, New York's Fourteenth District, in New York City, ranks first, and California's Twentieth District, around Fresno, ranks last. The average resident of New York's Fourteenth District earns over three times as much as the average resident of California's Twentieth District, lives four and a half years longer, and is ten times as likely to have a college degree.

By gender and ethnicity, Asian males have the highest human development score; African American males the lowest. The human development gap between the two groups is a staggering fifty years.

In other meaningful ways, as well, the American Human Development Index shows great variation among states and congressional districts, among racial/ethnic groups, and between women and men. The data that inform these analyses are derived in the following ways:

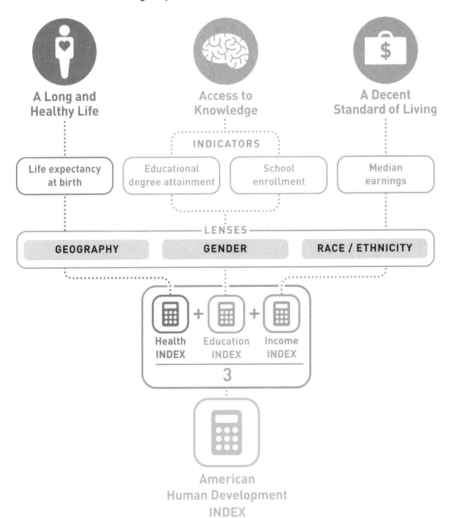

A Long and Healthy Life is measured using life expectancy at birth, calculated from mortality data from the Centers for Disease Control and Prevention, National Center for Health Statistics, and population data from the U.S. Census Bureau, 2005.

Access to Knowledge is measured using two indicators: school enrollment for the population age three and older, and educational degree attainment for the population twenty-five years and older. Both indicators are from the American Community Survey, U.S. Census Bureau, 2005.

A Decent Standard of Living is measured using median earnings of all full- and part-time workers sixteen years and older from the American Community Survey, U.S. Census Bureau, 2005.

A Long and Healthy Life

The United States spends roughly $5.2 billion every day on health care. But despite spending more per capita than any nation in the world, Americans live shorter lives than citizens of many other nations, including virtually every Western European and Nordic country. In addition, infant mortality rates are substantially higher in the United States than in other affluent nations. And homicide and suicide are significant contributors to premature death nationwide.

Here are some key findings of the report and index:

- In Washington, D.C., the average life expectancy is 73.8 years; in Hawaii, it is 81.7 years, a difference of almost 8 years.

- Kentucky's Fifth Congressional District, encompassing the southeastern part of the state, is at the bottom of the rankings with an average life expectancy of 72.6 years. Virginia's Eighth District, covering urban northern Virginia, is at the top of the table with a life expectancy of 82.9—a difference of more than a decade. Residents of Kentucky's Fifth District have an average life expectancy equal to that of the average American three decades ago.

- Asian females live on average to 88.8 years; African American females live to 76.3—a difference of more than 12 years.

- Among males, Asians live, on average, to 83.6; African Americans to 69.4—a difference of 14 years.

- The U.S. infant mortality rate is on par with that of Croatia, Cuba, Estonia, and Poland. If the U.S. rate were equal to that of first-ranked Sweden, twenty-one thousand more American babies would have lived to celebrate their first birthday in 2005.

- Two significant risk factors for premature death are obesity and lack of health insurance.

Americans live shorter lives than citizens of virtually every Western European and Nordic country.

Access to Knowledge

Access to knowledge is central to expanding people's choices and opportunities so that they can fulfill their human potential and lead long, creative lives that they value.

Research associates higher levels of education with a host of positive outcomes for individuals and society. Educated citizens, on average, vote more frequently, volunteer more time, make more charitable contributions, and are more tolerant. For individuals, more education is linked to better health, a longer life, higher income, more civic and political participation, greater ability to adjust to change, a more robust self-identity, stronger and more extensive social bonds, more stable relationships, and greater personal happiness.

Here are some key findings of the report and index:

- Washington, D.C., has the highest educational score among the states, followed by Massachusetts and Connecticut. However, the percentage of people in the nation's capital who did not graduate from high school is 16.4 percent, above the national average.

- California's Thirtieth Congressional District (from the Malibu coast east to Beverly Hills and West Hollywood) tops the list on the Education Index: 57 percent of adults over twenty-five have at least a bachelor's degree, and only 5 percent failed to graduate high school. In the lowest-scoring U.S. congressional district, Texas's Twenty-Ninth (predominantly eastern Houston city neighborhoods), only 6 percent of adults have earned a bachelor's degree, and 46 percent did not complete high school. In terms of high school completion rates, the Twenty-Ninth Congressional District in Texas is today roughly where the whole country was in 1970; in terms of bachelor's degree attainment, this district is behind the 1960 national average.

- High levels of educational attainment among Asians drives their number-one HD Index ranking by race/ethnicity. Half of all Asians have at least a college degree, compared to roughly 30 percent of whites, 17 percent of African Americans, 14 percent of Native Americans, and 12 percent of Latinos.

- By the end of fourth grade, African American and Latino children, and children of all races who are living in poverty, are two years behind their more affluent, predominantly white peers in reading and math. They have fallen three years behind by eighth grade, and four years behind by twelfth grade.

- Research shows that investment in intensive early childhood education pays high dividends in educational attainment and reduction of social problems, including crime, that correlate to high dropout rates.

Research associates higher levels of education with a host of positive outcomes for individuals and society.

A Decent Standard of Living

Income enables valuable options and alternatives, and its absence can limit life chances and restrict access to many opportunities. Income is a means to a host of critical ends, including a decent education; a safe, clean living environment; security in illness and old age; and a say in the decisions that affect one's life.

The measure used in the Human Development Index to represent standard of living is earnings and includes only income generated by labor. Median earnings in the United States in 2005 ranged from a high of $36,948 in Washington, D.C., to a low of $21,472 in Montana. The variations in earnings among the country's 436 congressional districts range from median earnings of more than $51,000 in New York's Fourteenth Congressional District to earnings one-third as much, less than $17,000, in California's Twentieth.

Here are some key findings of the report and index:

- Six of the ten states with the highest median earnings are in the Northeast (New Jersey, Connecticut, Massachusetts, New Hampshire, New York, and Rhode Island). The remaining four (Washington, D.C., Maryland, Virginia and Delaware) lie just to the south, also along the eastern seaboard.

- The average income in the top fifth of U.S. households in 2006 was $168,170. This is almost fifteen times the average income of the lowest fifth, with an average income of $11,352 per year.

- The top 1 percent of households possesses a full third of America's wealth. Households in the top 10 percent of income distribution hold more than 71 percent of the wealth, while those in the lowest 60 percent possess just 4 percent of wealth.

- Fifteen percent of American children—10.7 million girls and boys—live in families with monthly incomes of less than $1,500 per month.

- White males, the highest earners, make more than $37,000 per year, on average; at the low end of the scale, Latino females earn little more than $16,000.

- The United States is far behind other developed countries in its support to working families, particularly in terms of family leave, sick leave, and child care.

The United States is far behind other developed countries in its support to working families.

Advancing Human Development

Based on the data in the American Human Development Index and the information and analysis in the American Human Development Report, a steady, broad-based advance of human development in the United States will require attention to several priorities.

- For Americans to live longer, healthier lives, it is obvious from the report that progress depends in large part on a comprehensive resolution of the problem of health insurance. Today, some 47 million Americans lack health insurance, risking negative health outcomes and shorter life spans. The nation appears unlikely to make significant strides in health until every American has adequate health coverage.

  In addition, Americans are at risk from a wide range of preventable causes of death and disease, including obesity and violence. In a reflection of how complex social problems are linked, researchers have found that poor parents, living in neighborhoods they perceive to be dangerous, are often reluctant to allow their children to play outside. Lack of exercise contributes to childhood obesity, which lowers health scores. Restricted space to play can also have a negative impact on school performance, lowering education scores.

- In order to improve access to knowledge, research suggests that intensive intervention in early childhood is necessary to break the pattern by which parents with limited education raise children with limited education—short-circuiting their ability to command decent opportunities and wages in a high-tech, information-intensive, globalized economy. Superior preschool programs and intensive elementary schooling can offer students from poor families a chance to fulfill their potential, seize opportunities, and lead lives they value. The ideal of American opportunity, grounded in equal access to public education, is threatened by the lopsided educational realities of American schools. In addition, we are asking our schools to solve society's most intractable problems—social exclusion, chronic unemployment, dangerous neighborhoods, and more.

- For Americans to sustain, or obtain, a decent standard of living, the wages and opportunities of millions of Americans must improve. Growing inequality in income distribution and wealth raises a profound question for Americans: Can the uniquely middle-class nation that emerged in the twentieth century survive into the twenty-first century? Or is it fracturing into a land of great extremes?

  The answers to these questions will determine not only the future of America, but also the future of the idea of America—that of a land of opportunity where those who work hard and live honestly can prosper in freedom and security. The American Dream has drifted beyond the reach of many, while fading from view among others. To reinvigorate it, to make it real for millions of middle-class and poor Americans, the stagnation and decline of middle and low incomes must be reversed, and opportunity must once again reach down to the lowest rungs of society.

It may well be too late to help the generation of Americans who have just come of age. But a debate is long overdue on just how many generations America is willing to waste. We hope this American Human Development Report and American Human Development Index will help prod and inform that important discussion.

PART 1

Understanding Human Development

Human development is defined as **the process of enlarging people's freedoms and opportunities and improving their well-being.**

The human development model emphasizes the everyday experience of ordinary people, including the economic, social, legal, psychological, cultural, environmental, and political processes that shape the range of options available to us.

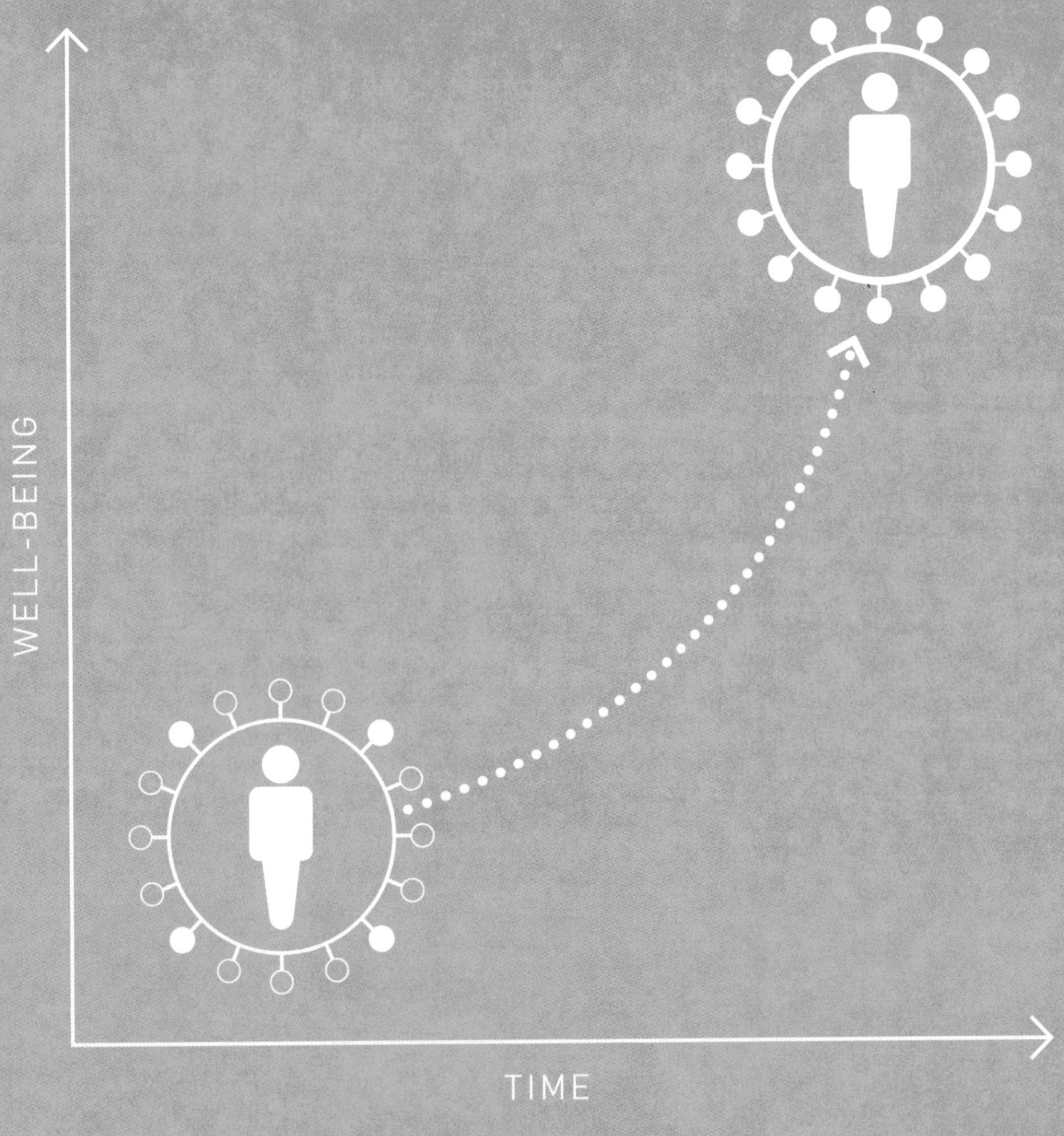
WELL-BEING
TIME

Introduction

"Human development is concerned with what I take to be the basic development idea: namely, advancing the richness of human life, rather than the richness of the economy in which human beings live, which is only a part of it."

AMARTYA SEN, Nobel Laureate, 1998

The Human Development Report

Commissioned by UNDP since 1990, the *Human Development Report* is an authoritative source on global development issues and a valued public policy tool. The *Human Development Report* is not widely known in the United States, but in some parts of the world, the report and its Human Development Index are household words. In Brazil, the HD Index has become such a staple of national development debates that a Brazilian television broadcast of World Cup soccer displayed the HDIs of all the countries competing.

Countries worldwide have embraced an idea that captures key dimensions of national well-being in one framework: human development. The human development concept was developed by economist Mahbub ul Haq. At the World Bank in the 1970s, and later as minister of finance in his own country, Pakistan, Dr. Haq argued that **existing measures of human progress failed to account for the true purpose of development—to improve people's lives**. In particular, he believed that the commonly used measure of Gross Domestic Product failed to adequately measure well-being. Working with Amartya Sen and other gifted economists, in 1990 Dr. Haq published the first *Human Development Report*, which had been commissioned by the United Nations Development Programme.

The human development model emphasizes the **everyday experience of ordinary people**, including the economic, social, legal, psychological, cultural, environmental, and political processes that shape the range of options available to

Two Approaches to Understanding Progress in America

How is the **economy** doing?		How are **people** doing?
TRADITIONAL Approach	**PROGRESS** In America	**HUMAN DEVELOPMENT** Approach

us. This approach soon gained support as a useful tool for analyzing the well-being of large populations. In addition to the global *Human Development Report* that comes out annually, more than five hundred national and regional reports have been produced in the last fifteen years, with an impressive record of provoking public debate and political engagement (see sidebars).

The *American Human Development Report 2008–2009* is the first to use this well-honed international approach to assess living standards in a wealthy, developed nation. Like previous reports, it includes a Human Development Index (see page 162). While the report is far-reaching, the index measures just three factors: life expectancy, as a key indicator of health; school enrollment and educational attainment, as a measure of access to knowledge; and earned income, as a measure of material well-being. All three components—longevity, knowledge, and income—are valued by people the world over as building blocks of a good life. In the Human Development Index (HD Index), all three are weighted equally.

The human development approach seeks a holistic measure of a country's progress. In the United States, the state of the nation is often expressed through Gross Domestic Product, daily stock market results, consumer spending levels, and national debt figures. But these numbers provide only a partial view of how we are faring. This report offers an alternative: **a first-ever American Human Development Index**, which combines key human-centered indicators into a single figure. While data are plentiful on the extremes of affluence and deprivation in the United States, the American Human Development Index (page 162) provides a single measure of well-being for all Americans, disaggregated by state and congressional district, as well as by gender, race, and ethnicity. The report also contains a host of useful data on economic, social, political, military, and environmental issues, enabling ordinary citizens to assess the state of the nation in a more comprehensive manner, using apples-to-apples comparisons. This information can be found in the tables in the back of the book.

The data included in the American Human Development Index will help us understand variations among regions and groups. It is a snapshot of America today. Moreover, the index will serve as a baseline for monitoring future progress. In a number of countries, the Human Development Index is now an official government statistic; its annual publication inaugurates serious political discussion and renewed efforts, nationally and regionally, to improve lives.

The United States is a country of unparalleled opportunity and personal freedom. We have vast natural resources, efficient institutions, tremendous ingenuity, a rich democratic tradition, and great prosperity. In the past half century, America has become a far more just and inclusive nation. The civil rights and women's movements enlarged the landscape of choices and chances available to millions of Americans, giving them greater freedom to decide what to do and who to become, enabling them to invest in themselves and their families, and allowing the country as a whole to benefit from a hugely expanded pool of talent.

National and Regional Human Development Reports

Developing nations from Afghanistan to Zimbabwe have adapted the global report methodology to assess progress within their own countries and regions.

The **Arab** *Human Development Report* series has challenged the status quo in such areas as women's empowerment, freedom, and knowledge. In response, a half dozen Arab countries partnered with Microsoft to train tens of thousands of boys and girls in the use of Internet technologies.

As a direct result of the **Botswana** 2000 national *Human Development Report*, which broke the nation's taboo on public discussion of AIDS, Botswana's president announced that the government would provide free antiretroviral drugs to every HIV-positive citizen. At the time, more than three in ten working-age adults were HIV-positive.

In **Brazil**, a Human Development Index is published for each of the country's more than five thousand municipalities. These indices have reshaped the way in which the federal budget is apportioned. Low-HD Index communities now receive targeted assistance through educational scholarships, improved water and sanitation facilities, support to family farms, and more. Private firms have used the HD Index to site manufacturing plants.

Yet despite great progress and the unmatched resources at our disposal, **the United States is still beset by challenges that undermine the capacity of many Americans to realize their full potential.** The United States ranks second in the world in per-capita income (behind Luxembourg), but thirty-fourth in survival of infants to age one.[1] If we were as successful in infant survival as number-one-ranking Sweden, another twenty-one thousand American babies born in 2005 would have lived to celebrate their first birthdays. We rank forty-second in global life expectancy and first among the world's twenty-five richest countries in the percentage of children living in poverty—exerting a drag on the prospects and futures of roughly one in six American girls and boys.[2]

Comparisons among different groups of Americans reveal much about who is being left out of improvements in health, education, and living standards: African American babies are two and a half times more likely to die before age one than white babies; Latinos are twice as likely to drop out of high school as African Americans and almost four times more likely to drop out than whites; and the earnings of American women are about two-thirds of men's earnings.

FIGURE 1.1 **Income and Human Development in the U.S. and Select Countries, 2005**

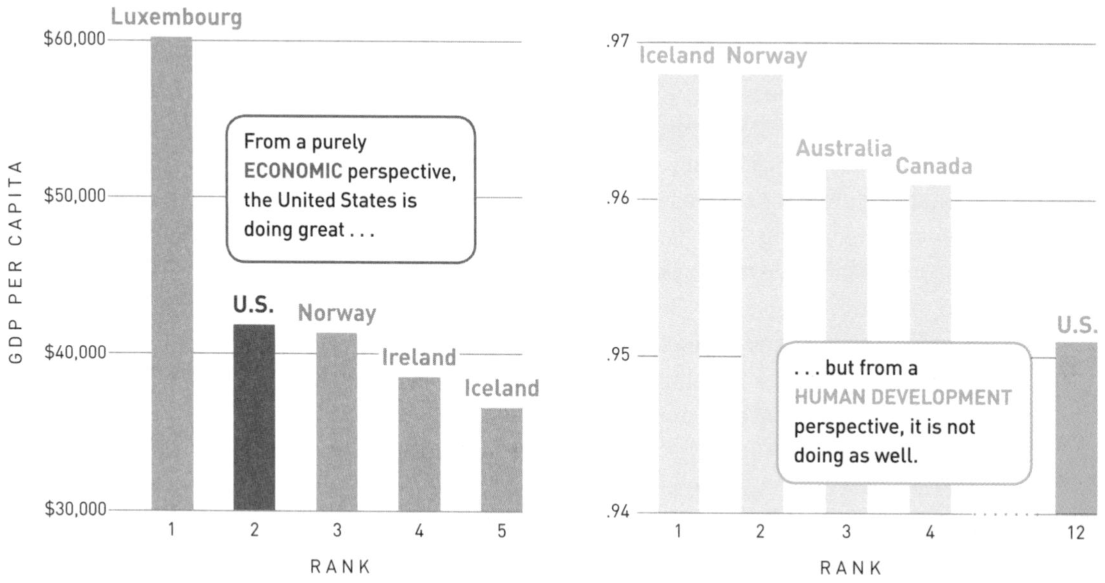

From a purely economic perspective, the United States is doing great; it ranks second among 177 countries in per-capita income. But from a human development perspective, it is not doing as well, occupying the 12th position overall, according to the global Human Development Index, published annually by the United Nations Development Programme. Each of the 11 countries ahead of the United States in the HD Index ranking has a lower per-capita income than does the United States, but all perform better on the health and knowledge dimensions.

Source: UNDP, *Human Development Report 2007/2008.*

Comparisons with affluent nations reveal some awkward truths. First, others have achieved better outcomes in many vital areas, including infant mortality and longevity, than we have. Second, they have achieved superior results with less spending per capita. This report explores some of those disparities. It also raises questions about the status of significant numbers of Americans whose opportunities are constrained by poor health, inadequate education, limited employment prospects, social and political exclusion, and economic insecurity.

American history is in part a story of expanding opportunity to ever-greater numbers of citizens. Practical policies such as the GI Bill, which opened the gates of higher education and expanded home ownership, and Social Security, Supplemental Security Income, and Medicare, which provide income and health security to the elderly, have allowed more Americans to realize their potential for a good life. **This report introduces a new tool and framework for measuring and analyzing well-being and human progress that can be used to build upon these policy successes of the past, and to create an infrastructure of opportunity that serves a new generation of Americans.**

FIGURE 1.2 **Top-Ranked Countries in Human Development, 1980–2005**

1980	1985	1990	1995	2000	2005
1 Switzerland	1 Canada	1 Canada	1 Norway	1 Norway	1 Iceland
2 **U.S.**	2 **U.S.**	2 **U.S.**	2 Canada	2 Sweden	2 Norway
3 Iceland	3 Switzerland	3 Iceland	3 Sweden	3 Australia	3 Australia
4 Norway	4 Norway	4 Japan	4 Netherlands	4 Netherlands	4 Canada
5 Canada	5 Iceland	5 Switzerland	5 Australia	5 Iceland	5 Ireland
6 Japan	6 Japan	6 Netherlands	6 **U.S.**	6 Canada	6 Sweden
7 Netherlands	7 Netherlands	7 Norway	7 Belgium	7 Switzerland	7 Switzerland
8 Denmark	8 Sweden	8 France	8 Japan	8 Belgium	8 Netherlands
9 Sweden	9 Denmark	9 Finland	9 UK	9 **U.S.**	9 Japan
10 France	10 France	10 Sweden	10 Switzerland	10 Japan	10 Finland
11 Belgium	11 Finland	11 Belgium	11 France	11 Finland	11 France
12 Australia	12 Belgium	12 Austria	12 Iceland	12 France	12 **U.S.**

America's score on the global Index increased steadily over the last twenty-five years but other countries have progressed more quickly. As a result, the United States dropped from **number 2** in 1980 to **number 12** in 2005, falling behind peer nations that have been more efficient in transforming income into positive health and education outcomes.

Source: UNDP, *Human Development Report 2007/2008.*

The OECD

Use of the terms "rich," "wealthy," "affluent," or "industrialized" countries refers to the thirty countries that make up the Organization for Economic Co-operation and Development (OECD). OECD countries include:

Australia
Austria
Belgium
Canada
Czech Republic
Denmark
Finland
France
Germany
Greece
Hungary
Iceland
Ireland
Italy
Japan
Korea
Luxembourg
Mexico
Netherlands
New Zealand
Norway
Poland
Portugal
Slovak Republic
Spain
Sweden
Switzerland
Turkey
United Kingdom
United States

What Is Human Development?

Human development is about the real freedom ordinary people have to decide who to be, what to do, and how to live. These diagrams illustrate the central ideas of human development and visually depict how we measure it using the American Human Development Index.

CONCEPT

Human development is defined as **the process of enlarging people's freedoms and opportunities and improving their well-being.**

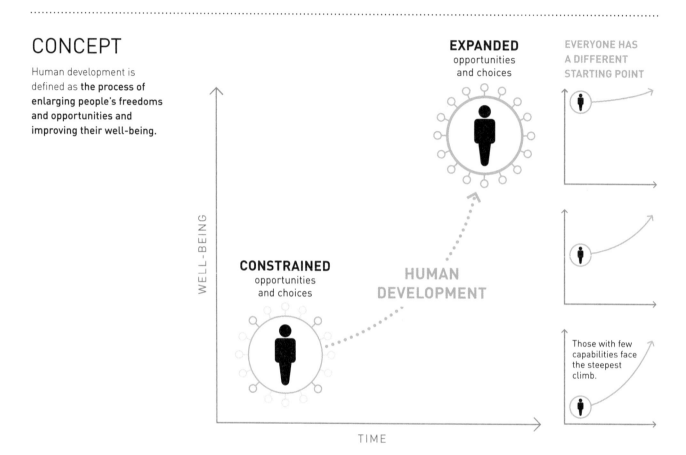

EXPANDED opportunities and choices

CONSTRAINED opportunities and choices

HUMAN DEVELOPMENT

WELL-BEING

TIME

EVERYONE HAS A DIFFERENT STARTING POINT

Those with few capabilities face the steepest climb.

JOURNEY

Human development can be understood as a journey. Even before one's life begins, **parents** play a role in setting the trajectory of one's human development. Numerous factors and experiences alter the course of one's journey through life, **helping** or **hindering** one's ability to live a life of choice and value.

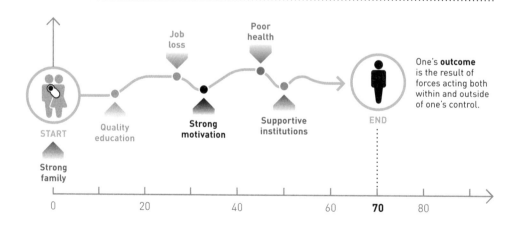

Job loss

Poor health

START

Quality education

Strong motivation

Supportive institutions

END

Strong family

One's **outcome** is the result of forces acting both within and outside of one's control.

0   20   40   60   **70**   80

THE MEASURE OF AMERICA

CAPABILITIES

Capabilities—**what people can do and what they can become**—are central to the human development concept. Many different capabilities are essential to a fulfilling life.

Our capabilities are expanded both by our own efforts and by the institutions and conditions of our society.

DIMENSIONS

Of all the capabilities, this report focuses in-depth on just **three**, all of which are relatively easy to measure. They are considered core human development dimensions.

LENSES

The results of the American Human Development Index reveal variations among regions, states, and congressional districts; between women and men; and among racial and ethnic groups.

INDEX

The modified American Human Development Index measures the same three basic dimensions as the standard HD Index, but it uses **different indicators** to better reflect the U.S. context and to maximize use of available data. The Index will serve as a **baseline** for monitoring future progress.

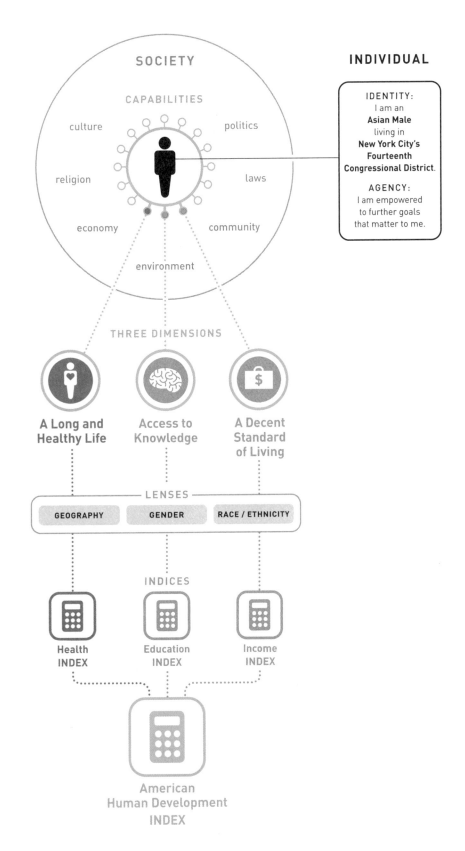

SOCIETY

INDIVIDUAL

CAPABILITIES

culture

politics

religion

laws

economy

community

environment

IDENTITY:
I am an
Asian Male
living in
**New York City's
Fourteenth
Congressional District.**

AGENCY:
I am empowered
to further goals
that matter to me.

THREE DIMENSIONS

**A Long and
Healthy Life**

**Access to
Knowledge**

**A Decent
Standard
of Living**

LENSES

GEOGRAPHY   GENDER   RACE / ETHNICITY

INDICES

Health
INDEX

Education
INDEX

Income
INDEX

American
Human Development
INDEX

Shared Aspirations and Values:
The American Dream

The foundation of the American Dream is an idealized vision of America as a level playing field, a land rich with possibilities for anyone willing to dream big, work hard, and "just do it." **Despite the variety of personal meanings invested in the American Dream, it connotes widely shared ideals such as mobility, freedom, security, and dignity.** Americans have long accepted profound inequality of outcomes, in part because of their steadfast belief in equality of opportunity. They generally believe responsibility for seizing opportunities lies with the individual. These intertwined beliefs in equal opportunity and individual responsibility are reinforced in textbooks and popular culture and widely shared across ethnic groups and income levels—though they are not universal. (Even reality television programming promotes the ideal. *American Idol* is a popular exponent of the American Dream, in which raw talent and moxie earn a meteoric, meritocratic rise to fame and fortune.)

The history of the twentieth century broadly supports the notion that the United States is a land of expanding opportunity. Women won the right to vote. Workers won landmark rights, including the eight-hour day, weekends off, and pensions. Committed civil rights activists won important legislation to prohibit discrimination in education, employment, housing, and all walks of public life. Businesses in a number of sectors have come to see the value of a diverse workforce. Significant investment in the construction and operation of schools and libraries brought free public education to everyone. The GI Bill helped to educate a generation of veterans. Taxpayers brought financial security and health to the vulnerable elderly with Social Security, Supplemental Security Income, and Medicare, dramatically reducing the number of older Americans living in poverty.

However, Americans are well aware that everyone does not share the same starting line. Many minorities, people with disabilities, older workers, and gay men and lesbians, for example, are especially aware of the ways in which discrimination and disadvantage keep the dreams of many out of reach. In a recent survey, only 33 percent of Americans said that everyone has the opportunity to succeed; 38 percent of respondents agreed that "most" have that opportunity; and 27 percent believed "only some" have it.

But to most Americans, unequal beginnings are not the end of the story. The same poll also revealed that about 80 percent of Americans agree that hard work and perseverance can usually overcome disadvantage.[3] These somewhat contradictory findings highlight the gap between the promise and practice of the American Dream (see BOX 1.1).

BOX 1.1 **Social Mobility: A Cornerstone of the American Dream**

Social mobility—the ability to move up the economic ladder—is a central tenet of the American Dream. But recent evidence suggests that, in some critical areas, social mobility has slowed or even reversed. Some groups have greater income and employment security than ever before. But for many others, realizing the American Dream—or even hanging on to it—is more difficult today than it was thirty years ago. For instance, a recent study found that nearly half of African Americans born to middle-class parents in the 1960s ended up among the bottom 20 percent of earners as adults.[4]

In 1987, Nobel Prize–winning economist Gary Becker wrote, **"Almost all the earnings advantages or disadvantages of ancestors are wiped out in three generations."**[5] However, improved methodologies and data are increasingly telling a different tale. A study by the Federal Reserve Bank of Boston, for example, found that income mobility in the United States was higher in the 1970s than it has been since. Of the poorest one-fifth of families in the 1980s, half were still poor in the 1990s.[6] Moreover, intergenerational mobility is on the wane. Researchers at the Chicago Federal Reserve and the University of California–Berkeley found that brothers born in the 1960s were more likely to have similar incomes than brothers born in the 1940s.[7] Today, fully half of poor children in the United States grow up to be poor adults.[8]

Parents who have done well in life are more likely to foster in their children the attitudes and values that society rewards, to make the investments and decisions that help children obtain competitive advantages, and to have the connections to help their children get into top schools and workplaces.[9]

The American meritocracy, the foundation of the American Dream, is at risk. Social mobility is now less fluid in the United States than in other affluent nations. Indeed, a poor child born in Germany, France, Canada, or one of the Nordic countries has a better chance to join the middle class in adulthood than an American child born into similar circumstances.[10]

Increasingly, the rich are staying rich . . .

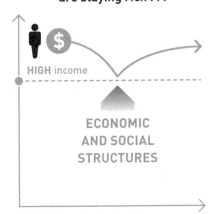

. . . while the poor are staying poor

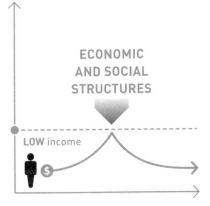

The same economic and social structures that help the wealthy stay at the **top** of the economic ladder can limit the upward mobility of those at the **bottom**.

Capabilities in the United States

People's Capabilities

What we can be and do—our capabilities—are expanded (or constrained) by our own efforts, by our family circumstances, and by the institutions of our society.

The capabilities approach was developed by Amartya Sen and others, including University of Chicago philosopher Martha Nussbaum. **Capabilities shape the real possibilities open to a person. Capabilities enable you to choose one direction over another because it is your preference rather than because you lack other opportunities.**

Basic capabilities valued by virtually everyone include physical and psychological health, access to knowledge, and a decent material standard of living. Other capabilities central to a fulfilling life are the ability to participate in the decisions that affect one's life, to have control over one's living environment, to enjoy freedom from violence, to experience love and friendship, to have societal respect, and to relax and have fun.

In effect, family background not only matters, but in some instances appears to be decisive. This has serious implications for American **capabilities**, a concept central to human development. Amartya Sen argues that **the measure of any society should be how much freedom people have to decide how to live and to act on their decisions**. This concept of freedom goes beyond civil and political freedoms, though it certainly embraces freedoms of assembly, religion, speech, and the like. But for Sen, the ultimate measure of freedom is the reach of human capabilities.

Capabilities define what people are truly able to do and be; they are the equipment one has to pursue a life of value (see sidebar). **People with extensive, well-developed capabilities have the tools they need to make their vision of "a good life" a reality.**

In the human development framework, the question of choice is critical because a good life is at least partly a life of genuine choice. Those poor in capabilities are less able to chart their own course and to seize opportunities. Without basic capabilities, human potential remains unfulfilled.

The exercise of real capabilities, on the other hand, is a gateway to freedom and fulfillment. The experience of one young immigrant to the United States is illustrative. Ekaterina, quoted at the beginning of this section, is a twenty-five-year-old Russian woman. She arrived in New York alone at age twenty with a suitcase, fifty dollars, and no more English than "hello." Five years later, Ekaterina says she is "living the American Dream." After learning English and working her way through college, she has a job that pays a living wage and a network of supportive friends. She is applying to graduate school programs.

Clearly, Ekaterina has capabilities. She is naturally intelligent. But she also benefited from an excellent education in her own country; although she knew no English upon her arrival, she already knew how to study and learn. Like many immigrants, she was resourceful and willing to take risks. In good health, she had the physical capacity to work long hours, attending school while working full-time. She also benefited from less tangible capabilities—confidence and poise engendered by a supportive family, previous scholastic achievements, and her social standing in her home country.

Ekaterina arrived in the United States poor in income and assets but rich in capabilities. This wealth of capabilities enables her to seize opportunities and create positive outcomes for herself. It also allows her to make valuable contributions to her workplace, community, and adopted country.

As the example of Ekaterina illustrates, **what we can be and do—our capabilities—are expanded both by our own efforts and by the institutions and conditions of our society.** Investing in people builds their capabilities, enabling them to take advantage of the full range of opportunities offered in the United States.

Human Poverty

Official U.S. poverty measures are linked to eligibility for government benefits. The official government poverty threshold is based on the cost of food. **There is strong consensus among experts that this is a woefully outdated measure.** For many impoverished children, the zip code into which they are born reveals more about their life chances than the amount of food in their cupboard. Dilapidated schools, overcrowded classrooms, shabby apartments shared with roaches and rodents, neighborhoods so dangerous that parents don't let their children play outside—these are all powerful signals of poverty. Poor children are very much aware of what they are missing. **What conclusions do they draw about themselves and about the value society places on their well-being and happiness? What are they learning about their chances in life?**

In purely monetary terms, one can argue that poverty does not exist in the United States. Most poor Americans have a material living standard that in Bangladesh or Rwanda—or even in the United States fifty years ago—would qualify as middle class or even higher. Nearly all Americans have running hot and cold water, a toilet and shower, a television, a telephone, and access to public roads, schools, and hospitals. Yet poverty exists—in extreme forms for people who lack the basic human necessities, and in less extreme forms for millions of Americans for whom opportunities are few and human potential is unrealized.

Many Americans would likely be surprised to learn that fundamental deprivations are far too prevalent. Despite a surfeit of inexpensive food, the U.S. Department of Agriculture reported that "on a typical day in November 2005, an estimated 531,000 to 797,000 households experienced very low food security,"[11] which means that normal eating patterns were disrupted due to lack of money or other resources. Homelessness is another persistent problem. **Over the course of a year, at least 1.35 million children are at some point homeless.** More families with children are homeless today than at any time since the Great Depression. For the hungry and homeless, the American Dream is especially elusive. It is hard to dream on an empty stomach, with no roof over your head or living in fear of violence.

Most poverty in America is not absolute; it is relative, meaning deprivation based on what is considered necessary by most of society. Research has shown that relative poverty can curb children's aspirations and limit their achievements.[12] Children are especially sensitive to the stress that relative deprivation imposes on their parents, who cannot provide their children with the opportunities available to other kids. Discouragement and hopelessness in families can lead to weakened self-esteem, marital tensions, and depression, all of which further undermine the quality of life, aspirations, and achievements of children.

Understanding the Difference between Human Poverty and Income Poverty

One of the cornerstones of the human development paradigm is the definition of poverty as more than a lack of income or a shortage of material goods. Income poverty is only one dimension of a broader concept of **human poverty**, which is defined as **a lack of basic human capabilities for sustaining a tolerable life**.

Human poverty is often closely related to a lack of money and material goods. But **the loss of dignity** that accompanies income poverty also stems from **a sense of powerlessness** to change one's living conditions, **a lack of autonomy and control** over many crucial decisions, and **a feeling that one is marginalized or excluded** politically, socially, or psychologically—and thus deprived of participation, choices, and opportunities.

Human poverty is generally harder to identify and measure than income poverty, but it is no less a burden on poor families and a drain on society. A more comprehensive definition of poverty is a predicate to more successful policies to fight poverty.

Human Security

Human security was comprehensively explored for the first time in the 1994 *Human Development Report*. **A human security approach expands the concept of security from nations to individuals,** from protection of national assets from foreign aggression to protection of individual rights to physical safety and health, basic freedoms, and economic security.

Human security entails **protection of the vital core of human lives** from critical threats. It is defined as safety from chronic threats, such as discrimination, unemployment, or environmental degradation, as well as protection from sudden crises, including economic collapse, environmental disaster, violence, or epidemic. Human insecurity can be a product of human actions or natural events, or of an interaction between the two.

Even in cases in which natural catastrophe cannot be prevented, action must be taken to safeguard lives and minimize damage, thus allowing us to face threats "with security." Absent preparation, sudden environmental shocks can, in days or even minutes, wipe out capabilities that communities have developed over generations. In addition to life itself, all human capabilities are at risk in the face of hurricanes, tornadoes, floods, fires, and earthquakes. Health suffers, schooling is disrupted, economies collapse, homes are destroyed, communities are scattered, and the secure landscape of the familiar vanishes.

Investing in infrastructure and emergency systems to mitigate risk saves lives. In California, $8 billion has been spent since 2000 just on retrofitting the state's bridges to withstand serious earthquakes;[13] public and private expenditures dedicated to other aspects of earthquake preparedness, like retrofitting houses and office buildings and educating the public about how to stay safe during earthquakes, are doubtless greater still. What difference does this investment make? Compare the impact of two roughly similar earthquakes in different parts of the world. Sixty people perished in 1994 in a magnitude 6.7 earthquake in Northridge, California. In southeastern Iran in 2003, roughly 31,000 people lost their lives in a slightly less powerful earthquake (magnitude 6.6). Most of those killed in Iran died when their buildings collapsed.[14]

How many lives would have been saved in New Orleans and along the Gulf Coast if Hurricane Katrina had been met by adequate levees, restored wetlands, and a realistic emergency evacuation plan?

Security from natural disasters has received a great deal of attention in a post-Katrina America coming to terms with the extreme weather events often associated with climate change. **But a different kind of security is the chief preoccupation of millions of Americans: security in one's own home and neighborhood.**

One in three female murder victims is killed by an intimate partner. This kind of violence is particularly pernicious because it often occurs in precisely the place where one should feel safest: the home. Intimate partner violence, which includes rape and domestic violence, has devastating psychological, physical, and economic consequences on the women who experience it—and on the children who far too often witness it. It also exacts a high cost to society—medical costs, justice system costs, reduced workforce productivity, and reduced capabilities of future generations.

In 2005, an estimated 899,000 American children were victims of abuse or neglect, and 1,460 of them died. Infants and toddlers up to age three had the highest rates of victimization. As with intimate partner violence, the abuse was centered in the home, in eight out of ten cases at the hands of the very people the children should trust most: their parents.[15]

Rates of violent crime and property crime have declined in the country as a whole in the past decade; New York City's murder rate in 2007 was the lowest since 1963. However, especially in low-income neighborhoods, crime and violence continue to act as a check on human freedom. Gang violence, in particular, persists. Ninety percent of large cities report gang activity; in Los Angeles and Chicago, more than half of all homicides are the result of gang activity. Gang members, mostly Latino and African American boys and young men, kill one another with heartbreaking frequency, but innocent bystanders are also caught in the crossfire and whole neighborhoods are terrorized by witness intimidation, threats of savage retaliation, and gang dominance of public space.

This report advocates for **an approach to security that enables all Americans to have the peace of mind and physical safety required to lead productive lives**.

Key Concepts of the Human Development Approach

Agency
People's ability to act, individually and collectively, to further goals that matter to them. Autonomy, control, empowerment, and the exercise of free choice are critical aspects of agency.

Capabilities
The personal and societal assets that enable people to fulfill their potential.

Human Development
A process of enlarging people's freedoms and opportunities and improving their well-being, enabling them to lead long, healthy lives; to have access to knowledge; to enjoy a decent standard of living; and to participate in the decisions that affect them.

Human Poverty
The lack of basic human capabilities and opportunities for living a tolerable life.

Human Security
Protection of the vital core of human lives from critical threats; it includes both safety from chronic threats and protection from sudden crises.

International Development
Long-term, sustainable strategies for people to generate secure livelihoods and improve their quality of life. It differs from humanitarian aid, which is aimed at short-term solutions to specific crises.

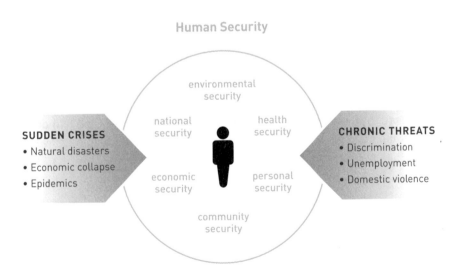

Human Security

SUDDEN CRISES
- Natural disasters
- Economic collapse
- Epidemics

environmental security
national security
health security
economic security
personal security
community security

CHRONIC THREATS
- Discrimination
- Unemployment
- Domestic violence

Measuring Human Development

The first Human Development Index was presented in 1990. It has been an annual feature of every *Human Development Report* ever since, ranking virtually every country in the world. **The HD Index has become one of the most widely used indices of well-being** and has succeeded in broadening the measurement and discussion of well-being beyond the important but nevertheless narrow confines of income. What's more, **the index has encouraged countries to invest in data collection on their citizens' well-being and spurred many countries to try to improve their rankings on the index**.

Over the years, the index has revealed **striking disparities between groups** and shed needed light on why different results were achieved. One comparison of Pakistan and Vietnam is illustrative. In 2000, annual per-capita income in both countries was virtually the same: $1,928 in Pakistan and $1,996 in Vietnam. However, in human development terms the two nations were far apart. Pakistan ranked 138 out of 173 countries while Vietnam ranked 109. Why? In Pakistan, only 43.2 percent of adults were literate, while the literacy rate in Vietnam was over 93 percent. A Pakistani born in 2000 could expect to live to about age 60. In Vietnam, life expectancy was 68.2 years.[16] The relative status of the two countries provided powerful proof that the link between income and well-being is not automatic.

Human Development Reports and the HD Index have always been published in tandem. **However, it is important to draw a distinction between the concept of human development and the index. The concept is holistic**, encompassing a wide range of human values, such as religious expression, environmental sustainability, cultural liberty, political participation, self-confidence, community bonds, dignity, nondiscrimination, and others.

By contrast, **the index is restricted to statistics on longevity, education, and material well-being**. Unlike measurements of empowerment or psychological well-being, for example, statistics in these three areas can be objectively measured and compared across regions and nations. Thus, the Human Development Index is used to identify major challenges in three critical areas and to monitor advances and declines over time. It provides a useful portrait of human lives and how well-being is evolving in different parts of the globe.

BOX 1.2 A Primer on the American Human Development Index

Why do we need an American Human Development Index?

Because national well-being cannot be measured by GDP alone. The American HD Index offers a more comprehensive and nuanced picture of the state of the nation.

What indicators does the American HD Index include?

The American HD Index is a composite measure of three basic areas of human development: health, knowledge, and standard of living. Health is measured in the modified American HD Index by life expectancy. Knowledge is measured by a combination of educational attainment and school enrollment. Standard of living is measured using median earnings. All data sources are from official 2005 U.S. government data.

Why these three components?

Most people would agree that health, knowledge, and adequate material resources are the basic ingredients of a decent life. These three areas are measured by the global HD Index as well as by most modified national HDIs, an indication that these core capabilities are universally valued. In addition, measurable, intuitively sensible, and easily understood proxy indicators exist for these three areas. Additional aspects and measures of well-being are discussed in the report, but the American HD Index is restricted to hard data on these three core dimensions.

Can one indicator measure complex concepts like health, knowledge, and standard of living?

People studying large populations use simple, easy-to-collect proxy indicators to represent complex phenomena that cannot be measured directly. Researchers assessing school readiness among children might use as a proxy the number of books in the child's home, the number of times she is read to each week, or how many shapes and colors a child can name. There is no way to directly measure a population's health. Even the proxies on which doctors rely to assess the health of a specific individual, such as blood pressure or body temperature, hardly capture the entirety of that person's health. However, they do reveal some important information. For large populations, life expectancy is a generally accepted proxy for health, though the length of a person's life does not tell us everything about the quality of that person's health. Similarly, degree attainment and school enrollment are reasonable stand-ins for the broad and elusive concept of knowledge. Income is a valuable proxy for living standards.

How can the American HD Index be used?

The American HD Index is a tool for assessing the relative socioeconomic progress of groups of Americans as well as different parts of the country. It provides a snapshot of how different groups stack up today and sets a benchmark by which to evaluate progress in the future.

What are the American HD Index's limitations?

The index does not capture information on important areas of human development beyond health, education, and income. The index cannot be used to measure the short-term impacts of policy changes, since its indicators do not change quickly. And, like all indicators, composite or otherwise, the index is only as reliable as the data upon which it is based.

> The American HD Index offers a comprehensive and nuanced picture of the state of the nation.

The Modified American Human Development Index

More than 150 countries have presented the Human Development Index in their national reports, sometimes using the standard HD Index formula seen in the annual global report, and in other cases modifying the formula to suit an individual country's situation.

The modified American Human Development Index measures the same three basic dimensions as the standard HD Index, but it uses different indicators to better reflect the U.S. context and to maximize use of available data. All data come from official U.S. government sources. The most recent year for which data are available is 2005, owing to the typical lag time of two to three years. (For full details, see the Methodological Notes.)

Calculating the Human Development Index

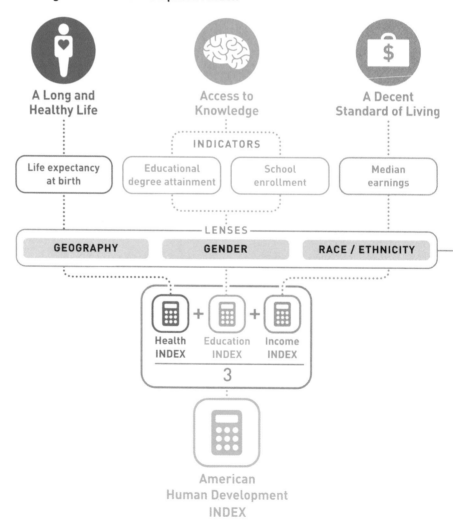

A Long and Healthy Life
is measured using life expectancy at birth, calculated from mortality data from the Centers for Disease Control and Prevention, National Center for Health Statistics, and population data from the U.S. Census Bureau, 2005.

Access to Knowledge
is measured using two indicators: school enrollment for the population age three and older, and educational degree attainment for the population twenty-five years and older. Both indicators are from the American Community Survey, U.S. Census Bureau, 2005.

A Decent Standard of Living
is measured using median earnings of all full- and part-time workers sixteen years and older from the American Community Survey, U.S. Census Bureau, 2005.

Lenses into Human Development by Group

Throughout the rest of the book, we will look at the American HD Index through several different lenses. We will use the Index to compare the levels of human development by geography, presenting Index scores and rankings by region, by state, and by congressional district. And we will use the Index to compare the levels of human development by racial and ethnic group as well as by gender.

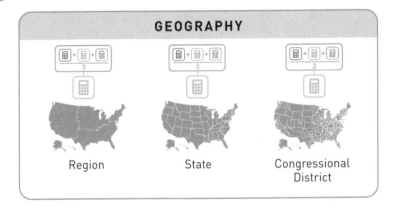

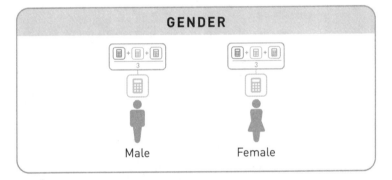

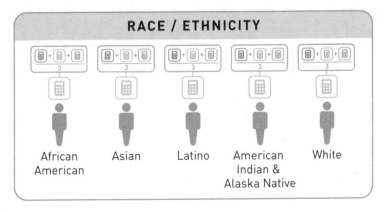

PART 2

What the American Human Development Index Reveals

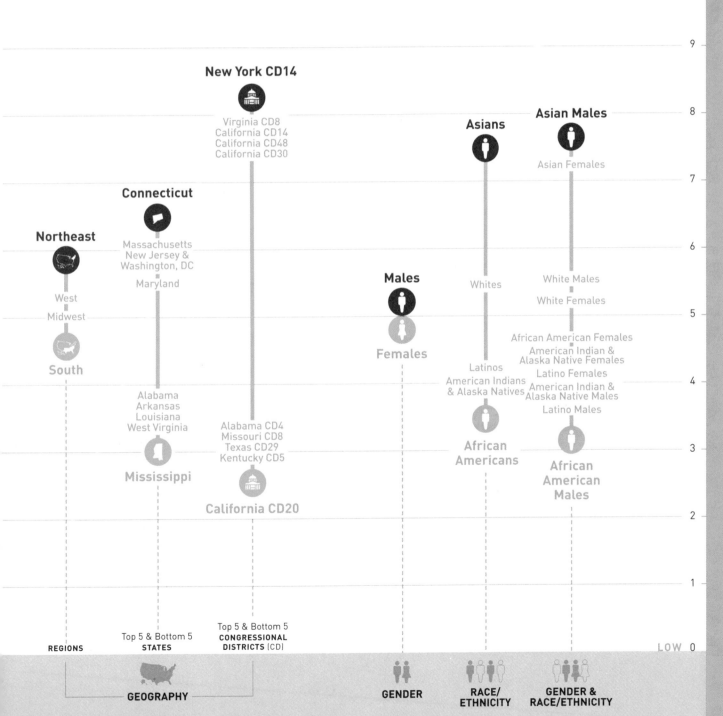

HUMAN DEVELOPMENT INDEX

How Do We Stack Up?

HD INDEX

HIGH 10

9

New York CD14

8

Virginia CD8
California CD14
California CD48
California CD30

Asians

Asian Males

Asian Females

7

Connecticut

Northeast

Massachusetts
New Jersey &
Washington, DC

Maryland

6

White Males

White Females

West

Males

5

Midwest

Whites

African American Females
American Indian &
Alaska Native Females

South

Females

Latinos
American Indians
& Alaska Natives

Latino Females
American Indian &
Alaska Native Males

Latino Males

4

Alabama
Arkansas
Louisiana
West Virginia

Alabama CD4
Missouri CD8
Texas CD29
Kentucky CD5

**African
Americans**

**African
American
Males**

3

Mississippi

California CD20

2

1

Top 5 & Bottom 5
**CONGRESSIONAL
DISTRICTS** (CD)

LOW 0

Top 5 & Bottom 5
STATES

REGIONS

GEOGRAPHY

GENDER

**RACE/
ETHNICITY**

**GENDER &
RACE/ETHNICITY**

Source: Census Bureau, "2005 American Community Survey."

Introduction

"The welfare of a nation can scarcely be inferred from a measure of national income. If the GDP is up, why is America down? . . . Goals for more growth should specify more growth of what and for what."

SIMON KUZNETS, Nobel Laureate, in a 1934 report to Congress

Do people living in Connecticut really have it so good? On average, they live to the age of eighty and earn more than $35,000 per year. More than one-third of Connecticut residents have graduated from college, and 15 percent have graduate degrees. All together, that makes Connecticut the number-one state in the American Human Development Index.

The American Human Development Index shows great variation among states and congressional districts, among racial/ethnic groups, and between women and men. Today, some groups experience levels of human development typical of the whole country ten, twenty, even fifty years ago. At the other end, if present trends continue, the country as a whole will not catch up to high-performing groups for many years. Income is an important part of the story, but not the only part. Health and education are critical factors in determining how much freedom people have and the quality of the lives they lead.

This first American HD Index provides a snapshot of the fifty states and the District of Columbia, and also looks at every congressional district, the five major ethnic groups, and the relative well-being of men and women. It reveals where we are today and sets a benchmark against which we will be able to assess where we are tomorrow—which parts of the country are moving forward and which are stalled or even falling behind.

The HD Index measures a limited number of indicators in three basic areas: life span, education, and earned income. These indicators represent good proxies for three key human development dimensions: health, knowledge, and standard of living, respectively. A particular individual's choices and opportunities may be constrained by any number of factors not captured in the index, such as a disability or a chronic lack of child care. Similarly, his or her life chances might be greatly enhanced by unmeasured variables ranging from superior athletic talent to inherited wealth.

The HD Index is an average that encompasses considerable variation. For example, the average income for people in Washington, D.C., is $36,948 a year. Yet some in the capital earn millions while others scrape by on $6.55 an hour.

In the state and congressional district rankings, very small differences may separate some states and districts. In some cases, differences are so small that they are not statistically significant. Even in cases in which the difference between two districts or states is statistically significant, the effect may be so slight that, for all practical purposes, the human development level of the two places is the same.

Historical Trends: Forty-Five Years of Human Development Progress

America has experienced tremendous progress during the past half century, not only in rising income but also in educational attainment and health. The American HD Index more than quadrupled between 1960 and 2005 (see TABLE 2.1). The biggest advance occurred in the education component, which grew more than six-fold. The percentage of the U.S. population with less than a high school education dropped from 58.9 percent in 1960 to 15.8 percent in 2005, while the percentage of college graduates almost quadrupled. Income and health also showed significant increases, with the average American earning almost twice as much in 2005 as in 1960 (with adjustments for inflation), and living eight years longer.

TABLE 2.1 **Historical Trends in Human Development**

YEAR	AMERICAN HD INDEX	LIFE EXPECTANCY AT BIRTH (years)	AT LEAST HIGH SCHOOL DIPLOMA (%)	AT LEAST BACHELOR'S DEGREE (%)	GRADUATE OR PROFESSIONAL DEGREE (%)	SCHOOL ENROLLMENT (%)	MEDIAN EARNINGS (2005 dollars)
2005	5.05	77.9	84.2	27.2	10.0	86.8	27,299
2000	4.67	77.0	80.4	24.4	8.9	82.8	27,382
1990	3.82	75.4	75.2	20.3	7.2	80.8	23,164
1980	2.86	73.7	66.5	16.2	5.6	71.9	21,432
1970	2.10	70.8	52.3	10.7	3.6	73.3	20,613
1960	1.23	69.7	41.1	7.7	2.5	76.9	15,732

Source: See Methodological Notes

America has experienced tremendous progress during the past half century.

While all three components of the HD Index increased each decade in the second half of the twentieth century (except for enrollment rate, where historical data are inconsistent), income has stagnated thus far in the twenty-first century. The overall HD Index grew on the strength of education and health improvements.

The remainder of this section paints a general picture of human development in America. A more in-depth look at each of the three dimensions of the index follows in subsequent chapters.

Presenting the American Human Development Index

Geography, Gender, and Race/Ethnicity

Mobility and Human Development

While some people are educated and work in or near the location where they were born, others relocate at different periods in their lives. This mobility has a significant impact on human development that the data cannot fully capture. The Human Development Index measures groups of individuals at one point in time. Thus, while Washington, D.C. offers highly educated people high salaries, most of them did not receive their education there.

The American HD Index for the country as a whole is 5.05. But that number has meaning only when compared to something else, such as the American HD Index for the country in 1960 (1.23) or 1980 (2.86). These comparisons reveal interesting information about the expansion of progress and opportunity over time. Another way to use the Index is to compare the scores of different groups of Americans today.

GEOGRAPHY: VARIATIONS AMONG REGIONS

The American HD Index reveals large disparities among the country's four major geographic regions. The Northeast is ranked number one and outperforms other regions in education and income, while the West, ranked number two, has the best performance in health. The South, ranked fourth, has the worst performance in all three dimensions of human development.

The ten states with the highest HD Index are mostly in the Northeast—Maryland and Minnesota being the only exceptions (see MAP 2.1). At the other end of the spectrum, nine of the ten states with the lowest HD Index are in the South—the exception being Montana.

TABLE 2.2 **American HD Index and Components, by Major Geographic REGION**

RANK	REGION	AMERICAN HD INDEX	LIFE EXPECTANCY AT BIRTH (years)	AT LEAST HIGH SCHOOL DIPLOMA (%)	AT LEAST BACHELOR'S DEGREE (%)	GRADUATE OR PROFESSIONAL DEGREE (%)	SCHOOL ENROLLMENT (%)	MEDIAN EARNINGS (2005 dollars)
1	Northeast	5.72	78.9	**86.2**	**31.3**	**12.6**	**89.6**	**31,037**
2	West	5.31	**79.2**	83.4	28.7	10.1	87.5	27,783
3	Midwest	5.04	78.0	87.0	25.5	9.0	86.9	27,015
4	South	4.64	**76.9**	**82.0**	**25.0**	**9.0**	**85.3**	**25,865**

Highest Performer   **Lowest Performer**

Note: The table highlights best and worst performers in each dimension of human development, not in each individual indicator. Unlike health and standard of living, each of which is measured using a single indicator, "access to knowledge" is captured using data on school enrollment and degree attainment, and the degrees included are high school diplomas, bachelor's degrees, and graduate degrees.

THE MEASURE OF AMERICA

MAP 2.1 **American Human Development Index, 2005**

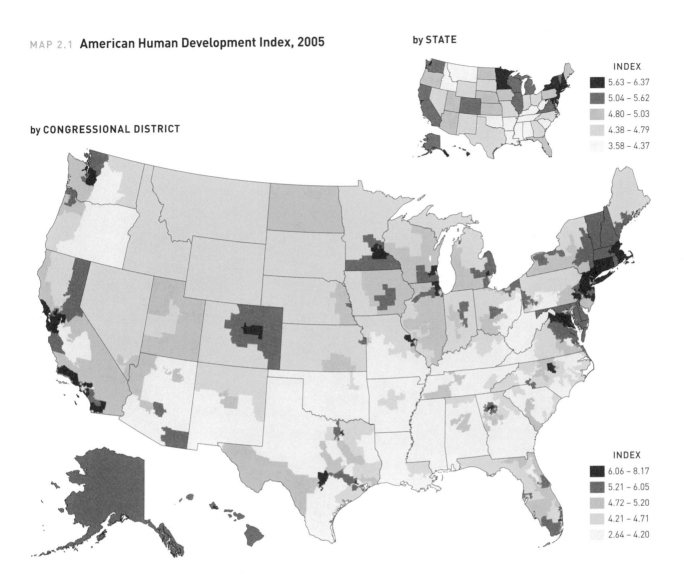

by **STATE**

INDEX
- 5.63 – 6.37
- 5.04 – 5.62
- 4.80 – 5.03
- 4.38 – 4.79
- 3.58 – 4.37

by **CONGRESSIONAL DISTRICT**

INDEX
- 6.06 – 8.17
- 5.21 – 6.05
- 4.72 – 5.20
- 4.21 – 4.71
- 2.64 – 4.20

GEOGRAPHY: VARIATIONS AMONG STATES

The level of overall human development in Connecticut is the highest in the United States, followed closely by Massachusetts (see TABLE 2.3). Neither of these states ranks highest on any of the three indices that make up the HD Index, but both score well across the board, yielding a balanced and high outcome. The District of Columbia, ranked third overall (tied with New Jersey), has the best performance on education; an impressive 45 percent of its residents have a college degree and one-quarter have a graduate or professional degree, far more than in any other state. It is also first in income. But the District of Columbia ranks last on health, with a life expectancy, at 73.8 years, approximately that of the average American in 1980. Wyoming has the highest percentage of the adult population with at least a high school diploma, but settles fairly far down on the overall state ranking table

NOTE: Each of the country's 436 congressional districts has approximately 650,000 inhabitants, except for a few districts located in states with small populations.

TABLE 2.3 **American HD Index and Components, by STATE**

RANK	STATE	AMERICAN HD INDEX	LIFE EXPECTANCY AT BIRTH (years)	AT LEAST HIGH SCHOOL DIPLOMA (%)	AT LEAST BACHELOR'S DEGREE (%)	GRADUATE OR PROFESSIONAL DEGREE (%)	SCHOOL ENROLLMENT (%)	MEDIAN EARNINGS (2005 dollars)
1	Connecticut	6.37	80.1	87.9	34.9	15.0	91.4	35,387
2	Massachusetts	6.27	79.8	88.0	36.9	15.7	92.4	33,544
3	District of Columbia	6.14	**73.8**	**83.6**	**45.3**	**25.2**	**99.8**	**36,948**
3	New Jersey	6.14	79.2	86.3	34.2	12.5	90.5	35,468
5	Maryland	5.99	78.0	87.0	34.5	15.2	89.9	35,144
6	Hawaii	5.82	**81.7**	88.1	27.9	9.1	87.5	29,287
7	New York	5.81	79.6	84.3	31.3	13.4	90.1	30,983
8	New Hampshire	5.80	79.5	89.9	31.8	11.7	88.0	31,054
9	Minnesota	5.72	80.5	90.9	30.7	9.7	86.1	29,687
9	Rhode Island	5.72	79.2	83.5	29.3	11.5	91.6	30,742
11	California	5.62	79.7	80.1	29.5	10.6	90.2	30,018
12	Colorado	5.59	79.1	88.7	35.5	12.3	86.0	29,438
13	Virginia	5.56	78.1	85.4	33.2	13.4	87.5	31,108
14	Illinois	5.42	78.1	85.7	29.2	10.9	89.3	29,598
14	Vermont	5.42	79.6	89.5	32.5	12.3	87.9	26,260
16	Washington	5.41	79.4	88.8	30.1	10.5	83.9	29,052
17	Alaska	5.35	78.5	91.0	27.3	10.1	83.1	30,388
18	Delaware	5.22	77.4	85.6	27.6	11.1	84.8	30,702
19	Wisconsin	5.20	79.0	88.8	25.0	8.1	86.6	27,387
20	Michigan	5.13	77.7	87.0	24.7	9.5	89.5	27,468
21	Iowa	5.03	79.3	89.6	23.8	7.3	85.3	25,618
21	Pennsylvania	5.03	77.7	86.7	25.7	9.8	86.7	27,395
23	Nebraska	5.00	79.2	89.5	27.3	8.5	85.1	24,865
24	Florida	4.96	78.5	84.6	25.1	8.8	86.7	25,951
25	Kansas	4.93	78.0	88.7	28.2	9.6	86.6	25,038
26	Arizona	4.90	78.2	83.8	25.6	9.3	83.9	26,764

Highest Performer   Lowest Performer

because it performs less well on the other indicators.

The five states at the bottom of the list, Alabama, Arkansas, Louisiana, West Virginia, and Mississippi, include the three Gulf states. Mississippi, where more than 21 percent of the state's population leaves high school without a diploma, and West Virginia, where only 17 percent receive a college degree, are tied for the lowest education index. Montana has the lowest income index, with median earnings almost $6,000 below the national average of $27,299.

Connecticut has an HD Index of 6.37, which, if current trends continue, will be the average HD Index of America as a whole in the year 2020. Mississippi, on the other hand, has an HD Index (3.58) lower than the HD Index for the whole country in 1990 (3.82). In other words, Mississippians today live like the average American lived more than fifteen years ago. Thus, a thirty-year gap in human development separates the two states. An average Connecticut resident earns 60 percent more, lives six years longer, and is almost twice as likely to have a college degree as a typical Mississippian.

TABLE 2.3 **American HD Index and Components, by STATE** *continued*

RANK	STATE	AMERICAN HD INDEX	LIFE EXPECTANCY AT BIRTH (years)	AT LEAST HIGH SCHOOL DIPLOMA (%)	AT LEAST BACHELOR'S DEGREE (%)	GRADUATE OR PROFESSIONAL DEGREE (%)	SCHOOL ENROLLMENT (%)	MEDIAN EARNINGS (2005 dollars)
26	North Dakota	4.90	79.8	88.2	25.5	6.7	84.6	23,789
26	Oregon	4.90	78.7	87.5	27.7	10.0	84.3	24,825
29	Maine	4.86	78.1	89.0	25.6	8.6	86.3	24,844
29	Utah	4.86	79.5	90.1	27.9	8.7	83.8	23,144
31	Ohio	4.79	77.1	86.3	23.3	8.5	85.7	26,706
32	Georgia	4.74	76.2	82.8	27.1	9.5	85.6	27,320
33	Indiana	4.64	76.9	85.3	21.3	7.7	84.4	26,442
34	North Carolina	4.61	76.6	82.3	25.1	8.0	87.5	25,111
35	Texas	4.57	77.6	78.8	25.1	8.2	84.5	24,952
36	Missouri	4.54	76.8	85.0	24.0	8.6	83.2	25,422
36	Nevada	4.54	76.3	82.8	20.6	6.6	81.0	28,486
38	South Dakota	4.53	78.6	88.6	24.7	7.0	80.9	23,110
38	Wyoming	4.53	77.8	91.3	23.2	7.7	81.7	23,752
40	New Mexico	4.49	77.7	82.0	25.1	10.9	87.0	22,131
41	Idaho	4.37	78.9	86.7	23.3	7.4	80.2	21,888
42	Montana	4.34	77.9	90.7	26.5	8.0	81.2	**21,472**
43	South Carolina	4.27	75.8	81.7	23.0	7.9	83.8	24,532
44	Kentucky	4.12	75.5	79.0	19.3	7.8	83.8	24,435
45	Tennessee	4.10	75.3	81.2	21.8	7.6	80.9	24,984
46	Oklahoma	4.02	75.1	84.3	22.4	7.2	83.2	22,901
47	Alabama	3.98	74.6	80.3	21.4	7.9	83.4	23,817
48	Arkansas	3.86	75.5	81.0	18.9	6.3	82.8	22,122
49	Louisiana	3.85	74.0	80.5	20.6	7.1	83.7	23,467
50	West Virginia	3.84	75.3	**81.2**	**16.9**	**6.8**	**82.1**	22,691
51	Mississippi	3.58	73.9	**78.5**	**18.7**	**6.5**	**82.6**	22,042

Highest Performer   **Lowest Performer**

Note: The table highlights the best and worst performers in each *dimension* of human development, not in each individual indicator.

GEOGRAPHY: VARIATIONS AMONG CONGRESSIONAL DISTRICTS

The map of HD Index by congressional district reveals a similar pattern (see MAP 2.1 and TABLE 2.4). The United States comprises 436 congressional districts, which include 435 voting districts plus the District of Columbia's nonvoting delegation. Each has approximately 650,000 inhabitants, with a few exceptions, such as in states with very small populations. We have broken all districts into five approximately equal groups by their HD Index ranking. Forty percent of the districts in the top group, or quintile, are in the Northeast, while 73 percent of the districts in the bottom fifth are in the South. The Northeast and the West regions have a large number of districts in the highest quintile, with a diminishing number of districts in each lower quintile. The South presents the inverse, with a large number of districts in the lowest quintile and a diminishing number of districts in each higher quintile. The Midwest has a relatively even distribution, with the largest number of districts in the middle quintiles. Supporting the value of looking beyond income to determine well-being, all three components—health, education, and income—play important roles in the regional variations revealed by the HD Index.

The variations among congressional districts are surprisingly lopsided in the overall HD Index and its component parts. The nation's number-one district on the HD Index—New York's Fourteenth Congressional District, which includes Manhattan's East Side, Roosevelt Island, and part of Queens, has an HD Index of 8.17. This is more than three times that of the 436th district—California's Twentieth Congressional District, which covers parts of Fresno, Kern, Kings, and Tulare counties, and has an HD Index of 2.64. In human development, these two districts are worlds apart: an average resident of New York's Fourteenth Congressional District earns almost three times as much as the average resident of California's Twentieth Congressional District, lives four and a half years longer, and is ten times as likely to have a college degree.

The two top-ranked districts—New York's Fourteenth and Virginia's Eighth (located in suburban Washington, D.C.)—have the best income and health indices, respectively. California's Thirtieth Congressional District (Hollywood, West Hollywood, Beverly Hills, Santa Monica, and Malibu), ranked number-five overall, has the best education index; while it does not have the highest score in any one of the education indicators, it scores well on all of them.

The three districts at the bottom of the list—Texas's Twenty-ninth (eastern portion of the greater Houston area), Kentucky's Fifth (eastern Kentucky), and California's Twentieth—have the worst education, health, and income indices, respectively. **The percentage of the adult population in Texas's Twenty-ninth District with less than a high school education today is at about the level of the U.S. average in the early 1970s. The life expectancy today in Kentucky's Fifth District is below that of the United States overall a quarter of a century ago.** California's Twentieth District has an earned income at the level of the country in the early 1960s.

The states with the largest internal variations of the HD Index among their congressional districts, as measured by their HD Index ranges, are California, New York, Virginia, and Texas. Connecticut and Massachusetts, the top two states on the HD Index, are among the states with a more balanced HD Index distribution among their congressional districts. Both states have low internal variation on the Index.

California, with fifty-three districts, spans the gamut in terms of human development status, with several districts in the top ten and one at the bottom. The state is home to the country's third-highest-ranking (Fourteenth District—Silicon Valley) as well as the nation's bottom district (Twentieth District—Kings County), located only about one hundred miles apart. Sometimes, the extremes are located within the same city: Los Angeles contains both a top-ten district (Thirtieth District—Hollywood, Beverly Hills, Santa Monica, and Malibu) and a bottom-thirty district (Thirty-first District—downtown Los Angeles).

California spans the gamut in terms of human development, with several districts in the top ten and one at the bottom.

TABLE 2.4 Top and Bottom 20 CONGRESSIONAL DISTRICTS on the American HD Index

RANK	STATE	AMERICAN HD INDEX	LIFE EXPECTANCY AT BIRTH (years)	AT LEAST HIGH SCHOOL DIPLOMA [%]	AT LEAST BACHELOR'S DEGREE [%]	GRADUATE OR PROFESSIONAL DEGREE [%]	SCHOOL ENROLLMENT [%]	MEDIAN EARNINGS (2005 dollars)
TOP 20 Congressional Districts								
1	CD 14, New York	8.17	81.6	90.4	62.6	27.3	94.6	**51,139**
2	CD 8, Virginia	8.14	**82.9**	90.1	58.2	28.7	96.7	46,031
3	CD 14, California	8.08	82.1	90.6	56.3	27.9	98.2	46,539
4	CD 48, California	7.89	81.6	93.8	51.9	20.5	99.2	45,999
5	CD 30, California	7.78	79.9	**95.0**	**56.7**	**24.0**	**102.6**	45,128
6	CD 11, Virginia	7.65	81.6	92.6	52.2	22.9	93.2	45,119
7	CD 8, New York	7.60	80.7	87.4	55.3	25.7	96.0	44,340
8	CD 8, Maryland	7.58	82.7	88.5	55.5	29.8	93.4	39,158
9	CD 12, California	7.50	81.7	89.5	45.6	15.8	103.9	41,947
10	CD 15, California	7.43	82.4	87.4	43.8	17.4	96.1	42,135
11	CD 7, New Jersey	7.42	80.6	91.9	47.6	18.9	94.7	44,838
12	CD 11, New Jersey	7.39	79.9	93.0	49.8	20.2	94.2	45,410
12	CD 12, New Jersey	7.39	80.2	92.5	48.8	21.2	95.6	43,714
14	CD 18, New York	7.26	81.3	88.0	48.5	24.5	93.1	40,813
15	CD 5, New Jersey	7.19	80.9	92.3	42.5	16.1	94.4	42,204
16	CD 8, California	7.16	80.8	83.7	49.0	18.2	111.6	38,434
17	CD 3, New York	7.07	80.8	91.8	34.7	14.5	96.0	41,761
18	CD 42, California	7.06	80.1	91.2	40.4	14.0	96.7	41,577
18	CD 9, Michigan	7.06	79.5	92.4	46.9	20.8	95.3	40,365
20	CD 46, California	7.05	81.2	87.6	39.6	15.4	98.3	38,634
BOTTOM 20 Congressional Districts								
417	CD 4, Arkansas	3.50	75.0	78.6	14.8	5.1	83.0	20,471
418	CD 8, Tennessee	3.49	74.3	78.8	14.2	4.9	79.9	22,511
419	CD 7, Alabama	3.47	74.2	77.6	15.9	5.9	83.5	20,863
420	CD 6, South Carolina	3.45	75.1	76.1	15.3	5.2	81.2	20,796
421	CD 1, Tennessee	3.42	74.9	77.7	17.0	6.0	76.9	21,639
422	CD 15, Texas	3.40	79.3	57.4	14.6	3.9	78.1	18,113
422	CD 16, New York	3.40	77.6	64.5	8.7	2.5	86.6	19,113
424	CD 4, Arizona	3.36	78.6	60.9	12.0	4.2	70.5	21,671
424	CD 4, Tennessee	3.36	75.0	75.4	13.1	4.4	76.4	22,233
426	CD 1, North Carolina	3.35	74.2	77.4	13.1	4.1	85.2	20,257
426	CD 5, Louisiana	3.35	73.4	74.7	17.3	6.0	83.0	20,892
428	CD 1, Arkansas	3.34	74.2	77.3	13.7	4.3	82.8	20,551
429	CD 2, Mississippi	3.30	73.0	74.8	18.7	6.3	84.1	20,572
430	CD 2, Oklahoma	3.29	74.0	80.0	14.9	5.0	79.7	20,763
431	CD 3, West Virginia	3.28	73.8	76.4	13.7	5.5	81.1	21,060
432	CD 4, Alabama	3.26	74.1	73.5	12.8	4.8	78.7	21,868
433	CD 8, Missouri	3.15	74.8	76.3	12.7	5.1	77.8	19,979
434	CD 29, Texas	2.81	77.4	**53.6**	**6.4**	**2.0**	**75.2**	18,811
435	CD 5, Kentucky	2.79	**72.6**	66.5	11.5	5.4	77.7	20,759
436	CD 20, California	2.64	77.1	52.6	6.5	1.6	79.7	**16,767**

Highest Performer   Lowest Performer

Note: This table highlights the best and worst performers in each *dimension* of human development, not in each individual indicator. For all 436 congressional districts, see the Indicator Tables.

New York has four of the top twenty districts and one in the bottom twenty. The district with the highest HD Index rank in the country, the Fourteenth Congressional District (Manhattan's East Side, Roosevelt Island, and part of Queens), is located less than three miles from the congressional district ranked number 423 (out of 436), the Sixteenth Congressional District (South Bronx; see BOX 2.1).

TABLE 2.5 **Range of CONGRESSIONAL DISTRICT Index Scores, by State**

RANK	STATE	NUMBER OF DISTRICTS	HD INDEX RANGE	MINIMUM HD INDEX	MAXIMUM HD INDEX
1	California	53	5.44	2.64	8.08
2	New York	29	4.77	3.40	8.17
3	Virginia	11	4.44	3.70	8.14
4	Texas	32	3.62	2.81	6.43
5	Georgia	13	3.32	3.61	6.93
5	North Carolina	13	3.32	3.35	6.67
7	Illinois	19	3.28	3.65	6.92
8	Michigan	15	3.16	3.90	7.06
9	Missouri	9	3.03	3.15	6.19
10	Washington	9	2.80	4.02	6.82
11	Arizona	8	2.62	3.36	5.98
12	Pennsylvania	19	2.56	3.72	6.29
13	New Jersey	13	2.55	4.87	7.42
14	Maryland	8	2.53	5.04	7.58
15	Florida	25	2.45	3.77	6.23
16	Colorado	7	2.43	4.55	6.99
17	Minnesota	8	2.27	4.53	6.80
18	Kentucky	6	2.24	2.79	5.03
19	Tennessee	9	1.84	3.36	5.20
19	Wisconsin	8	1.84	4.50	6.33
21	Kansas	4	1.77	4.27	6.04
21	Alabama	7	1.77	3.26	5.03
23	Ohio	18	1.73	3.82	5.55
24	South Carolina	6	1.51	3.45	4.96
25	Oregon	5	1.49	4.20	5.68
26	New Mexico	3	1.31	3.77	5.08
27	Indiana	9	1.30	4.25	5.55
27	Massachusetts	10	1.30	5.47	6.78
29	Nebraska	3	1.21	4.29	5.50
30	Oklahoma	5	1.20	3.29	4.50
31	Louisiana	7	1.18	3.35	4.53
32	Arkansas	4	1.13	3.34	4.47
33	Connecticut	5	0.96	6.07	7.03
34	West Virginia	3	0.87	3.28	4.15
35	Nevada	3	0.82	4.03	4.85
35	Iowa	5	0.82	4.61	5.43
37	Mississippi	4	0.64	3.30	3.94
38	Utah	3	0.46	4.67	5.12

Note: States with fewer than three congressional districts not included (Alaska, Delaware, District of Columbia, Hawaii, Idaho, Maine, Montana, New Hampshire, North Dakota, Rhode Island, South Dakota, Vermont, and Wyoming).

BOX 2.1 **A Tale of Two Districts: Five Subway Stops, A Half-Century Difference**

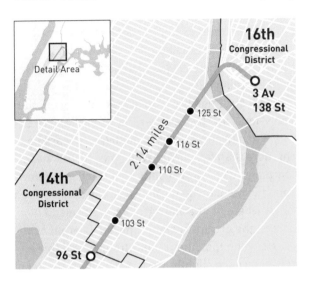

To travel more than half a century back in time, a New York City subway passenger need only board the #6 Train at Ninety-sixth Street in Manhattan and travel 2.14 miles uptown, emerging at the Third Avenue station in the Bronx. The Ninety-sixth Street station is located in New York's Fourteenth Congressional District, the top-ranked HD Index district in the country. Given the historical growth pattern between 1960 and 2005, the country as a whole can expect to reach the Fourteenth Congressional District's HD Index level of 8.17 sometime around the year 2041. However, for residents in New York's Sixteenth Congressional District, which includes the Third Avenue station in the Bronx, the wait will likely be longer. The Sixteenth Congressional District is a bottom-twenty district with an HD Index of 3.40, which corresponds to America's national average circa 1985.

Thus, these two districts have a fifty-six-year gap in human development. Separated by little more than 2 miles, they might just as easily be located in different hemispheres.

The ethnic profiles of the two districts are totally distinct: the Fourteenth Congressional District has an overwhelmingly white population (two-thirds of the total), with Latinos and African Americans together accounting for less than 19 percent. By contrast, Latinos and African Americans constitute more than 93 percent of the Sixteenth Congressional District's population, and whites only 2 percent.

On average, a resident of the Fourteenth Congressional District earns two and a half times as much, lives four years longer, is more than seven times as likely to have a college degree, and is four times less likely to be in poverty than a resident of the Sixteenth Congressional District.

EARNINGS (2005)

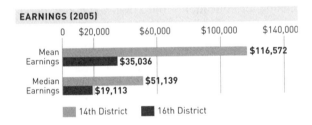

UNEMPLOYMENT AND POVERTY

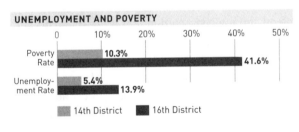

EDUCATIONAL ATTAINMENT

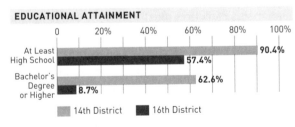

RACE / ETHNICITY

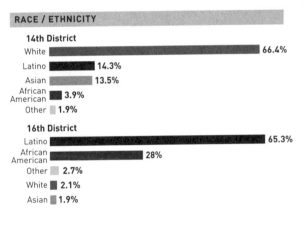

Source: Census Bureau, "2005 American Community Survey."

DIFFERENCES ACROSS GENDER AND RACE/ETHNICITY

Some of the largest disparities in human development outcomes occur across different gender and race/ethnicity combinations. When we look at gender alone, men have a slightly higher HD Index than women, but the difference is small; American men and women have virtually the same human development level. However, examining each of the three dimensions of the HD Index individually, outcomes for men and women are anything but equal.

Women have a higher education index (mostly due to higher rates of enrollment in school from ages three to twenty-four) and live, on average, about five years longer. But advantages in education and health are wiped out by lower earnings. American males earn 50 percent more than females.[17] (While the income measure used in this report is personal earnings, as a way to capture the gender differences in earnings and control over economic resources, this measure can underestimate women's standard of living in cases where household earnings are pooled.)

Turning to HD Index by ethnicity, the picture is highly uneven. Overall, Asians have the highest HD Index, outperforming the other ethnic groups in all three human development dimensions. They earn slightly more than whites, the second-ranked group, but have a large advantage in health and education.

Latinos have the lowest ranking for education—more than 40 percent don't have a high school diploma—and income, but score well on health, resulting in a number-three ranking overall. African Americans, on the other hand, rank third in income and education, but have a large gap in life expectancy—five years less than American Indians, the second lowest-ranking group on health, and more than thirteen years less than Asians. These factors result in a bottom ranking overall when compared by ethnic grouping.

Gender adds another layer of difference to an already highly unequal picture. At the top, men have an income advantage over women that more than compensates for their relative disadvantages in health (Asians and whites) and education (whites only). At the lower end of the spectrum, the opposite is the case. Among African Americans, American Indians, and Latinos, men all have lower HD Indices than women. While men's earnings are higher in these three groups, advantages in education or longevity, or a combination of the two, outweigh superior earnings to yield a higher HD Index for women.

Looking in more depth, Asian males rank first mostly because of educational differences. While Asian and white males have similar high school graduation rates, 53 percent of Asian males have at least a college degree, compared to 32 percent of white males. Asian females have the highest health index and rank second overall, followed by white males, who have the highest earned income.

Latino males score last on education (with less than 60 percent graduating from high school and only 12 percent graduating from college) and rank ninth out of ten overall; African American males have the lowest health index, and occupy the number-ten overall ranking, in spite of being ranked fourth in income.

> Latino males score last on education, with less than 60 percent graduating from high school and only 12 percent graduating from college.

America as a whole can expect to reach the HD Index of Asian males by the year 2035, while African American males are living at a level that prevailed in America circa 1986. In sum, the human development gap between Asian and African American males is half a century.

NOTE: The tables highlight the best performers in each dimension of human development, not in each individual indicator.

TABLE 2.6 **HD Index by GENDER**

RANK	GENDER	AMERICAN HD INDEX	LIFE EXPECTANCY AT BIRTH (years)	AT LEAST HIGH SCHOOL DIPLOMA [%]	AT LEAST BACHELOR'S DEGREE [%]	GRADUATE OR PROFESSIONAL DEGREE [%]	SCHOOL ENROLLMENT [%]	MEDIAN EARNINGS (2005 dollars)
1	Males	5.04	75.4	83.8	28.5	10.8	83.8	**32,850**
2	Females	5.01	**80.5**	**84.6**	**26.0**	**9.2**	**90.0**	22,000

Highest Performer

TABLE 2.7 **HD Index by RACE/ETHNICITY**

RANK	GENDER	AMERICAN HD INDEX	LIFE EXPECTANCY AT BIRTH (years)	AT LEAST HIGH SCHOOL DIPLOMA [%]	AT LEAST BACHELOR'S DEGREE [%]	GRADUATE OR PROFESSIONAL DEGREE [%]	SCHOOL ENROLLMENT [%]	MEDIAN EARNINGS (2005 dollars)
1	Asians	7.53	**86.3**	**85.6**	**49.1**	**19.9**	102.3	31,518
2	Whites	5.51	78.2	89.0	30.0	11.0	87.7	30,485
3	Latinos	3.97	82.1	59.5	12.2	3.9	78.8	20,255
4	American Indians	3.89	78.0	76.3	13.6	4.5	82.4	21,037
5	African Americans	3.81	**73.0**	79.9	17.3	5.9	89.5	23,025

Highest Performer   **Lowest Performer**

TABLE 2.8 **HD Index by GENDER and RACE/ETHNICITY**

RANK	GENDER	AMERICAN HD INDEX	LIFE EXPECTANCY AT BIRTH (years)	AT LEAST HIGH SCHOOL DIPLOMA [%]	AT LEAST BACHELOR'S DEGREE [%]	GRADUATE OR PROFESSIONAL DEGREE [%]	SCHOOL ENROLLMENT [%]	MEDIAN EARNINGS (2005 dollars)
1	Asian males	7.64	83.6	**88.3**	**53.1**	**24.3**	**98.8**	37,035
2	Asian females	7.30	**88.8**	83.1	45.6	16.0	106.0	26,138
3	White males	5.55	75.7	88.7	31.7	12.1	84.7	**37,269**
4	White females	5.32	80.7	89.3	28.3	10.1	90.9	23,388
5	African American females	4.18	76.3	80.2	17.8	6.3	92.7	20,915
6	American Indian females	4.17	81.1	77.3	23.0	4.1	85.3	17,589
7	Latino females	3.98	85.0	60.7	12.7	3.9	81.7	**16,147**
8	American Indian males	3.76	74.7	75.3	21.1	4.9	79.5	24,315
9	Latino males	3.67	79.1	58.3	11.8	3.9	76.1	22,471
10	African American males	3.45	**69.4**	79.5	16.6	5.4	86.4	26,086

Highest Performer   **Lowest Performer**

Income vs. Investment in People's Capabilities

Looking at congressional districts with similar income but highly divergent well-being outcomes helps to illustrate a key rationale of the human development approach: that consideration of income alone produces an exceedingly narrow and incomplete portrait of the human condition. For example, Vermont's only congressional district has about the same average income as Nevada's First District, about $26,300 per year. However, they are separated by 223 places on the HD Index. Why? Vermont residents can expect to live on average three and a half more years, and about 10 percent of Vermont's residents did not graduate from high school; in Nevada's First District, just under 25 percent did not. College and graduate school completion rates are higher as well in Vermont (see FIGURE 2.1).

In order to fully understand why two districts with nearly identical income levels have such different outcomes in health and education, one would need to examine a full range of indicators, analyzing each district's circumstances and historical backgrounds. But the data make clear that money is buying neither a better education nor a longer life for the average Nevadan.

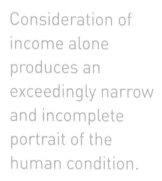

Consideration of income alone produces an exceedingly narrow and incomplete portrait of the human condition.

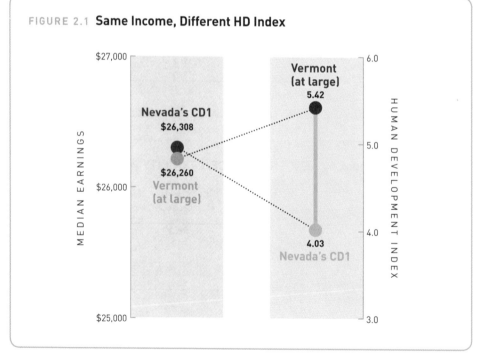

FIGURE 2.1 **Same Income, Different HD Index**

MEDIAN EARNINGS

HUMAN DEVELOPMENT INDEX

Nevada's CD1
$26,308

$26,260
Vermont
(at large)

Vermont
(at large)
5.42

4.03
Nevada's CD1

$27,000 — 6.0

$26,000 — 5.0

$25,000 — 4.0

3.0

FIGURE 2.2 plots each state's overall HD Index rank against its income rank. States that fall on the left side of the diagonal line rank higher on the HD Index overall than they rank on income. In other words, they are doing a better job in transforming income into positive health and education outcomes. States to the right of the line rank higher on income than on overall HD Index; their higher incomes are not buying them longer lives or better educations.

North Dakota and Utah are the most efficient states in terms of investing in residents' well-being, followed by Vermont, Nebraska, and Hawaii. Nevada is last on the efficiency list, followed by Tennessee, Georgia, Indiana, Delaware, and Alabama.

FIGURE 2.2 **Income and Human Development, States**

Some states do a better job than others in transforming income into positive health and education outcomes.

The global Human Development Report, as well as several country-specific reports using this model, show strong correlations between income and life expectancy—they tend to move in tandem. However, for Americans, the correlation is weaker.

In the U.S., income levels are no longer decisive in determining lifespan; other factors, such as lifestyle, environment, and health insurance, play significant roles.

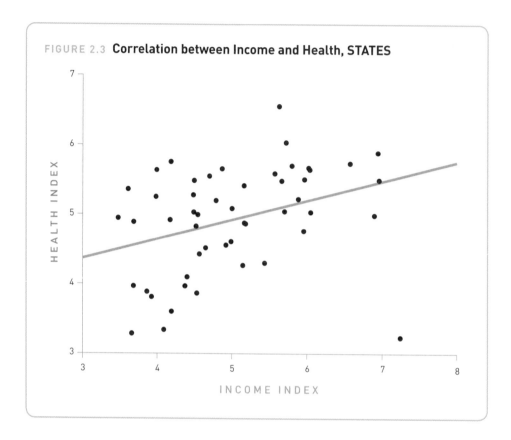

FIGURE 2.3 **Correlation between Income and Health, STATES**

Only 12 percent of the variation in life expectancy across states can be explained by variations in income. For congressional districts, the observed relationship is stronger—27 percent—but still much weaker than the values for low- and medium-income countries. Looking at 181 countries, 65 percent of the variance in life expectancy can be explained by the variance in income.[18] A closer look at the evidence explains this finding. Income and life expectancy are strongly correlated across countries, as first documented by demographer Samuel Preston.[19] FIGURE 2.4 shows an updated version of the Preston Curve, using data from the *Human Development Report 2007/2008*.

Among the countries with the lowest GDP per capita, shown at the left side of the graph, the slope of the curve is very steep. In these cases, small changes in income are associated with large changes in life expectancy. More than 30 percent of all deaths in these low-income countries are among children, and the vast majority can be prevented by low-cost interventions such as immunizations. Among the

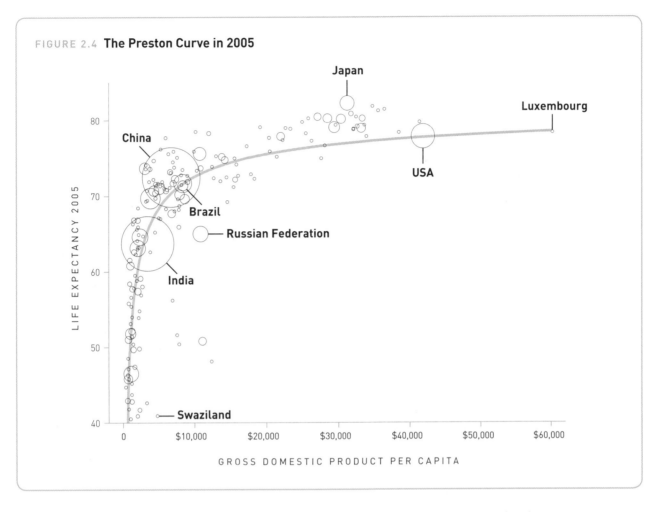

FIGURE 2.4 **The Preston Curve in 2005**

high-income countries, shown at the right side of the graph, the curve is almost flat, indicating that changes in income have little or no effect on life expectancy. In these countries, fewer than 1 percent of deaths occur before a child's fifth birthday. Most are due to chronic diseases, such as cancer and heart disease, that typically affect the elderly.[20]

The United States, with the second-highest per-capita GDP in the world, occupies the flat portion of the Preston Curve because infant deaths due to preventable diseases are mercifully rare. In the United States, income levels are no longer decisive in determining how long one is expected to live; other factors, such as diet, lifestyle, environment, and health insurance coverage, play significant roles. This is one reason that the multidimensional human development approach is highly relevant to affluent countries: income has a less decisive impact on human development in affluent countries than it generally has in less developed countries.

> In the poorest countries, small increases in income are associated with large gains in life expectancy.

The Building Blocks of the HD Index

Now that we know how different groups of Americans compare in terms of levels of human development, we turn our attention to the question of **why such differences exist**.

In the sections that follow, we unpack the HD Index, examining more closely the health, access to knowledge, and standard of living of Americans. We explore the **factors** that influence life expectancy, educational attainment, and earnings, and we weigh **efforts** to achieve greater progress in these critical areas.

A Long and
Healthy Life

Access to
Knowledge

A Decent
Standard
of Living

PART 3
The Building Blocks of the HD Index
A Long and Healthy Life

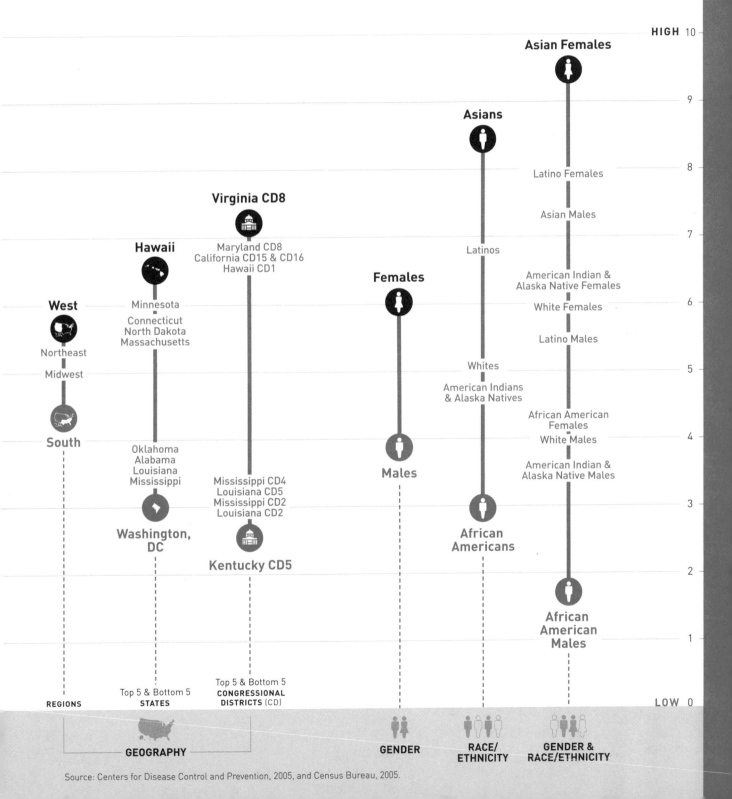

HEALTH INDEX: Life Expectancy at Birth

How Do We Stack Up?

HEALTH INDEX

HIGH 10

Asian Females

9

Asians

Latino Females

8

Asian Males

Virginia CD8

7

Maryland CD8
California CD15 & CD16
Hawaii CD1

Latinos

American Indian &
Alaska Native Females

Hawaii

White Females

6

West

Latino Males

Minnesota

Females

Connecticut
North Dakota
Massachusetts

5

Northeast

Whites

Midwest

American Indians
& Alaska Natives

African American
Females

4

White Males

South

Oklahoma
Alabama
Louisiana
Mississippi

Mississippi CD4
Louisiana CD5
Mississippi CD2
Louisiana CD2

Males

American Indian &
Alaska Native Males

3

**Washington,
DC**

**African
Americans**

2

Kentucky CD5

**African
American
Males**

1

REGIONS

Top 5 & Bottom 5
STATES

Top 5 & Bottom 5
**CONGRESSIONAL
DISTRICTS** (CD)

LOW 0

GEOGRAPHY

GENDER

**RACE/
ETHNICITY**

**GENDER &
RACE/ETHNICITY**

Source: Centers for Disease Control and Prevention, 2005, and Census Bureau, 2005.

Introduction

"In a nation as rich as ours, it is a shocking fact that tens of millions lack adequate medical care. . . . We must have without further delay—a system of prepaid medical insurance which will enable every American to afford good medical care."

HARRY TRUMAN, State of the Union Address, January 5, 1949

The Human Development Index reveals stark disparities in longevity among different groups.

In 1793, a yellow fever epidemic hit Philadelphia. In the absence of knowledge about either the cause or the cure for yellow fever, doctors told everyone to flee the city, then the nation's capital. About 10 percent of the population perished.

We've come a long way since then. Investments in a safe water supply and sanitary sewage disposal, in a safe food supply, in research on the causes and prevention of disease, and on campaigns and laws to prevent the spread of disease and to change social norms have all contributed to healthier lives.

Over the long haul, all Americans are living longer. In 1900, life expectancy at birth was forty-six for men and forty-eight for women. A century later, we have reached averages of seventy-five and eighty, respectively, and those with the best health have achieved some of the highest life spans on record anywhere. **The nation has made significant advances in public health, some of which have had a profound influence on longevity and quality of life.**

- The elderly are now protected from catastrophic medical expenses as a result of Medicare, enacted in 1965.

- The percentage of smokers has fallen, from about 42 percent of the U.S. population in 1965 to 17 percent in 2004.

- Implementation of the 1990 Americans with Disabilities Act has afforded disabled Americans more choices and opportunities in access to transportation, employment, communications, and many other areas.

- Vaccination rates increased from just over half of all children in 1995 to over 80 percent of nineteen- to thirty-five-month-olds a decade later.

- The U.S. leads the world in the availability of high-tech medicine and in new patents for biomedical technology, innovations that can contribute to healthier lives not only in this country, but for people around the world.

There is much to celebrate in this progress. Yet these critical advances are not enabling long and healthy lives across the full spectrum of American society. The Human Development Index reveals stark disparities in longevity among different groups.

Health and Human Development

The human development approach values the freedom to live a long and healthy life. Good health is required to feel secure and self-confident about the future. Good health is also a means to other ends, including undertaking meaningful work, raising educated and healthy children, and participating in society. Children suffering from chronic illness face tremendous challenges succeeding in school. Likewise, chronically ill adults are far more likely to face economic difficulties and are less able to seize opportunities and carry out their plans.

Health is also essential for the nation as a whole. Healthy people make a productive workforce and contribute to growth and global competitiveness. The National Academy of Sciences estimated in 2004 that the lost economic value due to poorer health and earlier deaths among uninsured Americans equals an average of $178 million to $356 million every day.[21] An effective, affordable health system is predicated on the existence of a predominantly healthy population whose needs will not overwhelm the health-care infrastructure or place undue financial burdens on employers, patients, or governments.

This section of the text looks at health from two different angles. The first is *quantitative.* The Human Development Index on health is based on life expectancy, a statistic that measures how long people are living based on data derived from death certificates and mortality patterns. We review the longevity status of various groups in the United States, based on the results of the Index, and look at factors leading to different causes of death among different groups.

Our second perspective on American health is *quality***—how we achieve physical, mental, and social wellness.** This section of the text evaluates some of the conditions that contribute to wellness throughout the life cycle, along with particular challenges America faces in achieving good health for all. Finally, we look at *whose* health we are investing in and how the issue of health insurance influences the quality and cost of American health.

What follows is a broad discussion of the status of health in America and how it impacts human development.

Critical advances are not enabling long and healthy lives across the full spectrum of American society.

What Does the HD Index Show?

The United States and Its "Peer Group"

Americans live
fewer years
than citizens of
Israel, Greece,
Singapore, Costa
Rica, and Korea.

American life expectancy in 1960 was 69.7 years. By 2005, more than 8 years had been added to American lives, with the average reaching 77.9. While worthy of celebration, this progress nonetheless represents a poor return on health-care investment compared with other countries. Japanese citizens can expect to outlive Americans, on average, by more than 4 years. Indeed, Americans live fewer years than citizens of Israel, Greece, Singapore, Costa Rica, Korea, and virtually every Western European and Nordic country (see **FIGURE 3.1**).

FIGURE 3.1 **Global Comparison: Life Expectancy, 2005**

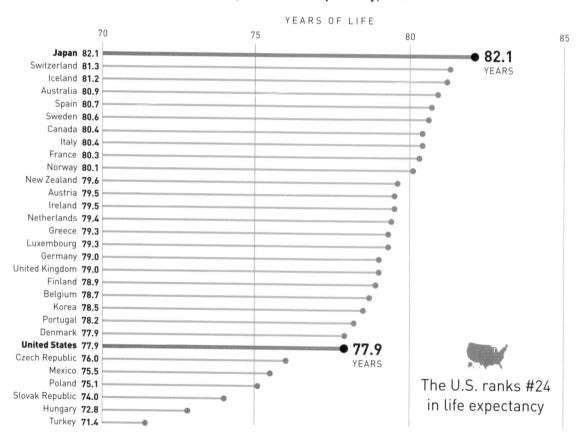

The U.S. ranks #24
in life expectancy

Source: Organisation for Economic Co-Operation and Development. *Health at a Glance*, 2007.

MAP 3.1 **Life Expectancy at Birth, 2005**

by **STATE**

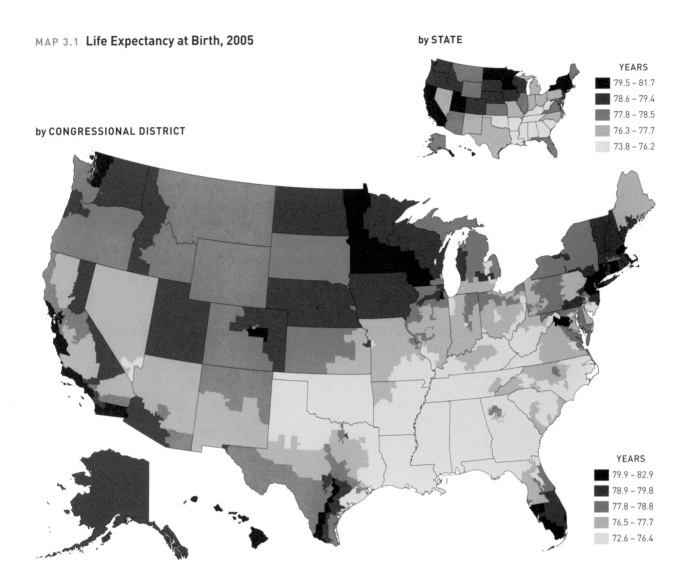

YEARS

■	79.5 – 81.7
■	78.6 – 79.4
■	77.8 – 78.5
■	76.3 – 77.7
■	73.8 – 76.2

by **CONGRESSIONAL DISTRICT**

YEARS

■	79.9 – 82.9
■	78.9 – 79.8
■	77.8 – 78.8
■	76.5 – 77.7
■	72.6 – 76.4

VARIATIONS IN HEALTH BY STATES

As MAP 3.1 **reflects, within the United States, there is great variation in lifespan depending on where one lives.** In Washington, D.C., the average life expectancy is 73.8 years; in Hawaii it is 81.7 years, a difference of almost eight years. Washington, D.C., which has the highest income of any state but the shortest average lifespan, is a reminder that looking at income alone does not tell the whole story of people's well-being.

Minnesota, the number-two state in life expectancy, can boast a handful of centenarians-plus—residents who have crossed the age of 110. What is Minnesota doing that the rest of us can study and implement? In terms of state expenditures on health, Minnesota spends at the rate of the national average—3.3 percent of

Regional Ranking in Health:

1. West
2. Northeast
2. Midwest
4. South

its gross state product.[22] Yet the state is maximizing its wealth and other favorable factors to produce exceptionally long lives for its people. BOX 3.1 discusses some of the factors that put Minnesota near the top.

In addition to wide lifespan variations among states, there are also wide variations within states. In Maryland, a resident of the Eighth Congressional District, Montgomery County, can expect to live an average of 82.7 years, while a resident of nearby District 7 (parts of Baltimore City, Baltimore County, and Howard County) will live, on average, about seven and a half years less. The average lifespan in District 7 is below the U.S. average from eighteen years ago. Florida also has extreme variations in life expectancy within the state. Residents of Florida's Thirteenth and Fourteenth districts live to over 80, while those in District 4 can expect to live on average six years less.

Looking at the range in the congressional district life expectancy (see Indicator Tables), Kentucky's Fifth District, at the bottom of the rankings, has an average life expectancy of 72.6 years, while in Virginia's Eighth Congressional District, at the top of the table, it is 82.9 years—a difference of more than a decade. Residents of Kentucky's Fifth District are living on average the same as the country average in the mid- to late 1970s.

Asian Americans have the highest life expectancy.

BOX 3.1 Why Is Minnesota Number Two?

Statewide health is based on a complex set of factors and their interrelationships. There is tremendous variation within state averages. Some of the following factors likely contribute to Minnesota's average life expectancy of 76.1 years, among the highest in the nation.

- **Physical activity.** In 2004, more Minnesotans reported engaging in recent leisure time physical activity than did residents of any other state. Also, residents of the state's most populous city, Minneapolis, have the second highest rate of bicycling to work in the nation.

- **Healthier newborns.** Minnesota has a low infant mortality rate, including the lowest rate of infant mortality for non-Hispanic black mothers in the United States.

- **Investment in public health.** While overall health spending in the state is at the national average, Minnesota's per-capita public health expenditures, including childhood immunization, food safety, and cancer screening clinics, are more than 50 percent higher than the national average.

- **Income equality.** An emerging body of research is examining the correlation between economic inequality and health. Minnesota is known for its relatively egalitarian culture. As measured by the Gini Index (a summary measure of income inequality), Minnesota is significantly less unequal than the U.S. average

- **Insurance coverage.** Nationally, 16 percent of the population lacks any form of health insurance. However, only 7 percent of Minnesotans are without health insurance. This is one of the lowest rates of uninsured citizens of any state.

Yes, Minnesotans come from hearty stock. But the state's institutions and policies have built on this strong foundation to yield one of the healthiest populations in the nation.

Sources: DeNavas-Walt, Proctor, and Smith, "Current Population Reports"; Centers for Disease Control and Prevention, "Results of Behavioral Risk Factor Surveillance System"; U.S. Census Bureau, "2005 American Community Survey"; Matthews and MacDorman, "Infant Mortality Statistics from the 2004 Period Linked Birth/Infant Death Data Set"; National Association of State Budget Officers. "Per Capita Health Spending"; Kawachi, "Income Inequality and Health."

VARIATIONS IN HEALTH BY RACE/ETHNICITY

Because of the difference in life expectancy between men and women, which stems from biological and behavioral causes and is found in virtually every country, it is important to weigh ethnic variations by gender. **Asians top the index, with female life expectancy at 88.8 years, followed by Latino, Native American, white, and then African American women, in that order. This ordering involves a twelve-year gap between the top and bottom groups and almost four years between Asian women and the next group down, Latino women.** The life expectancy of white women is 8 years less than Asian women and five years less than Latino women. In male life expectancy, the order shifts slightly, with white males above Native American men.

Among African Americans, overall trends in many aspects of life are positive, including higher college graduation rates and diminishing barriers to careers in business, law, public service, and other occupations. Yet in terms of basic health, obstacles abound. **The 13.3-year gap between Asians and African Americans can be compared to the gap between Japan and Guatemala.**

African Americans today have a lifespan shorter than the average American in the late 1970s. A group of physicians and health experts have calculated that from 1940 to 1999, 4.3 million African Americans died prematurely relative to whites in the same period[23] (see **FIGURE 3.2**). **Raising the average age at death of African Americans to the average age of whites could prevent tens of thousands of premature deaths each year.**

Overall life expectancy for Latinos is second to Asians. Latinos are not a monolithic group, and the health and overall human development challenges of Mexicans, Puerto Ricans, Cubans, Dominicans, and other Latino groups vary widely. **But one disturbing pattern suggests that the longer non-native-born Latinos reside in the United States, the lower their age at death and the higher**

> African Americans today have a lifespan shorter than the average American in the late 1970s.

TABLE 3.1 Life Expectancy for Race/Ethnicity by Gender

RACE/ETHNICITY BY GENDER	LIFE EXPECTANCY
Asian females	88.8
Latino females	85.0
Asian males	83.6
American Indian females	81.1
White females	80.7
Latino males	79.1
African American females	76.3
White males	75.7
American Indian males	74.7
African American males	69.4

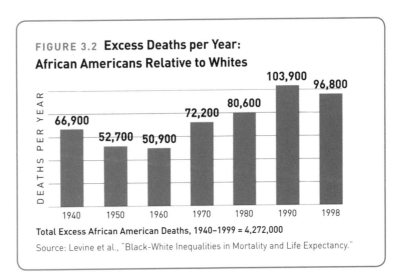

FIGURE 3.2 Excess Deaths per Year: African Americans Relative to Whites

DEATHS PER YEAR

1940	1950	1960	1970	1980	1990	1998
66,900	52,700	50,900	72,200	80,600	103,900	96,800

Total Excess African American Deaths, 1940–1999 = 4,272,000

Source: Levine et al., "Black-White Inequalities in Mortality and Life Expectancy."

their rates of certain risk factors and causes of death. Two particular areas of concern are obesity and high rates of uninsurance. Lack of health insurance is associated with fewer cancer screenings, less prenatal care, and lower utilization of other preventive services among some Latino groups.[24] These factors, in turn, lead to earlier mortality.

Child Survival

Contained in the data on life expectancy is critical information on child survival, the rate at which babies survive their fragile early years. Infant mortality, defined as death before the age of one, has been falling in the United States for five decades. Recently, however, progress has stalled. In 2004, an average of seventy-six babies died each day in the United States.

The U.S. infant mortality rate is on par with that of Croatia, Cuba, Estonia, and Poland. Nations generally regarded as U.S. peers, including Australia, Canada, Norway, and other affluent countries, perform far better.[25] As discussed earlier, every year over 21,000 babies could live to celebrate their first birthday if the United States under-one death rate were on a par with that of Sweden.

There is a surprising variation in child survival indicators by state. As the health indicator table reveals, the rate of infant deaths prior to their first birthday ranges from a high of 11.4 infant deaths per 1,000 in Washington, D.C., to a low of 4.7 in Vermont. Leading causes of infant death generally are linked to the situation of the mother; smoking during pregnancy, teen births, inadequate prenatal care, poor nutrition, and stressful working conditions such as long work days and lengthy periods on one's feet all can play a part. When expectant mothers face barriers in access to health care, such as lack of transportation, limited education, language barriers, and lack of health insurance, these preventable conditions can bring tragedy. Racial disparities in the rates of infant mortality are severe. The African American infant death rate is more than twice that of both whites and Latinos, and rates among Native Americans are very high as well. At the very least, the high rates among these groups suggest a need for targeted efforts at improving the health of expectant mothers in these communities.

A recent rise in infant mortality rates in a number of southeastern states, including Alabama, Louisiana, Mississippi, North Carolina, and Tennessee, has reversed steady progress made in the late 1990s. It is widely accepted that investment in a child's early years helps build a solid foundation for a healthy and productive life. Despite a period of great medical and technological advances and steady economic growth, Americans have failed to protect the health of one of our most vulnerable groups.

The U.S. infant mortality rate is on par with that of Croatia, Cuba, Estonia, and Poland.

The Many Determinants of Good Health

Our health is influenced by genetics and personal behavior, by factors in our physical environment, by our social and political environment, and by the interaction among these factors. Major health successes in recent years have much to do with medical advances, pharmaceuticals, and technology, but they also have roots in nonmedical efforts. For example:

- Research shows that one additional year of schooling increases life expectancy at age 35 by 1.7 years.[26] Education is a worthwhile investment for good health.

- A decent job is a powerful health intervention for individuals, and bringing jobs to a community can be very important for community health and vitality. Unemployment and the deprivations and stress it brings can have many harmful health effects for individuals and their families.

- Other nonmedical efforts, such as public awareness campaigns, laws, and regulations, have had major impacts on health and longevity. Laws like the Highway Safety Act, underage drinking legislation, and mandatory seat belts, motorcycle helmets, and child seats have helped dramatically reduce driving fatalities even as the number of cars on the road, and the number of miles driven, has soared. The annual death rate in the United States per hundred million miles traveled declined 90 percent from 1925 to 1997.[27]

Approximately 95 percent of current health spending is directed at medical treatment and research. Yet changes in behavior and the physical and social environment can help avoid about 70 percent of premature deaths.[28] One major front in protecting and promoting health is public health—collective actions to address present and future health challenges. The sidebar describes public health and the actors engaged in it.

Traffic safety campaigns are not public health's only victory. An estimated 1.6 million deaths from smoking were prevented between 1964 and 1992, an achievement aided by bans on smoking in public places, health warnings on cigarette packages, restrictions on tobacco advertising, and higher cigarette taxes. Other public health successes include children's immunization campaigns, school nurses, regulation and labeling of food, clean water and air standards, fluoridation of water supplies, and public parks and recreation sites to encourage exercise. These efforts sometimes require involvement of the medical community, but also of education, energy, housing, justice, and other sectors and agencies. Private employers provide important leadership on public health as well, through fitness centers, healthy cafeterias, flu shots, and treatment for substance abuse, stress, and smoking cessation.

What Is Public Health?

An old definition by one of the leading figures in the history of public health, C. E. A. Winslow, still stands today: "Public health practice is the science and art of disease prevention, prolonging life, and promoting health and well-being through organized community effort."

Public health has a role for everyone—for **individuals** in adopting healthy behaviors and taking an active role in building good health, for **academics and researchers** in making discoveries and advancing understanding, for **business** in promoting health in work settings and providing health coverage benefits and incentives for healthy choices, for the **media** in disseminating reliable information, for **community and non-governmental organizations** in lobbying, educating, and undertaking research to encourage healthy practices, for **health care professionals** in attending to patient health, and for **government agencies** at all levels and in all sectors, in providing leadership through policies, regulations, campaigns, and other levers to support long and healthy lives for everyone.

No single entity can do it all. Public health depends on a complex set of forces and factors that are constantly interacting.

Source: Turnock, *Public Health.*

By promoting health as a public good deserving of public investment, much like transportation, advocates have achieved positive outcomes. Moreover, community approaches to health, with an emphasis on **prevention, protection, and promotion,** offer a very good return on the public's investment.

Leading Causes of Death

About 70 percent of deaths in the United States, as in most affluent countries, are attributable to chronic diseases, which can often be prevented or controlled but not cured. This is a radical departure from the past, and in contrast to the situation in poor countries, where infectious diseases are responsible for a larger share of mortality.

TABLE 3.2 lists the top fifteen leading causes of death in the United States (for the most recent year available, 2005), as well as leading causes among major ethnic groups. The discussion that follows addresses two leading causes of mortality—*chronic diseases* and *violence*—and their impacts on human development.

Chronic Diseases: The Top Three Causes of Death

HEART DISEASE AND STROKE

Mortality from heart disease has declined virtually every year since 1980, as a result of improved medications and technology, in which the United States is a leader in adoption and diffusion, as well as better and faster care and individual lifestyle changes. **But heart disease and stroke are still the first and third leading causes of death and major causes of disability in the United States. Much work remains to be done by patients, health-care providers, and society to help people embrace lasting, healthy lifestyle changes to reduce heart disease and stroke.** Fatal heart disease cannot be fully prevented, but longevity and quality of life can be improved with attention to major risk factors. Chief among them are high blood pressure, high cholesterol, diabetes, smoking, physical inactivity, and obesity.

Discussion on nutrition and physical activity follow, but one persistent concern in these top killers is **the gap between African Americans and whites in prevention, treatment, and survival rates.** Taken together with diabetes, cardiovascular-related diseases account for 35 and 50 percent of this gap for males and females, respectively. Progress in this area could radically close this gap.

What contributes to the large and lasting African American–white disparity in heart disease? While contributing factors are a complex mix involving all of the determinants of our health, research increasingly points to two important risk factors: lack of access to effective treatments and hypertension rates.

About 70 percent of deaths in the United States, as in most affluent countries, are attributable to chronic diseases.

TABLE 3.2 **Leading Causes of Death in the United States, 2005**

	OVERALL UNITED STATES	AFRICAN AMERICAN NON-HISPANIC	AMERICAN INDIAN/ ALASKAN NATIVE	ASIAN AMERICAN/ PACIFIC ISLANDER	LATINO	WHITE NON-HISPANIC
1	Heart disease	Heart disease	Heart disease	Cancer	Heart disease	Heart disease
2	Cancer	Cancer	Cancer	Heart disease	Cancer	Cancer
3	Stroke	Stroke	Accidents (unintentional)	Stroke	Accidents (unintentional)	Stroke
4	Chronic lower respiratory diseases	Accidents (unintentional)	Diabetes	Accidents (unintentional)	Stroke	Chronic lower respiratory disease
5	Accidents (unintentional)	Diabetes	Stroke	Diabetes	Diabetes	Accidents (unintentional)
6	Diabetes	Homicide	Liver disease and cirrhosis	Influenza and pneumonia	Liver disease	Alzheimer's
7	Alzheimer's	Chronic lower respiratory diseases	Chronic lower respiratory diseases	Chronic lower	Homicide	Diabetes
8	Influenza and pneumonia	Kidney disease	Suicide	Kidney disease	Chronic lower respiratory disease	Influenza and pneumonia
9	Kidney disease	HIV	Influenza and pneumonia	Suicide	Influenza and pneumonia	Kidney disease
10	Septicemia	Septicemia	Kidney disease	Alzheimer's	Kidney disease	Suicide
11	Suicide	Influenza and pneumonia	Homicide	Hypertension	Alzheimer's	Septicemia
12	Liver disease and cirrhosis	Hypertension	Septicemia	Septicemia	Suicide	Liver disease and cirrhosis
13	Hypertension and hypertensive renal disease	Alzheimer's	Alzheimer's	Homicide	HIV	Hypertension
14	Parkinson's disease	Liver disease and cirrhosis	Hypertension	Liver disease and cirrhosis	Septicemia	Parkinson's
15	Homicide	Suicide	HIV	Aortic aneurysm (294 people in 2004)	Hypertension	Pneumonitis

Source: Centers for Disease Control and Prevention, "WISQARS Leading Causes of Death Reports, 1999–2005."

Varying access to treatment is affected by insurance benefits, patient decisions, and the availability of state-of-the-art cardiac equipment in hospitals used by different communities. Other factors come into play as well, including patient-provider communication and location of medical practices.[29] One issue related to communication is the need for greater diversity in the health-care workforce, which can sometimes contribute to greater patient choice, convenience, and satisfaction for racial and ethnic minority patients. For example, while the total population is approximately 26 percent nonwhite, only about 10 percent of physicians are nonwhite.[30] This issue is significant more broadly for health care and human development progress in the United States.

Heart disease, cancer, and stroke are the leading causes of death in the U.S.

Feelings of powerlessness and nagging worry about the future can result in chronic stress.

Lack of insurance plays a role in the significance of **hypertension rates** also. The uninsured are less likely to get screened for hypertension and to follow up on recommended actions. But another factor is also receiving increasing attention. The circumstances in which we live and work have a strong influence on our health. Researchers across a number of countries have been examining links between living standards and health, and are finding that **among people in the lower ranks of society, higher levels of human insecurity and lack of autonomy are contributing to worse health outcomes.** Feelings of powerlessness and nagging worry about the future can result in chronic stress, bringing on a set of conditions associated with worse health outcomes in areas such as heart disease, cancer, and diabetes. Greater levels of economic and social participation and expanded opportunities produce a health bonus.

CANCER

Pathbreaking research over the past few decades has brought new understanding about the causes of various cancers as well as new life-saving treatments. Links between some behaviors and cancers have been confirmed, especially smoking as a major risk factor for lung and other cancers. And the recent development of the human papillomavirus vaccine brings new protection against some cervical cancers, a major killer worldwide. While the list of questions on causes and treatments is still long, there are two issues of cancer prevention and treatment today that, within a human development context, merit closer attention:

- **Greater attention to psychosocial needs:** As of 2006, one in ten households had someone either diagnosed or treated for cancer within the five preceding years.[31] But that diagnosis is no longer a death sentence. **Because of progress in treating cancer, an area newly requiring attention is how to manage the financial, emotional, and physical impact of cancer on people's lives and the support needed to help with the difficult choices patients often face.** Studies have shown that cancer patients often feel that while physical needs are being met, their other needs are neglected. From transportation to work to medical bills to the emotional toll and stress that often come with illness and treatment, greater attention to these factors can significantly enhance the effectiveness of the treatments and bolster a patient's strength to fight the disease.

- **Wider, more even applications of state-of-the-art prevention and treatment techniques:** The question of why overall cancer mortality rates vary widely between racial and ethnic groups and across geographic regions in the United States has yet to be answered conclusively. In the meantime, fairness demands that the very best efforts be made for everyone across the board. However, there is another compelling reason as well: efficiency. **Numerous studies indicate that the lack of preventive care for people**

without health insurance is costly in the long run. Insured adults under sixty-five are 50 percent more likely to have had preventive screening, such as pap smears, mammograms, and prostate exams, than the uninsured.[32] Texas state health statistics indicate that the cost to treat advanced breast cancer is more than double the cost of treating it at an early stage, before it spreads.[33] In Wyoming, early detection of colon cancer brings a 90 percent chance of recovery. Late detection rates fall below 10 percent.[34]

Among some regions, geographic disparities in cancer mortality are glaring. Cancer death rates among men in southeastern states such as Louisiana, Kentucky, Georgia, and South Carolina are more than 30 percent higher than among men living in western states such as Colorado, Utah, and New Mexico. This geographic variation may in part be a function of the elevated cancer mortality rate among African Americans, who make up a relatively large proportion of the population of the southeastern states. However, it is also true that among African American men, those living in the southeastern United States and adjacent areas in the Midwest have higher lung, colorectal, and prostate mortality rates than African American men living elsewhere in the United States.

Among women, smaller geographic differences in cancer rates are apparent, with areas in the eastern half of the United States experiencing the highest rates. [35, 36]

> Insured adults under sixty-five are 50 percent more likely to have had cancer screening than the uninsured.

Violence: A Staggering Burden in the Top Fifteen

An American fortunate enough to avoid heart disease, diabetes, cancer, and other chronic diseases is still not guaranteed a long and healthy life. **Tens of thousands of Americans die each year as a result of violence.** Suicide and homicide are the eleventh and fifteenth top causes of death, respectively.

The goal of human development is to expand people's choices and freedoms and build a more just, cohesive society. Violence is the antithesis of that. In addition to spreading death, violence leaves lasting traumas, including fear, anger, and a sense of powerlessness. It tyrannizes the student who stays home from school to avoid a bully, the job seeker who foregoes nighttime employment in an unsafe neighborhood, the rape victim who avoids intimate relationships. It sometimes feeds further violence—leading to eye-for-an-eye vengeance—and creates more victims, including some who end up in jail.

SUICIDE

There is a suicide in the United States roughly every sixteen minutes—adding up to more than thirty-two thousand each year. About 57 percent of suicides among males are carried out using a firearm. While there is little variation between most states, one state, Alaska, stands out for its suicide rate. In 2004, suicide accounted for an average of 1.4 percent of total deaths in most states; in Alaska, the rate is more than triple that. This is partly due to elevated rates among Native Americans and Alaska Natives, for whom suicide is the number-two killer in the fifteen-to-thirty-four age group. But there are other factors as well. Despite tremendous oil wealth and annual household income more than $10,000 above the national median, Alaska faces a combination of unique challenges, not only related to its expansive geography and harsh environment. Seasonal employment—especially in the oil and fishing industries—is marked by periods of intense work followed by idle months during which employment opportunities are scarce. A more diversified economy, with expanded off-season employment opportunities, might be one path to increasing economic security and confidence in the future, potentially contributing to reduced risk factors that can lead to suicide.

HOMICIDE

The United States belongs to a community of affluent, democratic nations with relatively high education levels. Yet as this report reveals, we stand out from our peers in ways both good and bad. One such difference is the U.S. murder rate. Premature death from homicides in the United States is more than five times higher than the OECD average. If the U.S. rate were the same as Japan's, the number of murders recorded in 2003 would have been more on the order of fifteen hundred than fifteen thousand.

According to official government data, more than seventeen thousand Americans were murdered in 2006. Statistics for 2006 range from an annual rate of about twenty-nine murders per one hundred thousand residents in Washington, D.C., to fewer than two murders per one hundred thousand residents in North Dakota, Iowa, Maine, New Hampshire, Utah, Hawaii, Montana, South Dakota, Vermont, and Wyoming. **Yet even the lowest state murder rates still exceed rates in Japan, Germany, Greece, France, Austria, Italy, Norway, Switzerland, the United Kingdom, Ireland, Spain, Sweden, and the Netherlands.**[37]

Generally, murder rates in the United States are higher in the South and West, and lower in the Northeast and Midwest.[38] Sixty-eight percent of all U.S. homicides in 2006 were committed with a firearm.[39] **A Harvard School of Public Health study found a strong correlation between the prevalence of firearms and the likelihood of homicide.** Americans age five years or older are 2.5 times more likely to be victims of homicide in states where gun ownership rates are high than in states where ownership rates are low.[40]

Yet most murders take place in cities. In 2006, the murder rate in metropolitan areas was 6.2 per 100,000 residents, compared to 3.1 in nonmetropolitan counties.[41] Seventy-eight percent of all murder victims in 2006 were male. And while African Americans make up only 13 percent of the population, for every two murder victims in that same year, one was African American.

If the U.S. homicide rate were the same as Japan's, there would have been about **fifteen hundred** murders in 2003 instead of **fifteen thousand**.

INTIMATE PARTNER VIOLENCE

Intimate partner violence (IPV) is the term specialists use to describe violence between two people who share intimate lives, and can include rape, assault, and homicide. **IPV affects health in many ways, not only among victims and perpetrators but often among children when their parents or caregivers are involved. While many victims are injured physically, IPV can also have psychological, economic, and social impacts.**

Abusive intimate relationships are particularly pernicious because they often take place in a space that is supposed to be protective and where we develop central capabilities such as self-esteem and trust in others. The fear, anger, and stress that arise from abuse can lead to eating disorders, anxiety attacks, or depression. IPV is linked to other harmful health choices as well; victims are more likely to smoke, drink heavily, use drugs, or engage in risky sexual activity.[42] The physical and mental injury of IPV can have an economic impact also, affecting productivity and ability to perform with the necessary confidence and willingness to engage in social relationships.

Many victims do not report IPV crimes due to shame and stigma or fear of retribution, so they are widely underreported. But between 1976 and 2005, some 11 percent of all homicides were perpetrated by intimates.[43] The aggregate hides a stark gender difference: while only 3 percent of men murdered were killed by intimates, nearly a third of female murder victims were killed by an intimate.[44] Firearms are the most common instrument of death. From 1976 to 2005, 68 percent of wives murdered by their husbands were shot.[45]

> The fear, anger, and stress that arise from abuse can lead to eating disorders, anxiety attacks, and depression.

HIV and AIDS

With the introduction of significant new funding, life-saving drugs, accelerated medical efforts, public awareness campaigns, and more, overall AIDS-related deaths began to fall sharply in the United States in 1995 and continue to decline. From a peak of more than forty-three thousand AIDS deaths in 1995, by 2005 the number of deaths had declined to about seventeen thousand.[46]

AIDS is no longer a leading cause of death overall in the United States, and there are currently more than 1 million people living with HIV, the virus that causes AIDS, many of whom lead fully productive lives. However, AIDS is among the top-ten causes of death among African Americans, who account for half of all new HIV diagnoses[47] and have the lowest AIDS survival rate among ethnic or racial groups.

The unfinished agenda in the AIDS epidemic is reflected by some recent data points[48]:

- **Racial and ethnic differences.** As FIGURE 3.3 reveals, the rate of AIDS diagnoses for whites has declined dramatically since 1990, while the proportion of AIDS cases among African Americans has risen steadily. Latinos have experienced a slow but steady decrease. Diagnoses among Asian Americans/Pacific Islanders have remained relatively constant, while the AIDS case rate among Native American/Alaska Natives has nearly doubled.

- **Sexual orientation.** The share of HIV cases resulting from heterosexual transmission has risen from 3 percent in 1985 to more than 30 percent today.

- **Gender.** In 1985, 8 percent of new AIDS patients were women; by 2004, that number had jumped to 27 percent.

- **Regional distribution.** The share of AIDS cases in the South has increased from 40 percent of U.S. cases in 1996 to almost half in 2004. The share of AIDS cases in the Northeast and West has declined commensurately.

Despite enormous progress, the number of annual new infections has held steady at an estimated forty thousand since at least 1998. According to a recent study by the Open Society Institute's Public Health Program,[49] more than $16 billion was spent on the epidemic domestically in 2007, and numerous effective prevention and treatment programs exist in the United States. However, government response to the disease is fragmented. Countries such as Thailand, the Ukraine, and Australia made dramatic inroads against the disease after governments took decisive actions—establishing clear objectives, monitoring progress, and ensuring coordination among the many groups involved.

The share of HIV cases resulting from heterosexual transmission has risen from **3 percent** in 1985 to more than **30 percent** today.

Results in the United States are disappointing by comparison, due in part to a fragmented approach in lieu of national coordination and leadership. A more coherent approach could set clear benchmarks and hold government agencies and other stakeholders accountable for results. Strategies must account for differential impacts by gender, race, and other groupings. Given their high rates of infection, prevention and treatment for African Americans should be a primary focus, including efforts to improve social conditions that foster new HIV infections. Affordable housing and assistance to those making the transition from prison to community are two critical needs.

FIGURE 3.3 **The Unfinished Agenda in HIV and AIDS**

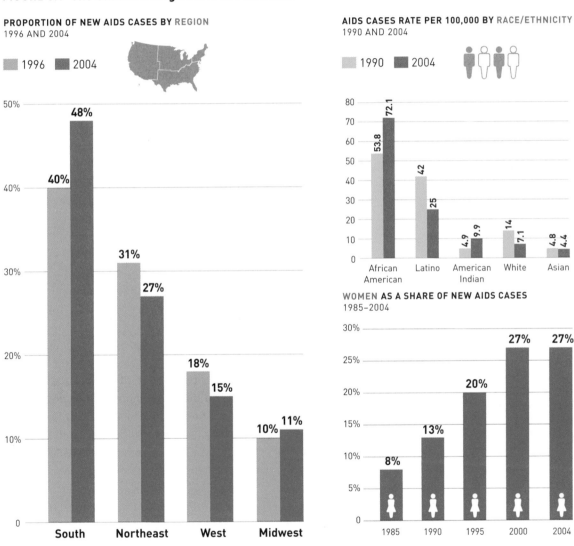

PROPORTION OF NEW AIDS CASES BY REGION
1996 AND 2004

1996 2004

	South	Northeast	West	Midwest
1996	40%	31%	18%	10%
2004	48%	27%	15%	11%

AIDS CASES RATE PER 100,000 BY RACE/ETHNICITY
1990 AND 2004

1990 2004

	African American	Latino	American Indian	White	Asian
1990	53.8	42	4.9	14	4.8
2004	72.1	25	9.9	7.1	4.4

WOMEN AS A SHARE OF NEW AIDS CASES
1985–2004

1985	1990	1995	2000	2004
8%	13%	20%	27%	27%

Source: Kaiser Family Foundation, *AIDS at 25.*

Essential Conditions for Health

We have made great strides in identifying and reducing risk factors that cause illness and mortality. We know how to prevent lead poisoning in children. We understand the behaviors that lead to obesity. We have the medical knowledge to transform asthma from a fatal disease to a manageable chronic illness. **But in each case, some groups of Americans are not benefiting from this knowledge.** As a result, large numbers of Americans have seen their capacities undermined and every aspect of their lives adversely affected. What follows is a discussion of select conditions essential for overall health, and causes of illness and death that have distinct profiles among certain groups.

Nutrition and Physical Activity

Evidence suggests that obesity is a problem with roots in a complex range of human development issues.

One American dies every ninety seconds from obesity-related problems. It is the fastest-growing underlying cause of disease and death in America today, and a strong predictor of type-2 diabetes, hypertension, coronary heart disease, and some types of cancer. Beyond the human and financial cost of obesity, which hampers the ability to contribute fully to society and often affects happiness and self-esteem, the cost to our health-care system is more than $110 billion per year—a full 1 percent of our Gross Domestic Product.[50]

How did we get to this point? Research shows that obesity rates have been edging upward since the 1980s.[51] A number of factors contribute to obesity in America: the price per calorie of food, particularly high-fat foods, has been steadily decreasing; changes in the nature of work have led to a far more sedentary society; and time pressures have increased in part due to the rapid evolution of two- and single-parent families, who often rely on quick, convenient food preparation or takeout. **BOX 3.2** examines why agricultural crops are less diversified at the expense of healthy fruits and vegetables and how government subsidies have helped foods and drinks laden with high-fructose corn syrup become cheap and common alternatives to healthier foods.

While fatty and sugary foods with poor nutritional content surely have an impact, a single, definitive cause of obesity is difficult to pinpoint. Consider, for example, a recent U.S. Census Bureau report showing that nearly 40 percent of Latino families keep their children indoors because they fear danger on the streets outside. Although the U.S. epidemic of overweight and obese adults is widespread, is it any surprise that childhood obesity is particularly severe among Latinos? Girls and boys of Mexican origin are nearly twice as likely as non-Latino white children to be overweight, and the rates are rising faster for Latinos than for non-Latino white youths.[52] **Nationwide, inactivity is considered a major factor in obesity among 66 million young people.**[53]

Women of lower socioeconomic status, regardless of racial or ethnic group, are about 50 percent more likely to be obese than those of higher socioeconomic status. Women (but not men) suffer economic harm from being overweight, research shows. An increase in a woman's body mass results in a decrease in her family income as well as a drop in in her occupational prestige; a higher body mass index also negatively correlates with the likelihood of marriage. The Census data reveals that, like poor Latino families, more than one-third of families living below the poverty line keep their children inside due to fear of neighborhood dangers. Thus, the evidence suggests that obesity is a problem with roots in a complex range of human development issues, including agricultural policy, poverty, employment, family structure, and violence. All these factors influence people's freedom to make choices and lead a healthy life.

BOX 3.2 Corn Subsidies: Expanded Markets or Expanded Waistlines?

From 1995 to 2006, more than $56 billion in federal subsidies were paid to American corn growers. Subsidies to American farmers to produce corn began in the 1930s as a way to stabilize farmers' livelihoods by paying them a fair and reasonable price in times of overproduction and lower market prices. The subsidies were designed to keep farms in business and to ensure a secure food supply for Americans.

Today, corn is the most subsidized crop in America, leading to overproduction and a surplus that is not necessarily in the best interests of health.

Expanded Markets for Corn Sweeteners

A common destination for surplus corn is the manufacture of high-fructose corn syrup (HFCS). Invented in the 1970s, HFCS is a much cheaper sweetener than cane or beet sugar. Big soft-drink brands, including Coca-Cola and Pepsi, changed recipes in the 1980s to exploit the price benefits of HFCS. Ice tea, juices, cereals, soups, luncheon meats, and countless other common processed foods have added HFCS—increasing their calories while reducing nutritional value. Often, farmers cannot justify devoting acreage to more healthful foods because growing highly subsidized corn is more profitable.

Many scientists suspect that the body does not break down HFCS as readily as it breaks down cane and beet sugars, and that this "produces high levels of insulin, and boosts a dangerous type of fat in the blood." Others are still researching these claims, but are concerned that the low cost of HFCS has prompted widespread and increasing use.

Alternatives

Reducing subsidies for corn production would lead to higher prices for HFCS, making it a less desirable sugar substitute. Large producers claim subsidies are necessary in part to spur biofuel production from corn. But other crops are more efficient and less polluting sources of biofuel. At the same time, markedly increasing funds for programs that aid family (rather than corporate) farmers and public health might yield additional health dividends. Compare the $4.9 billion spent in 2006 on corn subsidies to the $5 million earmarked nationwide for the innovative *Community Food Projects* program. Other potentially useful programs have similarly small budgets. The *Appropriate Technology Transfer for Rural Areas* (ATTRA) program receives $2.5 million while *Sustainable Agriculture Research and Education* (SARE) receives less than $20 million.

Projects that receive temporary funding under these two programs help family farmers to diversify crops, use environmentally sustainable production practices, and develop efficient ways to reach local consumer markets. They pay for the development of farmers markets, community-supported agriculture, and other programs, bringing healthful food directly to communities that otherwise have limited access to it.

While evidence suggests that obesity and corn subsidies are linked, many political leaders and industry executives maintain that every individual must take responsibility for his or her diet. True, individuals must take responsibility for their food choices. But shouldn't leaders also take responsibility for their policy choices?

Sources: Environmental Working Group, "Farm Subsidy Database"; Havel et al., "Fructose, Weight Gain, and the Insulin Resistance Syndrome"; Squires, "Sweet but Not So Innocent?"; Bantle et al., "Effects of Dietary Fructose on Plasma Lipids in Healthy Subjects"; Zeratsky, "Ask a Food and Nutrition Specialist."

A Safe, Clean Living Environment

Citizens whose communities serve as dumping grounds get a loud-and-clear message about the value society places on their lives.

A healthy living environment is necessary to our physical and psychological well-being; it helps us to adopt healthy behaviors that are a precondition for avoiding many diseases, and it is prerequisite to human dignity. Residents of urban neighborhoods with infrequent garbage collection, bustling garbage transfer stations, bus depots, and other sources of pollution play unwilling host to disease. Likewise, rural communities with more than their share of industrial hog farming, inadequate pesticide regulation, and more absorb numerous toxins and contaminants. Whether urban or rural, citizens whose communities serve as dumping grounds get a loud and clear message about the value society places on their lives.

Each of us has an equal right to clean air and clean water. We all deserve protection from environmental hazards and access to green spaces and the rejuvenating qualities of nature. Yet the distribution of natural resources, like that of pollution, is highly uneven, leading to uneven health outcomes. Pollution-producing facilities and environmental degradation are concentrated in disadvantaged communities of color and in very poor rural areas, leaving long-lasting effects that are particularly insidious for children.

CLEAN AIR

Many forms of exercise—including walking and other physical activities that Americans of all income levels can enjoy—take place out-of-doors. They also require clean air. Yet in the South alone, more than 20 million people breathe air that fails to meet federal health standards.[54]

Asthma is a chronic illness that is aggravated by poor air—indoors as a result of smoke or workplace irritants, or outdoors from particulates. Childhood asthma in the United States more than doubled from 1980 to the mid-1990s.[55] In 2005, nearly 9 percent of American children had asthma.

Despite this negative trend, huge progress has been made in transforming asthma from a life-threatening condition to a manageable disease. New medications and partnerships between parents, children, school personnel, and medical care providers have spread awareness, empowered parents and caregivers, and generally reduced mortality from the disease. Yet the gap in the death rate is increasing between major groups.

Consider the disparate situations of two children interviewed for this report:

Sophie and Alexa are two active eight-year old girls. They both have severe asthma and caring families struggling to cope with the disease. But their life chances are profoundly different due to compounded layers of advantage and disadvantage in their daily lives.

Sophie

CLEAN NEIGHBORHOOD ENVIRONMENT
FEW INDOOR POLLUTANTS
FIRST-RATE COMMUNITY PREPAREDNESS

Alexa

POLLUTED NEIGHBORHOOD ENVIRONMENT
POORLY MAINTAINED PUBLIC HOUSING
UNDER-RESOURCED PUBLIC HEALTH PROGRAMS

Sophie is a vibrant eight-year-old who was diagnosed with severe asthma when she was two. She lives in a house in a New York City suburb with a park down the street and fresh air outside—an environment with few asthma triggers.

Her family has private health insurance, a benefit of her father's job, with extensive provisions for preventative care and patient education. Her parents' jobs have personal and sick days that give them time off from work to take her to the doctor. After some early difficulty finding a suitable medication regime, she has settled into a routine of daily inhaled medications (at a cost of about $500 per month, fully covered by insurance), annual flu shots, and a special medication she takes only when she is sick with a cold. Sophie sees her pediatrician regularly, and a top-flight asthma specialist yearly, to monitor her progress; has a nebulizer for quick relief in case of a serious attack; and can rely on nebulizers in her school and after-school programs as well.

Sophie has never had to go to the emergency room for an attack, almost always participates in gym, and misses about two or three days of school a year due to asthma-related problems.

Alexa is also an active eight-year-old, first diagnosed with severe asthma at age three. She lives with her mother in a Brooklyn apartment three blocks from a waste transfer station that receives, sorts, and dispatches thirteen thousand tons of garbage each weekday. In addition to the acrid smell of garbage, the cockroaches that frequent her apartment also trigger Alexa's asthma attacks through allergens in their droppings. Her mother works at a minimum-wage job; she loses income when she takes Alexa to the doctor, fills emergency prescriptions, or stays home with Alexa when she is sick.

Alexa's mother could qualify for SCHIP, which would provide health insurance for Alexa, but she has never heard of it. Instead, Alexa is officially listed as living with her grandmother, whose Medicaid coverage extends to Alexa. Alexa sees a doctor annually, though her grandmother fears Alexa is not benefiting from the latest advances in asthma care.

Alexa misses twelve to fifteen days of school each year, does not participate in gym, and spends up to eight fearful nights each year in a hospital emergency room. When she misses consecutive days of school, she struggles with schoolwork. She wishes she could run around like her classmates.

African American children have a 500 percent higher asthma death rate than white children.

Sophie is representative of the best-case scenario. **For those with control over their circumstances and environments, managing the disease has become relatively straightforward.** However, for millions of American families, this is not possible. African American children have a 250 percent higher rate of hospitalization for asthma than white children and a 500 percent higher death rate. Environmental triggers for asthma abound, particularly in impoverished neighborhoods. Countering pollution, indoor smoking, and other public health menaces would contribute significantly to reducing the personal and social costs of asthma. In addition, a public information campaign highlighting existing programs and strategies for controlling asthma seems appropriate. About 40 percent of families eligible for SCHIP are not enrolled.[56] In a nation known for its creative advertising, surely more can be done to alert parents to the availability of this state-sponsored insurance program.

LEAD-FREE HOMES

Lead poisoning is caused primarily by eating or breathing paint chips or dust containing lead. It does not take much lead to affect the health of a small child. **High levels of lead exposure can hamper a child for a lifetime—leading to lower IQ, learning disabilities, hyperactivity, and sometimes violent behavior.** Like asthma, lead poisoning raises serious issues about health, the environment, and environmental justice.

The United States has achieved tremendous reductions in lead levels over the past fifteen years due to a shift to unleaded gas and to the removal of lead from food cans and residential paint products. This success resulted from substantial federal investment, enforcement by the EPA and Department of Justice, and a variety of vigorous state and local government and nongovernmental campaigns and actions.

The Centers for Disease Control have set a goal of eliminating elevated blood lead levels in all children by 2010. However, **lead remains a top environmental health hazard, particularly in low-income dwellings with remaining lead paint.** Nutrition matters as well; a healthy diet can help reduce lead absorption. The number of confirmed cases of elevated blood levels in 2005 ranged from 5,427 children in California and 5,443 in Illinois to 56 children in Delaware and 63 in Oregon.[57] **With sufficient effort, including targeted public education, mandatory blood lead tests for children, and safe, lead-free homes, lead poisoning can be conquered.**

Sound Mental Health

Although mental health is not, per se, a leading cause of death, it is a strong risk factor for suicide, the eleventh-leading cause of death overall but the third-leading cause of death among children and adolescents and eighth among Native Americans. More than 90 percent of those who die by suicide have had mental or substance-abuse disorders.[58] Mental and substance-use illnesses are the leading cause of combined death and disability among women and among men ages fifteen to forty-four.[59]

Sound mental health underpins people's capacity to fulfill their potential and live lives they value. Mental illness takes a heavy toll not just on sufferers but also on those who love them, in the form of lost wages, depletion of assets, psychological and other health disorders ("caregiver burnout"), and heartbreak. Even less severe mental disorders can have serious impacts on people's ability to care for themselves and others. Compounding the effects of illness is the **stigma** society still attaches to psychological disorders.

Mentally ill individuals in the United States today fare better overall than those who lived with mental illness half a century ago. This is due to a combination of medical and pharmaceutical advances; support from mainstream social programs, including Medicaid, Supplemental Security Income, housing vouchers, and food stamps; and legislation that has allowed more mentally ill individuals access to care and the potential to lead independent lives.[60] Legislation recognizing the autonomy of mentally ill individuals and acknowledging mental illness as a disability has increased their political and social power and expanded the services available to them.

While progress has been made over the long haul, mental health care falls very short in providing adequate social and support services to the mentally ill. The New Freedom Commission, established by President Bush in order to improve mental health services, concluded in 2002 that the nation's "mental health delivery system is fragmented and in disarray."[61]

This section addresses mental illness in two particularly vulnerable populations: the homeless and children. It will also examine how a capabilities approach might be extended to the mentally ill, enabling them to participate in key decisions that affect them and gain control over their lives (see **BOX 3.3**).

MENTAL ILLNESS AND HOMELESSNESS

Homelessness is an expensive, disturbing, and unyielding social problem that affects millions each year, including up to 1.4 million children. **The link between homelessness and mental health is quite strong**—more than one out of every four people with severe mental illness will lose their home at some point in their lives.[62] [63] In many cases, the homeless mentally ill cycle in and out of detoxification centers, shelters, hospital emergency rooms, psychiatric facilities, and jail. This extensive use of public systems is inefficient and expensive, and exacts a tremen-

Mental illness today:

OVERALL PREVALENCE

About 60 million Americans, or one in four adults, suffer from a diagnosable mental disorder in a given year.

SEVERE ILLNESS

About one in seventeen Americans (6 percent) suffers from severe mental illness.

UNINSURANCE

About one in five noninstitutionalized adults with severe and persistent mental illness lacks health insurance.[64]

URBAN/RURAL

Some research indicates that rural communities overall have lower mental illness rates than urban areas, but those who need treatment in rural areas have fewer provider choices and face a heavier reliance on primary care as well as greater stigma.[65]

CHILDREN

Only about one in five children and adolescents with mental health disorders use mental health services annually. Reasons include stigma, cost, and dissatisfaction with services. Of children who begin some form of treatment, 40 to 60 percent do not complete the full regimen.

Over 90 percent of those who die by suicide have had mental or substance-abuse disorders.

dous emotional toll on the homeless mentally ill, often exposing them to traumas that exacerbate their condition.

The need for alternative approaches seems plain. One response—**independent, affordable, permanent housing with a range of services on site**—would cost about the same (or less) than continuing to ignore the problem. Yet it is both a more sustainable and more humane approach. Permanent supportive housing units, like the one in Minnesota described in **BOX 3.4**, are increasingly being developed on a small scale. Construction is premised on a belief that homelessness is solvable, but only if its multiple causes, and not just the symptoms, are addressed. Public policy should pave the way for communities to create and operate permanent supportive housing on a larger scale.

MENTAL ILLNESS AND CHILDREN

Children are another group ill served by current policies.

One particularly disturbing finding is related to children with severe mental illness. The U.S. Government Accounting Office has found that many thousands of families resort to placing their children in foster care in order to access mental health services they otherwise cannot afford.[66] This drastic measure sometimes requires parents to surrender custody of their own child. A system that necessitates such a wrenching and inhumane course surely requires reform.

BOX 3.3 Creating Wellness by Allowing Patients to Manage Their Own Medication

Caring for individuals with disorders like schizophrenia or manic depression is extremely challenging. The medical profession has responded to the difficulty by focusing in many cases more on containment than recovery. From forced medication to restricted movement to outright restraint, institutionalized persons with psychiatric disorders are often controlled by caregivers around the clock. During acute episodes, this strategy is sometimes the only option. However, as a way to manage mental illness long-term, this approach has increasingly been under attack not only because of high costs and curtailed civil liberties but also because it fails to improve mental health.

Since the early 1960s, efforts have been made to move patients from large asylums into community alternatives; innovative efforts to improve patient quality of life have been developed across the country. One group, CommonGround in Kansas City, Missouri, is trying to empower outpatient clients to be active agents in their own treatment through a system that prepares them to participate in decisions about medications. It joins touch-screen technology with peer support to help

mental health clients review and organize medication issues for meetings with their psychiatrists. The Web-linked software guides service users through a detailed inventory of concerns and goals, and generates a report. CommonGround users also meet with recovering peers to discuss treatment experiences and how decisions about treatment options fit into life plans. Finally, the system provides patients with access to their treatment records so they can help monitor medication side effects and track progress in meeting goals. By equipping people to be more active in decisions that directly affect their treatment, CommonGround helps them to build the broader capabilities they will need to participate fully as citizens and to construct individual life plans.

Given the success of this model, plans are under way to open additional CommonGround sites in Kansas, Pennsylvania, and New York. With some adaptation, CommonGround-like software could empower other patients with long-term health conditions, such as asthma, diabetes, or HIV.

Source: Deegan, "CommonGround."

BOX 3.4 **Moving from Band-Aids to Real Solutions: Permanent Supportive Housing in Minnesota**

Permanent supportive housing—affordable housing linked to health, mental health, employment, and other support services—is a proven, cost-effective way to end homelessness for people who face complex challenges.[67][68]

One public-private collaboration, Project Quest in Minnesota, is an example of a successful supportive housing model for families with children. More than fifty families with extensive histories of homelessness live there, working with case workers to address a range of needs. Tenants in supportive housing sign leases and pay a portion of the rent. The project affords them a chance to become self-supporting again.

Project Quest was established in 2001 as a demonstration project led by Hearth Connection, a nonprofit organization in partnership with state and county government, supportive housing providers, health plans, consumers, advocates, and others. After successful results, the project was expanded in 2006.

Permanent supportive housing is cost-effective. Researchers tracked the costs associated with caring for nearly five thousand people with mental illness in New York City for two years while they were homeless and for two years after they were housed.[69] Permanent supportive housing and transitional housing created an average annual savings of $16,282 per unit by decreasing the use of public services.[70] The savings nearly covered the cost of developing, operating, and providing services in permanent supportive housing. Even without accounting for the positive impacts on health and employment status or positive changes in community life, it costs little more to permanently house and support people than it does to leave them homeless.

By Dr. Ellen Bassuk, National Center on Family Homelessness.

Eldercare with Dignity

As the baby boom generation reaches old age, caring for elders will increasingly be a key issue facing families, policymakers, and our social care system. While some may age at home, aided by visiting nurses and other home support, for many people the twilight years are likely to be considerably less comfortable. As families have grown busier and more geographically dispersed, more elderly Americans have resorted to living in nursing homes. About 1.5 million Americans live in the sixteen thousand nursing home facilities registered with Medicare and Medicaid.

Many families and health-care professionals are concerned about the quality of care—and quality of life—available in this country's nursing homes. The nursing home market has been restructured in recent years, with large private equity firms buying thousands of nursing homes, cutting services, reducing costs, and increasing profits. Although public funds foot much of the nursing home bill—$65 billion worth in 2003—about two-thirds of nursing homes are for-profit institutions.[71]

The New York Times reported that many of the nursing homes purchased by investment companies prior to 2006 achieved low scores from regulators who track ailments among long-term residents, including easily prevented conditions like bedsores.

Nationwide organizations Pioneer Network and the Eden Alternative work with nursing homes to help residents feel more like members of a community, increase their contact with nature, and lead more active lives. But these small efforts to change the culture of aging are exceptions to an often dismal rule.

1.5 million Americans live in nursing home facilities.

BOX 3.5 provides a glimpse of for-profit homes squeezing both caregivers and the cared for in unabashed pursuit of higher profits. Productivity quotas and forced therapy (to generate bills) feed the bottom line. **But who cares for the elderly?**

BOX 3.5 Squeezing Caregivers and the Cared For: For-Profit Nursing Home Operations

"Here is the Productivity for Last Week. We have to be at 83%—no excuses. Please email me how you plan to expand your utilization of group therapy in your facility."

—Sign taped to the wall of a rehabilitation company that operates in Texas nursing homes

The morning starts with a business meeting, calling out our rank by productivity compared to other area nursing homes, our profit margin, and our quotas for the day by the minutes. We are therapists—occupational, physical, etc. in the rehabilitation department of a 120-bed nursing home in Texas. We are given our client list and reminded that if any patient refuses treatment or is too ill for therapy, we will have to leave work. During the meeting I learn that four of my Medicare 'B' patients in the home have died in the night. Unless we have new admissions, in which case all the charges are covered by Medicare 'A' or private insurance, I must convince four residents to take occupational therapy by the end of the day in order to meet my quota. If I can get a group, I can bill multiple patients simultaneously. I then have to call their families and have them sign an agreement to pay 20 percent of the charges for my services.

But the first thing I have to do this morning is see Mr. V, a once robust ninety-seven-year-old who has just returned from the hospital for pneumonia. So Mr. V is signed up for 3.75 hours of rehabilitation therapy today, the highest category possible.

The home makes a profit on his bed only if he is receiving some form of rehab treatment.

"Good morning, Mr. V!" I am always happy to see him. He is genuine, cheerful, working hard in therapy. He and his wife managed their grocery store in a small Texas town for forty years.

Today, though, he is irritable and not sure of where he is or who I am. He is shouting, "No! Not today!" His voice is harsh. But I am assigned seventy-five minutes of occupational therapy with him, and without it I will fall far short of my quota. I make a wage of twenty-five dollars an hour. No paid lunch. No paid sick days. My mortgage is due. If Mr. V refuses today, I will only have five hours pay.

He is trembling, sweating; his eyes roll back in his head. "Put him back to bed," I tell the nurses and report his condition to the rehab director. "Have him do exercises in bed. We need at least forty minutes of therapy out of him," she replies.

I finish my day early, and check on Mr. V first thing the next morning. He has died in the night with his wife at his side. I will miss him. But I need to find seventy-five treatment minutes today, and I am still behind from yesterday. It has already been written up that I was uncooperative and unproductive yesterday. Lately, I wonder, what else, at fifty-six years old, can I do to make a living?

By Helen Nellie Donahue, occupational therapist, Texas nursing home.

Health Insurance: The Policy That Unlocks Many Doors

One in six Americans goes without health insurance.

For more than half a century, comprehensive reform of our health coverage has been delayed. It is a complex issue. However, every single affluent country in the world—except the United States—has found a way to provide health coverage to virtually every citizen. In the process, all of these nations spend less money per capita on health care than the United States, and most achieve better overall health results for their citizens. No health-care system is perfect. But, as costs rise and one in six Americans goes without health insurance, clearly there is much we can learn from the experiences of other countries (see BOX 3.6).

BOX 3.6 **Interesting Features of Health Coverage in Other Countries**

The rapidly rising cost of medical technology coupled with an aging population and a subsequent increase in demand for services renders health-care provision an increasingly challenging task for many affluent countries. In seeking ways to improve the health-care system in the United States, a number of foreign examples merit attention. The following health systems have achieved impressive health outcomes in terms of life expectancy (Japan), positive ratings in self-reported health and patient satisfaction (Denmark), and technology (Taiwan).

Japan is the clear leader in objective health outcomes. Japanese life expectancy (over 82 years on average) provides the benchmark toward which other countries strive. Japan's health-care system operates under a publicly funded, privately provided mechanism, similar to Canada and the United Kingdom. Public spending accounts for more than 80 percent of health-care expenditures. Despite its far more elderly population, Japan spent about half the portion of its GDP on health care in 2005 that the United States did. How does Japan spend less and achieve significantly better outcomes with an older population? One explanation is lifestyle and prevention. The rate of obesity in Japan is ten times lower than in the United States. Japan also has fewer physicians per capita and lower average pay for health-care providers.

If we use subjective measures of health to assess the quality of a system, **Denmark** stands out. According to the Eurobarometer, in 2005, almost nine of ten Danes considered themselves to have good health. In the European Union as a whole, the figure was 73 percent. According to the 2006 National Health Interview Survey, the corresponding number in the United States is 86 percent. Yet the Danes' superior satisfaction is achieved at a much lower price—less than half the per-capita expenditures the United States makes. Denmark

offers free public health, including general practitioners and hospital care, for all Danes. The decentralized system is administered locally and funded through local taxes, supplemented by the national government. Elected county officials assess the local need for general practitioners and hospitals. General practitioners (GPs), commonly self-employed private practitioners operating within the public system, play a key role. They are the primary point of patient contact and gatekeepers of the referral system. Patients are free to choose any GP, and anyone willing to pay a co-payment may bypass the GP and go directly to a specialist. However, few do, and polls suggest that they are content with the GP referral system. At a fraction of the cost of the U.S. system, this decentralized, government-funded approach provides high-quality medical care and outcomes in key areas, including lifespan and infant mortality, that are equal or superior to those in the United States.

In its effort to restrain growing health-care costs, **Taiwan** has turned to technology to improve efficiency. Taiwan is now testing a patient "smart-card" containing a patient's demographic profile along with clinical history, allergies, immunizations, test results, medications, and insurance details. The card, which features a secure personal identification number, was developed to minimize bureaucracy, avoid identity theft, reduce unnecessary procedures, eliminate accidents, and facilitate safer, less costly care.

Sources: Ariana, "Health Inequalities in America"; Fukawa and Izumida, "Japanese Healthcare Expenditures in a Comparative Context"; Cohen, "Smart Cards, Smarter Health Care"; Organisation for Economic Co-Operation and Development. *Health at a Glance*, 2007; World Health Organization, Europe., *Highlights on Health in Denmark*; K. Davis, "Danish Health System through an American Lens."

Public and private spending on health care in the United States adds up to $2 trillion, and it continues to rise. It is not a question of whether we can afford something better—we are already paying caviar prices. So the question is this: Can we reform health care so that our number-one rank in spending leads to a number-one rank in outcomes?

U.S. SPENDING ON HEALTH CARE

The proportion of national wealth absorbed by health care has been increasing in each of the thirty OECD countries. Much of this increase is due to more costly medical procedures and medications and an ever-rising demand for care among an aging population. In the United States, health-care costs have more than tripled from 5.1 percent of gross domestic product in 1960 to 16 percent of GDP in 2006

Spending on health care in the U.S. adds up to $2 trillion annually, and it continues to rise.

(see FIGURE 3.5). Our health-care expenditures, combining both public and private spending, are more than double those of Japan, which has the greatest life expectancy of any OECD country (see FIGURE 3.4).

FIGURE 3.4 **Global Comparison: Health Expenditures Per Capita, 2005**
Public and Private, Combined

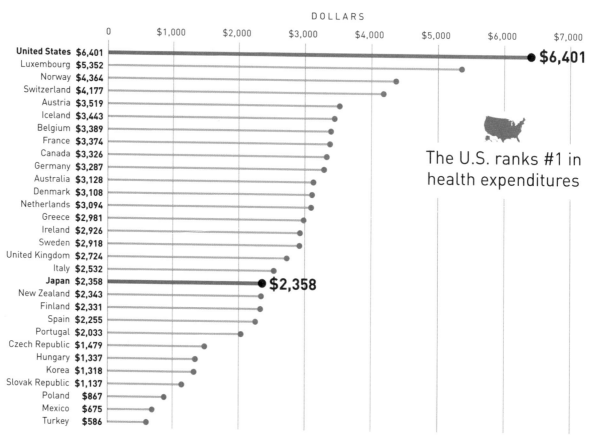

The U.S. ranks #1 in health expenditures

Source: Organisation for Economic Co-Operation and Development. Health at a Glance, 2007.

WHO PAYS FOR WHOM?

Financial support for health coverage is available for two out of three Americans through either favorable tax treatment or direct programs, such as the following:[72]

- **Tax deduction for private health insurance.** Over $188 billion in 2004 in foregone revenue from exempting employer and self-employed health benefits from federal taxes plus deduction for individual health expenses. About 180 million Americans benefit from these tax breaks.[73]

- **Medicare.** $400 billion in 2006 for an estimated 44 million Americans—all those over sixty-five and an additional 7 million with certain disabilities.[74 75]

- **Medicaid.** $310 billion for 38.3 million Americans in 2006.[76 77]

- **SCHIP.** $7.9 billion annually for an estimated 4.1 million children who are ineligible for Medicaid but whose families lack the resources to obtain private insurance.[78 79 80]

- **Military Tricare.** $35.4 billion annually for 9.2 million active and retired military personnel and their dependents through the Department of Defense's health-care program.[81]

While there is frustration with the health-care system, **there are also encouraging signs that insured people are taking a more active and informed role in their health care,** discussing treatment options more thoroughly with doctors and making doctor's visits more judiciously. However, for the 47 million people who lack insurance, the consequences are higher levels of insecurity and shorter lives. For society as a whole, the uninsured entail tremendous costs.

WHO ARE THE UNINSURED?

FIGURE 3.6 provides profiles of the 16 percent of the population without health insurance. The data reveal:

- The great majority of uninsured are employed.

- Four of five are adults.

- Rates of uninsurance are high in every nonpublic sector of the workforce.

The uninsured are generally connected to employment, and many are in their most productive years. While higher-income workers without employment-based insurance can afford to obtain coverage and can even deduct some out-of-pocket expenses from their taxes, there is little recourse for those in low-wage jobs, young adults, self-employed middle-class workers, and those who are on the cusp of Medicare eligibility without qualifying. **Many simply cannot afford private health insurance premiums.**

In addition to 47 million Americans without health insurance, more than 80 million go without coverage during a two-year period.[82] **Others avoid moving jobs to advance their careers or skills in order to maintain employer-based health coverage.** The economic impact of this "**job lock**" phenomenon is difficult to measure. However, it is clear from voluminous anecdotal evidence as well as surveys and studies that job lock constrains employment choices and likely creates an inefficiency drag on economic activity.

FIGURE 3.5

National Health Expenditures as a Percentage of GDP

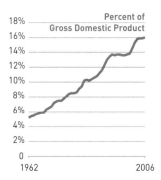

Percent of Gross Domestic Product

Source: Centers for Medicare and Medicaid Services, "National Health Expenditure Data."

> For the 47 million people who lack insurance, the consequences are higher levels of insecurity and shorter lives.

The United States will spend $230 million on health care in the next hour.

The human costs of uninsurance and underinsurance are high:

Personal Impact

- Some eighteen thousand people died prematurely in 2000 due to lack of insurance.[83]

- More than half of all personal bankruptcies in the United States are related to an inability to pay for illness or injury.[84]

- Lack of insurance causes increased anxiety for 47 million individuals.[85]

- Uninsured children are at higher risk of suffering developmental delays

Societal impact

- Communities with high rates of uninsured residents face overburdened health facilities, such as emergency rooms, and financial instability for health-care providers and institutions.[86]

- According to the Institute of Medicine, between $65 billion and $130 billion in workplace productivity is lost annually due to uninsurance.[87]

- As discussed above, the uninsured are less likely to benefit from early detection of diseases like cancer and hypertension, which makes treatment far more costly in the long run.[88] [89]

HEALTH-CARE REFORM: A WAY FORWARD

Many advocates of comprehensive health-care reform believe that the economic value derived from universal insurance would exceed the cost. They claim further that health-care costs in the United States have reached such an exorbitant level that universal care might be had at little additional cost. Given that the United States will spend $230 million on health care in the next hour, this claim grows more convincing by the minute.

How can we build a health-care system for the twenty-first century that nurtures health and protects human dignity while delivering the highest quality care in the most efficient, transparent, and cost-effective way possible? How can we improve the quality of life for the many Americans who experience premature mortality in an era of widespread prosperity?

There are many models and options to consider. In the absence of federal leadership, some states have taken bold steps to improve health care for their citizens. Massachusetts, Illinois, and California have each instituted ambitious plans to expand health-care coverage to children and the uninsured. One health insurer trade group, America's Health Insurance Plans, has developed a plan to guarantee coverage for all, and many nonprofit organizations have proposed long-term solutions of their own. There is no shortage of directions. But to support human development in the United States, we must summon the political will to take a bold first step without requiring that it be a perfect or final arrangement.

TABLE 3.3

Health Insurance Coverage Rates for Children, by Region

Coverage rates for children vary dramatically among regions. Nearly half of all children in the South are uninsured, compared with less than 10 percent in the Northeast. More children have discontinuous coverage (7.7 percent of all children in the United States under eighteen) than lack health coverage entirely.[90]

REGION	FULL-YEAR UNINSURED	PART-YEAR UNINSURED
West	31.5%	23.3%
Midwest	13.1%	22.7%
South	47.4%	41.1%
Northeast	8.0%	13.0%

Source: Olson, Tang, and Newacheck, "Children in the United States with Discontinuous Health Insurance Coverage."

FIGURE 3.6 **Six Views of the Uninsured in America**

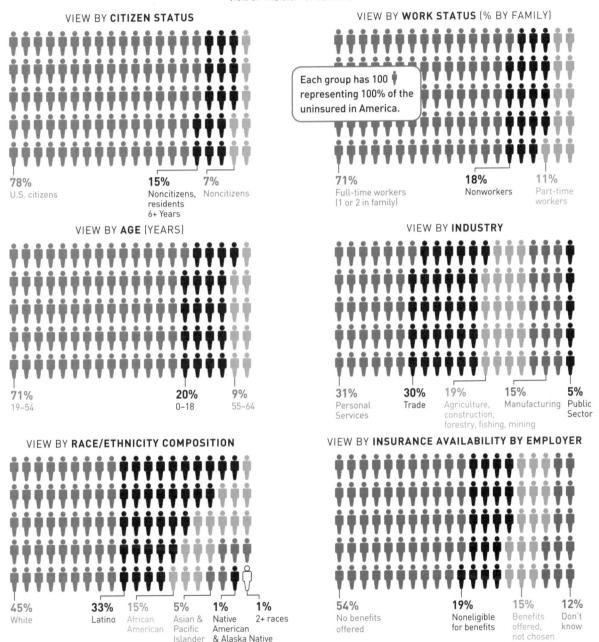

47 million Americans are Uninsured
(16% OF THE U.S. POPULATION)

VIEW BY CITIZEN STATUS

78%
U.S. citizens

15%
Noncitizens,
residents
6+ Years

7%
Noncitizens

VIEW BY WORK STATUS (% BY FAMILY)

Each group has 100 representing 100% of the uninsured in America.

71%
Full-time workers
(1 or 2 in family)

18%
Nonworkers

11%
Part-time
workers

VIEW BY AGE (YEARS)

71%
19–54

20%
0–18

9%
55–64

VIEW BY INDUSTRY

31%
Personal
Services

30%
Trade

19%
Agriculture,
construction,
forestry, fishing, mining

15%
Manufacturing

5%
Public
Sector

VIEW BY RACE/ETHNICITY COMPOSITION

45%
White

33%
Latino

15%
African
American

5%
Asian &
Pacific
Islander

1%
Native
American
& Alaska Native

1%
2+ races

VIEW BY INSURANCE AVAILABILITY BY EMPLOYER

54%
No benefits
offered

19%
Noneligible
for benefits

15%
Benefits
offered,
not chosen

12%
Don't
know

Source: Kaiser Family Foundation, *Uninsured*. The uninsured does not include those 65 and over, who receive Medicare. Data from 2006.

Conclusion

Evidence examined for this report yields the following conclusions:

The range of factors that contribute to a healthy society extend beyond medical solutions. We must reform strategies for wellness to focus on the cumulative factors, both medical and nonmedical, that contribute to a healthy life. Medical research, new technologies, and clinical services to treat illness are primary ingredients of a successful health-care system. But so are many other factors, including education, employment, housing, environment, the security of our homes and communities, and reverence for human dignity. Deprivation in these areas can affect health and longevity and inhibit people from realizing their full potential. Investment to ameliorate social conditions that cause, exacerbate, or prolong illness is just as necessary as investment in medical infrastructure.

Comprehensive reform of U.S. health care is urgently needed to build a more efficient system and get a higher return on our investment. Health care in the United States, including private and public spending, costs a staggering $2 trillion annually.[91] For reform to be successful, inefficiencies must be addressed.

- **Prevention and cure.** Despite overwhelming evidence of its efficacy, preventive medicine continues to be shortchanged. The United States spends about 95 percent of its health-care resources on medical research and treatment for existing conditions.[92] Yet disease prevention and early detection cost far less both in dollars and in terms of human suffering.

- **Public health and clinical approaches.** Public health victories of the twentieth century, most notably reducing smoking, car fatalities, and toxic emissions, contributed significantly to the increase in the American life span. Such public health campaigns should be given higher priority, targeting specific groups and communities and advocating practices and investments that improve health.

- **Technology to boost efficiency.** Information technologies, used judiciously, have tremendous potential to save money and improve health. Innovative technologies have revolutionized the way information is stored, shared, and used in many different industries. The health-care industry has been a notable laggard. Better use of information technologies, including digitized medical records, can improve safety and quality of care while reducing costs. In addition, improved technology can help patients gain more control over their medical decisions.

Comprehensive reform of U.S. health care is urgently needed to build a more efficient system and get a higher return on our investment.

Health outcomes for two large groups of Americans—children and African Americans—are bad and not improving. There is a need to build stronger public reporting and accountability for improving health outcomes. The U.S. government set commendable objectives in its Healthy People 2010 plan, including two major goals: to increase the quality and longevity of lives and to eliminate health disparities among different population groups. However, it is failing to reach its goals, particularly among children and African Americans. The United States ranks at the very bottom of twenty-four OECD countries in child health and safety.[93] Meanwhile, the gap in life expectancy between African Americans and whites remains large, with particular challenges in infant mortality rates and mortality from homicide, AIDS, and cardiovascular diseases. With focused public reporting on established goals and targeted strategies to reach them, and with attention from the media, political leaders, and the public on established benchmarks, we can develop a culture of accountability for progress in health outcomes.

Firearms contribute significantly to homicide and suicide, which are both among the top causes of death. Fifty-seven percent of suicides and two out of every three homicides[94] are committed with guns. There is a correlation between high levels of gun ownership in a state and higher rates of homicide and suicide. The United States has the highest civilian-owned gun rate in the world.[95] For children ages five to fourteen, the homicide rate from firearms is seventeen times higher in the United States than in any other industrialized nation—in short, children in other affluent countries are not dying from guns.[96] The evidence that the availability of guns in the home is contributing to these two leading causes of death, particularly among youth, is compelling.

Lack of health insurance limits opportunity. Access to health insurance directly influences age at death. In the lower forty-eight states, 43 percent of the variations in age at death can be explained by the percentage of a state's population without health insurance. In other words, those who lack insurance or experience periods without insurance generally live shorter, less healthy lives. Studies confirm that the uninsured also face agonizing choices between paying for health care or for other basic needs, such as food, heat, and even housing. In addition, the uninsured are more likely to postpone treatment, which often results in more severe illness. They frequently do not fill prescriptions for medicine that, if taken, would reduce future health-care needs.

Good health is a prerequisite for good school attendance and concentration, for good work attendance and performance, for basic control of one's life, and for developing one's talents. Like the United States, other countries around the globe are struggling to balance rising costs and quality care. But a pragmatic approach to comprehensive health coverage for all is both necessary and feasible.

For Future Consideration: Health Topics of Tomorrow

The United States has made tremendous progress increasing life span and quality of life. However, we must also secure these gains from sudden reversals. The growing interdependence of the world's economies, technologies, governance structures, cultures, and people creates new and often unpredictable challenges. In the health arena, we must be prepared for them. The increasing rate of movement across borders, heightened resistance to various antibiotics, changing intellectual property standards, and the emergence of new disease agents require new policies, new control measures, and new investments. These challenges, and others, will be discussed in future reports on American human development.

A pragmatic approach to comprehensive health coverage for all is both necessary and feasible.

PART 3
The Building Blocks of the HD Index

Access to Knowledge

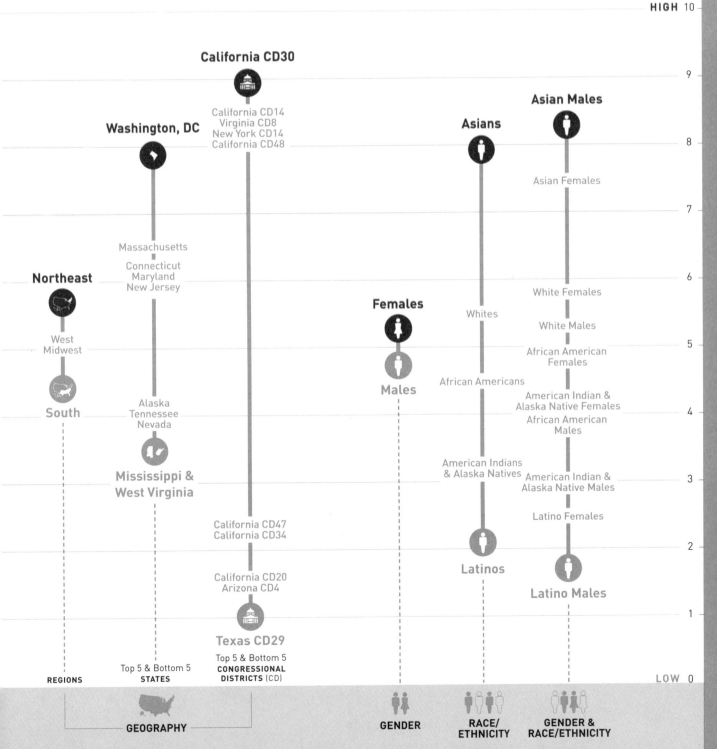

EDUCATION INDEX: Educational Attainment and School Enrollment

How Do We Stack Up?

EDUCATION INDEX

HIGH 10

9

California CD30

California CD14
Virginia CD8
New York CD14
California CD48

8

Asian Males

Asians

Washington, DC

Asian Females

7

Massachusetts

Connecticut
Maryland
New Jersey

6

Females

Whites

White Females

White Males

Northeast

Males

African Americans

African American
Females

5

West
Midwest

American Indian &
Alaska Native Females

4

South

Alaska
Tennessee
Nevada

American Indians
& Alaska Natives

African American
Males

American Indian &
Alaska Native Males

3

**Mississippi &
West Virginia**

Latino Females

California CD47
California CD34

2

Latinos

California CD20
Arizona CD4

Latino Males

1

Texas CD29

Top 5 & Bottom 5
**CONGRESSIONAL
DISTRICTS** (CD)

Top 5 & Bottom 5
STATES

REGIONS

LOW 0

GEOGRAPHY

GENDER

**RACE/
ETHNICITY**

**GENDER &
RACE/ETHNICITY**

Source: Census Bureau, "2005 American Community Survey."

Introduction

"The most important thing in America—
the most important thing—is information."

L, young immigrant woman from Belarus living in Brighton Beach, New York

The acquisition of knowledge is a lifelong process that includes, but goes beyond, formal schooling. It starts with what happens at home and during interactions with caregivers in the critical years of early childhood. It encompasses the K–12 educational system, but also experiences after school, on weekends, and in the summer. It includes various types of formal education and job training for young adults, as well as access to informal social networks that impart information about schools, jobs, health, and investment.

Access to knowledge affords the opportunity to develop capabilities, fulfill human potential, and break the heredity of disadvantage. Discovery, learning, and mastery are sources of satisfaction, even joy; thus, access to knowledge is intrinsically valuable. Conversely, not being able to read well, perform mathematical tasks fundamental to daily life, or communicate one's thoughts and feelings clearly are fundamental deprivations that cause frustration and shame. The government's most recent assessment of adult literacy in the United States found that such fundamental deprivations are astonishingly widespread. Fourteen percent of the population—some 30 million Americans—have "below basic" prose literacy skills, meaning that they cannot perform "simple and everyday literacy activities" like understanding newspaper articles or instruction manuals. Twelve percent have below basic document literacy—they cannot fill in a job application or payroll form, read a map or bus schedule, or understand labels on foods and drugs. And a whopping 22 percent of us—more than one in five Americans—have below basic quantitative skills, making it impossible to balance a checkbook, calculate a tip, or figure out from an advertisement the amount of interest on a loan.[97]

But access to knowledge is also a central capability for living a good life because of the many things it makes possible—its instrumental value. For the individual, access to knowledge, particularly formal education, can increase

College graduates can expect, on average, about **double** the lifetime earnings of high school graduates.

a person's self-confidence, self-awareness, and feelings of worth and dignity. Education enables economic self-sufficiency and is linked to better health, more stable relationships, and more effective parenting. Education fosters better understanding of one's rights, greater and more effective participation in the political process, and higher levels of civic engagement. It can teach tolerance, respect for the views of others, and an appreciation of the diversity and richness of the human experience. An educated population is also good for democracy and good for economic productivity, dynamism, and competitiveness.

Highly educated people tend to have extensive, well-developed capabilities; they thus have a great deal of freedom to decide how to live their lives, and they have the tools they need to make their vision of a good life a reality. They are also able to make a greater contribution to society.

SIX ISSUES EMERGE

When we look at the question of access to knowledge in the United States from a human development perspective, six issues emerge strongly.

1. Significant investment in early childhood education is money well spent.

Sizeable gaps in both cognitive and behavioral capabilities exist between poor and nonpoor children before their first day of kindergarten. The greatest documented social and economic returns on investment in education come not from programs for school-aged children but from high-quality interventions for at-risk infants, toddlers, preschoolers, and their parents. The early years are critical not just for elementary school readiness but also for setting a child's academic and, in some cases, even life trajectory. Every dollar invested in high-quality early childhood intervention yields benefits worth anywhere from $2 to $17.[98] Successful intervention pays dividends in greater educational attainment and higher-paying jobs as well as in lower rates of special education placement, repetition of grades, teenage pregnancy, use of social services, and criminal activity.

Interestingly, long-term benefits are derived less from better cognitive skills—like the ability to recognize letters, numbers, and shapes—and more from socialization and the development of noncognitive capabilities like persistence, impulse control, and emotional regulation.

However, quality programs require the resources to be able to afford college-educated teachers with early childhood expertise, low teacher-to-child ratios, developmentally appropriate materials, and enrichment activities. Early childhood intervention on the cheap—mediocre custodial care dressed up with flashcards and drills—does nothing to help poor children close the gaps with middle-class peers.

Some 30 million Americans have "below basic" prose literacy skills; they cannot perform "simple and everyday literacy activities" like understanding newspaper articles or instruction manuals.

In 2006,
4.5 million young
people ages
eighteen to
twenty-four were
not in school, not
working, and had
not graduated
high school.

2. The richest country in the world can afford to educate all its people.

Research and common sense suggest that the benefits of early education are maximized when children subsequently attend better-quality elementary and secondary schools and maintain access to enriching activities and environments. Even a model preschool cannot immunize the most at-risk children against all the effects of material deprivation, family stress, unsafe neighborhoods, and poor-quality schools. Helping at-risk girls and boys navigate the rocky shoals of adolescence, graduate high school, avoid too-early parenthood, and launch independent lives is in their interest as well as in the national interest. In 2006, 15 percent of young people ages eighteen to twenty-four were not in school, not working, and had not graduated high school. That's nearly 4.5 million Americans detached from the worlds of school and work. Doesn't it make sense to help provide them with a productive life of meaning and value rather than decades of disengagement, despair, and dependency?

3. We are asking schools to solve society's most intractable problems.

Historically, schools have played an important role in addressing major national challenges, most notably assimilating waves of immigrants in the first half of the twentieth century, providing newcomers with concrete skills as well as an identity as Americans. This assimilation task is not over: about 20 percent of school-aged children come from homes in which English is not the primary language.[99]

The educational system has never performed the class-leveling function that popular culture attributes to it. But today, many children confront problems that even the best schools would be hard pressed to solve. Nearly one in five American children lives in poverty (with more than one in thirteen living in extreme poverty), one in six lives in a family whose head didn't graduate high school, one in eight lives in overcrowded housing, one in ten is born to a teen mother, more than one in ten has no health insurance, and one in twenty lives in a household where no adult is working.[100] Two-thirds of all poor children have had at least one experience of prolonged food insufficiency in the past year.

Evidence shows that a good school can **significantly improve** the performance of low-income and minority children—but schools alone **cannot close the gap** in average performance between these children and middle-class and privileged children. A popular focus on how schools are failing distracts us from broader questions about societal failures. There are huge inequalities at the starting gate of formal education, making it extremely difficult for schools to provide anything close to "equal opportunity" for all.

Policy-makers but also the general public have found it easier to turn to educational reforms to solve these problems rather than directly addressing the root causes of poverty and inequality. Policies in areas like housing, employment, and health in some cases would do more to close the educational achievement gap than educational policies.

4. We give the fewest resources to schools that face the greatest challenges.

Rising income inequality has intensified residential segregation by earnings and ethnicity in recent decades. Poor families increasingly tend to be concentrated in high-poverty neighborhoods, and their children are likely to attend schools with other poor children. More affluent families with children tend to live in communities inhabited by other prosperous families. And the last twenty years have not seen greater integration but rather growing racial isolation in the public schools. African American and Latino children tend to be concentrated in struggling, high-poverty schools; white students have surprisingly little interaction, on the whole, with minority students.

The de facto result of this sorting-by-income-and-race is that America has two public education systems. The one serving predominantly white, suburban children is working—though there is considerable room for improvement. The other, serving low-income, almost entirely minority children in urban areas and poor rural areas, is in crisis. The two systems diverge on every measure of educational quality: the skills and qualifications of the teachers; the physical state of facilities; the breadth and rigor of their curriculums; funding and resources; the likelihood of instruction in art, music, and physical education; and the levels of student achievement, graduation rates, and college attendance.

In forty-eight of the one hundred largest school districts, where the vast majority of students are African American or Latino, fewer than half of all children who start ninth grade graduate with a high school diploma in four years.[101] Far from leveling the playing field, as Americans expect their schools to do, public education today actually exacerbates the gaps between affluent children and disadvantaged children.

For families with school-aged children, school quality is a hugely important issue with significant resource implications. Although public education is "free," accessing high-quality public education is anything but. It requires significant financial resources—money to rent or buy a home in a good school district or to send children to private school. For many families, the wide disparity in the quality of public education is the decisive factor in choosing where to live. In 2003, parents of about one-quarter of all students reported that they had moved to their current neighborhood to enable their children to attend a better school.[102]

5. We are not adequately preparing our children for tomorrow.

In the post–World War II years, unionized manufacturing jobs in workplaces like steel mills and auto plants brought a middle-class lifestyle to a generation of Americans. The credential required for this secure, well-paying work—other than being a man—was, at most, a high school diploma. Women's occupational choices were limited to clerical and retail jobs, domestic work, and a handful of professions (teachers, nurses, and librarians).

No Skills or Women's Skills?

Those who work at service-sector jobs in the bottom half of the hourglass are often referred to as "unskilled"—to differentiate them from those in the top of the hourglass, whose jobs require the creation and use of specialized knowledge, as well as those in manufacturing, who often have a specific set of technical skills. But do "unskilled" jobs really exist, or do we simply devalue them because such jobs—in customer service, retail, and caregiving of all sorts—require skills traditionally associated with women?

Experience confirms that these jobs do require skills—people skills or soft skills. In the past, male-dominated manufacturing jobs paid middle-class wages in part as a consequence of powerful unions, less global competition, and high economic growth.

If jobs like home health aide, customer service representative, or retail clerk came with a living wage, good benefits, job security, societal respect, and the power of collective bargaining, would we call them "unskilled"?

Today the world has changed. **The demand for skills is becoming increasingly hourglass-shaped—with high demand for highly educated workers at the top and high demand for less-educated, low-wage workers at the bottom.** The middle is becoming increasingly wasp-waisted as domestic demand for skilled manufacturing workers drains away.

Economists, business leaders, and others have sought to identify the types of skills that will be most desired in coming decades (see BOX 3.7). Future-oriented thinkers in the private sector, education researchers, and government policymakers alike are increasingly raising the alarm about the gap they see between the capabilities children acquire in school today and the capabilities they will need as adults in the world tomorrow. There is growing consensus that core subjects like **math and reading are critical, but that we must go well beyond the basic competency we target today in order to develop advanced academic skills as well as a host of noncognitive skills.** Schools need to help students acquire more complex, higher-order capabilities, such as communications skills, interpersonal skills, self-direction, problem identification, and media literacy.

> Schools need to help students acquire more complex, higher-order capabilities, such as communications skills, interpersonal skills, self-direction, problem identification, and media literacy.

BOX 3.7 Teaching Rocket Scientists to Use Plowshares

The last century saw a great democratization of learning across the globe. Education went from being a privilege to a right in most of the industrialized world. Yet the very thing that allowed primary and secondary education to flourish is also likely to be its greatest liability as we move into the next one hundred years. Education has been cast in the image of the factory. It has become a mass production engine of in-the-box learning. But in-the-box learning is the last thing that children thrust into a world of ever-increasing uncertainty need.

The very nature of the world these children inhabit is defined by on-demand and spontaneous interaction. Today's youngsters are connected through instant messaging, informed of world events via blogs, and immersed in an always-on world of constant interruptions. Their world is shaped by armies of one, extreme personalization (from the MP3s on their iPods to their personal Web sites), and a virtually unlimited pool of information sources. So how does the classroom education offered today help to prepare these children for the world? It doesn't. Yes, of course, there will be those few exceptional children who always stand out in their creativity and ability to achieve excellence in any setting. But for the mass of humanity being pumped through the current K–12 system, we are accomplishing the equivalent of teaching future rocket scientists to use plowshares.

The United States is capable of leading the charge by focusing on primary and secondary schools and incorporating the methods of creative problem-solving into mainstream classroom learning. But to succeed, a seismic shift must occur in the development of a new set of foundational skills and capabilities that will focus on problem solving, creativity, and innovation.

By Thomas Koulopoulos, Cofounder of Delphi Group, author and thought leader on technology, business, and globalization.

6. Testing regimes distort the mission of education and deepen educational inequities. America lags behind other affluent countries in math and science education, in the affordability of higher education, and in the number of graduates with the skills for high-tech jobs. Naturally we want kids to graduate from school competent at reading, writing, and computing. But for them to flourish in a globalized, knowledge-based world, we need a system that turns out independent thinkers, creative problem-solvers, lifelong learners, and responsible, effective, and engaged contributors to democratic society and an interdependent world.

The No Child Left Behind Act has worthy goals—ensuring that all children are proficient in reading and math and closing the achievement gap between minority and white children by 2014. However the Act has encouraged schools to narrow their mission dramatically. Activities central to the full development of the human being—music, art, social studies, creative writing, research projects, field trips, physical education, cultural enrichment—are increasingly deemed unnecessary frills because they are not tested.

All parents want their children to enjoy lives of meaning, opportunity, and happiness. Writing about developing countries, Amartya Sen argues that mothers and fathers "from even the poorest . . . families long to give basic education to their children, to make them grow up without the terrible handicaps from which they—the parents—had themselves suffered." But, he writes, "there are many obstacles in giving shape to the dreams of parents." The same can be said of the situation in the United States.

America lags behind other affluent countries in math and science education, in the affordability of higher education, and in the number of graduates with the skills for high-tech jobs.

> **BOX 3.8 American HD Index: Access to Knowledge**
>
> Access to knowledge has been a key component of the global HD Index since its inception in 1990. Education is critical to people's real freedom to decide what to do and who to be. Education builds confidence, confers status and dignity, and broadens the horizons of the possible—as well as allowing for the acquisition of skills and credentials.
>
> The global index uses literacy rates as a measure of access to knowledge. Internationally, higher literacy rates predict higher wages and higher life expectancies, fewer infant and childhood deaths, and lower birth rates.
>
> The American HD Index uses educational attainment and school enrollment as measures of access to knowledge. Affluent societies like the United States generally have very high literacy rates, and a more demanding indicator is required to show the variations in educational attainment, skills, and knowledge.

What Does the HD Index Show?

The American HD Index shows significant variation across racial and ethnic groups and among states and congressional districts. Over the course of this section of the report, we unpack the various components of the educational index, looking at preschool enrollments, aspects of K–8 schooling, high school completion rates, and college-going.

Among regions, the Northeast has the highest educational score, followed by the West, the Midwest, and the South. The Northeast and West have the greatest number of people with at least a college degree (31 percent and 29 percent, respectively), compared to about one-fourth of the population in the Midwest and South. The Midwest has the highest percentage of people who graduate high school—87 percent—while the South has the lowest, at 82 percent.

At 7.94, Washington, D.C., has the highest educational index among the states, followed by Massachusetts and Connecticut, the two states with the highest overall HD Index. However, the percentage of people in the nation's capital who did not graduate from high school is 16.4 percent, above the national average. **West Virginia, Mississippi, and Nevada (with educational index ranks, respectively, of 49, 50, and 51) are at the bottom of the educational scale.** The map of congressional districts shows that higher scores are found where population is denser (see MAP 3.2).

There is greater variation within states than among states, and even high-scoring states have low-scoring districts.

- **New York** ranks fifth in the education index. But the state's high aggregate ranking obscures the fact that New York has one of the best-performing and one of the worst-performing congressional districts in education. In the Fourteenth Congressional District, which includes Manhattan's Upper East Side, 63 percent of the population holds at least a college degree; just 9 percent did not graduate from high school. In the Sixteenth Congressional District in the South Bronx, only 9 percent of residents earned at least a college degree, and 43 percent left high school without a diploma.

- **California**, an above-average state in education overall, is home to the Fourteenth Congressional District (San Francisco/Silicon Valley), where 56 percent of the population has at least a bachelor's degree and only 9 percent are high school dropouts. California also includes the Twentieth Congressional District (Fresno), where 7 percent of the population has a bachelor's degree and 47 percent are high school dropouts.

- In **Illinois**, another above-average state, in the Tenth Congressional District, made up predominantly of white suburbs north of Chicago,

MAP 3.2 **Education Index, 2005**

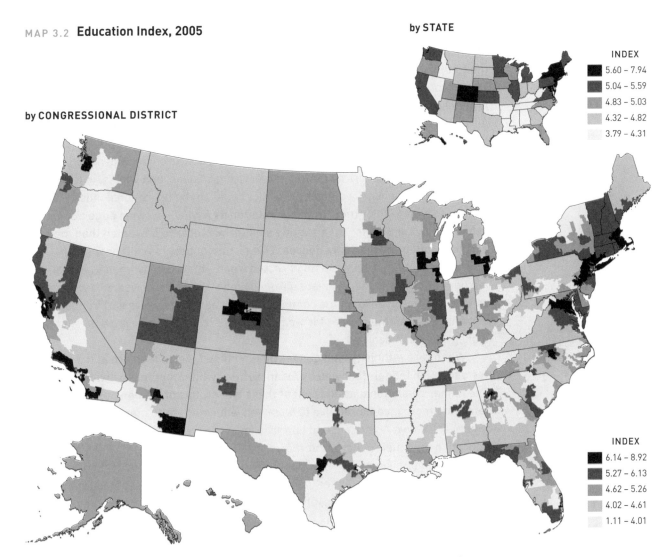

by **STATE**

INDEX
- 5.60 – 7.94
- 5.04 – 5.59
- 4.83 – 5.03
- 4.32 – 4.82
- 3.79 – 4.31

by **CONGRESSIONAL DISTRICT**

INDEX
- 6.14 – 8.92
- 5.27 – 6.13
- 4.62 – 5.26
- 4.02 – 4.61
- 1.11 – 4.01

9 percent are high school dropouts and 52 percent have at least a bachelor's degree. But in Illinois's Fourth Congressional District, which has a large Latino population, 40 percent of residents are high school dropouts and 17 percent have graduated college.

- **Texas**, which is below the national average on the educational index, has the country's worst-performing congressional district, the Twenty-ninth, in the greater Houston area, where 46 percent of the population have less than a high school diploma and only 6 percent have a bachelor's degree. But Texas also has one congressional district in the top quintile, the Twenty-first, northeast of San Antonio, where the numbers are almost exactly reversed—6 percent have less than a high school diploma and 46 percent have graduated college.

Regional Ranking
in Education:

1. Northeast
2. West
3. Midwest
4. South

Among ethnic groups, the high levels of educational attainment among Asians, reflected in their educational index score of 7.98, is a main driver for their number-one HD Index ranking. Asians score 44 percent higher than whites, 76 percent higher than African Americans, more than twice as high as Native Americans, and more than three and a half times higher than Latinos. Half of all Asians have at least a college degree, compared to roughly 30 percent of whites, 17 percent of African Americans, 14 percent of Native Americans, and 12 percent of Latinos. Latinos have the highest rate by far of those who do not finish high school, followed by Native Americans, African Americans, Asians, and whites, in that order.

In terms of gender, women have a slight lead on the educational index—5.32 compared with 4.79 for men. **In the population as a whole, women edge out men in high school diplomas, but a slightly smaller percentage of women than men earned a college or graduate degree.** This picture of today's adult population 25 years and older obscures a much-noted trend—that more women than men are now enrolling in and graduating from college. Women received 57 percent of college degrees in 2005. In the coming decades, barring a reversal of trends, the educational attainment index for women will rise to reflect their growing share of higher education degrees.

When race, ethnicity, and gender are combined, Asian men are at the top of the education ladder, followed by Asian women, white women, and white men. The higher educational attainment of these two groups of women has not translated into more income relative to less-well-educated white men. White, African American, Native American, and Latino women are all doing better in terms of education than their male counterparts, with Latino men having the lowest scores of any group by a significant margin. Although women's higher educational levels have not led to incomes higher than those of male counterparts, among African Americans, Native Americans, and Latinas they have contributed to higher overall levels of human development.

When looking at educational attainment in this report, we present the percentage of the population that has reached AT LEAST a specific educational level (for instance, "at least a high school diploma" includes those with bachelor's degrees and graduate degrees). In contrast, **TABLE 3.4** shows the HIGHEST educational level achieved, and thus the exact percentage of the population with a high school diploma, a bachelor's degree, or a graduate degree.

TABLE 3.4 **Education Rank: Gender by Race/Ethnicity**[103]

EDUCATION RANK	GENDER BY RACE/ETHNICITY	EDUCATION INDEX	LESS THAN HIGH SCHOOL (%)	HIGH SCHOOL GRADUATE (%)	COLLEGE GRADUATE (BA) (%)	GRADUATE OR PROFESSIONAL DEGREE (%)	SCHOOL ENROLLMENT (%)
1	Asian males	8.34	11.7	35.2	28.8	24.3	98.8
2	Asian females	7.54	16.9	37.6	29.5	16.0	106.0
3	White females	5.78	10.7	60.9	18.2	10.1	90.9
4	White males	5.30	11.3	57.0	19.7	12.1	84.7
5	African American females	4.94	19.8	62.4	11.5	6.3	92.7
6	American Indian females	4.12	22.7	54.3	18.9	4.1	85.3
7	African American males	4.11	20.5	62.9	11.3	5.4	86.4
8	American Indian males	3.34	24.7	54.2	16.2	4.9	79.5
9	Latino females	2.51	39.3	48.0	8.8	3.9	81.7
10	Latino males	1.75	41.7	46.5	7.9	3.9	76.1

Note: Enrollment can be over 100 percent if adults twenty-five and over are enrolled in school.

How We Fare Internationally

How is the United States doing in educating its people compared to other Group of Eight (G-8) countries (Canada, France, Germany, Italy, Japan, the Russian Federation, and the United Kingdom), which are among the world's most affluent nations? The United States spends the most on education at the combined primary and secondary education levels as well as at the higher education level. But we do not achieve the best results. In 2006:

- All or almost all three- and four-year-old children were enrolled in pre-school education in France and Italy. In Canada, Germany, Japan, Russia, and the United Kingdom, at least 75 percent were enrolled. In the United States, 53 percent were enrolled and there is significant regional variation within the United States.

- Japanese fourth-graders are far ahead of the rest of the G-8 children in their math skills; U.S. performance is average.

- About one-quarter of fifteen-year-old students in the United States scored at or below the lowest proficiency level on an international test of math-ematics literacy, a higher proportion of students than in Germany, France, Japan, or Canada.

How do we compare to OECD countries, a larger group of thirty nations? Worse. On the Program for International Student Assessment (PISA), a rigorous evaluation conducted by the OECD every three years to gauge the math, science, and reading performance of fifteen-year-olds, the United States consistently ranks near the bottom. It is difficult to make comparisons in reading, due to differences in age at which reading is taught, variations among languages, and other factors, but in the most recent assessment year, 2006, in math, the United States came in twenty-fourth, and in science, the United States came in seventeenth.

When race, ethnicity, and gender are combined, Asian men are at the top of the education ladder.

The Knowledge Journey

In the coming sections, we contrast "average" life experiences among children and adults of different social classes at different points in life. The powerful drive of parents and grandparents to give their children a better life is a constructive socioeconomic force the world over. **Although nearly all parents want to give their children the best possible start and the most secure future, the resources and knowledge they bring to bear on this task vary greatly.**

Low-income Americans have a long and painful experience with experts and middle-class society in general analyzing their parental abilities and finding them wanting—often with devastating consequences for children. The point here is to discuss what research has shown about the associations between early childhood experiences and human outcomes in important arenas like school. It is written with full appreciation that while parenthood is a uniquely joyous and life-affirming experience, day-to-day its demands are relentless and frequently isolating, exhausting, and frustrating. Poverty, stress, depression, illness, poor living conditions, and the legacy of one's own childhood pains (what Selma Fraiberg called "the ghosts in the nursery") can easily intensify the already formidable challenges of parenting. None of us is our best parenting self when the car breaks down and there's no money to fix it, when we're treated disrespectfully at work, when bill collectors are calling.

On average, affluent Americans are able to offer their children a constellation of advantages and resources in childhood, during the transition to independent adulthood and beyond. A variety of mechanisms—family structure, assets and intergenerational wealth transfers, community norms and amenities, government policies and public institutions—serve to reinforce those benefits, creating a "virtuous circle" of mutually reinforcing advantages. **Low-income families, on average, have fewer resources of all sorts—less education, worse health, less income, fewer assets, less safe neighborhoods, more stress, and more fragile family and**

The knowledge journey can be thought of as a lifelong process that starts at birth.

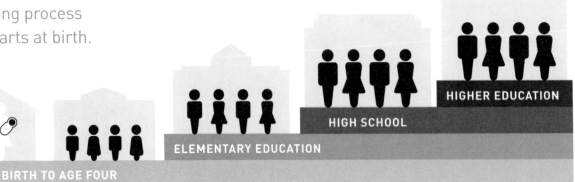

BIRTH TO AGE FOUR

ELEMENTARY EDUCATION

HIGH SCHOOL

HIGHER EDUCATION

community structures.[104] Their compounded disadvantages hamstring their ability to equip their children with capabilities on par with those of children of privilege.

Averages hide a great deal of variation. Not all highly educated mothers read to their children daily; not all teen mothers give birth to low-birth-weight babies. Typically, though, parents with higher incomes and more education are better able to equip their children to succeed in today's knowledge-based, globalized economy. Research indicates that the differences described below are particularly consequential for overall life chances.

Birth to Age Four: Where Knowledge Begins

A child's educational trajectory is set in the first years of life. Birth weight, household income, family structure, parent-child interactions, parental investment, and early childhood care and education are critical.

LOW BIRTH WEIGHT

Low income, low levels of maternal education, lack of prenatal care, teen motherhood, membership in a minority group, and smoking all correlate to low birth weight. Low birth weight, in turn, correlates to impairments in language acquisition and psychological and intellectual development. Controlling for other factors, low birth weight has been shown to be a detriment to timely high school graduation, which undermines access to opportunity.[105]

DEEP OR PERSISTENT POVERTY IN THE PRESCHOOL YEARS

Higher preschool family income is associated with higher rates of high school completion. Yet interestingly, higher income in the years of middle childhood and early adolescence is not associated with higher high school graduation rates. Jeannine Brooks-Gunn, an expert in the field, speculates, "Since low income is associated with less adequate preschool competencies, children are set on a trajectory for lowered school achievement that is difficult (although probably not impossible) to alter."

FAMILY STRUCTURE

Research overwhelmingly supports the view that, on average, children raised in homes with their two biological parents experience greater overall well-being and more positive future outcomes than children living with single parents or in non-intact families (i.e., with a stepparent or a biological parent's live-in companion). However, education helps to level the playing field.

Only 4 percent of births to college-educated women take place outside marriage. In addition, the divorce rate for college-educated women is less than the commonly cited 50 percent statistic for all marriages; only 17 percent of marriages of women with college degrees dissolve in the first ten years.[106] In addition, college-educated women have increasingly delayed both marriage and parenthood, and these delays

BIRTH TO AGE FOUR

A child's educational trajectory is set in the first years of life.

are associated with net benefits for the couple and their children, including higher levels of education, higher wages, and greater marital satisfaction and stability.

The increase in out-of-wedlock births is concentrated among the less educated and among African Americans. These groups delay marriage, but not childbearing. Two-thirds of African American children are born to single mothers. Factors contributing to this trend are discussed in the standard of living section of this report. Being born to a single mother is the strongest predictor of child poverty; it is also associated with behavioral problems, poor academic performance, leaving school before graduation, teen parenthood, and depressed adult employment and earnings.

PARENT-CHILD INTERACTION

Research stretching back decades has offered fairly consistent observations about the way in which low-income and high-income mothers and fathers interact with their children and the impact of these differing styles on educational outcomes. To use Annette Laureau's terminology, **middle- and upper-class parents use a parenting strategy of "concerted cultivation" while low-income parents allow children to experience "natural growth."** Edin and Kefalas argue that low-income mothers set the bar for what constitutes successful motherhood lower than do high-income mothers, in accord with their resources.

The result is that higher-income parents believe their role is to foster their children's cognitive and social skills, using methods and strategies in line with school expectations and supported by child-rearing experts. These include reading to children and limiting TV watching. They engage their children from infancy in frequent conversation; they encourage their children to engage adults in conversation on an equal footing; they offer frequent encouragement; and they provide a host of "enriching" activities. Low-income families are more inclined to tend to physical and emotional basics—food, clothing, shelter, stability, care during illness, affection, and the like. They tend to talk to their children less, to issue more direct commands, and to maintain a firm boundary between the world of children and the world of adults. Research indicates that many lower-income parents view middle-class parenting practices as indulgent.

The child who is read to in the early years has a higher likelihood of school success, research shows. The latest data from the U.S. Census Bureau indicate that non-Hispanic white children ages one to five are about four times more likely to have been read to in the past week than Hispanic children, and white children were about 50 percent more likely to have been read to than African American children.[107] Married parents, better-educated parents, and higher-income parents read to their young children more and put greater restrictions on TV watching than unmarried parents and parents with less education and income, the data show.

Clearly, these general trends do not hold true for every family. However, in aggregate, they have a significant effect: by age three, children of professionals have vocabularies nearly 50 percent greater than those of working-class

The child who is read to in the early years has a higher likelihood of school success, research shows.

children, and twice as large as those of children whose mothers receive public assistance.[108] Among four-year-olds (children between forty-eight and fifty-seven months of age), 40 percent of children from disadvantaged backgrounds were proficient in number and shape recognition, compared to 87 percent of children from privileged families.[109] A University of Kansas study more than twenty years ago found that professional parents spoke two thousand words per hour to their children, working-class parents thirteen hundred, and mothers receiving welfare six hundred. By age three, the children of affluent mothers had vocabularies twice as large as those of the children of low-income mothers. More recent studies continue to confirm that educated mothers use a richer vocabulary, engage in longer periods of conversation, and encourage child-directed conversation more frequently than less educated, less verbally skilled mothers, and that play and interaction are the pathways through which these mothers transmit verbal skills.[110]

The cumulative effect of the gap in oral vocabulary among children of different family backgrounds that is present by age three is substantial, putting the poorest students at a permanent disadvantage.[111] The consensus of researchers in this area is that these early interactions with parents develop a sense of entitlement among better-off children, who learn skills and behavioral styles in line with school expectations. Lacking these skills places children from low-income families at a disadvantage. Programs like the Nurse Family Partnership (see BOX 3.9) and Opportunity NYC (see BOX 3.10) are designed to address these disadvantages.

> By age three, the children of affluent mothers have vocabularies twice as large as those of the children of low-income mothers.

BOX 3.9 **Olds Nurse-Family Partnership**

When David Olds took a college job at a Baltimore day-care center in the early 1970s, he was surprised to observe that most of his efforts to help children seemed to be too little, too late. He wondered whether helping parents and children much earlier in their lives—before day-care age—was a better way to help them lead healthy, productive lives. He decided to dedicate himself to research and service that would help answer that question.

Dr. Olds went on to develop a home visitation program focused on first-time, low-income mothers, who receive visits by a registered nurse from pregnancy through the child's second birthday. Providing guidance on positive health behaviors, competent child-care, and personal development for mothers (educational achievement, workforce participation, family planning), nurses help inexperienced mothers with few resources to acquire a range of capabilities associated with positive early childhood development. Three separate clinical trials conducted over the last thirty years have demonstrated that the program reduces the rate of child abuse, mothers' drug use, and crime. Children in the program are healthier, and their parents pursue a more positive life path. A follow-up trial

in Memphis, Tennessee, for example, showed that children in the program incurred 80 percent fewer injuries or ingestions requiring hospitalization. An age six follow-up on the same population showed that mothers in the program spent 20 percent fewer months on welfare.

An analysis by RAND Corporation has shown that every dollar invested in the Olds program has yielded, on average, $2.88 worth of benefits—a figure that jumps to $5.70 for interventions targeting the children most at risk.

Now known as the Nurse-Family Partnership, the program has been expanding to communities across the country since 1996, with support from a central program team at the National Center for Children, Families and Communities (NCCFC), based at the University of Colorado Health Sciences Center. Programs that have sought to replicate this model with less trained personnel—such as nurse's aides rather than registered nurses—have not achieved similar results. The skills of providers are critical.

Source: Karoly, Kilburn, and Cannon. "Early Childhood Intervention."

Take your son for a physical or work an overtime shift? Encourage your daughter to finish high school or ask her to take a full-time job? Opportunity NYC is a pilot project aimed at changing the economics of this kind of decision making in three areas linked to poverty: child education, child health, and adult employment. Under the program, children in select schools in New York City can earn payments as high as six hundred dollars for good test scores and attendance. Their parents can earn payments for attending school conferences, working full-time, and ensuring that children accumulate school credits and receive regular health checkups. In broader terms, not only will families benefit in the long run, but so will society—through safer cities, reduced health-care costs, and a more productive economy.

The initiative is inspired by Oportunidades, a Mexican program rolled out in 1997, through which mothers get cash for ensuring that their children receive health checkups and attend school regularly. International studies show that the program has delivered results: attendance rates and preventive health visits are up, and more kids from poor families are growing up healthy, well fed, and better educated. The program has also shown immediate benefits—boosting the incomes of poor families enough to contribute to drops in the poverty rate and income inequality. These results have encouraged at least twenty-five countries to implement similar programs.

Opportunity NYC is funded by private foundations and donors. One of the lead funders of the program is the Rockefeller Foundation, whose president, Judith Rodin, said the goal of New York's program is to ensure "that beneficiaries make long-term investments in the health and education of their families."

Source: mikebloomberg.com., "Mayor Bloomberg Releases Incentives Schedule for Opportunity NYC" and "Mayor Michael Bloomberg and Delegation Visit Mexico's 'Oportunidades' Program"; World Bank, "Mexico's Oportunidades Program"; La Comisión Económica para América Latina, "Panorama Social de America Latina."

Highly educated fathers spend more time playing with, reading to, and going on outings with their preschoolers.

PARENTAL INVESTMENT

College-educated parents tend to spend more on their children as a proportion of total household expenditures and parental time. This trend seems to be on the rise. College-educated mothers spend more time on child care, the time they spend declines less steeply as children get older, and the activities mothers and children do together are more stimulating—less TV watching, more reading, more art projects. Highly educated fathers spend more time playing with, reading to, and going on outings with their preschoolers; they also spend more time caring for and playing with their infants than less educated fathers.[112]

EARLY CHILDHOOD EDUCATION AND CHILD CARE

The "new normal" in America is that most children live either in intact families where both the mother and father work outside the home or in single-parent homes headed by an adult (usually a woman) who is in the labor force. Our European peer countries have dealt with a similar influx of women into the labor force by offering high-quality, universal child care and a host of family-friendly policies that support mothers and fathers in their efforts to care for children and also earn a living. The United States has not. As a result, parents are on their own in finding ways to care for young children throughout the day. (See the section on income for more on this topic.)

THE MEASURE OF AMERICA

For *babies and toddlers under three* whose primary caretakers are in the workforce, slightly more than one in four were cared for by parents themselves (an option more open to two-parent families), slightly more than one in four were cared for by relatives, slightly fewer than one in four were cared for in a licensed child-care center, one in six was cared for in a home-based day care (a caregiver taking care of several children in her own home), and one in fourteen was cared for in the child's home by a babysitter or nanny, according to the Census Bureau.

In 2005, 20 percent of four-year-olds had no regular early care and education arrangement; 44.8 percent were in a center-based (non–Head Start) setting; 12.7 percent were in a Head Start setting; 13.1 percent were in a home-based relative care setting; and 7.6 percent were cared for by a babysitter or nanny.[113] These percentages vary by socioeconomic (SES) status, however. For instance, 31 percent of children from low SES families did not have regular child-care arrangements, compared to 20 percent of those from middle SES families, and 10 percent of children from high SES families.

Child care and nursery or preschool are not the same thing, though the lines separating them are increasingly blurry. Attending home-based day care for eight to ten hours per day in the apartment of a neighbor who did not graduate high school is a very different experience than attending a nursery school with college-educated teachers five mornings per week—though both would be categorized as "early childhood education" in many large surveys. According to this definition, 43 percent of three-year-olds and 69 percent of four-year-olds were enrolled in a center-based early childhood program in 2005.

Variation by state is striking, with several western states, Washington, Oregon, Idaho, Nevada, Utah, Arizona, and North Dakota, along with Wisconsin, West Virginia and Tennessee, showing very low rates of preschool enrollment (see MAP 3.3).

Some children receive little more than custodial care, whereas others enjoy a developmentally rich, nurturing environment. Cost is the key driver. The poorest families can qualify for Head Start and other reduced-cost programs—though for every child admitted to such a program, six qualified children are excluded due to a shortage of spaces. Middle-class and low-income families face a real crisis in finding decent care that they can afford; developmentally appropriate environments with trained teachers are often beyond their means.

Middle-class and low-income families face a real crisis in finding decent care that they can afford.

INTERVENTION IN THE PRESCHOOL YEARS: THE EVIDENCE

Children from different family backgrounds experience dramatically different qualities of learning in the preschool years, resulting in cognitive and noncognitive disparities measurable along class lines before children even start school.[114] This challenged development leaves some children so ill-prepared for education that they cannot take full advantage of primary school education, and they may never develop the cognitive and social abilities necessary to lead healthy, productive lives to their fullest potential.

A number of studies show, however, that interventions at the preschool level can result in a reduction of these disparities by the time the child begins primary school, with benefits lasting well into the adult years. Early intervention is vital because of the brain's high "plasticity" during the early years.

There is some controversy around the long-term effects of preschool, particularly Head Start, the most common preschool experience for poor children. There is little evidence of long-term benefits from this program, leading some to doubt the effectiveness of preschool interventions for disadvantaged children in general. However, robust evidence supports the effectiveness of high-quality programs.

The High/Scope Perry Preschool Project in Michigan, for example, provided high-quality preschool education to African American children between 1962 and 1967. The program focused on active learning and parent involvement as well as parenting skills development. It was staffed by college-educated teachers paid the same wages as public school elementary teachers and resulted in the following outcomes for students:[115]

- **44% higher** high school graduation rate (at age twenty-seven)

- **50% fewer** teen pregnancies (at age twenty-seven)

- **46% less likely** to have served time in jail or prison (at age forty)

- **42% higher** median monthly income (at age forty)

Another proven model, the Abecedarian Project of North Carolina, initiated in 1972, provided educational child care and high-quality preschool to mostly African American children from very disadvantaged backgrounds, focusing on development of language and cognitive skills through educational games. A study measured outcomes at age twenty-one for students who had attended the preschool:[116]

- An **increase** of more than one grade level in reading and math achievement;

- A **much higher percentage** of students having attended or attending four-year college (36 percent vs. 14 percent);

- A **much lower percentage** of teenaged parents (26 percent vs. 45 percent).

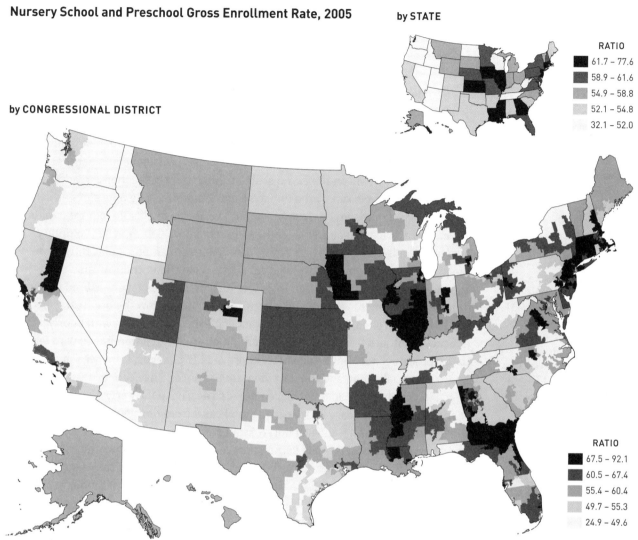

MAP 3.3

Nursery School and Preschool Gross Enrollment Rate, 2005

by **STATE**

RATIO
- 61.7 – 77.6
- 58.9 – 61.6
- 54.9 – 58.8
- 52.1 – 54.8
- 32.1 – 52.0

by **CONGRESSIONAL DISTRICT**

RATIO
- 67.5 – 92.1
- 60.5 – 67.4
- 55.4 – 60.4
- 49.7 – 55.3
- 24.9 – 49.6

The average annual cost of the Perry Preschool Project was about $12,000 per student: the Abecedarian Project cost about $13,000 (2002 dollars). And the payoff? One study estimated that benefits of Perry Preschool, minus the costs and including projected benefits like decreased crime, amounted to more than $31,000. Even excluding projected benefits, the results were impressive: more than $20,000 worth of net benefits. The benefit-cost ratio of the Abecedarian Project was about four-to-one.

Other small-scale, well-designed early intervention programs have also yielded impressive results. Chicago Child Parent Centers, the Houston Parent-

Redshirting Children

There is an increasing trend in some affluent communities for parents to give children born in the months immediately prior to the school cut-off date what is referred to as **"the gift of time"** by holding them out of school until the following year. "Redshirting" their children—and thus incurring an additional year's expense of preschool and/or child care—is a gift that low- and even many middle-income parents cannot make.

Although this strategy can help ensure that the redshirted child does not start school before he or she is developmentally ready, the trend exacerbates inequalities, putting six-year-olds with up to three years of preschool into class with four- and five-year-olds for whom kindergarten is their first formal school experience.

Child Development Center, the Syracuse Family Development Research Program, Project Care/Carolina Approach to Responsive Education, the Elmira New York Prenatal/Early Infancy Project, the Infant Health and Development Project, the Early Training Project, and others have demonstrated success in improving outcomes for disadvantaged children.

On a larger scale, many states are now implementing pre-K programs. Most focus on children with different risk factors, such as living in a low-income family or having a single parent, but a handful of states now offer truly universal pre-K. Oklahoma has perhaps gone furthest in expanding the successful elements of smaller experimental programs. Its teachers must have bachelor's degrees, for instance, and are paid on the same scale as public school teachers. In addition, the pre-K program is run by the public schools, not by private operators as is the case with most preschool programs. About two-thirds of eligible four-year-olds are enrolled. Recent evaluations of the Oklahoma program, which is voluntary but free for all, have shown that Latino youngsters benefited significantly from the program, particularly from full days. African American children also saw significant gains, as did children from low-income families (as measured by free or reduced-price lunch). The most disadvantaged children saw the greatest gains.[117]

In broad strokes, for the very poorest children and children with poorly educated mothers (less than high school), high-quality, center-based care leads to better school outcomes and vastly improved life chances, largely because of improved socialization and the development of noncognitive capabilities. Positive effects on math and reading achievement also accrue in the early elementary years. Center-based care with less qualified caregivers does not have these positive effects. For middle-class children, center-based care shows some benefits and some drawbacks; there is some improvement in certain academic readiness indicators, like number or letter recognition, and in third-grade math and reading achievement. But there is also a slight uptick in some behavioral problems, such as being disruptive in class, more conflict with teachers and parents, and having poorer social skills and work habits.

Essentially, children benefit from high-quality care, and don't benefit from poor-quality care. Studies have shown that the quality of care in U.S. child centers is, on average, poor—and that the care available to most low-income families is abysmal.

Elementary Education: The Gap Widens

Because public school is compulsory for elementary-school-aged children, there is no variation among states and congressional districts, among ethnic/racial groups, or between girls and boys in the level of enrollment for eligible children. Similarly, the educational attainment index of this Report starts with a high school diploma, and therefore educational attainment rates do not directly pertain to children in kindergarten through eighth grade. However, given the centrality of elementary school to an individual's experience, to the formation of capabilities that affect the life course, and to high school success and the likelihood of college attendance, we examine elementary school briefly here.

Many approaches have shown promise in improving schools in crisis. The challenge that bedevils reformers is that the most influential factors in school performance reside outside the classroom. The best way to do well in school is to have parents with college educations, high incomes, and plentiful assets. Children from lower-income families and children whose mothers have low levels of education actually learn more in school than do advantaged children—in that they cover more ground over the course of a school year—simply because school environments are more enriching than their home environments. Some proposals for school reform, including shortening the summer holiday or lengthening the school day to significantly increase instructional time, would benefit disadvantaged children. But they would be less likely to improve outcomes for privileged children, whose afternoons and summers are replete with opportunities for learning.

In this section, therefore, we look at the quality of public elementary education for different groups of children and argue that disparities in school quality and in the school-going experience widen the existing gap between disadvantaged children and everyone else on the first day of kindergarten. Overall, groups that perform at the bottom of the educational index, Latinos and African Americans, attend the worst schools and experience disproportionate school difficulties—a significant contributor to lower educational attainment in the teens and early twenties.

Disparities in school quality widen the gap between disadvantaged children and their middle-class peers.

DIFFERENCES IN EXPENDITURES PER PUPIL BY STATE

States spend different amounts of money educating their students. At the top, New Jersey and New York spend around $14,000 per pupil; at the bottom, Utah spends less than $6,000 per pupil.[118] Though expenditures are not a guarantee of quality, there is a strong correlation between what a state spends to educate each pupil and the score that state earns on this Report's Education Index (see FIGURE 3.7). What a state spends on each pupil explains about half the variation among states in the Education Index. It is possible that the higher elementary and secondary school expenditures are buying better teachers, better facilities, more enrichment, and a richer curriculum, all of which are boosting high school graduation rates and preparing kids to go to college. Another explanation is that states with better-

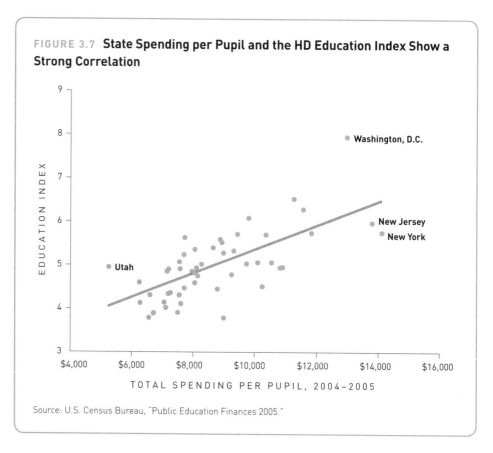

FIGURE 3.7 **State Spending per Pupil and the HD Education Index Show a Strong Correlation**

EDUCATION INDEX

TOTAL SPENDING PER PUPIL, 2004–2005

Source: U.S. Census Bureau, "Public Education Finances 2005."

The neediest schools often have the least qualified, least experienced, and least effective teachers, largely because of lower salaries and less desirable working conditions.

educated populations prioritize educational expenditures, or both trends could be working in tandem.

DIFFERENCES IN TEACHER QUALITY

The neediest schools often have the least qualified, least experienced, and least effective teachers, largely because of lower salaries and less desirable working conditions. Schools in low-income areas often pay less than those in high-income towns. For instance, one-third of teachers in wealthy Bronxville, New York, make more than one hundred thousand dollars per year; no teachers in the middle-income, majority African American town of Mount Vernon, directly adjacent to Bronxville, do. The median salary in suburban Westchester County in 2003–04 was seventy-four thousand dollars, compared to approximately fifty-two thousand dollars in bordering New York City.[119] Seniority allows more experienced teachers greater choice about where they teach, which can make a big difference in very large districts with wide variations in school quality. Working conditions in schools serving low-income students are much worse than those in schools serving affluent communities (see BOX 3.11). The result of differences in pay and working conditions leads to outcomes like these:

- Schools with high proportions of minority students, poor students (measured by those eligible for free or reduced-price lunch), and English-language-learners were more likely to hire novice teachers than schools with the lowest proportions of such students. Research shows that teachers become significantly more effective each year in the first five years of teaching (as measured by student achievement scores).

- Students in schools with high proportions of low-income and/or minority students are more likely to be taught English, science, and math by an "out-of-field" teacher than students in schools with few low-income and/or minority students. Research confirms the obvious: children learn more from math teachers who majored in math, from science teachers who majored in science, and so on.

Many parts of the country are facing teacher shortages fueled by the retirement of thousands of baby-boomer teachers and burnout among young teachers working in high-needs schools. At the start of the 2007 school year, for example, turnover in Guilford County, North Carolina, had become so severe in some high-poverty schools that principals had to hire new teachers every term for almost every class. Shortages in math and science are particularly severe nationwide; in Guilford, there were schools without a single certified math teacher.[120]

BOX 3.11 **School Environments Differ Sharply**

Working conditions in schools with more low-income and minority students are generally worse than those in wealthier, whiter schools.[121]

- African American tenth-graders were significantly more likely than white tenth-graders to attend schools with security guards, metal detectors, and bars on windows.

- African American students were more likely than white students to attend schools with trash on the floor, graffiti, and ceilings in disrepair.

- Students from the lowest socioeconomic quarter were more likely than students from the highest quarter to attend schools that had metal detectors.

- Schools with 51–100 percent of tenth-graders eligible for free or reduced-price lunch were more likely to have metal detectors and bars on classroom windows than other schools.

- Non-English-speaking tenth-graders were more likely than English-speaking tenth graders to attend schools that had security guards, metal detectors, bars on the windows, and fencing around the entire school.

Source: Planty and Devoe, "An Examination of the Condition of School Facilities Attended by 10th-Grade Students in 2002."

Fast Facts about K–12 Education

$489.4 billion
expenditure for public elementary and secondary schools in the 2007–08 school year.

49.6 million students
enrolled in public elementary and secondary schools in 2007–08.

97,000 public schools
(elementary and secondary) in 2005–06.

3.2 million teachers
employed in public elementary and secondary schools in 2007–08.

$9,969
average expenditure per pupil in public elementary and secondary schools in 2007–08.

1.1 million students
—about 2 percent of the total—homeschooled during the 2003 school year.

887,000 students
attended the nation's approximately thirty-three hundred charter schools during the 2004–05 school year.

6.1 million
students enrolled in private elementary and secondary schools in 2007–08.

Source: U.S. Department of Education, National Center for Educational Statistics, "Fast Facts.," 2007.

Spending per student is, on
average, higher in urban
school districts than in
suburban districts. This
is because urban districts
receive federal funds for
at-risk children, whose special
needs make their educations
more expensive. But in terms
of concrete educational
resources available to their
students, such as school
facilities, effective teachers,
and instructional resources,
urban districts fall short of
their suburban counterparts.
Rural districts spend the least
per enrolled student.

Low-income
children are
particularly ill-
served by our
short standard
school days
and long summer
breaks.

DIFFERENCES IN AVAILABLE SCHOOL RESOURCES

**Schools are funded primarily from local property taxes, so rich districts generally
have more money for teachers, specialists, enrichment programs, supplies, and
the physical plant and school grounds.** When affluent districts fall short, families
often make up the difference with fund-raising events, thus ensuring that foreign
language or music instruction, field trips to museums, fully equipped sports
teams, and the like are part of their children's educational experience. Parents
in Greenwich, Connecticut, for instance, raised money to have air-conditioning
installed in their children's school when the district declined to install it. Schools
with few poor children have more psychologists, more special education aides, and
more library staff than high-poverty schools.

DIFFERENCES IN CURRICULUM AND "TEACHING TO THE TEST"

Schools are under a great deal of pressure to improve test scores. NCLB made
great strides in requiring schools to disaggregate testing results as a first step
toward closing the racial gap in educational indicators. But **the resulting "teach to
the test" phenomenon is, in some schools, leading to a no-frills, basics-only curriculum that does not foster the creativity and independence of thought required
for higher education and high-skills jobs.** It also removes art, music, and other
developmentally critical activities from schools.

TRACKING

Ability grouping hurts children who are struggling with different subjects, and confers little benefit to high-performing students, according to research. Yet it appears
throughout school, from kindergarten "reading groups" to formalized high school
curricula. Advanced Placement and other advanced courses/sections are dominat-
ed by high-income kids; low-tracks, special education, and remedial classes are
disproportionately poor, minority, and male. African American students are three
times more likely than whites to be placed in special education programs, and
only half as likely to be in gifted programs.[122] In 2003, 45 percent of children whose
parents had advanced degrees were in gifted classes, compared with 10 percent of
children whose parents did not graduate high school. Children whose parents were
married and better off also were more likely to be in gifted classes than children of
the never-married or poor.[123]

ON-TRACK

African American and Latino children are 50 percent more likely to have repeated
a grade by age nine than white children, yet there is no evidence that holding a
child back has any academic benefits. Moreover, **high rates of retention can create
disciplinary and social difficulties in subsequent years, and children who are held
back are less likely to ever graduate high school than other children.**

PARENTAL SATISFACTION

Middle- and upper-income parents reported being more satisfied with their child's school, its academic standards, and its order and discipline than poor or near-poor parents. More white parents than African American parents report being satisfied with their child's school.

LEVEL OF SUPERVISION DURING THE SCHOOL YEARS

Maternal time investment declines less steeply as children get older among college-educated mothers than among mothers with less education. Children living in poverty spend 40 percent more time unsupervised than do more affluent children.[124]

TYPES OF ACTIVITIES

Participation in after-school activities offers children a chance to build capabilities as well as the self-esteem that comes with mastery and accomplishment. Participating in sports is good for health, participation in clubs teaches the skills of participation and civic engagement, and lessons directly target specific capabilities. A child facing academic difficulties or social awkwardness can find solace and a source of pride by rising in the ranks at her karate program or a sense of belonging from joining a Boy Scout troop or a church youth group. Because formal activities are supervised, they are also a good way to keep kids out of trouble. Children's participation in extracurricular activities moves in step with family income: 45.8 percent of children from families living below the poverty line participate in some sort of after-school activity—a club, a sport, or some sort of lesson—while 52.8 percent of children from families living between the poverty line and double the poverty line take part in such activities. But 70 percent of children from families living above 200 percent of the poverty line take part. White children, children with married parents, and children whose parents had more education and income participated in more enrichment activities than did the children of minority, unmarried, and less educated families in 2003.[125]

Low-income children are particularly ill-served by our short standard school days and long summer breaks. A recent study showed that during the summer after kindergarten, children from higher socioeconomic families were significantly more likely to visit libraries, state parks, museums, zoos, and historic sites, as well as attend plays, concerts, and camp programs than students of poorer, less-educated parents. Eighty percent of privileged children went to the library, for instance, compared to 46 percent of disadvantaged children.[126]

Children living in central cities are less likely to play outside than other children. Among children living in central cities, 48 percent of Hispanic children, 39 percent of African American children, 24 percent of Asian children, and 25 percent of white children were kept inside because of parental perceptions of neighborhood danger. Lack of exercise and opportunity for spontaneous play make it hard to focus in school.[128] Groups around the country are seeking ways to address these inequalities. Teach for America and KIPP are two well-known examples (see BOX 3.12 and BOX 3.13).

Are Charter Schools the Answer?

The National Center for Education Statistics defines a public charter school as a publicly funded school that has been granted a charter exempting it from selected state or local rules and regulations.

A charter school may be newly created, or it may previously have been a public or private school; it is typically governed by a group or organization under a contract or charter with the state. In return for funding and autonomy, the charter school must meet accountability standards.

A 2003 U.S. Department of Education pilot study of charter schools found that in reading and math, the performance of fourth-grade students with similar racial/ethnic backgrounds in charter schools and other public schools was not measurably different, and that, among students eligible for free or reduced-price lunch, fourth-graders in charter schools did not score as high in reading or mathematics, on average, as low-income fourth-graders in other public schools.[127]

Teach for America: Can It Solve the Teacher Crisis?

Teach for America, founded in 1989, has a corps of more than five thousand young teachers educating some 425,000 students annually. The program is highly competitive, attracting some of the nation's top college students and accepting just 17 percent of applicants. TFA participants are placed in struggling urban and rural school districts where fourth-graders are already three grade levels behind their higher-income peers and half the students do not graduate from high school on time.

The program has boosters and detractors. Almost no TFA recruits are education majors; they rely instead on an intensive five-week summer training program that some critics argue leaves the inexperienced beginners ill-prepared for the rigors and realities of the classroom. Approximately 10 percent to 15 percent of TFA participants drop out of the program before their two-year commitment is up, and most TFA alumni do not remain teachers.

TFA supporters counter that the goal is not to create lifelong teachers or to end the teacher shortage; rather the program aims to improve public education by building a network of alumni with firsthand knowledge of the challenges schools in low-income neighborhoods face. This cadre of advocates and supporters can then advance education reform from other fields—law, media, business, and so on. Some TFA alumni have gone on to dedicate themselves to public education, including the founders of the KIPP schools and the new, youngest-ever chancellor of the District of Columbia Public Schools.

Sources: Alliance for Catholic Education., "Teacher Formation Program"; Decker, Mayer, and Glazerman, "Effects of Teach for America on Students"; Gillers, "Learning Curve"; Karman, "Program Lures Quality Teachers to State"; NYC Teaching Fellows, "New York City Teaching Fellows"; Teach for America.

Knowledge Is Power Program

Most educators, principals, and families in low-income, high-minority communities would not expect their local school to outscore the majority of schools in the state in reading and math achievement, or to have a college matriculation rate 60 percentage points higher than the national average. However, fourteen thousand students across seventeen states have proven these outstanding results can be achieved through their Knowledge Is Power Program (KIPP) schools.

KIPP is a national network of fifty-seven public schools located in low-income, high-minority areas. Most are charter schools, with admissions open to students on a first-come basis. KIPP schools serve a higher percentage of minorities and recipients of free or reduced-price lunches than the average urban school, but, as one school director said, "At KIPP, there is no blaming 'downtown.' There is no blaming 'the system.'"

The network includes mostly middle schools. By the eighth grade, 100 percent of classes outscore local districts in reading and math. The program began in 1995, when two teachers opened a fifth-grade school in Houston after completing Teach for America.

Students, teachers, and parents commit to nine-hour school days with occasional Saturday classes and three weeks of summer school. Teachers are compensated for their extra time with salaries 15–20 percent higher than the district average. Even with the cost of an extended schedule, KIPP spends the same or less per student than mainstream schools.

KIPP's critics argue that the success of KIPP students is at least in part a result of parents who are more engaged than the average neighborhood parent—evidenced by their success in getting their children into a KIPP school. Unlike public schools, KIPP schools can expel students with relative ease. In addition, KIPP and other charter schools are criticized for removing the best students and most involved parents from public schools, exacerbating the problems of schools that are already struggling. Yet it seems indisputable that students who have escaped failing schools to attend KIPP schools face a new world of opportunity and the potential for brighter futures.

Sources: Knowledge Is Power Program; Matthews, "Inside the KIPP School Summit."

STUDENT ACHIEVEMENT

This report is critical of the perverse incentives created by the emphasis on testing. But it is important not to throw the baby out with the bathwater. Test results can impart valuable information about how different groups of American children are doing.

By the end of fourth grade, African American and Latino students, and poor students of all races, are on average two years behind their wealthier, predominantly white peers in reading and math. By eighth grade, they have slipped three years behind, and by twelfth grade, four years behind.[129] This trend is similar to that seen in other industrialized countries; in fourth and eighth grades, children in schools with few students from economically disadvantaged homes score significantly higher than do children attending schools with more than half their students from disadvantaged homes on math achievement tests.[130]

In 2007, Massachusetts fourth-graders and eighth-graders scored highest on the U.S. Department of Education National Assessment of Educational Progress Tests in reading and math. Other states with achievement in the top ten in both grades and in both subject matters were New Jersey, New Hampshire, Vermont, and North Dakota. States consistently ranked in the bottom 10 include Hawaii, Nevada, Louisiana, California, New Mexico, and Mississippi, with Washington, D.C. fourth- and eighth-grade students scoring the lowest in both subjects[131] (see TABLE 3.5).

TABLE 3.5 **Educational Progress National Assessment, 2007 Test Results**

4th Grade Math TOP TEN		4th Grade Reading TOP TEN		8th Grade Math TOP TEN		8th Grade Reading TOP TEN	
1	Massachusetts	1	Massachusetts	1	Massachusetts	1	Massachusetts
2	New Jersey	2	New Jersey	2	Minnesota	2	Vermont
3	New Hampshire	3	New Hampshire	3	North Dakota	3	Montana
4	Kansas	4	Vermont	4	Vermont	4	New Jersey
5	Minnesota	5	Connecticut	5	Kansas	5	Maine
6	Vermont	6	Virginia	6	New Jersey	6	New Hampshire
7	North Dakota	7	Montana	7	South Dakota	7	South Dakota
8	Indiana	8	Pennsylvania	8	Virginia	8	Minnesota
9	Ohio	9	North Dakota	9	New Hampshire	9	North Dakota
10	Wisconsin	10	Ohio	10	Montana	10	Ohio
BOTTOM TEN		BOTTOM TEN		BOTTOM TEN		BOTTOM TEN	
42	Hawaii	42	Alaska	42	Arkansas	42	West Virginia
43	Tennessee	43	South Carolina	43	Louisiana	43	Arizona
44	Arizona	44	Hawaii	44	Nevada	44	Louisiana
45	Nevada	45	New Mexico	45	California	45	Nevada
46	Louisiana	46	Nevada	46	West Virginia	46	Alabama
47	California	47	Arizona	47	Hawaii	47	Hawaii
48	Alabama	48	California	48	New Mexico	48	California
49	New Mexico	49	Mississippi	49	Alabama	49	New Mexico
50	Mississippi	50	Louisiana	50	Mississippi	50	Mississippi
51	District of Columbia	51	District of Columbia	51	District of Columbia	51	District of Columbia

Source: U.S. Department of Education, National Center for Education Statistics, "State Comparisons, National Assessment of Educational Progress 2007."

Massachusetts is top ranked in 4th and 8th grade math and reading test results.

Washington, D.C. is ranked lowest.

HIGH SCHOOL

High Schools: Paths Diverge

In general, a high school diploma is the bare-bones minimum for a job that pays a living wage and a prerequisite for higher education. It signals to employers—as well as others, such as potential mates—not only that a student has a certain minimum skill level, but also that he or she has the staying power to achieve long-term goals. High school graduation is also a rite of passage for Americans, an important achievement that marks and celebrates a young person's emerging adulthood. Those who fail to graduate high school are thus deprived of a socially and economically significant credential. They may seek adult status elsewhere—for instance, through early parenthood.

Among the country's most notable achievements in the last forty-five years has been the rise in high school graduation rates. In 1960, only 41 percent of the adult population had a high school degree, less than half the rate today. Since

FIGURE 3.8 **Global Comparison: Upper Secondary (High School) Graduation Rate, 2004**

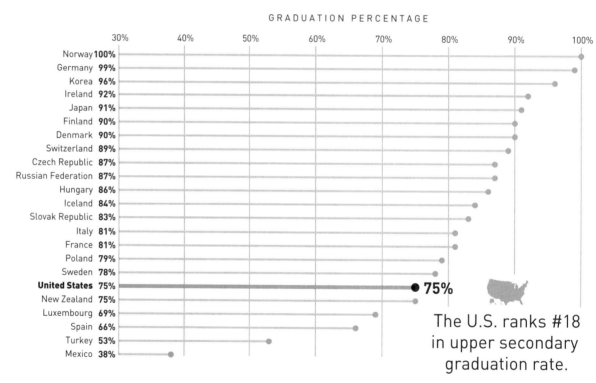

GRADUATION PERCENTAGE

Norway	100%
Germany	99%
Korea	96%
Ireland	92%
Japan	91%
Finland	90%
Denmark	90%
Switzerland	89%
Czech Republic	87%
Russian Federation	87%
Hungary	86%
Iceland	84%
Slovak Republic	83%
Italy	81%
France	81%
Poland	79%
Sweden	78%
United States	**75%**
New Zealand	75%
Luxembourg	69%
Spain	66%
Turkey	53%
Mexico	38%

75%

The U.S. ranks #18 in upper secondary graduation rate.

Note: Data for Denmark, Finland, and France are from 2003.
Source: Organization for Economic Co-Operation and Development. *Education at a Glance, 2006.*

THE MEASURE OF AMERICA

MAP 3.4 **Adults with at Least a High School Diploma, 2005**

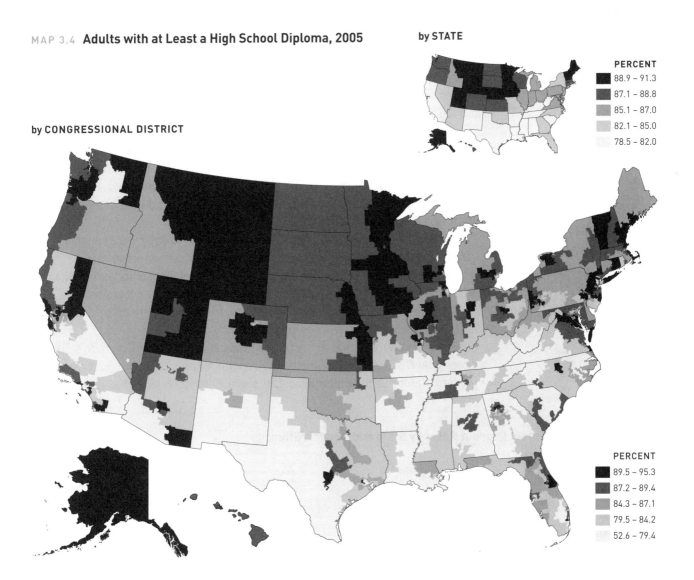

by STATE

PERCENT
- 88.9 – 91.3
- 87.1 – 88.8
- 85.1 – 87.0
- 82.1 – 85.0
- 78.5 – 82.0

by CONGRESSIONAL DISTRICT

PERCENT
- 89.5 – 95.3
- 87.2 – 89.4
- 84.3 – 87.1
- 79.5 – 84.2
- 52.6 – 79.4

1987, there has been a 17 percent increase in the graduation rates of students with disabilities.[132] Advanced Placement exams are taken by 1.2 million students—more than twice the number taking the exams in 1997.

Despite this progress, the United States is not doing as well as other countries in graduating students from high school. In 2004, it ranked eighteenth among the twenty-three affluent countries surveyed (see FIGURE 3.8). Only three-fourths of American public high school students graduated on time (within four years) with a regular diploma in 2003–04.[133]

Only 74 percent of American public high school students graduated on time (within four years) with a regular diploma in 2003–04.

Within the United States, the distribution of high school graduates follows very clear patterns. High dropout rates are concentrated in the South in general, and in high-poverty and high-minority pockets of the Midwest, South, and California. They are higher among men than women, with African American men and Latino men having the highest rates of leaving school.

TABLE 3.6 shows the percentage of the population in each state and ethnic/gender grouping that leaves high school without a diploma. Wyoming, Alaska, Minnesota, Montana, and Utah have the highest completion rates, with at least 90 percent of the population earning a high school diploma. Louisiana, Alabama, California, Kentucky, Texas, and Mississippi have the highest dropout rates, ranging from 19.5 percent to 21.5 percent.

The groups that, on average, face disproportionately greater challenges in their early childhood and elementary school years—African American and Latino children, especially boys—have the lowest rates of high school completion. One in five African Americans in today's population left school without a diploma, as did two in five Latinos. As a group, Latinos are about thirty years behind the country as a whole in terms of high school completion rates.

In terms of congressional districts, the range is remarkable. Colorado's Sixth Congressional District (Denver-Aurora Metropolitan Areas) has a dropout rate of 4.7 percent. California's Twentieth Congressional District (Fresno) has a dropout

TABLE 3.6 **High School Dropout Rates by State and Gender/Ethnicity**

STATE	LESS THAN HIGH SCHOOL (%)
Wyoming	8.7
Alaska	9.0
Minnesota	9.1
Montana	9.3
Utah	9.9
New Hampshire	10.1
Iowa	10.4
Vermont	10.5
Nebraska	10.5
Maine	11.0
Washington	11.2
Wisconsin	11.2
Colorado	11.3
Kansas	11.3
South Dakota	11.4
North Dakota	11.8
Hawaii	11.9
Massachusetts	12.0
Connecticut	12.1
Oregon	12.5
Maryland	13.0
Michigan	13.0

STATE	LESS THAN HIGH SCHOOL (%)
Pennsylvania	13.3
Idaho	13.3
New Jersey	13.7
Ohio	13.7
Illinois	14.3
Delaware	14.4
Virginia	14.6
Indiana	14.7
Missouri	15.0
Florida	15.4
New York	15.7
Oklahoma	15.7
Arizona	16.2
District of Columbia	16.4
Rhode Island	16.5
Georgia	17.2
Nevada	17.2
North Carolina	17.7
New Mexico	18.0
South Carolina	18.3
Tennessee	18.8
West Virginia	18.8

STATE	LESS THAN HIGH SCHOOL (%)
Arkansas	19.0
Louisiana	19.5
Alabama	19.7
California	19.9
Kentucky	21.0
Texas	21.2
Mississippi	21.5

GENDER BY RACE/ETHNICITY	LESS THAN HIGH SCHOOL (%)
White females	10.7
White males	11.3
Asian males	11.7
Asian females	16.9
African American females	19.8
African American males	20.5
American Indian females	22.7
American Indian males	24.7
Latino females	39.3
Latino males	41.7

rate of 47.4 percent, ten times greater. California's Twentieth District is where the country as a whole was in 1970. There are nineteen congressional districts in which one-third or more of the adult population did not earn a high school diploma. The majority of these districts are in either Texas or California.

THE TRANSITION TO ADULTHOOD

Evidence suggests the brain is not mature until the early twenties. The ability to make decisions and think long-term are the last functions to develop; recent research shows that teens lack the well-developed intuition that adults depend upon to make important decisions. Teens may assess risks rationally, but fail to recognize that when an action will have very severe consequences, more than the usual amount of care should be taken to avoid it. Many of the "bad decisions" that can dog young people for the rest of their lives—dropping out of school, becoming a mother at a young age, abusing drugs or alcohol, committing a crime—are first made when they are still in, or just out of, childhood.

Clearly, adolescents need adult supervision and guidance as well as financial support as they transition to adulthood. Middle-class and affluent parents are able to smooth this transition. Poor parents are less able to do so. Young people without capable, involved parents, such as teens aging out of foster care, often face this transition alone.

Compare the "precocious adulthood" or "rushed adolescence" of some low-income urban teenagers to the comparatively highly organized, supervised, and well-resourced lives of many middle-class teens, whose parents and communities are able both to provide them with appealing, life-enhancing opportunities (college, internships, etc.) and limit their scope for making self-destructive choices by enrolling them in supervised activities and by providing a host of incentives to mo-tivate positive behaviors. Of course, all teenagers can find ways to get into trouble, but some problems result from "crimes of opportunity" that never present them-selves to kids who are at soccer practice for two hours after school or are dashing from piano lessons to SAT classes, or who are spending their summer days in an internship rather than hanging around the neighborhood, bored and restless.

Investing in high-risk teens helps them lead lives they value and saves society money in the long run. People who do not graduate from high school face extremely limited job options and great challenges in achieving economic self-sufficiency. Less well known is the profound effect that low levels of education have on the likelihood of imprisonment, particularly for African American men. African Americans are imprisoned at six to eight times the rate of whites, but the rate is even higher for African American high school dropouts. By age thirty-five, 60 percent of African American high school dropouts will have spent time in prison. African American men who drop out of school are eight times more likely to be incarcerated than African American men who graduate college.[134] State and federal prison inmates average just eleven years of schooling.

By age thirty-five, 60 percent of African American high school dropouts will have spent time in prison.

HIGHER EDUCATION

Higher Education: Different Worlds

A college degree was long viewed as perhaps the chief engine of social mobility—a ticket to power, money, and status. Increasingly, however, college is seen as a prerequisite for virtually any job that pays a decent income, provides benefits, and offers a modicum of security. A typical high school graduate over age twenty-five earned around $26,000 in 2005, while peers with college degrees took home $18,000 more on average (see TABLE 3.7). The social meaning of college is also changing. In the public imagination, college has gone from a fairly elite pursuit centered on intellectual exploration and academics to a job-focused destination of choice for all high-schoolers.

Trends in college-going have changed for the better in many ways, among them the greatly expanded opportunities for academically able women, minorities, and low-income students as well as the increased proportion of high school graduates entering college. In 1972, about half of high school graduates entered college in the fall immediately after graduation, whereas in 2005, about seven in ten did,[135] with the largest rate of increase among women entering four-year colleges. Higher rates of enrollment indicate that college is both more accessible and more valuable than it was thirty years ago.

But the picture is less rosy when you look not at how many people start college but rather at how many finish: enrollment rates are up 40 percent, but the rates of completion have not changed.[136] College enrollment rates remain higher for white students than for African American or Latino students, higher for students from high-income than low-income families, and higher for children whose parents had a college degree than for those whose parents did not. Strikingly, college-going rates among high-achieving, low-income high school graduates are about the same as those among the lowest-achieving students from high-income families (see TABLE 3.8).[137]

> Despite claims and some genuine efforts to the contrary, most elite colleges and universities enroll primarily children of privilege.

TABLE 3.7 Median Earnings by Educational Attainment for the Population Twenty-five Years and Older, 2005

EDUCATIONAL ATTAINMENT	MEDIAN EARNINGS ($)
Less than high school graduate	18,435
High school graduate (includes equivalency)	25,829
Some college or associate degree	31,566
Bachelor's degree	43,954
Graduate or professional degree	57,585

Source: U.S. Census Bureau, "2005 American Community Survey."

TABLE 3.8 College-Going Rates by Income and Achievement Levels

SCHOLASTIC ACHIEVEMENT LEVEL	LOW-INCOME STUDENTS (%)	HIGH-INCOME STUDENTS (%)
Lowest quartile	36	77
Second quartile	50	85
Third quartile	63	90
Highest quartile	78	97

Source: Haycock and Gerald "Engines of Inequality."

In this section, we take a closer look at what the American HD Index reveals about college degree attainment as well as explore a few issues key to understanding trends in higher education. These issues include financial barriers to higher education, including recent shifts from need-based to merit-based aid; nonfinancial barriers, such as college readiness and the needs of nontraditional students; and the role of community colleges.

First, what do we mean by "college"? The word encompasses public and private universities; private four-year colleges; two-year community colleges that offer certificates, terminal associate degrees, opportunities to transfer to bachelor programs elsewhere, and adult basic skills and enrichment courses; and private, two-year "occupational" colleges that offer associate degrees and certificates. These different institutions offer distinct advantages and disadvantages and often serve widely disparate student populations.

Even colleges granting bachelor's degrees afford widely divergent opportunities. Prestigious private colleges and public universities perform a "sorting" function for society by conferring status on their graduates and facilitating social ties among the elite. Despite claims and some genuine efforts to the contrary, most elite colleges and universities enroll primarily children of privilege. Students from advantaged family backgrounds—those whose parents are well educated, have high-status occupations, and earn high salaries—are twenty-five times more likely to attend a "top-tier" college than students from disadvantaged backgrounds.[138] Contrary to public perception, research shows that highly selective schools give disadvantaged high school graduates "virtually no break" in the admissions process.[139]

WHO IS GRADUATING FROM COLLEGE?

MAP 3.5 shows the distribution of the adult population that has earned at least a four-year college degree by state and congressional district. **The congressional district map shows that college-educated Americans are concentrated in and around our largest cities.** The nineteen top-ranking congressional districts are located in the greater metropolitan areas of just four cities: New York (seven congressional districts), Washington, D.C. (five congressional districts), Los Angeles (four congressional districts), and San Francisco (three congressional districts). The metropolitan areas of Atlanta, Chicago, North Carolina's Research Triangle, Seattle, Denver, and San Antonio/Austin contribute to the remainder of the top twenty-five congressional districts.

At the top of the congressional districts list, between 51 percent and 63 percent of the adult population had at least a bachelor's degree in 2005. In the bottom ten congressional districts, the percentage of population with at least a college degree ranged from 6 percent to 12 percent. Four of these congressional districts were in California, two in Texas, and one each in Kentucky, Tennessee, West Virginia, and Ohio.

The Index Measures Bachelor's Degrees

The education index of the American HD Index measures three types of degree attainment: a high school diploma; a bachelor's degree from a four-year college or university; and a graduate or professional degree. We have not included "some college" or associate degrees in the scoring to best reflect the so-called sheepskin premium that a bachelor's degree confers in terms of lifetime earnings, occupational opportunities, potential for graduate study, cultural capital, and social prestige.

College for All?

In 2005, kids from high-income families were significantly more likely to enroll in college than those from low-income families. Likewise, white high school graduates were more likely to enroll than black or Latino high school graduates. Children whose parents have at least a college degree enter college at more than twice the rate of children whose parents did not graduate high school,[140] and disparities in degree attainment are greater still.

TABLE 3.9 **Top Ten Congressional Districts: Bachelor's Degrees**		
CONGRESSIONAL DISTRICT	METROPOLITAN REGION	AT LEAST A BACHELOR'S DEGREE (%)
CD 14, New York	New York	62.6%
CD 8, Virginia	D.C.	58.2%
CD 30, California	Los Angeles	56.7%
CD 14, California	Silicon Valley	56.3%
CD 8, Maryland	D.C.	55.5%
CD 8, New York	New York	55.3%
CD 6, Georgia	Atlanta	53.7%
CD 11, Virginia	D.C.	52.2%
CD 48, California	Los Angeles	51.9%
CD 10, Illinois	Chicago	51.8%

TABLE 3.10 **Percentage of the Population with at Least a Bachelor's Degree**	
GENDER BY RACE/ETHNICITY	AT LEAST A BACHELOR'S DEGREE (%)
Asian males	53.1%
Asian females	45.6%
White males	31.7%
White females	28.3%
American Indian females	23.0%
American Indian males	21.1%
African American females	17.8%
African American males	16.6%
Latino females	12.7%
Latino males	11.8%

Public University Aid Benefits Better-Off Families

"In 2003 the 'flagship' public universities in this country, along with other public research universities, spent $257 million on financial aid for students from families that earn more than $100,000 per year compared with $171 million they spent for families who earned less than $20,000 per year. Ultimately, families that earn more than $100,000 must come up with the amount equivalent to 12 percent of their yearly income to meet the remaining costs of these universities after grant aid; low-income families must come up with the amount equivalent to 80 percent of their annual income."[141]

—From "Engines of Inequality: Diminishing Equity in the Nation's Premier Public Universities"

In terms of gender, race, and ethnicity, Asians have the highest college graduation rates, followed by whites. Men are ahead of women in both cases. Native Americans, African Americans, and Latinos follow, with women ahead of men in each group (see TABLE 3.10).

FINANCIAL BARRIERS TO HIGHER EDUCATION

When analyzing why different groups of Americans attend college at different rates, cost immediately comes to mind. **The cost of earning a bachelor's degree is high and rising fast.** For the academic year 2004–05, the average price of one year of tuition, room, and board was $9,877 at public colleges and $26,025 at private colleges. **Between 1994 and 2004, costs increased 30 percent at public colleges and 26 percent at private colleges, even after adjusting for inflation.**[142]

Research has shown that parental net worth (family assets like a house or investments) is a powerful predictor of college enrollment and may affect degree attainment.[143] Somewhat counterintuitively, some research finds that the financial resources available to teens when they are making college-attendance decisions plays a relatively minor role in whether or not they attend college, once ability is accounted for.[144] Lack of resources keeps only about 8 percent of students from enrolling. However, even if credit constraints and limited family finances don't affect *whether or not* most kids go to college, financial resources can impact *where* students go to school, whether they go *full- or part-time*, whether they live on campus or commute, and how many hours of work they do during the academic year. All these factors have been shown to affect degree completion.

Several recent shifts in college funding have somewhat eased the financial burden of college for students from middle-class families while raising the

MAP 3.5 **Adults with a Four-Year College Degree or Higher, 2005**

by STATE

by CONGRESSIONAL DISTRICT

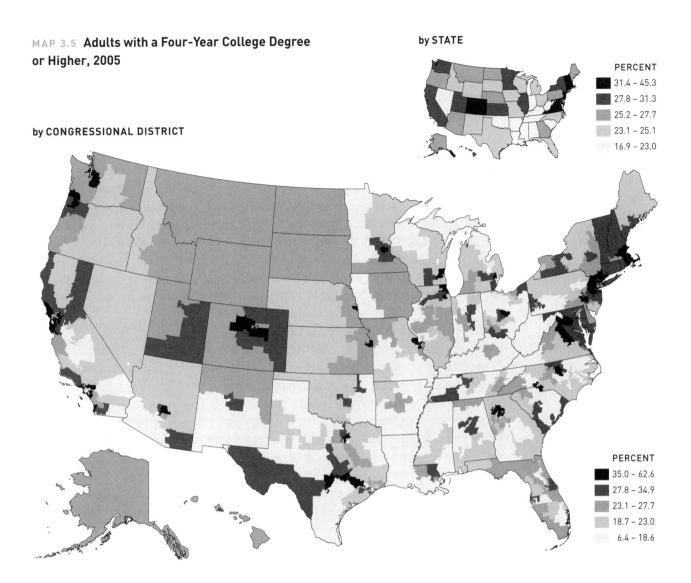

PERCENT
- 31.4 – 45.3
- 27.8 – 31.3
- 25.2 – 27.7
- 23.1 – 25.1
- 16.9 – 23.0

PERCENT
- 35.0 – 62.6
- 27.8 – 34.9
- 23.1 – 27.7
- 18.7 – 23.0
- 6.4 – 18.6

financial barriers for low-income students. **Whereas in the 1970s and 1980s, aid programs were primarily need-based and designed to promote access for low-income students, in recent decades the focus has shifted to making college more affordable to middle-class families and influencing where students attend college.** There is less reliance on grants and more on tax credits. Take, for instance, the Pell Grant, a need-based government program that benefits about 5 million low-income students; the typical Pell Grant recipient comes from a family earning less than $20,000 per year. The average Pell Grant in the 2005–06 academic year covered about one-third of college expense, representing a significant decline from 42 percent in 2001–02 and 75 percent in 1979. A low-income Pell Grant recipient now faces a funding gap of more than $6,000 per year to attend a public university.

Many so-called nonincome barriers to college are linked inextricably to income.

In addition, an increasing share of aid that public universities dispense is now allocated without regard to financial need. Merit-based programs like the University of Georgia's HOPE Scholarships, which cover the tuition costs of in-state residents maintaining a B average, have increased the number of talented students staying in Georgia while reducing the burden on their families, but the lion's share of benefits have bypassed low-income and minority students. Similarly, moves by Harvard University and other elite institutions to raise the income ceiling for aid eligibility to around $180,000—more than three-and-a-half times U.S. median household income—are clearly not geared toward poor families. Section 529 college savings, federal education tax credits, and the federal tuition tax deduction also serve to make college more affordable primarily for middle- and upper-income taxpayers.

Making a bachelor's degree more affordable for the middle class is a worthy goal. It is politically popular as well as socially and economically beneficial. But if efforts to increase affordability for the middle class come at the expense of those at the bottom of the income ladder, they raise serious issues of equity.

NONFINANCIAL BARRIERS TO COLLEGE

Many so-called nonincome barriers to college are linked inextricably to income. These barriers include inadequate high school preparation, poor noncognitive skills like persistence and goal orientation, and myriad challenges faced by students whose families lack familiarity with higher education. In low-income environments, significant obstacles to a four-year college degree first appear in early childhood and grow more difficult to surmount as life progresses. Research cited earlier in this report suggests a key to overcoming such barriers is to enrich early childhood environments. But progress will also require better schools in low-income communities, more opportunities for low-income students to develop skills and confidence, and programs to help teens stay in school and earn diplomas.

COMMUNITY COLLEGES: AN EVOLVING ROLE

Community colleges used to be known as junior colleges; they were primarily feeder schools set up to prepare students to transfer to a four-year college or university. In the last few decades, however, community colleges took on two new missions: increasing access to college and offering terminal degrees and certificates geared to getting jobs. **With open admissions and low fees, community colleges have dramatically lowered the barriers to entry** for higher education for previously excluded groups—minorities, immigrants, first-generation college-goers, low-income students, and students who did poorly in high school, as well as older students, parents, and full-time workers. The community college boom is the reason most high school graduates now continue their schooling the fall after receiving their diplomas.

Many scholars argue that community colleges have largely succeeded in their access mission, and now need to focus on the challenge of degree attainment. Eight years after starting community college, most students have neither transferred to a four-year college nor attained a terminal associate degree or certificate. Only two in five students ever manage to receive a degree, just one in five African American students. Those who do transfer to earn their bachelor's degree elsewhere tend to be white and middle class, so-called second-chancers who did badly in high school, but turned things around in community college.

Some researchers argue that community colleges maintain the existing social hierarchy by segregating low-income and minority students in a second-best system that will ultimately channel them into low-level technical careers, "cooling out" their ambitions and diminishing expectations along the way. The existence of community colleges arguably relieves pressure on elite public universities to make accommodations for students with greater challenges to college success, allowing them to remain selective and abandon remediation. Others maintain that the advising and academic structures of community college, which mirror those at four-year institutions, are simply not suited to the needs and constraints of the nontraditional students that community colleges attract. Students unfamiliar with college may find a structure that privileges choice and exploration distracting. They may benefit from fewer options and clearer paths to degree completion, less of an a la carte menu in the liberal arts model and more of a package deal. Some research suggests that occupational colleges are better meeting the needs of this student population, teaching social skills, guiding course selection, minimizing the scope for errors and disengagement, and focusing on job placement rather career counseling.[145][146]

Community colleges have performed a valuable function by opening the door to higher education to a wider range of students. Now perhaps the focus should turn to finding ways to ensure that those students emerge at the end of a two- or four-year course of study with a degree.

> Many scholars argue that community colleges have largely succeeded in their access mission, and now need to focus on the challenge of degree attainment.

BOX 3.14 **Immigrant Educational Attainments and Barriers**

The educational attainment of immigrants depends in part on how much education they have when they arrive. This not only affects their own prospects but also those of their children and grandchildren.[147]

Overall, recently arrived immigrants between twenty-five and thirty-four years of age have fewer years of education than native-born American peers. While 52 percent of immigrants have completed at least high school and 27.9 percent have obtained college degrees, some 61 percent of native-born Americans in the same age range (and who are not children of immigrants) have at least a high school diploma, and 31 percent are college graduates.

There is significant variation among immigrant groups. Hispanic immigrants overall have fewer years of education than other immigrants; 36 percent have graduated from high school, but only 8.5 percent have college degrees. At the other extreme, 71.8 percent of Asian immigrants have at least a high school degree, and 21.7 percent have graduated from college. Asian immigrants have more years of education than native-born Americans of nonimmigrant parents.

Source: Alba, "Immigrant Educational Attainments and Barriers."

Conclusion

Those without a high school diploma have few employment prospects save service-sector and retail jobs with poverty wages, often poor working conditions, and limited benefits.

Access to knowledge is a critical determinant of long-term well-being and is essential to individual freedom, self-determination, and self-sufficiency. Globalization and technological change have made it extraordinarily difficult for poorly educated Americans to achieve the economic self-sufficiency, peace of mind, and self-respect enabled by a secure livelihood. Those without a high school diploma have few employment prospects save service-sector and retail jobs with poverty wages, often poor working conditions, and limited benefits. Increasingly, even entry-level jobs require reading, arithmetic, and computer skills,[148] as well as some sort of credential, such as a high school diploma or vocational training. They also require soft skills like punctuality. College graduates can expect, on average, about double the lifetime earnings of high-school graduates.[149] A college degree is the minimum requirement for many jobs that allow for creativity, independence, and professional growth while conferring status, prestige, and authority. Technological change is sharply increasing rewards to a highly educated sliver of society while excluding many Americans, especially the roughly one in six who never finish high school.

Research associates higher levels of education with a host of positive outcomes for individuals and society. Educated citizens vote more frequently, volunteer more time, are more tolerant, and even donate blood more often. For individuals, more education is linked to better health, a longer life, higher civic and political participation, greater ability to adjust to change, a more robust self-identity, stronger and more extensive social bonds, more stable relationships, and greater personal happiness. Research suggests that educational levels are more predictive of good health than either income or health insurance coverage.[150]

Evidence suggests the following critical priorities:

- Establish a goal of universal access to two years of high-quality preschool; programs should meet families' needs for child care.

- Invest in high-quality early childhood care and education, with well-trained teachers who provide adequate and appropriate stimulation and interaction as well as low teacher-child ratios.

- Target poor teen mothers with home-visit programs.

- Focus on the needs of children until age twenty-one, including low-income adolescents/teens transitioning to productive, self-sufficient adulthood; kids aging out of foster care need special focus, as do very young parents and teens who have been processed by the criminal justice system.

- Support families in their efforts to help children learn (through conditional cash transfers and parenting programs). Deep poverty in the preschool years is particularly damaging to child development, with negative impacts reaching far into adulthood.

- Provide every child with a well-qualified, effective teacher in the class-room. Our education system should attract and support extraordinary teachers. But average teachers, like average students, should be able to succeed.

- Create more "enveloping" school environments, with longer days, on-site health clinics, after-school clubs and activities, mentoring programs, and so on to ensure that low-income kids get better supervision and more contact with adults, as well as enrichment activities.

- Equalize educational inputs in the public education system.

- Reform curriculum to teach twenty-first-century skills and relevant content.

- Reduce perverse incentives created by standardized testing regimes by expanding the scope of school assessments.

- View charter schools and teacher programs like Teach for America as laboratories for innovation. However, we must do more than provide a few lifeboats to students adrift in a sea of failure. We need to fix public education systems, especially those in urban districts that face severe challenges.

- Improve opportunities for the 70 percent of students who do not graduate from college. High school students not headed for college need a rich, meaningful curriculum that is linked to actual jobs and not stigmatized as "second best." Western European apprenticeship programs could offer valuable lessons.

- Expand efforts to make college affordable to middle-class families, but not at the expense of low-income families.

- Increase the real value of the Pell Grant to cover the majority of the cost of a public university. This important tool for educational equality has not kept up with costs and need.

Deep poverty in the preschool years is particularly damaging to child development.

A Decent Standard of Living

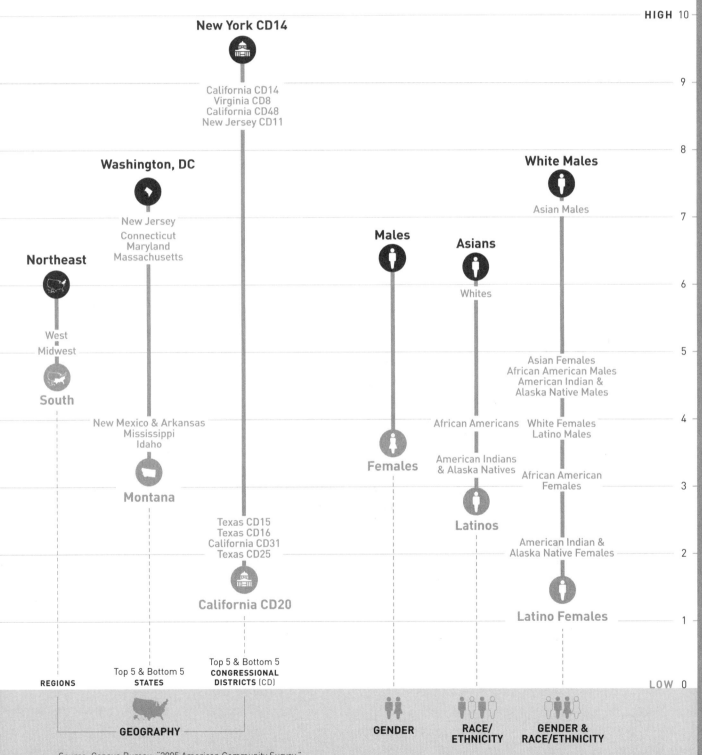

INCOME INDEX: Median Earnings for the Population 16 and Older

How Do We Stack Up?

INCOME INDEX

HIGH 10

New York CD14

9

California CD14
Virginia CD8
California CD48
New Jersey CD11

8

White Males

Washington, DC

Asian Males

7

New Jersey

Males

Asians

Connecticut
Maryland
Massachusetts

6

Northeast

Whites

West
Midwest

5

Asian Females
African American Males
American Indian &
Alaska Native Males

South

New Mexico & Arkansas
Mississippi
Idaho

4

African Americans

White Females
Latino Males

American Indians
& Alaska Natives

African American
Females

3

Montana

Females

Latinos

Texas CD15
Texas CD16
California CD31
Texas CD25

American Indian &
Alaska Native Females

2

California CD20

Latino Females

1

REGIONS

Top 5 & Bottom 5
STATES

Top 5 & Bottom 5
**CONGRESSIONAL
DISTRICTS** (CD)

LOW 0

GEOGRAPHY

GENDER

**RACE/
ETHNICITY**

**GENDER &
RACE/ETHNICITY**

Source: Census Bureau, "2005 American Community Survey."

Introduction

> "Wealth evidently is not the good of which
> we are in search, for it is merely useful
> as a means to something else."
>
> **ARISTOTLE,** *Nicomachean Ethics*

The "New Normal"

Family structures have changed, but institutions have been slow to adapt.

YESTERDAY

ONE-earner family

TODAY

ONE-earner family

ONE-earner family

TWO-earner family

Income is essential to meeting basic needs like food and shelter—and to moving beyond these necessities to a life of genuine choice and freedom. Income enables valuable options and alternatives, and its absence can limit life chances and restrict access to many opportunities. Income is a means to a host of critical ends, including a decent education; a safe, clean living environment; security in illness and old age; and a say in the decisions that affect one's life. Money isn't everything, but it's something quite important.

As a result of overall post–World War II economic growth and policies like Social Security, Medicaid, and Medicare, the United States experienced large drops in poverty from the postwar period to the early 1970s. FIGURE 3.9 traces poverty rates in three age groups starting in 1959. The United States made tremendous progress reducing poverty among children in the 1960s, as well as dramatic reductions in poverty among the elderly.

Yet for many families today, the cornerstones of middle-class life since the post–World War II era—steady, well-paying work; a home of one's own; security in ill health and old age; and a general confidence that life will be better for your kids—have cracked. Job security and many benefits have eroded for all but the wealthiest Americans. Well-paying manufacturing work has been shipped overseas, and many civil service jobs that once provided a toehold in the middle class have been eliminated. Today's families have a tenuous hold on middle-class status; the social safety net is frayed and frequently unable to support the weight of a serious shock such as natural disaster, death, divorce, job loss, or serious illness.

Stagnating wages, high child-care costs, and increases in housing and health prices mean that more families need two full-time workers to sustain the kind of middle-class life enabled by a single wage-earner just a few decades ago. "The American standard of living is based on the earnings of the main breadwinner,"

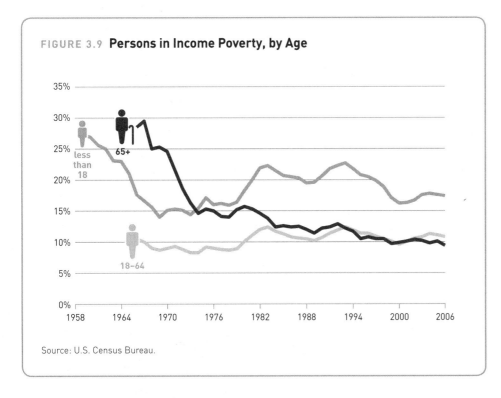

FIGURE 3.9 **Persons in Income Poverty, by Age**

Source: U.S. Census Bureau.

Poverty among the elderly has dramatically declined, thanks to Social Security and Medicare.

declared the United Steelworkers in 1945.[151] Few can make a similar claim today. **Despite a massive social and economic transformation from one-earner to two-earner families, neither social institutions nor expectations have significantly adjusted to the "new normal" of two parents in the workforce.** Overstretched families must cobble together the care and maintenance that families and communities alike require to function.

This section focuses on improving the ways in which we understand, describe and measure standard of living. New approaches and tools are critical.

The official measure for determining minimum income levels necessary for an adequate standard of living is published every year by the government's Census Bureau. The poverty thresholds, as they are formally called, determine the number of people each year who are officially considered "poor," based on a threshold for each family type (including size of family and number of children). The 2007 poverty threshold for a family of four (two adults and two children) is an income of $21,027 before taxes. All families whose incomes fall below this "line" are classified as poor—which in 2006 included more than 36 million Americans.

The formula for calculating this poverty threshold was developed in the 1960s and has a number of serious shortcomings: it reflects the consumption patterns of American families forty-five years ago; it does not include noncash benefits such as food stamps and does not deduct tax liabilities; and it does not account for today's essential costs of working, such as child care and transportation. As a

The formula for calculating the poverty threshold was developed in the 1960s and has a number of serious shortcomings.

result, the current poverty threshold fails to address the reality of the tens of millions of "near-poor," low-income, and moderate-income American families.

In order to respond to the inadequacy of the poverty threshold, researchers, policy makers, and advocates have developed other ways of determining what constitutes enough income to maintain an adequate standard of living. **This definition of "enough" goes beyond what it takes to stock the fridge** to include the costs of housing, health, transportation, and work-related expenses, as well as to account for the varied costs of living in different communities. It does not include funds for savings or retirement, takeout meals, or vacations. Research on basic and self-sufficiency budgets is being undertaken in every state. The methodologies and measures of these alternatives differ, but all offer a far more realistic picture of what is needed for a safe and decent standard of living in America today.[152.]

FIGURE 3.10 **Rethinking Today's Federal Poverty Measure**

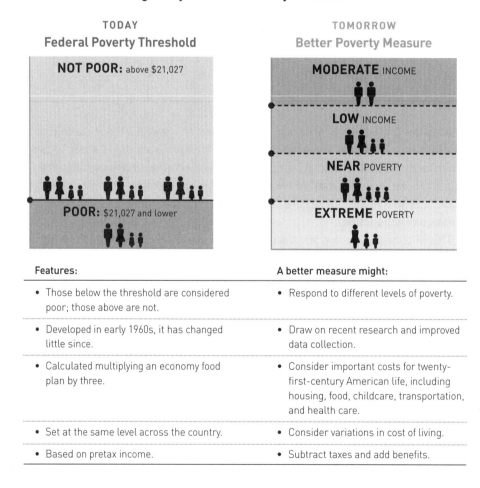

Features:	A better measure might:
• Those below the threshold are considered poor; those above are not.	• Respond to different levels of poverty.
• Developed in early 1960s, it has changed little since.	• Draw on recent research and improved data collection.
• Calculated multiplying an economy food plan by three.	• Consider important costs for twenty-first-century American life, including housing, food, childcare, transportation, and health care.
• Set at the same level across the country.	• Consider variations in cost of living.
• Based on pretax income.	• Subtract taxes and add benefits.

The official poverty guidelines and the basic family budget approach fall into the family of traditional poverty measures—an income threshold is set, and families or individuals whose income falls below this threshold are considered poor. In the human development approach, income is only part of the story, and no attempt is made to draw a line separating the poor and the nonpoor. The HD Index is not meant to replace a traditional poverty measure, but rather to complement it. The official poverty line is a key policy instrument used to determine eligibility for many antipoverty programs. Efforts to update it to better reflect our current reality should be energetically pursued (see FIGURE 3.10).

What Does the HD Index Show?

The measure used in the American Human Development Index to represent our standard of living is earnings—generally the largest portion of an individual's income. Drawing on data from the American Community Survey of the U.S. Census Bureau, the Index uses the median to measure the typical amount that working individuals over age sixteen receive from their labor. The year 2005 is the most recent for which these numbers were available at the level of congressional district and separated by gender at press time. The median earnings measure does not include welfare assistance or other government transfers (such as Social Security), nor does it include income other than that generated by labor. Thus, the measure leaves out stock dividends, interest income from savings, rental property income, returns on investments in small businesses, other sorts of investment income, and unreported income from both legal and illegal activities.

Overall median earnings in the United States for 2005 were $27,299. Keep in mind that this figure reflects earnings of both full- and part-time workers. The pool of workers spans the gamut from young people just getting started in the labor market, to seasoned workers at the height of their earning power, to retirees who are working part-time.

Overall median earnings in the United States for 2005 were **$27,299.**

VARIATIONS IN INCOME BY STATE

Looking across the fifty states and Washington, D.C., median earnings range from a high of $36,948 in Washington, D.C., to a low of $21,472 in Montana. TABLE 3.11 shows the five top and five bottom states.

TABLE 3.11 Median Earnings, Top Five and Bottom Five States, 2005

RANK	TOP FIVE STATES	MEDIAN EARNINGS ($)	RANK	BOTTOM FIVE STATES	MEDIAN EARNINGS ($)
1	District of Columbia	36,948	47	New Mexico	22,131
2	New Jersey	35,468	48	Arkansas	22,122
3	Connecticut	35,387	49	Mississippi	22,042
4	Maryland	35,144	50	Idaho	21,888
5	Massachusetts	33,544	51	Montana	21,472

Looking at income by state, some interesting facts stand out:

- New Jersey, Connecticut, and Maryland are the only states, along with the District of Columbia, with median earnings above $35,000; Idaho and Montana have the only median earnings below $22,000.

- Six of the ten states with the highest median earnings are in the Northeast (New Jersey, Connecticut, Massachusetts, New Hampshire, New York, and Rhode Island). The remaining four (Washington, D.C., Maryland, Virginia, and Delaware) lie just to the south, also along the eastern seaboard.

- Three of the bottom ten states are in the South (Louisiana, Arkansas, and Mississippi), and four (Utah, New Mexico, Idaho, and Montana) are in the West (see MAP 3.6).

- Of the top-ten income states, eight are also among the top ten in education, and four (Connecticut, Massachusetts, New Hampshire, and New York) are among the top ten in health.

- Washington, D.C., ranks first in income and education, but last in health.

- Montana, which ranks last in income, ranks number twenty-nine in health and number thirty-five in education.

Six of the ten states with the highest median earnings are in the Northeast.

MAP 3.6 **Median Earnings by State, 2005**

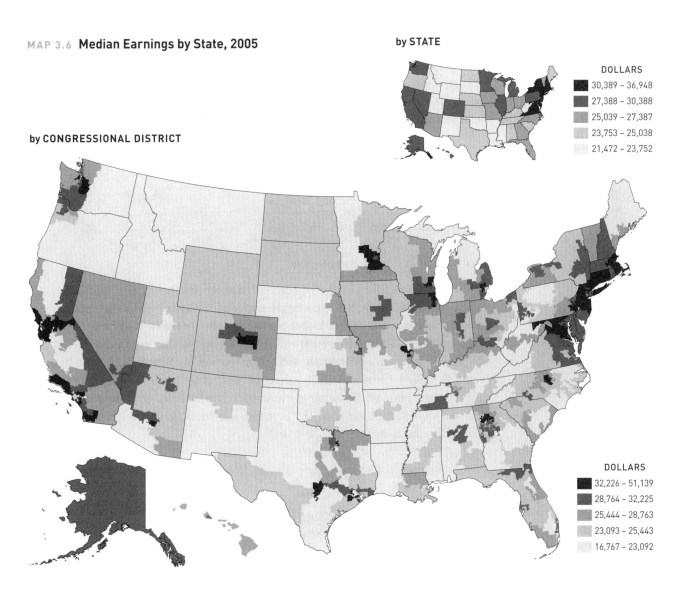

by **STATE**

DOLLARS
- 30,389 – 36,948
- 27,388 – 30,388
- 25,039 – 27,387
- 23,753 – 25,038
- 21,472 – 23,752

by **CONGRESSIONAL DISTRICT**

DOLLARS
- 32,226 – 51,139
- 28,764 – 32,225
- 25,444 – 28,763
- 23,093 – 25,443
- 16,767 – 23,092

Regional Ranking
in Earnings:

1. Northeast
2. West
3. Midwest
4. South

The Earned Income Tax Credit Helps Lift Millions out of Poverty

The Earned Income Tax Credit (EITC) is a program for working, low-income families. Administered by the Internal Revenue Service, the EITC was created in 1975 to offset the burden of Social Security taxes and to provide an incentive to work. It is the largest income transfer program for low-income workers.

Evaluations of the program confirm that it has produced substantial increases in employment, especially for mothers with low education levels, as well as reduced the receipt of public welfare by single parents. It has also been a catalyst for large decreases in poverty. Research indicates that families use the EITC to pay for necessities, repair homes and vehicles needed to commute, and in some cases, to boost their employability and earning power by obtaining additional education or training. One striking result: In 2003, the poverty rate among children would have been one-fourth higher without the EITC.

The success of the federal EITC has led about eighteen states to enact their own EITCs to supplement the federal program. In 2000, the United Kingdom introduced a Working Families Tax Credit modeled on the EITC that is credited with contributing to a substantial decrease in child poverty in that country.

Source: Greenstein, "The Earned Income Tax Credit."

There are several critical policies and patterns that may be contributing factors to the variation in income across states. What are the links between state incomes and their employment, food security, health insurance and other rates, and the impact of such policy levers as the Earned Income Tax Credit? To illustrate these patterns, we grouped the states into four clusters based on their income:

- **LOW**-Income States

- **MEDIUM-LOW**-Income States

- **MEDIUM-HIGH**-Income States

- **HIGH**-Income States

From this clustering we can observe:

Various states, even including some in the high-income group, have large numbers of families unable to generate enough income to meet basic expenses for food, clothing, and a place to live, as well as other necessities of life, such as day care for children whose parents are at work, transportation to and from jobs, health insurance premiums, and out-of-pocket medical bills. Among the twenty-two low-income states, 30.9 percent of families have incomes insufficient to support a basic budget. Surprisingly, among the thirteen states with medium-high incomes, a similar proportion—29.9 percent—cannot provide enough income to meet a basic budget (see TABLE 3.12).

A number of factors contribute to the economic challenges faced by many American families:

- **Education.** The percentage of residents with at least a college degree is higher in high-income states, underscoring the link between education and earnings.

- **Unionization.** In high-income states, union membership rates are higher as well. The average union member earns 22.9 percent more than non-union workers.

- **Public policy.** The Earned Income Tax Credit (EITC) is a refundable tax credit that provides low- and moderate-income families with a boost in income (see sidebar). As is demonstrated in TABLE 3.12, states with their own EITC programs that complement the federal program have far higher median incomes.

TABLE 3.12 Characteristics of States Clustered by Income Groups

Some **80 million** Americans are unable to generate enough income to meet basic expenses.

VARIABLE	LOW INCOME STATES	MEDIUM-LOW INCOME STATES	MEDIUM-HIGH INCOME STATES	HIGH INCOME STATES
Median Earnings	$24,206	$26,705	$30,112	$34,919
Required Annual Income for 2 Parent–2 Child Family	$37,833	$39,740	$44,615	$50,916
People unable to generate enough income to meet basic expenses (Income Less than Basic Budget)	30.9% (21 MillionPeople)	25.2% (26 Million People)	29.9% (25 Million People)	25.2% (7.6 Million People)
Union Membership (%)	6.4%	11.0%	16.5%	16.2%
Employed civilians (%)	67.7%	69.7%	69.2%	72.3%
States with EITC (%)	36%	45%	54%	80%
State EITC in place (years)	4.0	12.8	10.0	11.0
College Graduates (%)	23.7%	24.8%	30.2%	35.3%
Food Insecure (%)	13.9%	11.0%	10.0%	8.4%
Health Uninsured (%)	17.9%	14.0%	15.1%	12.6%
States within Clusters	Alabama Arkansas Idaho Kansas Kentucky Louisiana Maine Mississippi Montana Nebraska New Mexico North Carolina North Dakota Oklahoma Oregon South Carolina South Dakota Tennessee Texas Utah West Virginia Wyoming	Arizona Florida Georgia Indiana Iowa Michigan Missouri Ohio Pennsylvania Vermont Wisconsin	Alaska Colorado California Delaware Hawaii Illinois Minnesota Nevada New Hampshire New York Rhode Island Virginia Washington	Connecticut Maryland Massachusetts New Jersey Washington, D.C.

> Most high income states have a state Earned Income Tax Credit (EITC) in addition to the federal EITC program.

Source: Authors' calculations, Basic Budget from Economic Policy Institute online calculator. Indicators are weighted to take state size into consideration.

VARIATIONS IN INCOME BY CONGRESSIONAL DISTRICT

The variation in earnings among the country's 436 congressional districts ranges from median earnings of more than $51,000 in New York's Fourteenth Congressional District to earnings one third as much, $17,000, in California's Twentieth Congressional District.

The ten wealthiest districts are all located in the metropolitan areas of Washington, D.C., New York, San Francisco, or Los Angeles. Both New Jersey and California have three districts in the top ten; New York and Virginia have two each.

TABLE 3.13 shows the range of incomes within each state, by congressional district. States with the widest gulf in incomes among their districts, as measured by their median earnings ranges, are New York, California, and Virginia. New York is home to the country's top-ranked income district (Fourteenth District, East Side, Roosevelt Island, and part of Queens), while less than three miles away, New York's Sixteenth District (South Bronx) ranks number 429, in the bottom ten, with median earnings below $20,000—a $32,000 gap.

California has three districts in the top ten and one at the very bottom. The state is home to the country's second-highest-ranking (Fourteenth District, Silicon Valley) as well as its bottom district (Twentieth District, Kings County), located only about one hundred miles apart.

Virginia has two top-ten districts, the Eighth Congressional District and the Eleventh Congressional District, in suburban Washington, D.C., both of which have median earnings above $45,000. At the other end of the scale, Virginia's Ninth Congressional District, covering much of the southwestern part of the state, ranks number 414, near the bottom nationally, with median earnings barely above $20,000.

Prior to Hurricane Katrina, three of the Gulf Coast states—Alabama, Mississippi, and Louisiana—were at or near the bottom in measures of income. Only one congressional district in these three states, Alabama's Sixth Congressional District, has median income that exceeds the U.S. average. The region's other seventeen districts, from Louisiana's Second (ranked number 397) to Mississippi's Second (ranked number 429), are in the bottom quartile. Mississippi's Second Congressional District has median earnings equivalent to those of the United States nationally in the late 1960s. Louisiana's Second Congressional District, which includes the largely poor Ninth Ward, has median earnings of $22,344, roughly equivalent to median income in the United States in the mid-1980s.

The ten wealthiest districts are all located in the metropolitan areas of Washington, D.C., New York, San Francisco, or Los Angeles.

TABLE 3.13 **Variation among Congressional District Incomes, by State**

VARIATION RANK	STATE	NUMBER OF DISTRICTS	Median Earnings (2005 dollars)		
			MINIMUM	MAXIMUM	RANGE
1	New York	29	19,113	51,139	32,026
2	California	53	16,767	46,539	29,772
3	Virginia	11	20,808	46,031	25,223
4	Texas	32	17,378	37,993	20,615
5	Michigan	15	21,215	40,365	19,150
6	Georgia	13	21,338	40,246	18,908
7	Illinois	19	21,334	39,755	18,421
8	New Jersey	13	27,532	45,410	17,878
9	Washington	9	21,162	38,488	17,326
10	Colorado	7	23,151	39,101	15,950
11	Missouri	9	19,979	34,457	14,478
12	Minnesota	8	22,863	36,871	14,008
13	Pennsylvania	19	22,038	35,992	13,954
14	North Carolina	13	20,257	33,520	13,263
15	Florida	25	20,636	32,211	11,575
16	Arizona	8	21,671	32,319	10,648
17	Maryland	8	29,736	39,714	9,978
18	Alabama	7	20,863	30,646	9,783
19	Wisconsin	8	24,954	34,722	9,768
20	Tennessee	9	21,639	31,037	9,398
21	Ohio	18	22,362	31,402	9,040
22	Kansas	4	21,983	30,738	8,755
23	Massachusetts	10	29,112	36,754	7,642
24	Indiana	9	24,387	31,995	7,608
25	Oregon	5	21,705	28,946	7,241
26	Kentucky	6	20,759	27,509	6,750
27	Connecticut	5	32,918	39,550	6,632
28	New Mexico	3	18,174	24,759	6,585
29	Nebraska	3	21,630	27,741	6,111
30	Louisiana	7	20,892	26,853	5,961
31	South Carolina	6	20,796	26,549	5,753
32	Iowa	5	24,212	29,181	4,969
33	Oklahoma	5	20,763	25,652	4,889
34	West Virginia	3	21,060	25,513	4,453
35	Arkansas	4	20,471	24,805	4,334
36	Nevada	3	26,308	30,577	4,269
37	Mississippi	4	20,572	23,455	2,883
38	Utah	3	22,164	23,796	1,632

Note: States with fewer than three congressional districts (Hawaii, Idaho, Maine, New Hampshire, Rhode Island, Alaska, Delaware, District of Columbia, Montana, North Dakota, South Dakota, Vermont, and Wyoming) not included.

Mississippi's Second Congressional District has median earnings equivalent to those of the U.S. nationally in the late 1960s.

In every ethnic group, men earn more than women.

TABLE 3.14 Ranking Earnings by Gender and Race/Ethnicity

GROUPING	MEDIAN EARNINGS (2005 dollars)
White males	37,269
Asian males	37,035
Asian females	26,138
African American males	26,086
American Indian males	24,315
White females	23,388
Latino males	22,471
African American females	20,915
American Indian females	17,589
Latino females	16,147

Note: The difference in median earnings of white males and Asian males is not statistically significant; the difference in median earnings of Asian females and African American males is not statistically significant.

As TABLE 3.14 shows, in every ethnic group, men earn more than women. White and Asian men have median earnings of more than $37,000. At the other end of the scale, Latina females earn less than half that amount. Asian females, however, earn more than African American, American Indian, and Latino males (although the difference in earnings between Asian females and African American males is not statistically significant). **The difference between the top two groups, white men and Asian men, and the next two groups, Asian females and African American males, is more than $10,000.**

Trends in U.S. Income and Wealth

Income inequality is inevitable in any society that places a high value on individualism, entrepreneurship, and a market economy. In fact, it is human nature to look over our shoulder and have the success of others motivate us to develop ourselves to the fullest. Through this motivation, we may innovate, seek new skills, create new ideas, and work smarter and faster. **Thus, income inequality can reinforce incentives in the marketplace to spur entrepreneurship and economic growth.**

However, inequality can also waste human potential by limiting the ability of certain groups and individuals to invest in themselves. Extremes of inequality also have the potential to sharpen existing divisions among classes and races. Wall Street executives who are paid $30,000 an hour have little common cause with the janitors who clean their offices for under $10 an hour. While awareness of extreme income inequality has heightened, there is less awareness of extremes of inequality in other areas, particularly health, education, neighborhood safety, the quality of the local environment, and access to information.

Current INCOME Distribution of the Population

With several interruptions, the United States has enjoyed tremendous economic growth since the end of World War II. **Real mean income has more than doubled since 1947,**[153] **but the way that income is distributed across society is increasingly top-heavy.**

Social scientists study how income is allocated by dividing the total population into five equal groups, or quintiles. Our current income distribution resembles a margarita glass, with a large rim atop a very narrow stem. The richest 20 percent of all U.S. households earned more than half (50.5 percent) of the nation's total income in 2006. The next quintile had 22.9 percent and the third quintile had 14.5 percent. The bottom 40 percent of households earned only 12 percent of the nation's total income (see FIGURE 3.11).

The average income in the top quintile of U.S. households in 2006 was $168,170. This is almost fifteen times the average income of the lowest quintile, with an average income of $11,352 per year.

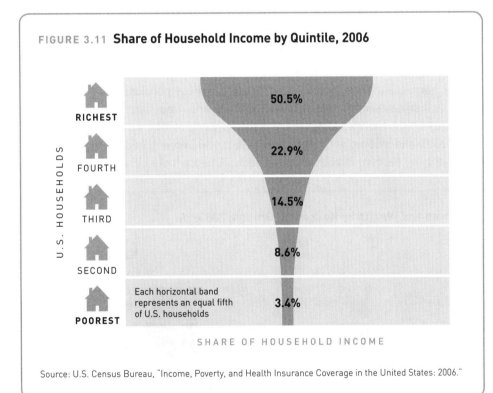

FIGURE 3.11 **Share of Household Income by Quintile, 2006**

U.S. HOUSEHOLDS

RICHEST — 50.5%
FOURTH — 22.9%
THIRD — 14.5%
SECOND — 8.6%
POOREST — 3.4%

Each horizontal band represents an equal fifth of U.S. households

SHARE OF HOUSEHOLD INCOME

Source: U.S. Census Bureau, "Income, Poverty, and Health Insurance Coverage in the United States: 2006."

The richest 20 percent of all U.S. households earned more than half of the nation's total income in 2006.

Current WEALTH Distribution of the Population

While income is critical for life's necessities, wealth, also called net worth, provides financial security and opportunity. Wealth allows families to keep their homes and maintain their standards of living in the event of illness, job loss, natural disaster, divorce, or death. It enables parents to invest in the next generation—to buy a home in a safe neighborhood with good public schools, finance a college education, or help an adult child with a down payment on a house or financing for a new business venture. It can buy autonomy, influence, and power. At the opposite end of the spectrum, debt is negative net worth, which often absorbs income and can make it harder to get an affordable loan, a car, or an apartment.

A study commissioned by the Federal Reserve in 2006 demonstrated the strength of a patchwork of federal asset-building policies, but found that they are largely reaching higher-income households. Through various incentive programs, the federal government subsidizes home buying, retirement savings, and small businesses, through direct outlays from the federal budget and from tax deductions (considered an expenditure for the government) such as the mortgage interest deduction. The study estimated a total cost of $367 billion in 2005 for these programs. However, the study found that over 45 percent of the benefits went to households with annual incomes of more than $1 million. These households received an average benefit of $169,150. By contrast, the bottom 60 percent of the population shares among them less than 3 percent of the benefits of these policies.[154]

BOX 3.15 discusses innovative approaches to helping Americans build assets.

FIGURE 3.12 provides a summary of the holdings of different groups—tracing both wealth and income of the top 1 percent, top 10 percent, middle 30 percent, and bottom 60 percent of households. The top 1 percent of households reap 20

> The top 1 percent of households holds **one-third** of America's wealth. The bottom 60 percent of households only holds **4 percent** of all wealth.

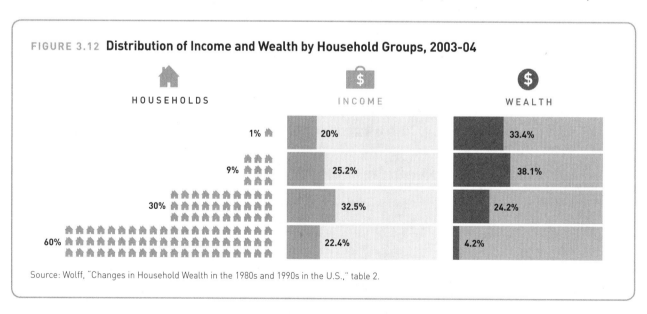

FIGURE 3.12 **Distribution of Income and Wealth by Household Groups, 2003-04**

HOUSEHOLDS   INCOME   WEALTH

	INCOME	WEALTH
1%	20%	33.4%
9%	25.2%	38.1%
30%	32.5%	24.2%
60%	22.4%	4.2%

Source: Wolff, "Changes in Household Wealth in the 1980s and 1990s in the U.S.," table 2.

percent of total income, the top 10 percent just about 45 percent of income, and the bottom 60 percent of households only 22.4 percent of income. The right bar shows household wealth among these same categories, indicating even greater disparities. The top 1 percent of households possesses 33.4 percent—one-third—of America's wealth, and the bottom 60 percent of households only 4.2 percent of all wealth held by U.S. households.[155]

BOX 3.15 **Saving for a Rainy Day: How Can We Help Americans Build Assets?**

Few would disagree that saving money is important, but many find it extremely difficult. In 2004, the Federal Reserve's Survey of Consumer Finances reported that 47.1 percent of Americans have a savings account, and 76.4 percent are carrying some form of debt at any given time.

There is growing interest in new approaches to building assets for low-income Americans. One obvious way is to pay wages that allow for surplus and that help to make up the growing gap that too many people experience between housing costs and wages. But targeted efforts to help families build assets are helpful as well. Here are three approaches with promise:

INTERNATIONAL PRACTICE:
The United Kingdom's Baby Bond Act[156]
Launched in 2005, the United Kingdom's Child Trust Fund (CTF) initiative provides a universal, long-term savings and investment account that ensures all British young people begin adulthood with at least a modest level of financial assets. At birth and again at age seven, all children automatically receive £250 (just under $500) from the government, which is deposited into their personal account held in a private bank. Children in low-income families receive an additional £250 at both time periods as well. Families can contribute up to £1,200 ($2,350) annually in this tax-free account, thereby creating an incentive for further savings. At age eighteen, the accountholder is permitted to withdraw the funds and has complete discretion regarding their use. The KIDS Account Fund, which is very similar to this approach, has been introduced in the U.S. Congress several times, but has yet to be enacted into law.

U.S. GOVERNMENT:
Assets for Independence[157]
Passed in 1998, the Assets for Independence Act created a national pilot program to determine the impact of Individual Development Accounts (IDAs) on savings and asset ownership among low-income families. Implemented through community-based organizations, eligible individuals receive matching funds allocated toward specific expenditures: the purchase of a first home, postsecondary training and education, or small business capitalization. Along with the funds, participants also receive financial education, credit counseling, and assistance in accessing refundable tax credits. Despite having low incomes, thus far they have found that participants do manage to save and that IDA recipients are significantly more likely than nonrecipients to purchase a home.

PRIVATE-SECTOR INITIATIVES:
Blistex Teams Up with Heartland Alliance[158]
In addition to government and foundation-funded asset initiatives, private companies have begun to develop asset-building programs for their employees, including savings incentives, financial and homeowner education, and assistance with tax preparation. Partnering with the Chicago-based not-for-profit agency Heartland Alliance for Human Needs & Human Rights, Blistex Inc. offers a $100 match for employees who save at least $5 weekly for a year. By investing in employees through programs such as this, companies can enhance employee satisfaction, productivity, and workforce stability, ultimately yielding returns for the corporation as well as individual families.

From the Homestead Act to the GI Bill, the United States has a long history of asset-building policies. Assets provide greater household security in the short term by enabling families to weather fluctuations in income, but also foster long-term social mobility through education as well as business and homeownership opportunities that can provide benefits for generations to come. The initiatives above offer potential asset-building opportunities for all Americans that, combined with living-wage policies, can stimulate savings and investment for the future.

Sources: Wheary, Shapiro, and Draut, "By a Thread"; Woo and Bucholz, "Subsidies for Assets"; Child Trust Fund, "Key Facts about the Child Trust Fund"; Loke and Sherraden, "Building Assets from Birth"; Sodha, "Lessons from across the Atlantic"; U.S. Department of Health and Human Services, "About the Assets for Independence Act"; Mills, Patterson, Orr, and DeMarco, "Evaluation of the American Dream Demonstration"; Mohn, "Building Employees' Nest Eggs."

Income and Wealth: Distribution over Time

From just under $30,000 in 1953, median family income grew to more than $56,000 in 2005—with all numbers adjusted for inflation. Yet because of a tremendous surge in incomes at the high end, the gap between different groups of the U.S. population in both income and wealth began to expand in the 1970s and continued in the first half of the 1990s.

In FIGURE 3.13, the four lowest quintile "slices" of families had a smaller share of total income in 2005 than they had in 1953, with significant losses (ranging from 15 to 23 percent) for the 60 percent of households at the lower end of the income spectrum. Only the wealthiest quintile increased their share of total income, by more than 17 percent. The share of total income belonging to the richest 5 percent grew by more than 34 percent, from 15.7 percent in 1953 to 21.1 percent in 2005.[159]

The average income of the top 5 percent of families more than doubled from just over $133,000 in 1966 (using 2005 dollars) to about $308,600 in 2005; for the lowest one-fifth of families, income grew only from about $12,000 to $14,800 during the same period, also adjusting for inflation.[160] In one especially stark example of the trend, in 1980, the average executive earned forty-two times as much as the average factory worker; today, executives earn some four hundred times what factory workers in their industries earn.[161]

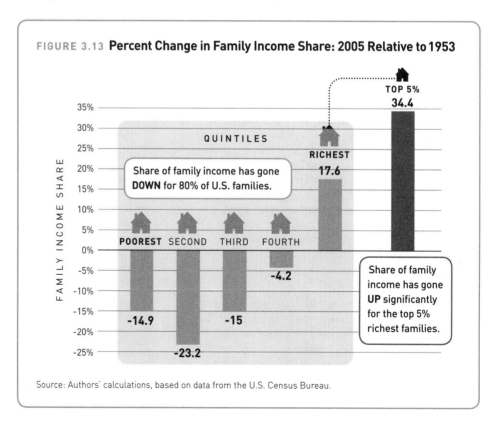

FIGURE 3.13 **Percent Change in Family Income Share: 2005 Relative to 1953**

TOP 5%
34.4

QUINTILES

RICHEST
17.6

Share of family income has gone **DOWN** for 80% of U.S. families.

FAMILY INCOME SHARE

POOREST SECOND THIRD FOURTH

-4.2

-14.9   -15

-23.2

Share of family income has gone **UP** significantly for the top 5% richest families.

Source: Authors' calculations, based on data from the U.S. Census Bureau.

RACIAL AND ETHNIC GAPS IN WEALTH OVER TIME

FIGURE 3.14 traces net worth by race and ethnicity starting in 1989. From this figure, you can see that nonwhites experienced the largest gains in wealth, or net worth, during the 1990s. Still, a large racial gap persists: in 2004, the median net worth of whites was almost six times bigger than that of nonwhites. An important component of disparities in wealth can be attributed to differences in home ownership: African American and Latino home ownership rates are more than 20 percentage points lower than ownership rates for whites. Home ownership helps families accumulate assets and is associated with many other positive outcomes, including increased political involvement, urban revitalization, decreased crime, and more.

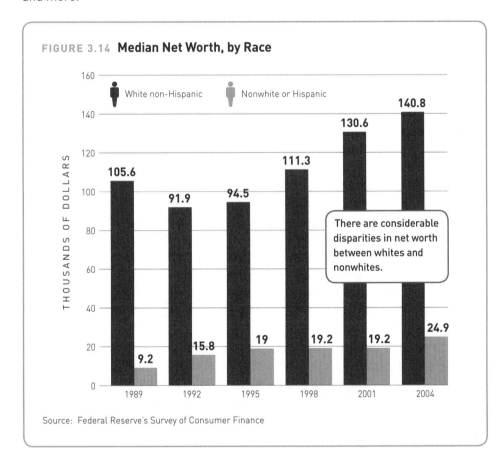

FIGURE 3.14 **Median Net Worth, by Race**

Source: Federal Reserve's Survey of Consumer Finance

In 2004, median net worth was **$140,800** for whites, and **$24,900** for nonwhites.

Factors That Fuel Growth in Earnings Inequality

Growing disparities in earnings over the last half century have been attributed to a number of factors, including changes in the economy wrought by technological change and globalization, the lagging growth of the U.S. minimum wage, the rise of women in the labor force, soaring earnings among the wealthiest, the decline in union membership, and lower levels of educational attainment among the poor and new immigrants. The section that follows will address these factors in turn.

GLOBALIZATION AND TECHNOLOGICAL CHANGE

Changes in labor demand have contributed significantly to the growth in income and earnings inequality. Globalization and technological innovation, particularly the information technology revolution, have dramatically changed how we work, where we work, with whom we work, and when we work. They have served as catalysts for the nation's shift from producing goods to supplying services. These trends have generated many benefits to Americans. Companies like Wal-Mart and Costco have harnessed technology and global supply chains to reduce prices while providing consumers with more choices. But globalization and the IT revolution have brought costs as well as benefits.

The "New Economy," the hallmark of which is increased adoption of IT, has adversely impacted the employment and earnings of less-skilled and less-educated Americans. As was discussed in-depth previously, evidence suggests that a new set of skills and capabilities is needed to succeed in today's knowledge-based economy. Employers need workers with soft skills, as well as skills in math and computers, communications and teamwork, problem-solving and critical thinking, and entrepreneurship and customer service.[162] Individuals lacking these skills have been devalued in the workplace.

Particular communities and industries have also borne the costs of globalization. The shift of manufacturing jobs from the North and Midwest first to the South and then abroad, as well as the corporate downsizings of the 1990s, has hit some local communities hard. The nation's textile industry is a notable example. In 1990, almost 500,000 Americans worked in the industry. Today, just over 170,000 do.

At the national level, the loss of jobs due to outsourcing and plant restructuring continues. However, outsourcing increasingly is associated with the creation of new jobs abroad rather than the displacement of existing jobs overseas. For example, manufacturing jobs once typically created in the United States are now created in Asia. Recent evidence indicates that service-sector jobs are increasingly in danger of being outsourced as well. Jobs that can be parceled into discrete processes are at greatest risk.[163]

Globalization and the IT revolution have brought costs as well as benefits.

DECLINING REAL VALUE OF THE MINIMUM WAGE

The United States is the leading economy in the world, and we have enjoyed tremendous and steady economic growth since the end of World War II, with only a few exceptions. Yet for those who are at the lower end of the wage scale, things are heading in the opposite direction. Since 1968, inflation rates have varied from 1.6 percent to as much as 13.5 percent annually. **But the federal minimum wage has not kept pace with inflation, and thus its real value has decreased by approximately 40 percent in the past forty years.** Even with the 2007 increase in the minimum wage set by Congress, full-time minimum wage work is not sufficient to lift a family of four above the poverty threshold if only one member of the family is working. FIGURE 3.15 shows real values of the federal minimum wage from 1960 to 2009, using projections for 2008 and 2009 based on recent law. Yet, even after the two projected increases have been enacted, the federal minimum wage will be $2.50 lower than its 1960s peak value of almost $10.00 per hour.

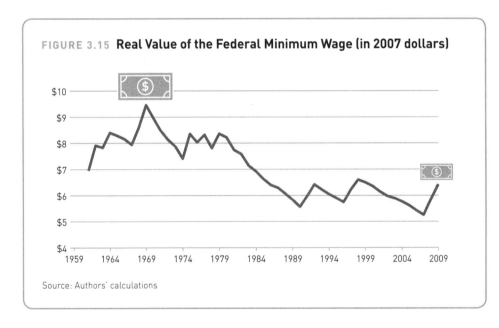

FIGURE 3.15 **Real Value of the Federal Minimum Wage (in 2007 dollars)**

Source: Authors' calculations

The real value of the minimum wage has decreased by **40 percent** in the past forty years.

A large-scale study of low-wage work and public assistance in California demonstrates vividly the hidden public costs of low-wage jobs. Half of all public assistance dollars for programs for people who meet the test of need are going to families who are working. The study assessed many of the largest means-tested programs, such as food stamps, WIC nutrition, energy assistance, and rental assistance, and concluded that full-time employment at the federal minimum wage does not bring self-sufficiency and that small improvements in wages could move many people off public programs. If all of California's workers earned a minimum of $8.00 per hour, aid program costs would be reduced by $2.7 billion.[164]

Currently Washington, Oregon, Vermont, and Missouri index their state minimum wages to reflect the cost of living. Washington's state minimum wage began to reflect changes in the state's cost of living in 2001. Although many economists argue that increasing the minimum wage hurts the very people that the policy seeks to help by raising the cost of labor, leading to cutbacks in hiring, their experience over these seven years shows that Washington state employment has not suffered since indexing began. In fact, since this time, cumulative private-sector employment growth has been just under 5 percent overall and about double that in the state's low-wage leisure and hospitality sector.

This experience is consistent with many studies since the early 1990s showing that moderate increases in the minimum wage do not have adverse impacts on employment of minorities and the least skilled.

In an attempt to ameliorate the situation, twenty states over the past five years have raised their state minimum wages above the federal minimum wage. In addition, several states now link their minimum wage to the Consumer Price Index, which tracks annual changes in the prices of household goods (see sidebar).

WOMEN IN THE LABOR FORCE
Since the mid-1960s, the labor force participation of women has surged. Some have argued that the dramatic rise in women's participation, which has increased the supply of workers overall, has led to a decrease in wages for the typical American, particularly among the least-skilled. However, the evidence does not support this view; during the 1980s, when most American men's wages were stagnating or falling, women's wages continued to rise.

If we look at households, however, the fact that women have fewer constraints on their ability to compete for highly paid jobs than they did in the past does contribute to the widening income gap among families. Prior to the 1980s, nearly all high-earning professionals were men; thus men were largely unable to marry their income-earning equals. Today they can and, increasingly, do. For all the attention paid to professional women who opt out of professional careers, well-educated women are more likely to work than less-well-educated women, even when they have small children. And they are more likely to contribute to a dual-high-earner couple, fueling a large and growing gap between high-earning households and others.

DECLINE IN UNION MEMBERSHIP
Changes in labor market institutions also influence patterns in U.S. earnings. Prior to the 1980s, more than 20 percent of American workers belonged to a union. Membership has fallen to 12 percent today.

How does this decline explain some of the growth in income inequality and the decline in the wages of the typical American worker? Simply put, the average union member earns more than the average nonunion worker—**nonunionized workers earn 77 cents for every dollar earned by unionized workers.** It matters as well for key benefits: unionized workers are 18.3 percent more likely to have health insurance and 22.5 percent more likely to have pension coverage.[165]

LEVELS OF EDUCATIONAL ATTAINMENT AMONG IMMIGRANTS
Changes in the skills composition of immigrants is another contributor to rising income inequality. In recent decades, the country of origin of immigrants has shifted from Europe to Central and South America and Asia, a change that has led to a less educated immigrant population overall, with diminished capacity to command high wages.

Explaining Persistent, Growing Gaps by Race and Ethnic Origin

Today, the usual median weekly earnings of African Americans who work full-time are about 80 percent of the earnings of whites, while Latinos who work full-time earn 70 percent of what whites earn. The African American unemployment rate remains double the white jobless rate. The factors fueling these continuing divides include the following: differing educational levels and work experiences, discrimination, residential segregation, and higher rates of incarceration.

EDUCATION

Differences in the quantity and quality of education are a primary reason for the continued inequality between whites, African Americans, Latinos, and Asians. Thirty percent of whites hold at least a college degree, while only 17.3 percent of African Americans possess at least a college diploma. At the educational extremes are Asians, almost half of whom have at least a college degree, and Latinos, 12.2 percent of whom have at least a college degree. Most experts agree that education remains a key to long-term progress among African Americans and Latinos.

WORK EXPERIENCE

Racial differences in the accumulation of work experiences as young adults are also important for understanding racial inequality later in life. Young African Americans, particularly those who end their formal education after high school, have difficulty transitioning from school to work. They have longer spells of unemployment, preventing them from accumulating early work experience. **Early experience has been shown to be instrumental to future stability in employment and earnings growth.**

DISCRIMINATION

The days when overt racial and ethnic discrimination was legally permitted or socially acceptable are behind us. **Nonetheless, discrimination lives on in stereotypes and often unacknowledged preconceptions.** For instance, many employers perceive African Americans to have weaker soft skills, such as attitude and communications.

In one experiment, researchers submitted resumes from fictional job seekers. The resumes were identical save for the first names of the "applicants." Half the names submitted were commonly associated with African Americans ("Imani"), while the other half were more readily associated with whites ("Molly"). The applicants with typically African American names were 50 percent less likely to be called for interviews than those with "white-sounding" names.[166]

Most experts agree that education remains a key to long-term progress among African Americans and Latinos.

RESIDENTIAL SEGREGATION

Racial residential segregation, discussed above, has proven highly resistant to change. **Low-income minority families often reside in highly segregated communities with concentrated poverty and weak job markets.** Because they live far from jobs and lack reliable transportation options, they have fewer opportunities.

Segregated, concentrated neighborhood poverty did not develop by accident. A Brookings Institution study[167] describes how concentrated poverty emerged due to "decades of policies that confined poor households, especially poor African American ones, to these economically isolated areas." The legacy of these policies can be seen in large cities today, such as New York City (see BOX 3.16).

INCARCERATION

5% **24%**

The United States has **5 percent** of the world's people—but **24 percent** of the world's prisoners.

The United States has 5 percent of the world's people—but 24 percent of the world's prisoners. We lock up more people in aggregate and more as a percentage of our population than any country in the world, including China and Russia. We incarcerate people at a rate **five to nine times greater** than that of our peer nations: over 7 out of every 1,000 U.S. residents are in prison.[168]

From the mid-1920s to the mid-1970s, the U.S. incarceration rate was stable at about 110 per 100,000 population[169]—roughly the same as in our peer nations today. But rates since then have soared, driven not by increases in violent crime but rather by **changes in criminal justice and sentencing policies, especially those related to drug offenses.**[170]

African American men and their communities bear the brunt of skyrocketing incarceration rates. If current incarceration rates continue, nearly one-third of African American males will spend some portion of their lives in state or federal prison.[171] In low-income minority communities, criminal justice system involvement is so pervasive as to be a normative life experience.

What impact does this have on the incomes and lifetime earnings of African Americans? Numerous studies show that employers rate young African Americans as the least desirable pool to draw from. Some of the lack of willingness on the part of employers to hire African Americans is based on a perception that many are involved in criminal activity though the majority are not.[172] Imprisoned men miss out on key career-building years, and their lifetime earnings are reduced as a result. **Their children often suffer emotionally and materially from their absence; children whose parents serve time in prison are, on average, more likely to end up behind bars at some point in their own lives than other children.** Finally, prison exposes many to extreme violence and health threats endemic in correctional facilities as well as behavioral norms that do not translate well to mainstream work and family life. All these experiences make rejoining the workforce difficult.

About 1,900 people with criminal records are released every day and, according to the Department of Justice, two-thirds of them will eventually end up back in prison: **our current system has failed to prepare the majority of prisoners for**

BOX 3.16 **Human Development Index for New York City**

New York University's Women of Color Policy Network has developed a modified Human Development Index to assess well-being in different neighborhoods, or community districts, in New York City. The Network sorted the fifty-nine community districts into three groups based on their HDI score.

The nine districts in the **HIGH human development** group shared the following characteristics:

- **RACE/ETHNICITY:** Three-fourths of residents were white. The majority of nonwhite residents were of Asian descent (Japanese, Chinese, Korean, and Indian).

- **HEALTH:** Infant mortality and birth rates were the lowest in the city.

- KNOWLEDGE: Thirty-seven percent of the city's residents with postgraduate degrees resided in these nine areas, which are home to just 13 percent of the city's population.

- INCOME: Residents earned about 34 percent of total New York City income. More than four of every ten earned at least $100,000.

The thirty-nine districts in the **MEDIUM human development** group are home to immigrant communities: white ethnic communities settled prior to 1965, recent Eastern European immigrants, and immigrants from Asia and Latin America who came after the 1965 Immigration Act. Index values rose in only two of these communities from 1990 to 2000, and declined in the rest. Some of their characteristics include:

- **RACE/ETHNICITY:** Thirty-five percent of the residents were white, 26 percent were Latino, 24 percent were African American, and 10 percent were Asian. Eighty percent of the city's foreign-born population resides in these communities.

- **HEALTH:** Despite moderate incomes and levels of educational attainment, the communities had relatively positive health indicators, which raised their human development status. Infant mortality rates were lower than the city average, as were deaths from diabetes.

- KNOWLEDGE: Twenty-two percent of adults 25 and above had completed college.

- INCOME: Per-capita income in these districts was $18,115, lower than the city average of $22,406.

Ten of the eleven **LOW human development** districts saw declines in their Index score from 1990 to 2000. These communities, home to native-born African Americans, Puerto Ricans, and immigrants from the Dominican Republic and Mexico, share the following characteristics:

- **RACE/ETHNICITY:** Nearly half of New York City's Latinos and African Americans live in these districts.

- **HEALTH:** Infant mortality rates were three times the city average.

- KNOWLEDGE: Fewer than one in ten adults had at least a college degree. Less than one-quarter of children aged five to twelve can read at a first-grade level.

- INCOME: Forty percent of the population was living below the poverty level, nearly twice the citywide rate. Thirty-eight percent of families earned $15,000 or less.

The New York City Human Development Index is a fine example of how the human development approach and indexing methodology can be adapted to varied local contexts. Its results paint a more nuanced picture of human well-being in the Big Apple than would simpler income measures.

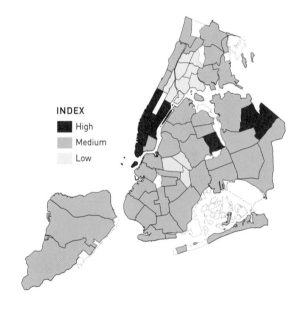

INDEX
- High
- Medium
- Low

Source: Women of Color Policy Network, Wagner School of Public Service, New York University.

a stable, law-abiding life on the outside. That effort must begin at the moment of arrest, through skills and transitional job programs, greater attention to mental health care and substance abuse treatment in prison, more realistic penalties imposed on prisoners so as to avoid credit scores that make housing difficult to obtain, and better efforts to maintain parent-child bonds. (see BOX 3.17, 3.18).

BOX 3.17 **Employment Opportunities for Those Who Face Major Economic and Social Barriers**

Social enterprises employing thousands of people belie the conventional wisdom that some people just can't work—particularly those who are homeless or mentally ill, have had alcohol or drug problems, or have been incarcerated.

Over the past decade, REDF, formerly known as the Roberts Enterprise Development Fund, has invested in and advised social enterprises—nonprofits and small businesses that have successfully created employment opportunities for more than 3,000 individuals. The five nonprofits REDF has partnered with over the past several years have established businesses that operate efficiently, hit their financial targets, and contribute needed goods and services to their communities, while employing 650 people each year.

Two years after being hired, 74 percent of employees were still working—many in private-sector jobs. Another 11 percent were enrolled in vocational education programs.

The results affirmed the role of stable employment in reducing recidivism to the streets and jail.

The San Francisco Bay Area nonprofits that REDF partnered with included: Community Gatepath, Community Vocational Enterprises, Juma Ventures, New Door Ventures, and Rubicon Programs. Their enterprises are focused on a wide variety of industries—light manufacturing, ballpark food sales, landscape gardening, janitorial work, screen printing, and bicycle sales and repair.

REDF has recently entered into partnerships with several new nonprofits, including Community Housing Partnership, San Francisco Clean City, San Francisco Conservation Corps, and St. Vincent de Paul of Alameda County, which intend to employ people who are generally shut out of the workforce. Jobs are designated in recycling, property management, infrastructure building, and street cleaning.

BOX 3.18 **Keeping Faith with the Children of Prisoners**

Like America's prison population itself, the nation's more than 2 million children of prisoners are disproportionately urban, poor, and African American or Hispanic. A low-income, inner-city minority child faces dim life prospects that grow even dimmer in cases where a parent is behind bars. These children suffer extreme risks of failing in school, abusing illegal drugs, remaining jobless, getting arrested, being violent crime victims, and being incarcerated.

One approach to breaking the poverty-and-crime cycle is youth mentoring. The nation's largest youth mentoring program is Big Brothers Big Sisters of America (BBBSA). Much scientific research proves that low-income children who are matched by BBBSA with an adult mentor in their community are less likely to get into trouble, more likely to stay drug-free, and more likely to succeed in school and later in life.

Traditionally, however, children with one or both parents incarcerated have been underrepresented in youth mentoring programs. Also, youth mentoring organizations have normally experienced difficulties in mobilizing inner-city minority men to mentor young males.

To overcome these barriers, in 2000 I helped develop a program specifically for the children of prisoners. Piloted in Philadelphia in 2001, it involved partnerships between BBBSA and urban church leaders in the city's predominantly African American and Latino sections. These clergy mobilized male mentors from their respective communities. Private foundations contributed seed funding.

The program's partners named it Amachi, an Ibo-Nigerian phrase signifying that every child is a gift from God. The program reached out to thousands of children and to prisoners to match them with mentors.

Public/Private Ventures, a national research organization, tracked the Amachi program's early progress in reaching out to prisoners, locating children, recruiting pastors, mobilizing mentors, and making matches. Their 2003 report on Amachi declared, "The results were overwhelming." In little more than a year, they had succeeded in mobilizing mentors in Philadelphia for 517 children of prisoners, from ages five to fifteen. Participants included 238 male mentors for boys. Amachi had instigated the fastest mentor mobilization in any city in the more than one-hundred-year history of BBBSA.

BBBSA became dedicated to expanding Amachi to other cities. By late 2006, there were about 25,000 Amachi matches in local affiliates in scores of cities nationwide. As one Philadelphia pastor observed, "We had prison outreach and youth study groups. But when Amachi executive director and former Philadelphia mayor Rev. Dr. W. Wilson Goode came to see me, I immediately recognized that in our mission we had totally overlooked one group and their particular needs. Sometimes you don't see the innocent victims."

If the program's partners maintain its post-2005 rate of growth, Amachi could reach over 100,000 matches before 2011. It costs about $1,000 a year to make, manage, study, and sustain an Amachi match. It would cost a maximum of about $2 billion a year to accommodate all children of prisoners whose parents or guardians might enable access to the program. That seems like a huge sum until one recalls that America now spends about $80 billion a year on prisons.

As Mark Scott, an Amachi coordinator and former associate director of the White House Office of Faith-Based and Community Initiatives, reminds us: "We're spending 40 times more on locking up their parents than it would take to change and save the lives of their innocent children. This must change if we are ever to break the crime-and-violence cycle. We need everyone—religious, secular, government, nonprofit—to step up." Amen.

By John J. DiIulio Jr., Frederic Fox Leadership Professor of Politics, Religion, and Civil Society at the University of Pennsylvania. In 2001, he served as first director of the White House Office of Faith-Based and Community Initiatives.

Explaining the Persistent Gender Earnings Gap

Is discrimination against women the key issue, or is it discrimination against mothers?

Although women's earnings have risen steadily since 1965, **women still take home 78 percent, on average, of what men earn**. If benefits are factored in, the disparity is even larger. Women's smaller paychecks typically lead to smaller retirement accounts, smaller pensions, and smaller Social Security checks.

Two of the last century's most far-reaching socioeconomic transformations have been **the wholesale entry of women into the paid workforce** and **a sharp increase in single motherhood**. Yet our policies, workplaces, social institutions, and societal expectations have been slow to adapt to the altered landscape. As a consequence, we have millions of **overstretched, overstressed families** trying to cobble together ways to function while still paying the bills.

Yet amid the stress of transformation, there are powerful signs of progress. More women than men have been graduating college since the 1980s. Laws prohibit gender discrimination in hiring and promotion. Fields once closed to women are now open. For a variety of reasons, however, the earnings gap remains. Some of the factors behind this gap include:

- **Women tend to study different subjects than men.** Fewer women major in science and engineering, for instance, than in education and psychology, fields that have lower economic payoffs in the work world.

- **Women work different jobs.** Studies have found that approximately 28 percent of women's lower earnings stem from differences in rates of union membership and the concentration of women in lower-paying occupations, industries, and professional specialties. Women with low levels of education make up almost the entire labor force of child-care providers and home health aides, jobs that pay less even than unskilled work like security guard or parking attendant. This pay disparity is particularly alarming given that child-care providers and home health aides are trusted with society's most vulnerable members and, in the case of child-care workers, with nurturing the next generation of adults.

- **Research shows that women pay a penalty for leaving the marketplace to care for children**; about one-third of the gap between male and female earnings stems from lost job experience during child rearing. One study showed that for every year a women in her twenties delays having her first child, her lifetime earnings rise by 10 percent.[173]

- **Some argue that women are consciously trading off wages for greater control over their time**, choosing lower-paying jobs that offer greater flexibility and thus making it easier to balance the demands of home and work. However, economist Elaine McCrate finds strong evidence to the contrary:[174] **Low-wage jobs are actually less flexible than high-wage jobs in terms of scheduling shifts and taking time off for illness.**

- **Discrimination also plays a role.** Evidence shows women are hired less frequently in high-wage firms, receive less training and fewer promotions, and are assigned lower-paying jobs within the same occupation as men. Men often earn more than women in jobs in which women vastly outnumber men, such as schoolteachers. One question that researchers ask with increasing frequency is as follows: is discrimination against women the key issue, or is it discrimination against mothers? Ann Crittenden demonstrates that, for workers under age thirty-five, the earnings gap between women with and without children is greater than that between women and men.[175] Another study found that, controlling for factors like education and experience, a woman pays, on average, a 5 percent wage penalty for each child she has.[176]

FAMILY-FRIENDLY POLICIES

The critical career-building years of one's twenties and thirties collide with the prime family-building years, creating work-life conflicts for dual-career couples. The social changes prompted by women's entry into the paid labor force have not been symmetrical: women have taken on paid work, but men have not made a commensurate foray into the unpaid world of domestic work.

How does the United States compare to other countries in terms of helping working families balance their responsibilities?[177]

- One hundred sixty-three countries guarantee paid maternity leave; 66 countries guarantee paid paternity leave. Ninety-eight countries have fourteen or more weeks of paid leave for mothers, 31 have fourteen or more weeks of paid leave for men as well. **The United States has no federally mandated paid childbearing leave for mothers or fathers.**

- At least 107 countries protect the right to breastfeed, with 73 offering paid breaks. **This right is not guaranteed in the United States.**

- One hundred thirty-seven countries mandate annual paid leave. **U.S. firms are not required to provide annual paid vacation.**

- One hundred forty-five countries have paid sick leave for short- or long-term illness, with 136 having at least one week annually, and 81 allowing at least twenty-six weeks or until recovery. **Sick leave is offered in the United States through the Family and Medical Leave Act, but it is unpaid and does not cover all workers.**[178]

In 98 countries, new mothers have 14 or more weeks of paid leave. The U.S. has no federally mandated paid maternity leave.

Conclusion

Americans are offsetting the higher costs of gasoline, college tuition, and medical bills with their credit cards. The trend is not sustainable.

Since 2001, the income of the typical American family has stagnated. Along with a growing number of low-wage workers who cannot support their families even with full-time work, moderate-wage workers are also facing difficulties. To survive in today's high-tech, global economy, families all along the income scale have been forced to develop coping behaviors. First, many low-income families have reduced consumption as their incomes failed to keep pace with inflation.[179] Second, income stagnation and decline has led many middle-class families to take on more debt. In 2004, middle-income households spent almost one-fifth of their income paying off debt.[180] Americans are offsetting the higher costs of gasoline, college tuition, and medical bills with their credit cards. The trend is not sustainable.

Easing the struggles of middle- and low-income Americans is vital to our country's future.[181] Here are some approaches to consider:

- **Make work pay for low- and moderate-income families.** To return economic stability to working families and to fuel upward mobility, full-time workers need to be paid a living wage. In addition, we need to shift from current outdated economic frameworks and measures to a standard of self-sufficiency for families in the setting of wages, benefits, and safety nets. Opposition to increases in the minimum wage, and to the use of family budgets to determine safety nets is often based on fears of increased labor cost and reduced profits. Yet studies consistently show that higher wage costs are offset by increased productivity, higher employee retention, and lower absenteeism.[182] Business profit margins are often bolstered as a result of higher worker morale, leading to increases in efficiency and commitment.[183][184] Living-wage ordinances have multiplier effects as well, creating economic stimulus as new income is circulated in the community.

- **Revitalize institutions to reflect the economy and workforce of our era.** The United States lags behind all our peer countries in adopting tools such as paid maternity/paternity leave, sick leave, and other policies to enable parents to remain productive in careers and earning income while also attending to family responsibilities. As a nation, we need to help families provide care and support to their members while also making ends meet. This approach is especially important for women, who shoulder the demands of child-rearing and elder care disproportionately.

- **Help people with significant employment challenges participate in the labor market.** There will always be people who cannot be self-sufficient. However, families, communities, churches, the private sector, and government can create opportunities for everyone who is capable of work to participate in the labor market, thereby earning income and playing a rewarding role in society. Philanthropic organizations have an important role to play in testing new approaches, assessing their impact, and documenting what works (see BOX 3.19).

- **Asset-building programs are vital to creating economic security for all families.** While households with incomes of $1 million or more receive an average benefit of about $170,000 from current federal policies that reward asset-building, the poorest one-fifth of households receive, on average, about $3 from these same policies.[185] More efforts are needed to help low- and moderate-income Americans to save, to reduce debt, and to build assets for a more secure future, with a role for the public and private sectors alike.

- **Greater financial, economic, and business literacy is required for the public to wisely invest money, prepare for retirement, and set and meet financial goals for themselves and their children.** Families who lost their homes—and life savings—due to their inability to meet subprime mortgage payments offer stark examples of the hazards of both a lack of transparency in business and financial naïveté among consumers. Consumers must be better educated about basic finance.

BOX 3.19 Getting Better Returns on Our Philanthropic Investments

Philanthropic giving in the United States is on the rise. Giving by U.S. foundations has nearly tripled since 1996, with grants to nonprofits around the world exceeding $40 billion as of 2006. U.S. foundations have been instrumental in creating programs we all take for granted. The 911 emergency response system, resulting from work by the Robert Wood Johnson Foundation, is but one example.

Philanthropy not only sponsors the basics; it also fosters the things that make life worth living such as the arts, open spaces, and higher education. The more than seventy-one thousand U.S. foundations run the gamut in terms of size and scope—from large, private foundations that tackle a variety of issues worldwide to small community foundations that focus on helping local citizens. But the differences go far beyond size and scope: every foundation takes its own approach to addressing problems, and some are clearly more effective than others.

In fact, an increasing number of funders want to achieve the most impact possible for the resources they expend and are willing to make the tough choices that this requires.

First, many are embracing focused strategies to achieve impact. Increasingly dissatisfied with mere "charity," more

foundation leaders are defining clearer goals and coherent strategies to achieve them. For them, it's not enough to get dollars out the door to worthy organizations. These foundation leaders are establishing a clear logic between their grant-making decisions and the achievement of specific outcome goals. In the face of many worthy efforts, this kind of focus takes discipline, and often requires making fewer, larger grants—which means saying "no" more often.

Second, more foundations are assessing their work. By defining indicators that relate to the achievement of their goals, foundations can measure how well their activities are moving the needle on the issues they address and make adjustments when their tactics are not effective. Many foundations use critiques from outsiders—grantees, for example—as one such indicator of performance.

At a time when their governmental safety net is shrinking, more and more U.S. citizens must look elsewhere for help in fulfilling their basic needs. Fortunately, philanthropy is improving its ability to create positive impact in their lives.

By Phil Buchanan, president, Center for Effective Philanthropy

---

PART 4

8-Point Human Development Agenda

What will it take to boost scores on the American Human Development Index?

Progress depends on us all:

People, Public Sector, Business Community, Civic Groups, Philanthropy, Religious Institutions, and the Media.

1. Promote prevention.

2. Make health care affordable for all Americans.

3. Modernize K–12 education.

4. Invest in at-risk kids, the earlier the better.

5. Strengthen and support families.

6. Boost incomes and aid asset-building.

7. Launch a Marshall Plan for the Gulf.

8. Take responsibility for the most vulnerable.

Introduction

The best gauge of human development is the capacity of ordinary people to decide who to be, what to do, and how to live, and the degree to which real freedom and possibility are open to them as they seek to realize their vision of a good life. We have argued that the way to promote human development is to invest in people, particularly in people's capabilities—the tools required to lead lives of choice and value. Capabilities enable people to capitalize on opportunities, invest in their families and communities, and contribute to society.

In this first *American Human Development Report*, we have focused on three core capabilities: health, knowledge, and a decent standard of living. Many factors beyond health, knowledge, and material living standards affect human development overall and the life chances of individuals. Future volumes in this series will explore additional capabilities, such as living in physical security, participating in decision making, and enjoying a healthy natural environment. Much remains to be done in these areas. However, this year's report seeks to highlight actions that would have the most significant impacts on the three core capabilities measured by the index.

What will it take for Americans to make significant gains in health, education, and income—particularly those Americans who today lag behind? What can we do to yield better American HD Index scores in five, ten, or twenty years?

Progress depends on us all. **People** themselves, individually and collectively, can do a tremendous amount to build capabilities. Actions and investments from both the **public sector** and the **business community** are also needed to put the American Dream of mobility, freedom, security, and dignity within everyone's reach. **Philanthropy** plays an increasingly important role in addressing many of the challenges we face. **Religious institutions**, long dedicated to the relief of human suffering, speak with moral authority on our obligations to one another. **The media** has a vital part to play in educating the public, stimulating civic engagement, holding leaders accountable, and contributing to transparency.

To expand choices and opportunities for more Americans, action in the following eight areas holds great potential.

> The way to promote human development is to invest in people, particularly in people's capabilities—the tools required to lead lives of choice and value.

For a Long and Healthy Life

PRIORITY 1:

Promote prevention.

While the lion's share of health care resources go for medical treatment, the great-est gains in life expectancy over the past half century have come from public health efforts and the spread of private behaviors designed to prevent rather than treat disease and disability, such as mass immunizations, seatbelts, and health warn-ings on cigarette packages. Medical interventions remain vital to fighting chronic illnesses like cancer and cardiovascular disease. But prevention, consumer infor-mation necessary to make healthy decisions, early detection, and maintenance can reduce health costs while improving the quality and lengthening the span of people's lives. To make headway against our leading causes of death today, we must take action to reduce risk—for instance, by maintaining a healthy weight, avoiding tobacco and excessive alcohol, exercising regularly, and getting recom-mended screenings. Similarly, research has shown that early, effective treatment for addiction is vastly less expensive and more effective than addressing drug use with incarceration. Tackling the life expectancy gaps revealed by the American HD Index requires public health campaigns targeted at Americans living the shortest lives: African Americans as well as the populations of the Gulf states, Washington, D.C., and residents of the lowest-life-expectancy congressional districts.

PRIORITY 2:

Make health care affordable for all Americans.

All Americans should have access to high-quality health care, including mental health care, regardless of employment status, preexisting conditions, or income level. The United States is a global leader in medical technologies; we have the know-how to help our people enjoy healthy lives and survive to old age. And we are already spending on health care at the highest levels in the world. Yet today, 47 million people do not have health insurance. Still others are afraid to change jobs or start their own business for fear of losing their health insurance, hamper-ing individual opportunity and acting as a drag on the economy. There are many models and options to consider, drawing on both American plans and the experi-ence of other countries. We must summon the political will to take a bold first step without requiring that it be a perfect or final arrangement.

Today, 47 million Americans do not have health insurance.

For Access to Knowledge

PRIORITY 3:

Modernize K–12 education.

Public education is the cornerstone of equal opportunity. A quality education, prerequisite to a life of value and choice, is the right of every American. Likewise, an educated population of lifelong learners, independent thinkers, and responsible citizens is vital to our democracy and economy. The educational index shows that our system falls short in two basic measures: relevance and fairness.

In terms of **relevance**, the days when basic skills were sufficient to ensure a life of reasonable economic security and full participation in society are past; the labor market today is unkind to those who lack high school diplomas, and jobs that afford financial security increasingly require college degrees. Yet only 74 percent of American public high school students graduated on time (within four years) with a regular diploma in 2003–04.[186] The content of education needs revitalization as well. To seize opportunities brought by globalization and technological change, young people need to know how to think, create, and relate—to work with others unlike themselves to solve problems. Schools need to teach twenty-first-century skills and content, expand the scope of school assessment, and create meaningful career education tracks for teens who are not headed for college.

In terms of **fairness**, we must tackle the appalling disparities in educational quality that persist more than half a century after the landmark *Brown v. Board of Education* ruling. The American Human Development Index reveals vast educational attainment gaps among congressional districts and racial and ethnic groups that undermine America's claim to a level playing field. None of the country's ten largest public school districts—which serve 8 percent of all American K–12 students, nearly all of them members of minority groups—graduate more than 60 percent of their students. In comparison, sixty-seven congressional districts have graduation rates above 90 percent. In 2003, the graduation rates for Latino and African American high school students were just 53 percent and 55 percent, respectively.[187] Public school children attending well-funded suburban schools paid for by local property taxes generally receive excellent educations; too many poor and minority children receive educations that are second-rate by any measure. Equalizing factors that contribute to excellence—money; physical plant; teacher training, salaries, and qualifications; support staff; and the depth, breadth, and rigor of curriculum—is vital to closing gaps in outcomes and increasing American HD Index educational attainment scores.

> The days when basic skills were sufficient to ensure a life of reasonable economic security and full participation in society are past.

154

PRIORITY 4:

Invest in at-risk kids, the earlier the better.

Intervening early, intensely, and consistently in the lives of at-risk children is an investment that pays for itself many times over. Many of the disparities we see in the American Human Development Index are rooted in the significant differences children experience in their everyday lives from birth onward. Often lacking adequate and developmentally appropriate stimulation in the critical early years, disadvantaged children start school far behind in their cognitive and noncognitive skills—and rarely catch up. These early deficits, coupled with other obstacles— inadequate health care, poor schools, neighborhood crime, material depriva- tions—reinforce one another, with their cumulative negative impacts compounding over the life course. The odds are against such children. Indeed, someone born into poverty who rises to prominence in adulthood is said to have beaten the odds. But research has shown that the odds can be changed, and that doing so pays huge dividends to individuals and society.

We can change the odds by scaling up effective programs supported by robust evidence. First, we should expand early intervention to reach all at-risk mothers and infants. Second, we should invest in high-quality early childhood education, modeled on successful interventions, for at-risk children ages two to four. High- quality preschools with college-educated, well-paid teachers; low teacher/student ratios; and programs that build social, behavioral, and cognitive skills lead to higher levels of scholastic achievement, less crime, lower rates of teen pregnancy, and less dependence on public assistance.

In addition, we should continue to reach out to at-risk children in school. Elementary schools serving low-income communities should provide more envel- oping school environments, including longer school days; more socially, culturally, and cognitively enriching activities; and a greater bridge to home life. Teens who drop out of high school earn $9,000 less than high school graduates, are more likely to become parents at an early age, and are more likely to be unemployed, in poor health, living in poverty, in prison, or on public assistance. There is a need for rigorous research on how to best reach disconnected adolescents with second- chance programs that help them make a successful transition to independent adulthood. Extending income support to low-income young people through age twenty-one would also help them invest in their futures, as would greater support to young people exiting the foster-care system.

There is something that each one of us can do: make a meaningful, long-term commitment to an at-risk child. There are many ways to do this, such as building a relationship with a boy or girl through a mentoring program or becoming a special advocate for a neglected or abused child.

"It is a rare public policy initia- tive that promotes fairness and social justice and at the same time promotes produc- tivity in the economy and in society at large. Investing in disadvantaged young children is such a policy."

James Heckman
Nobel Prize–winning economist[188]

Become a Mentor/Advocate

Big Brothers Big Sisters is a mentoring program with a successful track record (www. bbbs.org); National CASA recruits, trains, and supports volunteers to act as Court Ap- pointed Special Advocates for abused children (www.nation- alcasa.org). Both programs operate nationwide.

For a Decent Standard of Living

PRIORITY 5:

Strengthen and support families.

Families play the most influential role in the development of human capabilities. But today, most adults, especially women, must juggle family and work responsibilities, often feeling overwhelmed in the process. Three in four married mothers of school-aged children are in the workforce. Rates for single mothers are even higher.[189] In addition, 44 million Americans care for adult relatives, usually elderly parents, with the typical caregiver providing at least twenty hours per week of care; six in ten such caregivers are also employed. Yet workplaces and community institutions, including schools, have been slow to adjust to this new reality. The caring penalty that women pay in the labor market is reflected in lower paychecks and smaller retirement accounts—and significantly lower scores on the American Income Index. Forty percent of job loss can be attributed to the need to care for family members who are ill.

Businesses can do a lot to ease the strain on families by offering employees flexibility to balance the competing demands on their time—without penalizing them. Companies that have implemented flextime, shorter workdays or workweeks, job-sharing, on-site day care, emergency child care for sick kids, and on and off ramps for parents who take time out to raise children find that their investment in family-friendly policies pays off in terms of recruitment, retention, productivity, morale, and commitment, as well as fewer sick days.[190]

Investment, including incentives and tax breaks to help moderate- and low-income families secure quality child care, as well as expansion of the country's family leave policies, would help all of us to balance our responsibilities and better care for our children and elderly. Our peer nations and many far less affluent countries—163 in all—guarantee their citizens paid maternity leave.[191] In 2004, California mandated six week's leave at 55 percent of salary (up to $840 per week) to allow men and women to care for seriously ill parents, partners, and children as well as to bond with a newborn or newly adopted child. The California law mandates paid leave, and it covers nearly all workers. Research shows that small businesses and the general public broadly support the program, and that nearly all workers return to their job in six weeks or less.[192]

PRIORITY 6:

Boost incomes and aid asset-building.

Income and assets work together to expand our range of choices and opportunities; they are fundamental determinants of life-shaping decisions, such as where to live and where we can send our children to school. Adequate incomes are essential to securing the goods and services needed to live our lives with choice and dignity and

> Our peer nations and many far less affluent countries—163 in all—guarantee their citizens paid maternity leave.

to participate fully in society. Assets, or wealth, provide security and allow for investment in the future, making it possible for families to weather job loss or illness, to put down roots in a community through homeownership, to invest in education, and to maintain their standard of living during retirement. Income and assets both impact the American HD Index, though only income from earnings is measured.

The income index shows that African Americans, Latinos, and Native Americans are earning significantly less than Asians and whites; large disparities among congressional districts are also apparent. The income index also reveals that many American families are earning less than it takes to meet a monthly budget in their communities, and many more barely cover basic expenses. Indexing the federal minimum wage to inflation would help working families keep up with the rising cost of living. A full-time worker earning the minimum wage cannot support a family of three above the federal poverty line, despite recent increases. Pegging wage minimums to the actual cost of basic necessities like housing, transportation, and health care would be one way to help full-time workers achieve self-sufficiency. Whether these specific ideas are politically viable, or even desirable, is a matter for American voters and political leaders to decide. But if one accepts the premise that America's unique strengths reside in a broad and resilient middle class, it seems beyond question that arresting the erosion of middle-class security and strengthening its numbers, in part by enabling the poor to work and save their way into it, are vital national priorities.

In addition, more must be done to connect less-educated workers to the job force, which means easing school-to-work transitions for non-college-bound teens. It also requires creating pathways that reconnect ex-prisoners to the working world. The prison boom has had a devastating impact on African Americans and Latinos in a host of ways. It depresses lifetime earnings for those who serve time and creates barriers to labor force participation for many law-abiding young black and Latino men who are deemed guilty by association. Moreover, workers who have lost their jobs need greater support. Stronger links between training and unemployment benefits would help. Better income support for workers in transition would also help keep them from falling out of the middle class as they retool for new opportunities.

The distribution of assets in the United States is even more top heavy than the distribution of income, with the wealthiest 10 percent of American households holding more than double the share of wealth of the other 90 percent combined.

There are significant racial and ethnic differences as well. Census Bureau data indicate the net worth of white households is about ten times greater than that of African American or Latino households.[193] The Earned Income Tax Credit has provided a boost in income to working families that have kept many out of poverty; expanding this credit and adding a savings component would help them invest in the future as well. Asset-building programs that have worked elsewhere—such as the U.K. Baby Bond and conditional cash transfers in Brazil and Mexico—may also hold promise in the United States.

Effects on Income

Educational attainment accounts for a significant share of the earnings differential, which reinforces the need to address the educational inequalities highlighted in priorities 3 and 4. In addition, improving our approach to health care, elder care, and child care, as outlined in priorities 1, 2 and 5, would free up income and allow poor and middle-class families to begin building assets.

To Raise the American Index for States and People Left Behind

PRIORITY 7:

Launch a Marshall Plan for the Gulf.

For generations, Alabama, Louisiana, and Mississippi have lagged behind the nation as a whole on key indicators. Hurricanes Katrina and Rita revealed the significant deprivations that persist in this part of our country while simultaneously exacerbating them. These three Gulf states combined, home to 12 million Americans, have the lowest American HD Index scores of any region in the country. On key measures of human development, the region today is at the level of development the country as a whole experienced eighteen years ago. It has the nation's lowest levels of educational attainment, shortest life expectancy, and lowest incomes. If the whole region were a single state, it would rank second to last—surpassing only Mississippi itself.

Three years after the storms put the birthplace of jazz under water and wiped out towns south of I-10 from New Orleans to Mobile, promises of support and rebuilding have yet to bear fruit. Church groups and concerned individuals continue to volunteer their time, showing solidarity and helping some communities rebuild. But tens of thousands of flood victims are still living in FEMA trailers. Families and communities are scattered, many longing to return home. Even those whose homes are intact face tremendous human insecurity and financial hardship as they wait to see if their hometowns are reborn.

Yet America faced a far greater reconstruction challenge in the not-too-distant past. Six decades ago, Americans supported a plan to rebuild war-torn Europe. Totaling $13 billion (equivalent to $100 billion today), the Marshall Plan reconstructed Western Europe, modernizing the region and setting it on a path to the prosperity it now enjoys. The Gulf States seem equally deserving of reconstruction. Given the need to rebuild many institutions from the ground up, there is also a unique opportunity to test innovative approaches that, if successful, could be applied to struggling communities elsewhere in the United States.

A Gulf Coast Reconstruction Plan, encompassing far-reaching humanitarian, social, political, and economic aims, would expand choice and opportunity for the people of Alabama, Louisiana, and Mississippi. Only a concerted and sustained effort can address the significant shortfalls revealed by the American HD Index.

Alabama, Louisiana, and Mississippi have some of the country's lowest levels of educational attainment, shortest life expectancies, and lowest incomes.

PRIORITY 8:

Take responsibility for the most vulnerable.

The height to which a talented individual can ascend tells us something about a society; by this measure, America is a dynamic and inspiring place. But how the vulnerable fare tells us something equally important and, measured by this value, America fares significantly less well. The HD Index for the United States as a whole—5.06—tells us very little on its own; the figure becomes meaningful only when we disaggregate the population into geographic, gender, racial, and ethnic groups, and see how the data stack up. But we are unable to compare the American HD Index scores of some groups because of the specific data points chosen and the way the information is collected (by household). For Instance, we were not able to calculate an HD Index for physically disabled people, for adults with developmental disabilities, or for people with persistent and severe mental illnesses, though we are investigating possible approaches for future volumes in this series. But most of us realize that the American HD Index scores of our brothers and sisters in these population groups would be at the bottom of the scale. Take, for example, adults with schizophrenia, who make up about 1 percent of the population. Since the illness typically strikes in the late teens and early twenties, educational attainment is often limited. Earnings tend to be scant. And schizophrenia shortens life expectancy by fifteen years on average, due to greater risk of suicide, violence, injury, and chronic medical illnesses.[194] These factors would add up to an extremely low HD Index score.

The needs of vulnerable populations are not addressed in humane, sustainable ways.[195] Our attempts to care for these groups out of sight in large psychiatric hospitals, orphanages, and "homes" of all sorts have too often led to horrific, large-scale abuse. Yet while mass institutionalization is clearly hazardous, the shift to decentralized, community-based care has not worked for many people. Kids in the foster-care system suffer much higher rates of abuse than other children; parents of adult children with Down syndrome fear their children will outlive them, then be cast adrift in an uncaring society. The penal system houses more men and women grappling with mental illness and substance abuse than do psychiatric hospitals. Hundreds of thousands of people with serious mental illnesses are living on the streets rather than receiving treatment to help them live with self-respect and physical safety.

America's affluent peer countries provide comprehensive safety nets that protect vulnerable populations and help families and communities care for them with dignity and human security. These nations provide supportive housing, medical care, education and job assistance, and income supplements. America, too, can provide stronger safety nets to protect human dignity, minimize stigmatization, and extend to the disabled or dispossessed the tools to build lives of meaning and value. The care we provide our most vulnerable citizens is not the only measure of a great and civilized nation, but it is an extremely important one.

> The care we provide our most vulnerable citizens is not the only measure of a great and civilized nation, but it is an extremely important one.

PART 5

Human Development Indicators

The following indicator tables were prepared using official U.S. government data to the maximum extent possible. In the case of the cross-country comparisons, all data are from international organizations recognized as data providers for those indicators, and all data are standardized in order to ensure comparability.

This process of standardization is time consuming, and there is typically a delay of two to three years. For every indicator, we have tried to present the most updated data. In some cases, one column will contain a mix of years due to problems with data availability.

AMERICAN HUMAN DEVELOPMENT INDEX
by Gender, Race/Ethnicity, and Region

RANK / AMERICAN HD INDEX GROUPING	HD INDEX	LIFE EXPECTANCY AT BIRTH (years)	LESS THAN HIGH SCHOOL (%)	AT LEAST HIGH SCHOOL DIPLOMA (%)	AT LEAST BACHELOR'S DEGREE (%)	GRADUATE DEGREE (%)	EDUCATIONAL ATTAINMENT SCORE	SCHOOL ENROLLMENT (%)	MEDIAN EARNINGS (2005 dollars)	HEALTH INDEX	EDUCATION INDEX	INCOME INDEX
United States	5.06	78.0	15.8	84.2	27.2	10.0	1.214	86.8	27,299	5.00	5.04	5.14
GENDER												
1 Males	5.04	75.4	16.2	83.8	28.5	10.8	1.231	83.8	32,850	3.90	4.79	6.43
2 Females	5.01	80.5	15.4	84.6	26.0	9.2	1.198	90.0	22,000	6.05	5.32	3.65
RACE/ETHNICITY												
1 Asian	7.53	86.3	14.4	85.6	49.1	19.9	1.546	102.3	31,518	8.48	7.98	6.14
2 White	5.51	78.2	11.0	89.0	30.0	11.0	1.300	87.7	30,485	5.10	5.53	5.91
3 Hispanic/Latino	3.97	82.1	40.5	59.5	12.2	3.9	0.755	78.8	20,255	6.71	2.12	3.07
4 American Indian/Alaska Native	3.89	78.0	23.7	76.3	13.6	4.5	0.944	82.4	21,037	4.98	3.35	3.34
5 Black/African American	3.81	73.0	20.1	79.9	17.3	5.9	1.031	89.5	23,025	2.93	4.53	3.96
GENDER AND RACE/ETHNICITY												
1 Asian males	7.64	83.6	11.7	88.3	53.1	24.3	1.656	98.8	37,035	7.33	8.34	7.26
2 Asian females	7.30	88.8	16.9	83.1	45.6	16.0	1.447	106.0	26,138	9.50	7.54	4.84
3 White males	5.55	75.7	11.3	88.7	31.7	12.1	1.326	84.7	37,269	4.05	5.30	7.30
4 White females	5.32	80.7	10.7	89.3	28.3	10.1	1.277	90.9	23,388	6.12	5.78	4.07
5 Black/African American females	4.18	76.3	19.8	80.2	17.8	6.3	1.044	92.7	20,915	4.30	4.94	3.30
6 American Indian/Alaska Native females	4.17	81.1	22.7	77.3	23.0	4.1	1.044	85.3	17,589	6.28	4.12	2.10
7 Hispanic/Latino females	3.98	85.0	39.3	60.7	12.7	3.9	0.772	81.7	16,147	7.92	2.51	1.50
8 American Indian/Alaska Native males	3.76	74.7	24.7	75.3	21.1	4.9	1.013	79.5	24,315	3.62	3.34	4.34
9 Hispanic/Latino males	3.67	79.1	41.7	58.3	11.8	3.9	0.739	76.1	22,471	5.46	1.75	3.79
10 Black/African American males	3.45	69.4	20.5	79.5	16.6	5.4	1.015	86.4	26,086	1.43	4.11	4.83
REGION												
1 Northeast	5.72	78.9	13.8	86.2	31.3	12.6	1.301	89.6	31,037	5.38	5.74	6.03
2 West	5.31	79.2	16.6	83.4	28.7	10.1	1.222	87.5	27,783	5.50	5.15	5.27
3 Midwest	5.04	78.0	13.0	87.0	25.5	9.0	1.215	86.9	27,015	4.99	5.05	5.07
4 South	4.64	76.9	18.0	82.0	25.0	9.0	1.160	85.3	25,865	4.52	4.64	4.77

A Note on Racial and Ethnic Groups

These indicator tables draw on different data sets, which categorize racial and ethnic groups differently. For instance, some sources collect information about "African Americans," whereas others collect information on "African Americans and blacks" (to reflect Americans of Caribbean heritage). Similarly, some sources collect data on "Asians," while others include "Asians and Pacific Islanders." Clearly there is significant overlap among these categories, but they are not exactly the same. For the sake of consistency, we have used Census Bureau categories throughout the Indicator Tables. For any indicator whose source is not the Census Bureau, please consult the indicator source (listed at the end of the table) for a precise definition of the ethnic groups used.

Symbols and Acronyms

...   Data not available

—   Not applicable

ACS   American Community Survey

CDC   Centers for Disease Control and Prevention

EPA   Environmental Protection Agency

FBI   Federal Bureau of Investigation

NHCS National Center for Health Statistics

USDA United States Department of Agriculture

AMERICAN HUMAN DEVELOPMENT INDEX
by State

RANK	STATE	HD INDEX	LIFE EXPECTANCY AT BIRTH (years)	LESS THAN HIGH SCHOOL (%)	AT LEAST HIGH SCHOOL DIPLOMA (%)	AT LEAST BACHELOR'S DEGREE (%)	GRADUATE DEGREE (%)	EDUCATIONAL ATTAINMENT SCORE	SCHOOL ENROLLMENT (%)	MEDIAN EARNINGS (2005 dollars)	HEALTH INDEX	EDUCATION INDEX	INCOME INDEX
1	Connecticut	6.37	80.1	12.1	87.9	34.9	15.0	1.378	91.4	35,387	5.89	6.28	6.94
2	Massachusetts	6.27	79.8	12.0	88.0	36.9	15.7	1.406	92.4	33,544	5.73	6.52	6.57
3	District of Columbia	6.14	73.8	16.4	83.6	45.3	25.2	1.540	99.8	36,948	3.23	7.94	7.24
3	New Jersey	6.14	79.2	13.7	86.3	34.2	12.5	1.330	90.5	35,468	5.49	5.97	6.96
5	Maryland	5.99	78.0	13.0	87.0	34.5	15.2	1.368	89.9	35,144	4.99	6.08	6.89
6	Hawaii	5.82	81.7	11.9	88.1	27.9	9.1	1.251	87.5	29,287	6.55	5.28	5.63
7	New York	5.81	79.6	15.7	84.3	31.3	13.4	1.290	90.1	30,983	5.67	5.75	6.02
8	New Hampshire	5.80	79.5	10.1	89.9	31.8	11.7	1.334	88.0	31,054	5.64	5.71	6.04
9	Minnesota	5.72	80.5	9.1	90.9	30.7	9.7	1.314	86.1	29,687	6.03	5.40	5.72
9	Rhode Island	5.72	79.2	16.5	83.5	29.3	11.5	1.243	91.6	30,742	5.50	5.70	5.97
11	California	5.62	79.7	19.9	80.1	29.5	10.6	1.202	90.2	30,018	5.70	5.36	5.80
12	Colorado	5.59	79.1	11.3	88.7	35.5	12.3	1.365	86.0	29,438	5.48	5.63	5.67
13	Virginia	5.56	78.1	14.6	85.4	33.2	13.4	1.320	87.5	31,108	5.03	5.59	6.05
14	Illinois	5.42	78.1	14.3	85.7	29.2	10.9	1.259	89.3	29,598	5.04	5.52	5.70
14	Vermont	5.42	79.6	10.5	89.5	32.5	12.3	1.343	87.9	26,260	5.65	5.74	4.87
16	Washington	5.41	79.4	11.2	88.8	30.1	10.5	1.294	83.9	29,052	5.58	5.07	5.58
17	Alaska	5.35	78.5	9.0	91.0	27.3	10.1	1.284	83.1	30,388	5.22	4.94	5.89
18	Delaware	5.22	77.4	14.4	85.6	27.6	11.1	1.243	84.8	30,702	4.76	4.95	5.96
19	Wisconsin	5.20	79.0	11.2	88.8	25.0	8.1	1.218	86.6	27,387	5.41	5.03	5.17
20	Michigan	5.13	77.7	13.0	87.0	24.7	9.5	1.212	89.5	27,468	4.86	5.33	5.19
21	Iowa	5.03	79.3	10.4	89.6	23.8	7.3	1.207	85.3	25,618	5.55	4.85	4.70
21	Pennsylvania	5.03	77.7	13.3	86.7	25.7	9.8	1.221	86.7	27,395	4.87	5.06	5.17
23	Nebraska	5.00	79.2	10.5	89.5	27.3	8.5	1.253	85.1	24,865	5.48	5.02	4.50
24	Florida	4.96	78.5	15.4	84.6	25.1	8.8	1.185	86.7	25,951	5.19	4.90	4.79
25	Kansas	4.93	78.0	11.3	88.7	28.2	9.6	1.265	86.6	25,038	4.99	5.24	4.54
26	Arizona	4.90	78.2	16.2	83.8	25.6	9.3	1.187	83.9	26,764	5.08	4.60	5.01
26	North Dakota	4.90	79.8	11.8	88.2	25.5	6.7	1.204	84.6	23,789	5.75	4.75	4.19
26	Oregon	4.90	78.7	12.5	87.5	27.7	10.0	1.251	84.3	24,825	5.27	4.93	4.48
29	Maine	4.86	78.1	11.0	89.0	25.6	8.6	1.232	86.3	24,844	5.03	5.06	4.49
29	Utah	4.86	79.5	9.9	90.1	27.9	8.7	1.267	83.8	23,144	5.63	4.95	4.00
31	Ohio	4.79	77.1	13.7	86.3	23.3	8.5	1.181	85.7	26,706	4.61	4.78	4.99
32	Georgia	4.74	76.2	17.2	82.8	27.1	9.5	1.194	85.6	27,320	4.26	4.82	5.15
33	Indiana	4.64	76.9	14.7	85.3	21.3	7.7	1.143	84.4	26,442	4.56	4.45	4.92
34	North Carolina	4.61	76.6	17.7	82.3	25.1	8.0	1.155	87.5	25,111	4.43	4.85	4.56
35	Texas	4.57	77.6	21.2	78.8	25.1	8.2	1.121	84.5	24,952	4.83	4.36	4.52
36	Missouri	4.54	76.8	15.0	85.0	24.0	8.6	1.176	83.2	25,422	4.51	4.47	4.65
36	Nevada	4.54	76.3	17.2	82.8	20.6	6.6	1.100	81.0	28,486	4.30	3.89	5.44
38	South Dakota	4.53	78.6	11.4	88.6	24.7	7.0	1.204	80.9	23,110	5.25	4.34	3.99
38	Wyoming	4.53	77.8	8.7	91.3	23.2	7.7	1.222	81.7	23,752	4.92	4.51	4.18
40	New Mexico	4.49	77.7	18.0	82.0	25.1	10.9	1.180	87.0	22,131	4.89	4.91	3.69
41	Idaho	4.37	78.9	13.3	86.7	23.3	7.4	1.174	80.2	21,888	5.36	4.13	3.61
42	Montana	4.34	77.9	9.3	90.7	26.5	8.0	1.252	81.2	21,472	4.94	4.59	3.48
43	South Carolina	4.27	75.8	18.3	81.7	23.0	7.9	1.126	83.8	24,532	4.10	4.31	4.40
44	Kentucky	4.12	75.5	21.0	79.0	19.3	7.8	1.061	83.8	24,435	3.97	4.02	4.38
45	Tennessee	4.10	75.3	18.8	81.2	21.8	7.6	1.106	80.9	24,984	3.87	3.90	4.53
46	Oklahoma	4.02	75.1	15.7	84.3	22.4	7.2	1.139	83.2	22,901	3.81	4.31	3.93
47	Alabama	3.98	74.6	19.7	80.3	21.4	7.9	1.096	83.4	23,817	3.60	4.14	4.20
48	Arkansas	3.86	75.5	19.0	81.0	18.9	6.3	1.062	82.8	22,122	3.97	3.91	3.69
49	Louisiana	3.85	74.0	19.5	80.5	20.6	7.1	1.082	83.7	23,467	3.34	4.11	4.09
50	West Virginia	3.84	75.3	18.8	81.2	16.9	6.8	1.049	82.1	22,691	3.89	3.79	3.86
51	Mississippi	3.58	73.9	21.5	78.5	18.7	6.5	1.036	82.6	22,042	3.28	3.79	3.66

AMERICAN HUMAN DEVELOPMENT INDEX
by Congressional District

RANK	CONGRESSIONAL DISTRICT	HD INDEX	LIFE EXPECTANCY AT BIRTH (years)	LESS THAN HIGH SCHOOL (%)	AT LEAST HIGH SCHOOL DIPLOMA (%)	AT LEAST BACHELOR'S DEGREE (%)	GRADUATE DEGREE (%)	EDUCATIONAL ATTAINMENT SCORE	SCHOOL ENROLLMENT (%)	MEDIAN EARNINGS (2005 dollars)	HEALTH INDEX	EDUCATION INDEX	INCOME INDEX
1	CD 14, New York	8.17	81.6	9.6	90.4	62.6	27.3	1.804	94.6	51,139	6.49	8.52	9.50
2	CD 8, Virginia	8.14	82.9	9.9	90.1	58.2	28.7	1.770	96.7	46,031	7.05	8.61	8.77
3	CD 14, California	8.08	82.1	9.4	90.6	56.3	27.9	1.748	98.2	46,539	6.71	8.68	8.84
4	CD 48, California	7.89	81.6	6.2	93.8	51.9	20.5	1.662	99.2	45,999	6.51	8.41	8.76
5	CD 30, California	7.78	79.9	5.1	95.0	56.8	24.0	1.756	102.6	45,128	5.80	8.92	8.63
6	CD 11, Virginia	7.65	81.6	7.4	92.6	52.2	22.9	1.677	93.2	45,119	6.51	7.81	8.63
7	CD 8, New York	7.60	80.7	12.6	87.4	55.3	25.7	1.684	96.0	44,340	6.14	8.16	8.51
8	CD 8, Maryland	7.58	82.7	11.5	88.5	55.5	29.8	1.739	93.4	39,158	6.97	8.11	7.64
9	CD 12, California	7.50	81.7	10.5	89.5	45.6	15.8	1.509	103.9	41,947	6.56	7.82	8.12
10	CD 15, California	7.43	82.4	12.5	87.4	43.8	17.4	1.487	96.1	42,135	6.84	7.29	8.15
11	CD 7, New Jersey	7.42	80.6	8.1	91.9	47.6	18.9	1.584	94.7	44,838	6.10	7.56	8.58
12	CD 11, New Jersey	7.39	79.9	7.0	93.0	49.8	20.2	1.630	94.2	45,410	5.77	7.71	8.67
12	CD 12, New Jersey	7.39	80.2	7.4	92.5	48.7	21.2	1.626	95.6	43,714	5.90	7.85	8.41
14	CD 18, New York	7.26	81.3	11.9	88.0	48.4	24.5	1.611	93.1	40,813	6.36	7.50	7.93
15	CD 5, New Jersey	7.19	80.9	7.7	92.3	42.5	16.1	1.509	94.4	42,204	6.19	7.20	8.16
16	CD 8, California	7.16	80.8	16.3	83.7	48.9	18.2	1.509	111.6	38,434	6.15	7.82	7.52
17	CD 3, New York	7.07	80.8	8.1	91.8	34.6	14.5	1.410	96.0	41,761	6.18	6.93	8.09
18	CD 42, California	7.06	80.1	8.7	91.2	40.3	14.0	1.457	96.7	41,577	5.89	7.22	8.06
18	CD 9, Michigan	7.06	79.5	7.6	92.4	46.9	20.8	1.600	95.3	40,365	5.62	7.70	7.86
20	CD 46, California	7.05	81.2	12.4	87.6	39.6	15.4	1.426	98.3	38,634	6.33	7.26	7.55
21	CD 4, Connecticut	7.03	81.1	11.5	88.5	44.7	19.0	1.521	92.9	39,550	6.29	7.08	7.71
22	CD 6, Colorado	6.99	80.8	4.7	95.3	47.4	16.0	1.586	91.1	39,101	6.16	7.17	7.63
23	CD 36, California	6.95	79.9	13.9	86.1	41.9	15.2	1.432	101.9	38,757	5.80	7.48	7.57
24	CD 6, Georgia	6.93	78.3	5.4	94.6	53.7	18.3	1.667	93.7	40,246	5.13	7.82	7.83
25	CD 13, Illinois	6.92	79.9	6.5	93.5	45.2	16.5	1.552	93.0	39,755	5.79	7.23	7.75
26	CD 10, Illinois	6.89	78.9	8.8	91.1	51.8	21.8	1.648	93.7	38,667	5.38	7.73	7.56
27	CD 10, Virginia	6.87	80.3	9.5	90.5	48.3	19.4	1.582	85.8	41,644	5.97	6.56	8.07
28	CD 7, Washington	6.82	80.9	9.2	90.8	49.2	18.7	1.587	98.5	32,094	6.20	8.00	6.27
29	CD 19, New York	6.81	79.9	9.5	90.5	37.3	16.2	1.440	93.9	40,103	5.79	6.83	7.81
30	CD 3, Minnesota	6.80	80.5	5.3	94.7	43.7	13.5	1.519	93.1	36,871	6.06	7.10	7.23
31	CD 7, Massachusetts	6.78	80.6	11.6	88.5	43.0	19.6	1.510	94.7	35,770	6.08	7.23	7.02
32	CD 50, California	6.77	80.1	11.0	89.0	44.4	18.6	1.519	94.9	36,345	5.88	7.29	7.13
33	CD 13, California	6.76	80.2	14.2	85.8	35.8	13.2	1.349	94.5	40,430	5.91	6.50	7.87
34	CD 4, New York	6.73	81.4	12.6	87.5	35.6	15.0	1.380	93.0	37,448	6.40	6.47	7.34
35	CD 6, Massachusetts	6.70	80.3	8.6	91.4	39.3	16.1	1.469	93.6	36,754	5.96	6.93	7.21
36	CD 4, North Carolina	6.67	78.8	9.3	90.7	51.6	21.6	1.638	97.4	33,520	5.34	8.10	6.57
37	CD 9, New York	6.65	81.3	13.7	86.3	34.9	13.0	1.340	95.9	35,553	6.38	6.61	6.98
38	CD 10, California	6.61	80.0	9.7	90.3	39.4	15.2	1.448	88.9	39,252	5.85	6.31	7.66
38	CD 24, California	6.61	81.0	11.2	88.8	34.0	12.7	1.355	94.5	36,102	6.24	6.52	7.08
38	CD 8, Washington	6.61	80.3	6.4	93.6	40.8	14.0	1.484	87.9	38,488	5.94	6.37	7.53
41	CD 6, California	6.59	81.1	10.5	89.6	42.1	16.2	1.478	91.1	34,591	6.30	6.69	6.78
41	CD 4, Massachusetts	6.59	79.7	14.2	85.8	40.6	19.6	1.460	93.9	36,488	5.69	6.92	7.16
43	CD 16, California	6.58	82.4	21.3	78.7	33.4	11.4	1.235	93.3	35,902	6.84	5.86	7.04
43	CD 9, Massachusetts	6.58	79.7	10.7	89.3	38.2	15.8	1.432	94.2	36,636	5.71	6.84	7.18
45	CD 2, New York	6.52	79.3	10.5	89.5	34.1	15.0	1.387	92.3	38,858	5.55	6.41	7.59
46	CD 10, Massachusetts	6.51	80.3	7.3	92.7	35.8	12.9	1.415	93.0	35,329	5.98	6.62	6.93
46	CD 9, New Jersey	6.51	81.3	15.0	85.0	34.3	12.2	1.314	92.4	35,919	6.38	6.10	7.05
48	CD 9, Illinois	6.48	77.8	10.3	89.6	45.9	19.4	1.551	98.9	33,820	4.92	7.88	6.63
48	CD 1, New York	6.48	79.2	9.6	90.4	32.3	14.8	1.376	91.3	39,502	5.48	6.26	7.71
50	CD 5, Massachusetts	6.47	80.6	12.7	87.2	36.4	16.5	1.402	90.4	36,053	6.07	6.27	7.07
51	CD 26, California	6.46	78.6	11.3	88.7	36.0	13.5	1.381	96.7	37,047	5.25	6.88	7.26

AMERICAN HUMAN DEVELOPMENT INDEX
by Congressional District *continued*

RANK	CONGRESSIONAL DISTRICT	HD INDEX	LIFE EXPECTANCY AT BIRTH (years)	LESS THAN HIGH SCHOOL (%)	AT LEAST HIGH SCHOOL DIPLOMA (%)	AT LEAST BACHELOR'S DEGREE (%)	GRADUATE DEGREE (%)	EDUCATIONAL ATTAINMENT SCORE	SCHOOL ENROLLMENT (%)	MEDIAN EARNINGS (2005 dollars)	HEALTH INDEX	EDUCATION INDEX	INCOME INDEX
52	CD 21, Texas	6.43	78.9	6.3	93.6	45.4	16.4	1.555	94.6	33,095	5.38	7.42	6.48
53	CD 29, California	6.41	79.9	17.0	83.1	38.1	14.2	1.353	103.3	32,194	5.80	7.13	6.29
53	CD 7, Texas	6.41	77.4	9.7	90.4	49.2	18.8	1.582	90.2	37,993	4.75	7.05	7.44
55	CD 9, California	6.39	80.2	16.4	83.5	41.0	18.6	1.433	96.7	31,594	5.91	7.12	6.16
56	CD 52, California	6.35	80.1	10.3	89.7	33.1	12.6	1.353	92.0	35,267	5.88	6.24	6.92
56	CD 6, Illinois	6.35	79.9	11.8	88.2	34.9	12.9	1.362	92.9	35,208	5.78	6.38	6.91
58	CD 4, Maryland	6.34	79.4	13.3	86.6	34.0	15.2	1.360	91.8	36,544	5.60	6.25	7.17
59	CD 5, Wisconsin	6.33	79.7	6.2	93.7	38.5	12.6	1.449	90.5	34,722	5.70	6.50	6.81
60	CD 2, Connecticut	6.32	80.3	9.5	90.5	31.9	13.4	1.358	90.5	35,313	5.94	6.09	6.93
61	CD 7, Pennsylvania	6.29	78.4	9.4	90.5	39.9	16.1	1.466	91.2	35,992	5.15	6.65	7.06
62	CD 3, Connecticut	6.28	79.7	12.3	87.7	32.4	15.7	1.357	92.2	34,874	5.72	6.28	6.84
63	CD 2, Minnesota	6.27	80.8	6.7	93.3	34.6	10.0	1.379	86.7	35,019	6.16	5.76	6.87
64	CD 53, California	6.26	80.1	15.5	84.4	38.5	14.9	1.380	98.3	30,221	5.88	7.05	5.85
64	CD 1, Washington	6.26	79.7	7.8	92.2	38.9	13.4	1.444	86.9	35,606	5.71	6.08	6.99
66	CD 8, Illinois	6.25	79.3	10.2	89.7	35.8	12.3	1.379	90.7	35,672	5.54	6.21	7.00
66	CD 5, New York	6.25	81.7	18.8	81.2	37.8	15.9	1.349	91.5	31,008	6.56	6.16	6.03
68	CD 8, Massachusetts	6.24	78.9	16.1	83.9	43.8	21.6	1.493	97.5	30,313	5.39	7.47	5.87
68	CD 6, New Jersey	6.24	80.1	13.4	86.6	33.8	13.0	1.334	90.1	35,240	5.86	5.94	6.91
70	CD 22, Florida	6.23	79.9	10.6	89.4	36.3	13.1	1.387	93.9	32,150	5.81	6.60	6.28
71	CD 5, Maryland	6.20	77.2	10.3	89.7	31.5	12.9	1.342	92.3	39,714	4.65	6.22	7.74
71	CD 6, Pennsylvania	6.20	79.5	10.2	89.8	38.3	15.3	1.434	88.3	34,734	5.62	6.18	6.81
73	CD 1, Connecticut	6.19	79.6	13.8	86.2	31.4	12.8	1.304	91.8	35,097	5.68	6.00	6.89
73	CD 2, Missouri	6.19	78.6	7.5	92.6	40.4	14.3	1.472	90.2	34,457	5.24	6.56	6.76
73	CD 8, Pennsylvania	6.19	78.8	7.6	92.3	33.6	12.6	1.387	91.6	35,137	5.32	6.35	6.89
76	CD 1, Hawaii	6.18	82.2	12.5	87.5	31.1	10.2	1.288	92.2	30,080	6.74	5.97	5.82
77	CD 3, Maryland	6.17	76.6	12.3	87.7	40.8	17.8	1.463	92.4	37,322	4.42	6.77	7.31
77	CD 3, Massachusetts	6.17	79.3	13.0	86.9	35.1	13.3	1.354	92.8	33,909	5.54	6.33	6.65
77	CD 3, New Jersey	6.17	79.2	9.7	90.3	30.8	10.2	1.313	90.8	35,998	5.51	5.93	7.06
77	CD 3, Texas	6.17	79.5	11.9	88.1	42.5	13.6	1.441	86.4	35,124	5.61	6.00	6.89
81	CD 11, California	6.14	78.6	13.4	86.6	31.6	10.3	1.285	89.2	38,561	5.24	5.62	7.54
81	DD District of Columbia	6.14	73.8	16.4	83.5	45.2	25.2	1.540	99.8	36,948	3.23	7.94	7.24
81	CD 13, New York	6.14	79.0	14.8	85.2	27.9	11.3	1.244	93.6	36,031	5.42	5.93	7.07
84	CD 4, Minnesota	6.13	80.0	9.2	90.8	37.1	14.0	1.419	91.3	31,334	5.85	6.45	6.10
85	CD 20, Florida	6.10	79.2	10.2	89.8	35.4	13.7	1.388	93.3	32,211	5.48	6.53	6.29
86	CD 5, Connecticut	6.07	79.9	13.4	86.5	34.4	14.1	1.351	89.7	32,918	5.81	5.97	6.44
87	CD 7, Illinois	6.05	77.8	18.1	81.9	38.0	17.9	1.379	93.2	34,366	4.92	6.48	6.74
87	CD 5, Minnesota	6.05	80.5	11.2	88.8	39.8	13.5	1.420	91.0	29,468	6.06	6.43	5.67
89	CD 3, Kansas	6.04	79.2	8.2	91.8	43.4	14.7	1.499	89.9	30,738	5.51	6.65	5.97
90	CD 11, Michigan	6.03	76.3	9.1	90.8	34.7	13.9	1.395	93.2	36,970	4.29	6.55	7.25
91	CD 5, Arizona	5.98	78.6	7.4	92.6	41.0	15.4	1.491	89.9	31,128	5.27	6.61	6.05
92	CD 7, California	5.97	79.8	15.3	84.7	25.6	7.1	1.174	94.0	33,257	5.74	5.67	6.51
92	CD 11, New York	5.97	80.0	16.6	83.5	32.0	12.7	1.281	94.8	30,327	5.82	6.23	5.87
94	CD 3, California	5.96	78.4	9.8	90.2	29.9	9.3	1.294	91.6	34,618	5.15	5.93	6.79
94	CD 4, California	5.96	79.8	9.1	90.9	30.0	9.1	1.299	92.4	31,430	5.73	6.04	6.12
94	CD 4, New Jersey	5.96	79.7	12.8	87.2	29.0	9.4	1.256	88.4	34,500	5.71	5.41	6.77
97	CD 40, California	5.95	81.6	18.4	81.6	30.0	9.0	1.207	91.6	30,066	6.51	5.54	5.81
97	CD 7, Georgia	5.95	78.3	11.1	88.9	35.3	10.1	1.343	88.9	35,119	5.11	5.85	6.89
99	CD 2, Wisconsin	5.93	80.1	8.8	91.2	34.9	13.2	1.393	91.2	29,060	5.89	6.32	5.58
100	CD 2, Colorado	5.91	79.2	8.7	91.2	42.0	14.7	1.481	86.4	31,146	5.48	6.18	6.06
100	CD 6, New York	5.91	81.9	21.0	79.0	21.8	7.0	1.079	93.3	30,598	6.62	5.17	5.93
102	CD 8, Michigan	5.90	79.1	8.4	91.5	31.4	11.7	1.348	92.9	30,439	5.48	6.32	5.90

AMERICAN HUMAN DEVELOPMENT INDEX
by Congressional District *continued*

RANK	CONGRESSIONAL DISTRICT	HD INDEX	LIFE EXPECTANCY AT BIRTH (years)	LESS THAN HIGH SCHOOL (%)	AT LEAST HIGH SCHOOL DIPLOMA (%)	AT LEAST BACHELOR'S DEGREE (%)	GRADUATE DEGREE (%)	EDUCATIONAL ATTAINMENT SCORE	SCHOOL ENROLLMENT (%)	MEDIAN EARNINGS (2005 dollars)	HEALTH INDEX	EDUCATION INDEX	INCOME INDEX
103	CD 1, New Hampshire	5.83	79.6	9.5	90.5	31.7	11.9	1.341	87.9	31,394	5.66	5.73	6.11
104	CD 6, Minnesota	5.82	80.5	7.7	92.4	28.4	8.1	1.288	84.7	32,311	6.02	5.14	6.31
104	CD 13, Pennsylvania	5.82	77.0	11.1	88.9	32.1	13.1	1.341	92.4	34,058	4.57	6.23	6.68
106	CD 17, New York	5.78	79.5	18.7	81.3	30.3	13.2	1.248	91.1	31,198	5.61	5.67	6.07
107	CD 15, New York	5.77	81.4	27.1	72.8	33.9	15.8	1.227	93.0	27,210	6.40	5.79	5.12
107	CD 1, Rhode Island	5.77	79.3	17.0	83.0	29.6	12.0	1.246	92.7	30,524	5.55	5.84	5.92
109	CD 5, Illinois	5.75	77.8	17.0	83.0	38.2	15.0	1.362	90.7	31,779	4.92	6.13	6.20
109	CD 2, New Hampshire	5.75	79.5	10.8	89.2	31.9	11.5	1.326	88.2	30,573	5.62	5.69	5.93
111	CD 15, Michigan	5.73	77.6	11.6	88.4	30.1	14.1	1.326	95.9	30,083	4.82	6.55	5.82
112	CD 19, Florida	5.71	80.0	11.5	88.5	29.4	10.4	1.284	87.8	30,060	5.85	5.47	5.81
112	CD 22, Texas	5.71	78.1	13.8	86.2	34.5	11.8	1.324	88.5	32,496	5.06	5.71	6.35
114	CD 1, Oregon	5.68	79.6	9.5	90.5	36.0	13.3	1.399	86.5	28,946	5.68	5.83	5.55
115	CD 25, New York	5.67	78.9	10.7	89.4	29.7	12.0	1.310	90.8	29,731	5.36	5.91	5.74
115	CD 2, Rhode Island	5.67	79.1	16.0	83.9	29.0	10.9	1.240	90.4	30,901	5.45	5.56	6.00
117	CD 24, Texas	5.66	77.8	13.9	86.2	36.1	11.1	1.332	89.3	31,978	4.91	5.84	6.24
118	CD 9, North Carolina	5.65	77.2	11.4	88.7	38.1	11.0	1.376	88.9	32,225	4.65	5.99	6.29
119	CD 6, Arizona	5.63	78.5	12.3	87.6	27.7	9.0	1.244	88.5	32,319	5.20	5.37	6.31
119	CD 4, Georgia	5.63	78.3	12.4	87.6	37.1	14.9	1.397	88.7	29,562	5.12	6.07	5.70
121	CD 27, California	5.62	79.9	20.6	79.3	28.7	8.6	1.167	91.4	29,654	5.80	5.34	5.72
121	CD 1, Maryland	5.62	78.1	11.2	88.9	30.9	12.2	1.318	87.4	32,043	5.04	5.57	6.25
123	CD 18, Pennsylvania	5.61	77.8	7.9	92.2	32.0	11.9	1.360	90.4	30,041	4.93	6.08	5.81
123	CD 1, Virginia	5.61	78.8	11.9	88.1	30.0	11.5	1.295	85.6	31,924	5.34	5.27	6.23
125	CD 6, Maryland	5.59	78.5	11.6	88.4	28.4	10.5	1.272	85.9	32,568	5.20	5.20	6.37
125	CD 10, Texas	5.59	78.2	13.1	86.9	35.1	10.6	1.326	87.4	31,375	5.07	5.60	6.11
127	CD 12, Michigan	5.58	78.7	15.0	85.0	21.7	7.3	1.140	93.8	30,595	5.30	5.49	5.93
127	CD 7, Virginia	5.58	77.5	12.6	87.4	36.6	12.8	1.369	86.7	31,935	4.81	5.72	6.23
129	CD 5, Indiana	5.55	77.8	8.9	91.1	34.0	12.0	1.372	84.6	31,995	4.92	5.49	6.24
129	CD 12, Ohio	5.55	77.2	9.2	90.8	37.1	12.8	1.407	86.6	31,402	4.66	5.88	6.11
131	CD 14, Illinois	5.54	79.4	14.6	85.4	29.1	9.3	1.237	87.8	29,947	5.59	5.26	5.79
131	CD 1, Massachusetts	5.54	79.3	11.8	88.2	29.7	12.1	1.300	87.6	29,112	5.53	5.51	5.59
131	CD 8, New Jersey	5.54	78.4	20.7	79.4	31.2	11.5	1.221	89.0	31,608	5.15	5.31	6.16
134	CD 3, Arizona	5.53	78.6	9.4	90.6	30.6	11.1	1.322	85.4	30,679	5.27	5.36	5.95
134	CD 5, Georgia	5.53	77.2	15.1	84.9	43.6	16.5	1.450	85.4	30,846	4.65	5.93	5.99
134	CD 14, Ohio	5.53	78.0	11.2	88.8	30.3	10.7	1.299	89.1	30,552	5.01	5.67	5.92
137	CD 15, Pennsylvania	5.52	79.4	13.1	87.0	26.6	9.6	1.231	86.5	30,275	5.60	5.08	5.86
138	CD 2, Virginia	5.51	77.9	10.5	89.5	28.9	10.0	1.283	89.9	30,375	4.97	5.69	5.88
139	CD 2, Nebraska	5.50	78.7	9.7	90.3	35.7	11.3	1.373	88.7	27,741	5.29	5.95	5.25
140	CD 2, Hawaii	5.49	81.3	11.3	88.6	24.5	8.0	1.212	83.8	28,371	6.37	4.70	5.41
141	CD 2, Massachusetts	5.47	78.6	15.0	85.0	27.3	10.8	1.232	88.1	30,474	5.25	5.27	5.91
141	CD 4, Pennsylvania	5.47	77.6	8.7	91.3	31.4	11.2	1.339	89.4	29,453	4.85	5.88	5.67
143	CD 9, Florida	5.45	77.7	11.4	88.7	29.2	10.1	1.278	89.1	30,458	4.88	5.58	5.90
144	CD 8, Arizona	5.43	78.0	9.0	91.0	34.0	13.6	1.386	90.8	26,868	4.99	6.25	5.03
144	CD 3, Iowa	5.43	79.3	10.0	90.0	26.7	7.7	1.245	86.6	29,181	5.52	5.15	5.61
144	CD 26, New York	5.43	78.5	9.8	90.1	27.5	11.7	1.294	88.5	28,784	5.21	5.59	5.51
147	CD (at Large), Vermont	5.42	79.6	10.5	89.5	32.5	12.3	1.343	87.9	26,260	5.65	5.74	4.87
148	CD 21, New York	5.41	78.2	10.9	89.1	28.6	13.3	1.310	86.4	29,664	5.10	5.42	5.72
149	CD 1, Colorado	5.40	77.7	17.9	82.1	38.9	15.3	1.363	85.6	29,842	4.87	5.57	5.76
150	CD 1, Maine	5.39	79.0	8.8	91.2	31.3	10.5	1.330	87.9	26,976	5.42	5.68	5.06
150	CD 26, Texas	5.39	78.5	13.7	86.2	31.0	9.0	1.264	87.1	29,517	5.19	5.30	5.69
152	CD 25, Florida	5.36	80.0	20.2	79.8	24.0	7.5	1.113	92.9	26,719	5.83	5.27	4.99
152	CD 1, Wisconsin	5.36	78.0	10.6	89.4	23.0	7.2	1.197	88.5	30,638	4.99	5.15	5.94

AMERICAN HUMAN DEVELOPMENT INDEX
by Congressional District *continued*

RANK	CONGRESSIONAL DISTRICT	HD INDEX	LIFE EXPECTANCY AT BIRTH (years)	LESS THAN HIGH SCHOOL (%)	AT LEAST HIGH SCHOOL DIPLOMA (%)	AT LEAST BACHELOR'S DEGREE (%)	GRADUATE DEGREE (%)	EDUCATIONAL ATTAINMENT SCORE	SCHOOL ENROLLMENT (%)	MEDIAN EARNINGS (2005 dollars)	HEALTH INDEX	EDUCATION INDEX	INCOME INDEX
154	CD (at Large), Alaska	5.35	78.5	9.0	91.1	27.3	10.1	1.284	83.1	30,388	5.22	4.94	5.89
155	CD 33, California	5.34	79.9	23.9	76.1	32.1	11.1	1.194	93.9	24,844	5.80	5.74	4.49
155	CD 5, Colorado	5.34	78.3	8.4	91.6	32.2	12.0	1.357	89.5	26,448	5.13	5.98	4.92
155	CD 10, Michigan	5.34	78.4	12.1	87.9	19.6	6.9	1.144	88.3	30,680	5.18	4.89	5.95
155	CD 7, New York	5.34	79.5	23.2	76.8	22.1	8.0	1.069	89.6	29,423	5.64	4.71	5.66
159	CD 44, California	5.33	79.1	20.4	79.5	24.9	8.2	1.127	87.7	29,975	5.44	4.75	5.79
160	CD 7, Colorado	5.32	79.4	14.9	85.1	27.4	9.0	1.214	82.4	30,063	5.59	4.55	5.81
160	CD 10, New York	5.32	80.0	24.3	75.7	22.2	8.9	1.068	87.2	29,579	5.82	4.44	5.70
162	CD 2, Illinois	5.31	77.9	15.4	84.6	21.2	7.0	1.128	94.6	28,588	4.94	5.52	5.46
162	CD 20, New York	5.31	78.7	11.4	88.5	27.2	11.9	1.277	85.2	28,847	5.27	5.14	5.53
164	CD 17, California	5.29	81.0	24.3	75.6	27.4	10.4	1.136	89.4	25,343	6.26	4.98	4.63
164	CD 1, Minnesota	5.29	81.4	10.1	90.0	24.6	8.2	1.226	83.0	25,947	6.40	4.67	4.79
164	CD 13, Ohio	5.29	77.7	11.7	88.3	26.1	9.5	1.240	90.4	28,550	4.87	5.55	5.45
167	CD 21, Florida	5.28	79.3	22.7	77.2	26.7	9.3	1.133	95.8	25,251	5.55	5.68	4.60
167	CD 15, Ohio	5.28	76.3	11.9	88.1	34.3	12.9	1.353	88.2	29,819	4.28	5.82	5.76
169	CD 49, California	5.27	79.5	18.3	81.7	24.6	7.5	1.139	86.2	28,937	5.64	4.64	5.55
170	CD 4, Colorado	5.26	79.7	12.5	87.5	32.6	10.9	1.312	85.1	25,933	5.70	5.28	4.79
170	CD 2, Washington	5.26	80.1	11.3	88.7	24.8	8.4	1.220	83.1	27,745	5.86	4.66	5.26
172	CD 24, Florida	5.25	78.0	10.3	89.7	27.8	8.7	1.263	91.9	26,487	5.00	5.83	4.93
173	CD Delaware	5.22	77.4	14.4	85.5	27.5	11.1	1.243	84.8	30,702	4.76	4.95	5.96
174	CD 9, Washington	5.21	79.5	10.9	89.0	23.4	6.9	1.195	80.1	29,921	5.62	4.22	5.78
175	CD 2, Iowa	5.20	79.5	10.5	89.5	27.1	9.1	1.257	88.0	25,358	5.62	5.36	4.63
175	CD 7, Tennessee	5.20	75.4	12.3	87.7	32.8	11.6	1.321	88.1	31,037	3.91	5.66	6.03
175	CD 31, Texas	5.20	78.3	12.4	87.5	28.3	8.6	1.246	85.8	28,243	5.14	5.07	5.38
178	CD 16, Illinois	5.19	78.3	11.9	88.1	22.2	7.0	1.174	86.2	29,431	5.11	4.80	5.66
179	CD 3, Illinois	5.16	77.8	18.6	81.4	22.6	8.3	1.124	86.6	30,604	4.92	4.62	5.94
179	CD 2, Maryland	5.16	76.8	16.3	83.7	22.8	8.1	1.146	87.6	31,661	4.49	4.82	6.17
181	CD 1, Nebraska	5.15	79.7	10.2	89.8	26.7	8.1	1.246	85.9	25,469	5.69	5.09	4.66
181	CD 22, New York	5.15	78.9	13.4	86.6	26.7	12.2	1.253	89.2	25,168	5.38	5.48	4.58
183	CD 10, Florida	5.14	77.8	12.3	87.7	25.8	8.6	1.221	89.4	27,290	4.92	5.36	5.14
183	CD 29, New York	5.14	78.3	10.8	89.3	28.7	12.7	1.306	87.0	26,090	5.13	5.47	4.83
185	CD 19, Pennsylvania	5.13	78.9	13.4	86.6	23.5	8.5	1.188	85.4	27,764	5.37	4.77	5.26
186	CD 2, Utah	5.12	79.7	8.7	91.3	31.3	10.2	1.328	86.1	23,796	5.72	5.47	4.19
187	CD 23, California	5.11	80.8	23.0	76.9	27.2	9.7	1.140	91.5	22,955	6.15	5.23	3.94
188	CD 1, California	5.10	77.9	12.8	87.2	29.0	12.0	1.281	88.8	25,854	4.96	5.56	4.77
188	CD 1, New Jersey	5.10	76.7	14.7	85.3	24.6	7.0	1.169	87.6	30,484	4.48	4.93	5.91
188	CD 8, Wisconsin	5.10	79.4	10.9	89.2	22.4	6.6	1.181	85.2	26,633	5.60	4.71	4.97
191	CD 14, Florida	5.08	80.3	12.9	87.1	27.1	10.0	1.243	79.1	26,616	5.97	4.31	4.97
191	CD 4, Indiana	5.08	77.7	11.3	88.7	25.1	8.9	1.226	87.6	27,492	4.88	5.19	5.19
191	CD 3, Michigan	5.08	78.5	13.2	86.8	26.3	9.2	1.223	86.7	26,538	5.22	5.06	4.95
191	CD 1, New Mexico	5.08	77.9	14.3	85.6	31.0	14.1	1.309	89.9	24,759	4.98	5.80	4.47
195	CD 2, Ohio	5.07	76.5	14.7	85.3	30.8	11.2	1.274	83.6	30,524	4.35	4.95	5.92
195	CD 5, Oregon	5.07	79.3	12.3	87.7	29.2	11.0	1.278	84.3	25,345	5.52	5.05	4.63
197	CD 25, California	5.06	79.0	20.7	79.4	20.3	6.3	1.058	83.9	29,647	5.42	4.03	5.72
197	CD 5, California	5.06	78.1	20.1	79.9	24.6	8.3	1.128	88.6	27,809	5.04	4.86	5.27
197	CD 11, Illinois	5.06	78.3	12.1	87.8	21.2	7.1	1.163	86.0	28,025	5.13	4.73	5.33
197	CD 10, Ohio	5.06	76.9	13.8	86.3	25.3	8.2	1.197	89.5	28,312	4.54	5.26	5.40
201	CD 8, Florida	5.05	78.2	13.4	86.5	27.5	8.9	1.231	85.3	27,200	5.08	4.95	5.12
201	CD 13, Florida	5.05	80.4	13.3	86.7	26.6	9.8	1.231	81.3	25,412	6.00	4.51	4.65
203	CD 7, Maryland	5.04	75.1	18.0	82.0	31.7	15.1	1.289	88.8	29,736	3.80	5.59	5.74
204	CD 6, Alabama	5.03	75.1	11.8	88.2	33.5	12.2	1.339	84.9	30,646	3.77	5.38	5.95

AMERICAN HUMAN DEVELOPMENT INDEX
by Congressional District *continued*

RANK	CONGRESSIONAL DISTRICT	HD INDEX	LIFE EXPECTANCY AT BIRTH (years)	LESS THAN HIGH SCHOOL (%)	AT LEAST HIGH SCHOOL DIPLOMA (%)	AT LEAST BACHELOR'S DEGREE (%)	GRADUATE DEGREE (%)	EDUCATIONAL ATTAINMENT SCORE	SCHOOL ENROLLMENT (%)	MEDIAN EARNINGS (2005 dollars)	HEALTH INDEX	EDUCATION INDEX	INCOME INDEX
204	CD 7, Florida	5.03	78.3	12.4	87.6	27.0	9.2	1.238	85.6	26,690	5.11	5.01	4.99
204	CD 3, Kentucky	5.03	76.4	14.5	85.5	27.7	11.2	1.244	90.3	27,509	4.32	5.56	5.20
207	CD 13, North Carolina	5.01	77.7	16.4	83.6	31.7	9.3	1.246	87.6	26,279	4.88	5.27	4.88
208	CD 15, Florida	5.00	79.0	13.8	86.2	25.0	9.0	1.203	87.2	25,105	5.40	5.03	4.56
208	CD 1, Illinois	5.00	77.8	18.3	81.7	21.2	9.0	1.119	89.7	27,267	4.92	4.94	5.14
208	CD 4, Iowa	5.00	79.5	8.8	91.1	23.7	7.4	1.223	84.2	25,078	5.64	4.79	4.56
208	CD 3, Oregon	5.00	77.8	13.8	86.3	29.0	9.7	1.248	86.9	26,287	4.92	5.20	4.88
212	CD 2, Arizona	4.99	77.3	12.5	87.5	21.3	7.2	1.158	86.1	28,922	4.71	4.71	5.54
212	CD 8, Georgia	4.99	75.8	13.7	86.3	26.0	8.6	1.209	85.2	31,163	4.07	4.84	6.06
214	CD 1, Missouri	4.98	77.3	15.9	84.1	25.7	11.0	1.208	90.0	26,284	4.69	5.37	4.88
214	CD 10, New Jersey	4.98	78.0	21.3	78.7	21.5	6.6	1.068	89.8	27,532	5.00	4.73	5.20
214	CD 3, Washington	4.98	78.2	10.1	89.9	23.3	7.8	1.211	79.8	29,055	5.10	4.25	5.58
217	CD 13, New Jersey	4.97	79.0	26.6	73.4	26.4	8.2	1.080	83.1	28,656	5.41	4.04	5.48
218	CD 3, Ohio	4.96	77.0	14.1	85.8	24.7	9.3	1.200	88.4	27,186	4.60	5.15	5.11
218	CD 2, South Carolina	4.96	77.1	12.8	87.2	31.5	11.5	1.303	85.7	26,549	4.62	5.31	4.95
220	CD 14, Pennsylvania	4.95	77.3	12.0	88.0	26.2	10.6	1.248	93.4	23,842	4.72	5.93	4.20
221	CD 16, Pennsylvania	4.94	79.2	18.6	81.4	26.1	8.9	1.165	79.0	28,138	5.51	3.95	5.35
221	CD 6, Wisconsin	4.94	79.2	12.7	87.3	19.2	5.4	1.119	84.2	26,642	5.50	4.33	4.97
223	CD 2, Pennsylvania	4.93	74.1	18.3	81.6	29.1	13.5	1.244	95.5	27,803	3.39	6.14	5.27
223	CD 2, Texas	4.93	76.0	15.2	84.8	25.1	7.8	1.176	87.6	29,421	4.17	4.97	5.66
223	CD 4, Virginia	4.93	76.6	16.2	83.9	22.2	7.9	1.139	84.8	30,426	4.41	4.48	5.90
226	CD 18, Florida	4.91	79.1	24.6	75.3	29.9	12.1	1.174	90.0	23,371	5.46	5.22	4.07
226	CD 18, Illinois	4.91	77.4	10.0	90.0	23.6	7.6	1.213	86.2	26,767	4.74	4.97	5.01
228	CD 51, California	4.90	79.9	29.3	70.7	17.2	5.2	0.932	90.1	25,748	5.80	4.15	4.74
228	CD 2, Michigan	4.90	79.1	12.8	87.1	21.5	7.3	1.160	83.3	26,061	5.46	4.42	4.82
228	CD 3, Missouri	4.90	76.5	15.9	84.1	26.2	9.5	1.197	85.3	28,763	4.39	4.80	5.51
228	CD North Dakota	4.90	79.8	11.8	88.1	25.4	6.7	1.204	84.6	23,789	5.75	4.75	4.19
232	CD 1, Iowa	4.89	79.3	10.7	89.3	23.3	7.6	1.201	85.2	24,212	5.56	4.81	4.31
232	CD 3, Wisconsin	4.89	79.9	10.9	89.1	21.9	7.2	1.182	81.9	25,038	5.77	4.36	4.54
234	CD 7, Michigan	4.88	77.6	11.2	88.9	22.3	8.2	1.193	85.3	26,823	4.83	4.78	5.02
235	CD 19, California	4.87	78.0	18.7	81.3	21.2	7.0	1.096	87.0	27,004	5.02	4.54	5.07
235	CD 2, New Jersey	4.87	75.7	16.6	83.3	22.4	6.8	1.125	86.9	30,379	4.06	4.66	5.88
235	CD 23, Texas	4.87	78.6	22.6	77.4	29.7	10.9	1.181	87.5	24,424	5.26	4.98	4.37
238	CD 27, New York	4.86	77.9	13.8	86.3	22.0	9.1	1.173	86.1	26,073	4.97	4.78	4.83
238	CD 6, Texas	4.86	77.0	15.4	84.5	24.2	7.0	1.158	85.2	28,314	4.58	4.61	5.40
240	CD 3, Nevada	4.85	76.2	14.3	85.7	23.0	7.3	1.158	83.3	30,577	4.23	4.40	5.93
241	CD 11, Ohio	4.82	76.9	17.7	82.4	25.5	11.8	1.195	90.8	25,004	4.54	5.40	4.53
241	CD 17, Pennsylvania	4.82	77.7	14.9	85.0	19.8	6.9	1.118	83.2	28,331	4.85	4.22	5.40
243	CD 6, Michigan	4.81	77.6	12.9	87.1	24.1	9.9	1.211	87.4	24,890	4.84	5.09	4.50
244	CD 12, New York	4.80	80.6	32.9	67.1	22.0	7.6	0.968	84.7	25,294	6.08	3.71	4.61
244	CD 1, Utah	4.80	79.4	10.2	89.7	27.1	8.5	1.254	81.8	23,680	5.58	4.66	4.16
246	CD 4, Florida	4.79	74.5	11.1	88.9	27.5	9.1	1.256	85.7	29,589	3.56	5.11	5.70
246	CD 15, Illinois	4.79	77.3	10.8	89.2	26.1	9.7	1.249	89.3	23,756	4.71	5.47	4.18
248	CD 22, California	4.78	77.3	16.0	83.9	20.9	7.1	1.121	85.7	27,222	4.71	4.50	5.12
248	CD 45, California	4.78	78.7	21.4	78.6	21.2	7.7	1.074	83.0	26,911	5.30	4.00	5.04
248	CD 16, Florida	4.78	79.3	15.9	84.1	21.0	7.7	1.127	82.3	25,369	5.56	4.15	4.64
248	CD 28, New York	4.78	78.5	16.6	83.4	23.4	10.2	1.171	88.8	23,346	5.22	5.07	4.06
248	CD 6, North Carolina	4.78	77.1	17.8	82.2	23.5	6.3	1.120	88.4	26,446	4.62	4.81	4.92
253	CD 5, Tennessee	4.77	75.9	15.0	85.1	29.6	10.8	1.254	85.0	27,339	4.13	5.01	5.15
254	CD 41, California	4.75	77.1	17.4	82.5	18.6	7.7	1.090	87.5	27,014	4.62	4.56	5.07
254	CD 4, Kansas	4.75	76.7	12.6	87.4	23.2	7.4	1.181	88.4	25,624	4.47	5.08	4.70

AMERICAN HUMAN DEVELOPMENT INDEX
by Congressional District *continued*

RANK	CONGRESSIONAL DISTRICT	HD INDEX	LIFE EXPECTANCY AT BIRTH (years)	LESS THAN HIGH SCHOOL (%)	AT LEAST HIGH SCHOOL DIPLOMA (%)	AT LEAST BACHELOR'S DEGREE (%)	GRADUATE DEGREE (%)	EDUCATIONAL ATTAINMENT SCORE	SCHOOL ENROLLMENT (%)	MEDIAN EARNINGS (2005 dollars)	HEALTH INDEX	EDUCATION INDEX	INCOME INDEX
254	CD 5, Missouri	4.75	76.3	14.3	85.7	27.1	9.7	1.226	83.0	27,803	4.31	4.66	5.27
257	CD 19, Illinois	4.74	77.1	12.7	87.3	20.8	7.4	1.155	88.0	25,535	4.62	4.91	4.68
257	CD 6, Washington	4.74	78.3	12.6	87.4	23.5	7.9	1.188	80.9	26,199	5.11	4.26	4.86
259	CD 7, Ohio	4.73	76.5	12.8	87.2	21.1	8.4	1.167	85.3	27,285	4.39	4.67	5.14
260	CD 24, New York	4.72	78.7	13.2	86.8	22.9	10.0	1.196	84.3	23,830	5.28	4.68	4.20
260	CD 9, Ohio	4.72	76.8	14.0	86.1	21.9	8.0	1.159	87.4	25,975	4.48	4.87	4.80
262	CD 6, Missouri	4.71	77.5	10.7	89.3	24.2	7.6	1.211	79.8	27,119	4.79	4.24	5.10
262	CD 16, Ohio	4.71	78.3	11.9	88.1	20.9	7.0	1.161	82.3	25,667	5.11	4.31	4.72
264	CD 1, South Carolina	4.70	76.6	11.7	88.2	27.8	9.4	1.255	84.5	25,623	4.42	4.96	4.70
265	CD 2, Nevada	4.69	76.7	15.4	84.6	22.0	7.0	1.136	82.4	28,471	4.44	4.20	5.44
266	CD 5, Washington	4.68	78.9	10.5	89.5	25.1	9.3	1.239	85.7	21,892	5.39	5.03	3.61
266	CD 7, Wisconsin	4.68	79.2	12.1	87.9	18.3	5.6	1.119	81.6	24,954	5.49	4.04	4.52
268	CD 2, Kansas	4.67	77.5	9.7	90.3	24.9	9.6	1.247	86.0	23,547	4.80	5.10	4.12
268	CD 3, Utah	4.67	79.4	10.7	89.2	24.9	7.2	1.215	83.8	22,164	5.59	4.71	3.70
270	CD 6, Florida	4.66	77.0	13.3	86.7	23.7	9.1	1.194	86.0	24,984	4.59	4.87	4.53
271	CD 2, Florida	4.65	76.1	15.8	84.2	25.9	9.9	1.199	90.1	24,598	4.20	5.34	4.42
271	CD 3, Indiana	4.65	78.0	15.7	84.3	19.8	6.9	1.110	80.9	26,800	5.02	3.93	5.02
273	CD 8, Minnesota	4.64	79.6	10.3	89.6	19.3	5.8	1.149	80.3	23,945	5.65	4.02	4.23
273	CD 32, Texas	4.64	77.4	25.6	74.4	36.2	12.5	1.230	81.0	25,621	4.74	4.47	4.70
275	CD 37, California	4.63	79.9	29.9	70.1	18.2	4.7	0.931	86.9	24,182	5.80	3.79	4.30
276	CD 39, California	4.62	79.9	33.9	66.0	16.6	4.9	0.876	87.8	24,569	5.80	3.65	4.41
276	CD 6, Kentucky	4.62	76.6	17.8	82.1	27.0	11.2	1.205	85.8	25,183	4.40	4.88	4.58
276	CD 4, Michigan	4.62	77.9	12.8	87.1	20.5	7.6	1.154	89.2	22,639	4.98	5.04	3.85
276	CD 1, Ohio	4.62	76.2	14.6	85.5	24.3	8.8	1.184	85.2	26,325	4.23	4.73	4.89
280	CD 5, Iowa	4.61	79.0	12.2	87.9	18.0	4.8	1.105	82.6	24,252	5.41	4.09	4.32
281	CD 5, Ohio	4.59	77.9	12.2	87.9	15.6	5.7	1.090	83.6	25,487	4.97	4.13	4.67
282	CD 13, Georgia	4.57	77.1	18.3	81.8	20.8	6.0	1.084	83.9	26,591	4.62	4.14	4.96
283	CD 28, California	4.56	79.9	32.4	67.6	26.2	8.0	1.018	85.6	22,600	5.80	4.03	3.83
283	CD 6, Virginia	4.56	77.5	17.7	82.3	23.6	8.0	1.140	82.8	25,348	4.78	4.27	4.63
285	CD 3, Colorado	4.55	78.5	13.2	86.8	26.0	8.0	1.209	81.6	23,151	5.22	4.44	4.00
285	CD 1, Indiana	4.55	76.2	14.3	85.8	19.2	6.8	1.117	84.2	26,956	4.27	4.32	5.06
287	CD 9, Indiana	4.54	76.9	16.7	83.3	17.3	7.0	1.076	86.9	25,447	4.54	4.43	4.66
287	CD 3, New Mexico	4.54	77.9	17.4	82.6	25.4	10.9	1.190	83.9	23,272	4.97	4.61	4.04
289	CD 1, Louisiana	4.53	74.4	13.8	86.2	28.9	10.3	1.254	85.3	26,853	3.49	5.06	5.03
289	CD 7, Minnesota	4.53	80.2	12.8	87.3	18.6	5.3	1.111	79.3	22,863	5.92	3.75	3.91
289	CD 8, Ohio	4.53	77.3	14.6	85.3	19.0	6.7	1.111	81.4	26,319	4.72	3.98	4.89
289	CD South Dakota	4.53	78.6	11.4	88.6	24.6	7.0	1.204	80.9	23,110	5.25	4.34	3.99
289	CD Wyoming	4.53	77.8	8.7	91.4	23.2	7.7	1.222	81.7	23,752	4.92	4.51	4.18
294	CD 12, Texas	4.52	77.2	19.3	80.8	23.3	7.4	1.114	80.6	26,653	4.68	3.90	4.98
295	CD 5, Michigan	4.51	76.3	14.8	85.2	18.0	6.2	1.093	87.2	25,544	4.29	4.55	4.68
296	CD 5, Florida	4.50	77.4	15.2	84.8	18.9	6.2	1.099	83.9	25,047	4.75	4.20	4.55
296	CD 1, Oklahoma	4.50	75.3	12.6	87.4	27.9	8.1	1.234	84.7	25,652	3.87	4.90	4.71
296	CD 4, Oregon	4.50	78.1	12.0	88.0	23.2	8.8	1.199	86.1	21,705	5.03	4.90	3.55
296	CD 3, Pennsylvania	4.50	77.7	11.9	88.1	20.5	6.4	1.150	84.2	23,683	4.89	4.47	4.16
296	CD 4, Wisconsin	4.50	76.3	19.1	80.8	19.9	6.5	1.073	88.9	25,059	4.29	4.65	4.55
301	CD 10, Pennsylvania	4.49	77.4	13.0	87.0	20.4	7.7	1.151	83.8	24,123	4.76	4.42	4.29
301	CD 4, Texas	4.49	76.4	17.0	83.0	20.9	6.3	1.103	83.6	26,465	4.35	4.18	4.93
303	CD 32, California	4.48	79.9	33.5	66.5	15.1	3.9	0.854	89.5	22,767	5.80	3.74	3.88
303	CD 23, New York	4.48	78.3	14.2	85.8	19.3	8.4	1.135	80.3	24,376	5.11	3.97	4.36
305	CD 2, Arkansas	4.47	75.6	13.2	86.8	25.5	8.8	1.211	85.8	24,805	4.01	4.92	4.48
305	CD 38, California	4.47	79.9	36.3	63.7	13.7	3.9	0.813	88.0	23,868	5.80	3.39	4.21

AMERICAN HUMAN DEVELOPMENT INDEX
by Congressional District *continued*

RANK	CONGRESSIONAL DISTRICT	HD INDEX	LIFE EXPECTANCY AT BIRTH (years)	LESS THAN HIGH SCHOOL (%)	AT LEAST HIGH SCHOOL DIPLOMA (%)	AT LEAST BACHELOR'S DEGREE (%)	GRADUATE DEGREE (%)	EDUCATIONAL ATTAINMENT SCORE	SCHOOL ENROLLMENT (%)	MEDIAN EARNINGS (2005 dollars)	HEALTH INDEX	EDUCATION INDEX	INCOME INDEX
307	CD 4, Ohio	4.46	77.7	13.7	86.3	15.1	5.1	1.066	82.0	25,443	4.87	3.84	4.66
307	CD 5, Virginia	4.46	76.6	22.3	77.8	21.3	9.0	1.080	87.7	24,557	4.43	4.55	4.41
309	CD 11, North Carolina	4.45	76.8	16.2	83.9	24.0	8.4	1.161	88.4	22,673	4.51	4.99	3.86
310	CD 1, Idaho	4.44	78.9	13.0	86.9	22.1	6.8	1.160	81.4	22,357	5.37	4.19	3.76
310	CD 6, Louisiana	4.44	74.5	14.8	85.2	25.0	9.1	1.193	87.4	25,836	3.56	5.01	4.76
310	CD 17, Ohio	4.44	77.1	13.9	86.1	17.5	6.0	1.096	85.3	24,231	4.64	4.35	4.32
310	CD 4, South Carolina	4.44	75.9	19.3	80.6	24.0	8.1	1.129	84.4	26,005	4.13	4.39	4.81
314	CD 4, Kentucky	4.43	75.6	18.3	81.7	18.6	6.6	1.070	85.7	26,790	4.00	4.28	5.01
315	CD 17, Florida	4.42	79.3	24.0	76.0	16.3	5.5	0.978	91.6	20,636	5.54	4.52	3.20
315	CD 5, North Carolina	4.42	76.7	20.8	79.2	21.3	6.5	1.069	87.2	24,344	4.46	4.44	4.35
317	CD 2, Indiana	4.41	77.1	16.6	83.5	17.7	7.1	1.082	82.0	25,524	4.62	3.92	4.68
317	CD 14, Texas	4.41	76.3	19.3	80.7	22.1	6.7	1.096	84.6	25,440	4.31	4.27	4.65
319	CD 6, Indiana	4.40	76.6	16.2	83.8	16.9	6.2	1.068	87.1	24,387	4.42	4.42	4.36
319	CD 2, Tennessee	4.40	76.6	17.2	82.8	25.1	8.9	1.168	81.0	25,257	4.40	4.19	4.60
321	CD 12, Illinois	4.39	76.0	15.4	84.5	19.7	6.9	1.112	88.1	24,099	4.17	4.74	4.28
321	CD 5, Pennsylvania	4.39	78.1	13.5	86.4	19.2	7.4	1.131	84.8	22,038	5.05	4.45	3.66
321	CD 5, Texas	4.39	76.6	19.7	80.3	20.8	6.3	1.074	80.7	26,720	4.43	3.74	4.99
324	CD 5, Alabama	4.37	75.8	18.6	81.5	26.7	9.1	1.171	84.5	24,652	4.07	4.60	4.44
324	CD 2, North Carolina	4.37	76.6	19.1	80.9	17.3	5.7	1.038	85.7	25,073	4.41	4.13	4.55
324	CD 3, North Carolina	4.37	75.7	15.1	84.9	21.7	6.5	1.131	87.7	24,130	4.06	4.77	4.29
327	CD 1, Florida	4.35	76.4	13.4	86.7	22.9	7.4	1.167	84.4	23,725	4.32	4.57	4.17
328	CD (at Large), Montana	4.34	77.9	9.3	90.7	26.4	8.0	1.252	81.2	21,472	4.94	4.59	3.48
328	CD 11, Pennsylvania	4.34	77.1	14.8	85.3	18.1	6.4	1.096	83.9	23,781	4.64	4.19	4.19
330	CD 11, Florida	4.32	77.4	21.0	79.0	21.6	6.9	1.075	80.9	24,729	4.74	3.77	4.46
330	CD 1, Michigan	4.32	78.2	13.3	86.8	18.0	6.0	1.107	86.0	21,215	5.09	4.47	3.40
330	CD 9, Missouri	4.32	77.1	15.4	84.5	23.0	8.6	1.162	81.3	23,586	4.64	4.20	4.13
333	CD 2, California	4.31	77.2	16.1	83.8	20.1	6.3	1.103	86.7	22,283	4.65	4.53	3.74
334	CD 12, Pennsylvania	4.30	77.7	13.9	86.1	16.6	6.0	1.086	84.2	22,592	4.89	4.19	3.83
335	CD 7, Indiana	4.29	75.5	19.1	80.9	22.1	8.0	1.110	83.8	25,527	3.96	4.24	4.68
335	CD 14, Michigan	4.29	74.9	18.8	81.3	15.1	5.6	1.019	90.7	25,064	3.72	4.61	4.55
335	CD 3, Nebraska	4.29	79.0	11.6	88.3	19.2	5.9	1.135	80.0	21,630	5.41	3.93	3.53
338	CD 2, Idaho	4.28	78.8	13.6	86.4	24.6	8.0	1.191	79.1	21,307	5.35	4.08	3.43
338	CD 2, Maine	4.28	77.2	13.3	86.7	19.7	6.7	1.131	84.6	22,378	4.66	4.42	3.77
340	CD 1, Kansas	4.27	78.4	14.8	85.2	19.7	6.1	1.110	81.4	21,983	5.18	3.98	3.64
341	CD 8, Indiana	4.25	76.5	14.7	85.4	17.5	6.3	1.091	82.3	24,505	4.37	4.00	4.40
341	CD 8, North Carolina	4.25	75.9	18.4	81.6	20.1	6.1	1.077	86.3	23,955	4.14	4.38	4.24
343	CD 35, California	4.24	79.9	33.5	66.6	15.4	4.6	0.864	85.0	21,979	5.80	3.29	3.64
343	CD 9, Georgia	4.24	76.2	22.1	77.9	20.2	7.8	1.059	82.9	25,099	4.23	3.92	4.56
345	CD 17, Illinois	4.23	77.8	14.4	85.6	16.7	5.7	1.080	84.1	21,964	4.92	4.14	3.64
346	CD 8, Texas	4.22	76.1	16.9	83.2	21.5	6.2	1.107	81.6	24,830	4.19	3.99	4.49
347	CD 12, Florida	4.21	77.2	17.7	82.3	18.3	6.0	1.065	78.2	25,066	4.65	3.42	4.55
347	CD 23, Florida	4.21	79.7	24.8	75.3	15.6	4.7	0.954	82.2	21,706	5.70	3.37	3.55
349	CD 4, Oklahoma	4.20	75.6	13.6	86.4	21.0	6.9	1.143	85.8	23,209	3.98	4.61	4.02
349	CD 2, Oregon	4.20	78.5	15.2	84.8	21.2	7.1	1.131	78.0	22,167	5.19	3.70	3.70
351	CD 12, North Carolina	4.19	77.2	21.6	78.4	20.8	6.0	1.051	82.3	23,382	4.68	3.82	4.07
352	CD 3, Virginia	4.18	75.4	19.6	80.4	19.6	6.4	1.063	84.6	24,829	3.92	4.13	4.49
353	CD 5, Oklahoma	4.17	75.3	16.4	83.6	27.8	9.4	1.208	83.5	23,186	3.86	4.64	4.01
354	CD 1, Arizona	4.15	76.5	19.0	81.0	19.8	7.8	1.085	83.3	23,098	4.39	4.07	3.99
354	CD 2, West Virginia	4.15	75.6	17.7	82.2	18.6	7.2	1.081	80.9	25,513	3.99	3.79	4.67
356	CD 1, Georgia	4.14	74.6	17.7	82.2	21.3	8.2	1.118	84.6	24,796	3.59	4.36	4.48
356	CD 10, North Carolina	4.14	76.0	21.2	78.8	17.8	5.4	1.019	86.4	23,585	4.17	4.13	4.13

AMERICAN HUMAN DEVELOPMENT INDEX
by Congressional District *continued*

RANK	CONGRESSIONAL DISTRICT	HD INDEX	LIFE EXPECTANCY AT BIRTH (years)	LESS THAN HIGH SCHOOL (%)	AT LEAST HIGH SCHOOL DIPLOMA (%)	AT LEAST BACHELOR'S DEGREE (%)	GRADUATE DEGREE (%)	EDUCATIONAL ATTAINMENT SCORE	SCHOOL ENROLLMENT (%)	MEDIAN EARNINGS (2005 dollars)	HEALTH INDEX	EDUCATION INDEX	INCOME INDEX
358	CD 9, Pennsylvania	4.12	77.9	16.9	83.1	15.0	5.4	1.035	77.4	23,844	4.96	3.20	4.21
359	CD 10, Georgia	4.10	75.9	23.7	76.3	18.7	5.6	1.005	78.9	26,556	4.11	3.24	4.95
359	CD 2, Kentucky	4.10	76.5	19.7	80.3	16.8	6.8	1.040	82.8	23,479	4.38	3.83	4.10
361	CD 3, Arkansas	4.09	77.3	18.8	81.1	21.0	6.9	1.092	79.6	22,684	4.71	3.70	3.86
362	CD 7, Arizona	4.08	79.2	27.0	73.0	15.7	5.7	0.944	79.9	22,021	5.51	3.07	3.65
362	CD 6, Ohio	4.08	75.9	15.5	84.6	15.9	6.3	1.066	86.7	22,362	4.10	4.37	3.76
362	CD 20, Texas	4.08	77.9	24.4	75.6	14.9	5.0	0.955	85.1	21,845	4.95	3.70	3.60
365	CD 7, Missouri	4.06	76.9	14.7	85.3	19.4	6.5	1.112	81.6	21,918	4.54	4.01	3.62
365	CD 3, South Carolina	4.06	75.7	20.3	79.7	19.8	6.8	1.063	83.8	23,478	4.04	4.03	4.10
365	CD 9, Texas	4.06	77.8	28.7	71.4	23.0	7.3	1.015	84.9	21,039	4.90	3.95	3.34
368	CD 47, California	4.05	81.6	43.3	56.7	12.2	3.8	0.727	81.4	21,081	6.51	2.28	3.35
368	CD 1, West Virginia	4.05	76.6	15.1	84.9	18.4	7.5	1.109	84.5	21,297	4.42	4.32	3.42
370	CD 1, Nevada	4.03	76.2	22.6	77.5	16.5	5.4	0.993	77.1	26,308	4.23	2.98	4.89
370	CD 3, Tennessee	4.03	75.4	19.2	80.8	21.6	8.3	1.107	78.7	25,003	3.90	3.66	4.53
372	CD 17, Texas	4.02	76.5	19.9	80.2	22.9	8.0	1.109	86.1	20,668	4.36	4.50	3.21
372	CD 4, Washington	4.02	79.0	22.8	77.1	19.6	7.0	1.039	77.7	21,162	5.44	3.25	3.38
374	CD 6, Tennessee	4.01	76.0	19.7	80.3	19.4	5.7	1.053	78.1	25,001	4.15	3.36	4.53
375	CD 11, Georgia	3.98	75.9	21.4	78.7	19.9	7.2	1.056	80.8	23,712	4.10	3.67	4.17
376	CD 12, Georgia	3.97	75.1	19.4	80.6	19.4	7.5	1.075	89.1	21,338	3.79	4.67	3.44
376	CD 9, Tennessee	3.97	74.0	17.9	82.0	23.4	8.3	1.137	83.0	24,114	3.34	4.28	4.28
378	CD 21, California	3.95	77.3	29.4	70.6	17.0	5.0	0.927	82.0	22,839	4.72	3.24	3.91
378	CD 16, Texas	3.95	79.1	32.3	67.8	17.5	5.8	0.910	90.6	18,024	5.47	4.11	2.27
380	CD 3, Mississippi	3.94	74.2	19.1	80.9	22.9	8.2	1.119	84.0	23,455	3.42	4.31	4.09
381	CD 1, Alabama	3.93	74.8	16.9	83.1	21.1	7.6	1.118	84.4	22,382	3.68	4.35	3.77
381	CD 1, Texas	3.93	76.1	18.8	81.2	18.3	6.2	1.057	84.9	21,360	4.21	4.13	3.44
381	CD 27, Texas	3.93	78.7	30.3	69.7	17.2	5.9	0.927	86.4	19,383	5.29	3.72	2.77
384	CD 3, Oklahoma	3.91	75.6	15.7	84.4	20.2	6.6	1.109	82.2	22,029	4.02	4.06	3.66
385	CD 13, Michigan	3.90	74.9	24.3	75.7	15.8	6.7	0.982	88.4	22,459	3.72	4.18	3.79
386	CD 2, Alabama	3.89	74.5	20.7	79.3	19.6	7.3	1.063	84.5	23,165	3.56	4.11	4.01
386	CD 7, North Carolina	3.89	75.8	19.4	80.6	20.7	6.0	1.073	85.4	21,009	4.09	4.25	3.33
386	CD 11, Texas	3.89	77.2	22.8	77.2	17.9	5.2	1.001	80.9	21,653	4.68	3.44	3.54
389	CD 4, Missouri	3.86	76.6	17.1	82.9	16.1	5.2	1.041	79.5	22,207	4.40	3.46	3.71
390	CD 13, Texas	3.84	75.8	20.1	79.9	18.5	5.5	1.039	82.7	21,885	4.08	3.81	3.61
391	CD 18, Ohio	3.82	76.7	19.8	80.2	12.4	4.6	0.972	78.2	23,124	4.46	3.02	3.99
392	CD 2, Georgia	3.80	74.8	24.6	75.4	16.2	6.1	0.976	87.5	22,115	3.66	4.06	3.68
392	CD 5, South Carolina	3.80	74.6	23.3	76.7	17.4	5.8	0.998	82.8	23,778	3.58	3.63	4.19
392	CD 19, Texas	3.80	76.2	23.2	76.7	20.1	6.6	1.035	83.8	20,684	4.26	3.92	3.22
395	CD 3, Florida	3.77	76.4	20.4	79.5	13.4	4.5	0.976	81.3	21,934	4.32	3.37	3.63
395	CD 2, New Mexico	3.77	77.3	22.7	77.3	18.3	7.3	1.030	87.3	18,174	4.72	4.28	2.32
397	CD 2, Louisiana	3.76	72.8	20.2	79.8	24.1	9.3	1.132	86.8	22,344	2.85	4.67	3.75
398	CD 18, Texas	3.74	77.4	33.4	66.6	16.7	6.1	0.893	80.5	21,675	4.75	2.91	3.54
399	CD 1, Pennsylvania	3.72	74.3	26.6	73.3	16.9	7.5	0.978	84.5	23,131	3.44	3.74	3.99
400	CD 9, Virginia	3.70	75.1	25.4	74.5	17.0	6.9	0.985	86.9	20,808	3.80	4.04	3.26
401	CD 30, Texas	3.68	77.4	33.6	66.4	17.2	6.6	0.903	78.0	21,897	4.74	2.68	3.61
402	CD 28, Texas	3.66	78.4	32.1	67.9	12.5	3.3	0.838	83.8	19,435	5.15	3.03	2.79
403	CD 3, Alabama	3.65	73.9	22.3	77.8	18.6	7.7	1.039	83.1	22,425	3.31	3.85	3.78
403	CD 18, California	3.65	77.5	33.8	66.2	10.9	3.1	0.802	82.2	21,396	4.79	2.70	3.45
403	CD 4, Illinois	3.65	77.8	40.0	60.0	16.9	5.8	0.827	80.2	21,334	4.92	2.59	3.43
403	CD 3, Louisiana	3.65	74.4	24.3	75.7	12.7	3.5	0.918	81.0	24,448	3.50	3.07	4.38
407	CD 31, California	3.64	79.9	43.0	56.9	17.7	4.9	0.796	84.6	17,790	5.80	2.94	2.17
408	CD 4, Louisiana	3.63	74.3	19.0	81.0	18.2	5.9	1.052	81.2	22,282	3.45	3.70	3.74

AMERICAN HUMAN DEVELOPMENT INDEX
by Congressional District *continued*

RANK	CONGRESSIONAL DISTRICT	HD INDEX	LIFE EXPECTANCY AT BIRTH (years)	LESS THAN HIGH SCHOOL (%)	AT LEAST HIGH SCHOOL DIPLOMA (%)	AT LEAST BACHELOR'S DEGREE (%)	GRADUATE DEGREE (%)	EDUCATIONAL ATTAINMENT SCORE	SCHOOL ENROLLMENT (%)	MEDIAN EARNINGS (2005 dollars)	HEALTH INDEX	EDUCATION INDEX	INCOME INDEX
409	CD 3, Georgia	3.61	73.9	22.7	77.2	14.1	5.7	0.971	83.2	23,092	3.30	3.56	3.98
410	CD 43, California	3.60	76.6	36.7	63.4	9.2	2.8	0.753	83.6	22,275	4.43	2.64	3.73
410	CD 34, California	3.60	79.9	46.5	53.5	10.6	2.4	0.666	83.5	19,311	5.80	2.24	2.74
412	CD 1, Kentucky	3.58	75.5	22.5	77.4	13.9	5.4	0.967	80.1	21,785	3.96	3.20	3.58
413	CD 1, Mississippi	3.55	74.6	23.7	76.4	15.6	5.1	0.969	81.4	22,203	3.57	3.36	3.71
414	CD 7, Louisiana	3.52	74.2	22.3	77.7	17.4	5.7	1.007	81.3	21,930	3.42	3.52	3.63
414	CD 25, Texas	3.52	80.1	34.9	65.2	17.9	5.6	0.886	78.8	17,378	5.85	2.69	2.01
416	CD 4, Mississippi	3.51	73.6	18.6	81.4	17.7	6.5	1.058	81.1	22,010	3.18	3.71	3.65
417	CD 4, Arkansas	3.50	75.0	21.4	78.6	14.8	5.1	0.986	83.0	20,471	3.73	3.61	3.15
418	CD 8, Tennessee	3.49	74.3	21.2	78.8	14.2	4.9	0.978	79.9	22,511	3.45	3.23	3.81
419	CD 7, Alabama	3.47	74.2	22.3	77.6	15.9	5.9	0.995	83.5	20,863	3.41	3.70	3.28
420	CD 6, South Carolina	3.45	75.1	23.9	76.1	15.3	5.2	0.967	81.2	20,796	3.77	3.31	3.26
421	CD 1, Tennessee	3.42	74.9	22.3	77.7	17.0	6.0	1.006	76.9	21,639	3.71	3.02	3.53
422	CD 16, New York	3.40	77.6	42.6	57.4	8.7	2.5	0.685	86.6	19,113	4.85	2.66	2.67
422	CD 15, Texas	3.40	79.3	35.5	64.5	14.6	3.9	0.829	78.1	18,113	5.53	2.37	2.30
424	CD 4, Arizona	3.36	78.6	39.0	60.9	12.0	4.2	0.772	70.5	21,671	5.27	1.26	3.54
424	CD 4, Tennessee	3.36	75.0	24.5	75.4	13.0	4.4	0.930	76.4	22,233	3.75	2.62	3.72
426	CD 5, Louisiana	3.35	73.4	22.6	77.4	17.3	6.0	1.007	83.0	20,892	3.07	3.70	3.29
426	CD 1, North Carolina	3.35	74.2	25.3	74.7	13.1	4.1	0.918	85.2	20,257	3.42	3.55	3.08
428	CD 1, Arkansas	3.34	74.2	22.7	77.3	13.7	4.3	0.953	82.8	20,551	3.40	3.44	3.18
429	CD 2, Mississippi	3.30	73.0	25.2	74.8	18.6	6.3	0.998	84.1	20,572	2.93	3.78	3.18
430	CD 2, Oklahoma	3.29	74.0	20.1	80.0	15.0	5.0	0.998	79.7	20,763	3.34	3.29	3.25
431	CD 3, West Virginia	3.28	73.8	23.7	76.4	13.7	5.5	0.955	81.1	21,060	3.25	3.25	3.34
432	CD 4, Alabama	3.26	74.1	26.5	73.5	12.8	4.8	0.911	78.7	21,868	3.37	2.80	3.61
433	CD 8, Missouri	3.15	74.8	23.7	76.3	12.8	5.1	0.941	77.8	19,979	3.66	2.82	2.98
434	CD 29, Texas	2.81	77.4	46.4	53.6	6.4	2.0	0.619	75.2	18,811	4.75	1.11	2.56
435	CD 5, Kentucky	2.79	72.6	33.5	66.5	11.4	5.4	0.834	77.7	20,759	2.77	2.34	3.24
436	CD 20, California	2.64	77.1	47.4	52.6	6.5	1.6	0.608	79.7	16,767	4.61	1.56	1.76

U.S. INDICATOR TABLES
Demographics

STATE	POPULATION 2007[1]	POPULATION UNDER 18 [%] 2006[2]	POPULATION OVER 65 [%] 2006[3]	URBAN POPULATION [%] 2000[4]	RURAL POPULATION [%] 2000[5]
United States	301,621,157	24.6	12.4	79.0	21.0
Alabama	4,627,851	24.2	13.4	55.4	44.6
Alaska	683,478	27.1	6.8	65.6	34.4
Arizona	6,338,755	26.4	12.8	88.2	11.8
Arkansas	2,834,797	24.6	13.9	52.5	47.5
California	36,553,215	26.1	10.8	94.4	5.6
Colorado	4,861,515	24.6	10.0	84.5	15.5
Connecticut	3,502,309	23.3	13.4	87.7	12.3
Delaware	864,764	23.8	13.4	80.1	19.9
District of Columbia	588,292	19.8	12.3	100.0	0.0
Florida	18,251,243	22.2	16.8	89.3	10.7
Georgia	9,544,750	26.2	9.7	71.6	28.4
Hawaii	1,283,388	23.2	14.0	91.5	8.5
Idaho	1,499,402	26.9	11.5	66.4	33.6
Illinois	12,852,548	25.1	12.0	87.8	12.2
Indiana	6,345,289	25.0	12.4	70.8	29.2
Iowa	2,988,046	23.8	14.6	61.1	38.9
Kansas	2,775,997	25.2	12.9	71.4	28.6
Kentucky	4,241,474	23.8	12.8	55.8	44.2
Louisiana	4,293,204	25.4	12.2	72.6	27.4
Maine	1,317,207	21.3	14.6	40.2	59.8
Maryland	5,618,344	24.2	11.6	86.1	13.9
Massachusetts	6,449,755	22.5	13.3	91.4	8.6
Michigan	10,071,822	24.5	12.5	74.7	25.3
Minnesota	5,197,621	24.3	12.1	70.9	29.1
Mississippi	2,918,785	26.1	12.4	48.8	51.2
Missouri	5,878,415	24.2	13.3	69.4	30.6
Montana	957,861	23.1	13.8	54.1	45.9
Nebraska	1,774,571	25.2	13.3	69.8	30.2
Nevada	2,565,382	25.4	11.1	91.5	8.5
New Hampshire	1,315,828	22.6	12.4	59.3	40.7
New Jersey	8,685,920	23.9	12.9	94.4	5.6
New Mexico	1,969,915	26.0	12.4	75.0	25.0
New York	19,297,729	23.4	13.1	87.5	12.5
North Carolina	9,061,032	24.3	12.2	60.2	39.8
North Dakota	639,715	22.8	14.6	55.9	44.1
Ohio	11,466,917	24.1	13.3	77.4	22.6
Oklahoma	3,617,316	25.0	13.2	65.3	34.7
Oregon	3,747,455	23.1	12.9	78.7	21.3
Pennsylvania	12,432,792	22.5	15.2	77.1	22.9
Rhode Island	1,057,832	22.2	13.9	90.9	9.1
South Carolina	4,407,709	24.1	12.8	60.5	39.5
South Dakota	796,214	24.9	14.2	51.9	48.1
Tennessee	6,156,719	23.9	12.7	63.6	36.4
Texas	23,904,380	27.6	9.9	82.5	17.5
Utah	2,645,330	31.0	8.8	88.2	11.8
Vermont	621,254	21.4	13.3	38.2	61.8
Virginia	7,712,091	23.6	11.6	73.0	27.0
Washington	6,468,424	23.9	11.5	82.0	18.0
West Virginia	1,812,035	21.4	15.3	46.1	53.9
Wisconsin	5,601,640	23.6	13.0	68.3	31.7
Wyoming	522,830	23.6	12.2	65.1	34.9

1. Source: Table 1: Annual Estimates of the Population for the U.S., Regions, States, and Puerto Rico: April 1, 2000 to July 1, 2007. U.S. Census Bureau. http://www.census.gov/popest/states/NST-ann-est.html.

2 and **3.** Source: Table 1: Estimates of the Population by Selected Age Groups for the United States and States and for Puerto Rico: July 1, 2006, State Population Estimates-Characteristics, U.S. Census Bureau. http://www.census.gov/popest/states/asrh/SC-EST2006-01.html

4 and **5.** Source: Table 29. Urban and Rural Population, and by State: 2000 Census of Population and Housing, Population and Housing Unit Counts PHC-3, U.S. Census Bureau. www.census.gov/compendia/statab/tables/08s0029.xls.

U.S. INDICATOR TABLES

A Long and Healthy Life

GROUPING	LIFE EXPECTANCY (years) 2005[1]	INFANT MORTALITY RATE (per 1,000 live births) 2002–2004[2]	UNDER 5 MORTALITY RATE (per 1,000 live births) 2002–2004[3]	FOOD-INSECURE HOUSEHOLDS (%) 2005[4]	CHILD IMMUNIZATION RATE (% fully immunized) 2006[5]	DIABETES (% age 18 and older) 2004–2006[6]	OBESITY (% age 20 and older) 2004–2006[7]	
United States	78.0	6.86	30.9	11.4	83.2	10.2	…	
GENDER								
Female	80.5	…	27.4	…	…	8.9	29.6	
Male	75.4	…	34.2	…	…	11.7	30.1	
RACE/ETHNICITY								
American Indian/Alaska Native	78.0	8.6	49.8	…	80	…	27.6	
Asian/Pacific Islander	86.3	4.76	22.6	…	84.9	…	…	
Black/African American	73.0	13.7	47.4	23.6	79.1	14.2	41.4	
Hispanic/Latino	82.1	5.6	29.1	19.6	82.3	…	28.3	
White	78.2	5.72	27.2	8.6	84.7	8.8	26.6	
STATE								
Alabama	74.6	8.82	42.5	12.3	83.4	8.9	30	
Alaska	78.5	6.36	44.5	12.2	76	5.6	25.8	
Arizona	78.2	6.55	35.9	12.2	78.3	7.4	22.2	
Arkansas	75.5	8.47	46.2	14.7	77.1	7.4	27.5	
California	79.7	5.25	26.5	11.7	82	7.8	23	
Colorado	79.1	6.11	26.8	12	82.2	5.1	17.9	
Connecticut	80.1	5.75	19.8	8.2	88.9	6	20.3	
Delaware	77.4	8.88	35.5	6.6	88	7.7	24	
District of Columbia	73.8	11.42	25.7	11.4	84	8.4	23	
Florida	78.5	7.33	35.2	9.4	84.1	7.5	23.4	
Georgia	76.2	8.65	33.7	12.4	85.6	8.8	26.6	
Hawaii	81.7	6.95	30	7.8	83.7	7.3	20.5	
Idaho	78.9	6.14	39.7	14.1	79.3	6.6	23.5	
Illinois	78.1	7.53	29.1	9.1	82.4	7.3	24.9	
Indiana	76.9	7.78	35.2	11.1	82.6	7.9	27.5	
Iowa	79.3	5.36	25.8	10.9	87.4	6.3	25.5	
Kansas	78.0	7.04	40.9	12.3	83.6	6.7	24.8	
Kentucky	75.5	6.94	37.2	12.8	86.5	8.5	27.6	
Louisiana	74.0	9.95	49.3	12.8	75.4	8.8	28.7	
Maine	78.1	5.01	34.4	12.3	84.7	6.7	23.4	
Maryland	78.0	8.09	29.9	9.4	83.7	7.4	24.7	
Massachusetts	79.8	4.8	17.9	7.8	90.8	5.9	20.1	
Michigan	77.7	8.09	27.6	11.5	82.6	8	27.3	
Minnesota	80.5	4.85	28.8	7.7	86.4	5.5	24.1	
Mississippi	73.9	10.32	48.1	16.5	79.1	10	31.1	
Missouri	76.8	7.95	37.1	11.7	86.4	7.1	27	
Montana	77.9	6.42	35	11.2	75	5.5	20.9	
Nebraska	79.2	6.34	36.5	10.3	82.7	6.7	25.9	
Nevada	76.3	6	29.5	8.4	71.6	7.1	22.8	
New Hampshire	79.5	4.93	19.9	6.5	84.6	6.6	22.6	
New Jersey	79.2	5.62	22	8.1	82	7	22.5	
New Mexico	77.7	6.11	40.2	16.8	77.5	6.8	22.5	
New York	79.6	6.08	23.3	10.4	85.7	7.5	22.6	
North Carolina	76.6	8.35	30.1	13.2	86.5	8.6	25.9	
North Dakota	79.8	6.48	26	6.4	86	6	25.5	
Ohio	77.1	7.74	31	12.6	83.6	7.1	26.4	
Oklahoma	75.1	7.95	42.2	14.6	83.4	8.6	27.3	
Oregon	78.7	5.59	33	11.9	79.5	6.4	23.5	
Pennsylvania	77.7	7.4	28.7	9.8	86.1	7.5	24.9	
Rhode Island	79.2	6.4	19	12.4	83.9	6.7	20.8	

GROUPING	TEENAGE PREGNANCY (per 1,000 girls age 15–19)[8]	PRACTICING PHYSICIANS (per 100,000 population)[9]	TOBACCO CONSUMPTION (% 18 and over) 2004–2006[10]	PEOPLE WITHOUT HEALTH INSURANCE (%) 2004–2006[11]	MEDICARE ENROLLMENT (thousands) 2004[12]	MEDICAID RECIPIENTS (thousands) 2004[13]	CHILDREN ON MEDICAID (% age 0–18) 2005–2006[14]
United States	41.1	26.3	20.8	16.6	40,784	55,553	27
Female	—	…	18.4	15.1	…	…	…
Male	—	…	23.3	18.2	…	…	…
American Indian/Alaska Native	52.5	…	26.9	35.1	…	…	…
Asian/Pacific Islander	17.3	…	11.7	16.2	…	…	…
Black/African American	63.1	…	20.9	17.7	…	…	…
Hispanic/Latino	82.6	…	14.6	34.2	…	…	…
White	26.7	…	22.6	12.2	…	…	…
Alabama	52.4	21.1	25	19.6	734	808	31
Alaska	38.9	23.2	24	18.4	50	118	28
Arizona	60.1	22.2	19	23.4	763	1,070	30
Arkansas	60.3	20.5	25	23.5	461	708	39
California	39.5	25.2	15	20.1	4,122	10,015	29
Colorado	43.9	26.6	19	18.6	507	503	16
Connecticut	24.4	35.0	18	11.3	523	501	21
Delaware	43.5	25.9	23	10.4	123	157	21
District of Columbia	66.7	74.2	20	11	73	158	48
Florida	42.4	25.1	22	25.2	2,997	2,952	24
Georgia	53.4	22.0	20	18.6	1,000	1,929	29
Hawaii	36.1	31.0	18	9.6	178	218	22
Idaho	38.6	17.7	17	21	185	206	25
Illinois	40.2	27.2	21	17.1	1,673	2,032	22
Indiana	43.5	21.6	26	18	889	946	24
Iowa	31.6	21.0	21	12.9	485	383	25
Kansas	40.7	23.2	19	15.5	398	365	26
Kentucky	49.2	22.7	28	19.2	661	861	30
Louisiana	56.2	25.3	23	25.9	628	1,108	31
Maine	24.3	29.6	22	14.2	231	294	30
Maryland	32.4	39.3	19	12.6	683	750	20
Massachusetts	22.3	41.7	18	10.9	965	1,074	21
Michigan	34.1	27.1	23	14.8	1,462	1,799	27
Minnesota	26.7	27.5	20	9	686	698	18
Mississippi	61.9	18.4	24	23.5	446	726	35
Missouri	43.4	25.7	24	15.6	897	1,140	28
Montana	35.8	22.7	20	22.9	145	113	23
Nebraska	35.9	23.5	20	16.2	259	244	20
Nevada	51.1	19.2	23	25.6	287	237	14
New Hampshire	18.2	26.2	21	13.3	186	119	16
New Jersey	24.1	31.6	19	17	1,220	960	17
New Mexico	60.8	23.8	21	25.7	258	474	36
New York	26.9	37.1	20	16.4	2,759	4,712	32
North Carolina	48.8	24.5	23	21.7	1,240	1,513	28
North Dakota	27.2	23.8	20	14.5	103	78	20
Ohio	38.5	27.2	24	15	1,738	1,896	27
Oklahoma	55.6	20.3	26	25.2	530	654	34
Oregon	33.3	26.3	19	20.4	527	559	24
Pennsylvania	30.5	31.7	23	13.4	2,117	1,835	26
Rhode Island	32.9	34.6	20	13.7	172	208	31

A Long and Healthy Life *continued*

GROUPING	LIFE EXPECTANCY (years) 2005[1]	INFANT MORTALITY RATE (per 1,000 live births) 2002–2004[2]	UNDER 5 MORTALITY RATE (per 1,000 live births) 2002–2004[3]	FOOD-INSECURE HOUSEHOLDS (%) 2005[4]	CHILD IMMUNIZATION RATE (% fully immunized) 2006[5]	DIABETES (% age 18 and older) 2004–2006[6]	OBESITY (% age 20 and older) 2004–2006[7]
South Carolina	75.8	8.98	34.9	15.5	84.5	9.2	28.2
South Dakota	78.6	7.11	48.5	9.5	84.1	6.1	25.5
Tennessee	75.3	9.05	34.3	13	85.3	9.1	28.4
Texas	77.6	6.37	33.8	16	79.5	8.3	26.7
Utah	79.5	5.26	34.9	14.5	82.8	6.3	22.2
Vermont	79.6	4.68	...	9.5	87	5.4	20.3
Virginia	78.1	7.48	27.5	8.4	84.9	7.2	24.9
Washington	79.4	5.62	24.5	11.2	83.2	6.6	23.5
West Virginia	75.3	7.98	28.5	8.9	81.7	10.1	30.1
Wisconsin	79.0	6.43	28.8	9.5	90.2	5.9	25.3
Wyoming	77.8	6.99	46	11.1	76	6.1	23.1

1. Source: Life expectancy at birth is calculated from mortality data from the CDC, NCHS, and population data from the U.S. Census Bureau, 2005. See Methodological Note for full details.

2. Source: Table 3. Infant mortality rates per 1,000 live births by race and Hispanic origin of mother: United States and each state, Puerto Rico, Virgin Islands, and Guam, 2002–2004 linked files, National Vital Statistics Reports, Vol. 55, No. 14, May 2, 2007, NCHS, CDC, U.S. Department of Health and Human Services. http://www.cdc.gov/nchs/data/nvsr55/nvsr55_14.pdf.

3. Source: Mortality rate, children 1 to 4 years old, per 100,000 population, 2002–2004. Child and adolescent mortality by cause: US/state, 2002-2004 (Source: NVSS), Health Data for All Ages, NCHS, CDC, U.S. Department of Health and Human Services. http://209.217.72.34/HDAA/TableViewer/tableView.aspx?ReportId=248.

4. Source: Table 5. Number of individuals by food security status of households and selected household characteristics, Table 7. Prevalence of household-level food insecurity and very low food security by State, average 2003–05. Household Food Security in the United States, 2005, By Mark Nord, Margaret Andrews, and Steven Carlson, Economic Research Report No. (ERR-29) 68 pp, November 2006. Economic Research Service, USDA. http://www.ers.usda.gov/Publications/ERR29/ERR29.pdf.

5. Source: Estimated Vaccination Coverage with Individual Vaccines and Vaccination Series Among Children 19–35 Months of Age by Race/Ethnicity and by State and Local Area—U.S., National Immunization Survey, Q1/2006-Q4/2006. CDC, U.S. Department of Health and Human Services. http://www.cdc.gov/vaccines/stats-surv/nis/data/tables_2006.htm. 4 or more doses of DTaP, 3 or more doses of poliovirus vaccine, and 1 or more doses of MMR.

6. Source: Diabetes (self-reported) among adults age 18+: State, 1997–2006 (Source: BRFSS) Health Data for All Ages, NCHS, CDC, U.S. Department of Health and Human Services. http://209.217.72.34/hdaa/ReportFolders/ReportFolders.aspx?IF_ActivePathName=P/Health%20Conditions%20and%20Risk%20Factors. National data are not directly comparable with state data.

7. Source: Obesity (self-reported) among adults age 20+: State, 1997-2006 (Source: data from Behavioral Risk Factor Surveillance System). Health Data for All Ages, NCHS, CDC, U.S. Department of Health and Human Services. http://209.217.72.34/hdaa/ReportFolders/ReportFolders.aspx?IF_ActivePathName=P/Health%20Conditions%20and%20Risk%20Factors.

GROUPING	TEENAGE PREGNANCY (per 1,000 girls age 15–19)[8]	PRACTICING PHYSICIANS (per 100,000 population)[9]	TOBACCO CONSUMPTION (% 18 and over) 2004–2006[10]	PEOPLE WITHOUT HEALTH INSURANCE (%) 2004–2006[11]	MEDICARE ENROLLMENT (thousands) 2004[12]	MEDICAID RECIPIENTS (thousands) 2004[13]	CHILDREN ON MEDICAID (% age 0–18) 2005–2006[14]
South Carolina	52.1	22.6	23	20.5	627	857	31
South Dakota	38.5	22.1	21	14.6	123	128	26
Tennessee	52.1	25.4	25	15.1	894	2,205	30
Texas	62.6	21.2	19	30.8	2,458	3,604	27
Utah	34	21.0	10	17.3	228	307	19
Vermont	20.9	35.1	19	14	94	149	38
Virginia	35.2	26.5	20	13.6	967	732	17
Washington	31.3	26.2	18	17.2	797	1,109	25
West Virginia	43.8	24.6	27	21.3	350	377	37
Wisconsin	30.2	25.3	21	11.8	814	896	24
Wyoming	42.7	19.2	22	20.8	70	68	23

8. Source: Tables 8 and 11. National Vital Statistics Reports, Vol. 55, No. 1, September 29, 2006. NCHS, CDC, U.S. Department of Health and Human Services. http://www.cdc.gov/nchs/data/nvsr/nvsr55/nvsr55_01.pdf. Live births per 1,000 women ages 15–19 years, 2004.

9. Source: Table 104. Active physicians and doctors of medicine in patient care, by geographic division and states. Selected years 1975–2004. NCHS, CDC, U.S. Department of Health and Human Services. http://www.cdc.gov/nchs/hus.htm.

10. Source: Mortality rate, children 1 to 4 years old, per 100,000 population, 2002–2004. Child and adolescent mortality by cause: US/state, 2002–2004 (Source: NVSS), Health Data for All Ages, NCHS, CDC, U.S. Department of Health and Human Services. http://209.217.72.34/HDAA/TableViewer/tableView.aspx?ReportId=248. National data are not directly comparable with state data.

11. Source: Health insurance, lack of coverage among adults (%): State, 2002–2006, Health Data for All Ages, NCHS, CDC, U.S. Department of Health and Human Services. http://209.217.72.34/HDAA/TableViewer/tableView.aspx?ReportId=245. National data are not directly comparable with state data.

12. Source: Table 148. Medicare enrollees, enrollees in managed care, payment per enrollee, and short-stay hospital utilization in thousands, by geographic region and state: United States, 1994 and 2004. NCHS,CDC, U.S. Department of Health and Human Services. http://www.cdc.gov/nchs/data/hus/hus07.pdf#148.

13. Source: Table 149. Medicaid recipients, recipients in managed care, payments per recipient, and recipients per 100 persons below the poverty level, by geographic region and state: United States, selected fiscal years 1989–2004. Health, United States, 2007. NCHS, CDC, U.S. Department of Health and Human Services. http://www.cdc.gov/nchs/data/hus/hus07.pdf#148.

14. Source: Obesity (self-reported) among adults age 20+: State, 1997–2006 (Source: data from Behavioral Risk Factor Surveillance System). Health Data for All Ages, NCHS, CDC, U.S. Department of Health and Human Services. http://209.217.72.34/hdaa/ReportFolders/ReportFolders.aspx?IF_ActivePathName=P/Health%20Conditions%20and%20Risk%20Factors.

Access to Knowledge

GROUPING	LESS THAN HIGH SCHOOL (%) 2005[1]	HIGH SCHOOL GRADUATE (%) 2005[2]	BACHELOR'S DEGREE (%) 2005[3]	GRADUATE OR PROFESSIONAL DEGREE (%) 2005[4]	HIGH SCHOOL GRADUATE OR HIGHER (%) 2005[5]	BACHELOR'S DEGREE OR HIGHER (%) 2005[6]	COMBINED GROSS ENROLLMENT RATIO (%) 2005[7]
United States	15.8	57.1	17.2	10.0	84.2	27.2	86.8
GENDER							
Female	15.4	58.6	16.8	9.2	84.6	26.0	90.0
Male	16.2	55.4	17.6	10.8	83.8	28.5	83.8
RACE/ETHNICITY							
American Indian/Alaska Native	23.7	62.7	9.1	4.5	76.3	13.6	82.4
Asian/Pacific Islander	14.4	36.5	29.2	19.9	85.6	49.1	102.3
Black/African American	20.1	62.6	11.4	5.9	79.9	17.3	89.5
Hispanic/Latino	40.5	47.2	8.3	3.9	59.5	12.2	78.8
White	11.0	59.0	18.9	11.0	89.0	30.0	87.7
STATE							
Alabama	19.7	58.9	13.5	7.9	80.3	21.4	83.4
Alaska	9.0	63.8	17.2	10.1	91.0	27.3	83.1
Arizona	16.2	58.3	16.2	9.3	83.8	25.6	83.9
Arkansas	19.0	62.1	12.6	6.3	81.0	18.9	82.8
California	19.9	50.5	18.9	10.6	80.1	29.5	90.2
Colorado	11.3	53.2	23.1	12.3	88.7	35.5	86.0
Connecticut	12.1	53.0	20.0	15.0	87.9	34.9	91.4
Delaware	14.4	58.0	16.4	11.1	85.6	27.6	84.8
District of Columbia	16.4	38.3	20.0	25.2	83.6	45.3	99.8
Florida	15.4	59.5	16.3	8.8	84.6	25.1	86.7
Georgia	17.2	55.6	17.6	9.5	82.8	27.1	85.6
Hawaii	11.9	60.1	18.8	9.1	88.1	27.9	87.5
Idaho	13.3	63.4	15.9	7.4	86.7	23.3	80.2
Illinois	14.3	56.5	18.3	10.9	85.7	29.2	89.3
Indiana	14.7	64.1	13.5	7.7	85.3	21.3	84.4
Iowa	10.4	65.8	16.5	7.3	89.6	23.8	85.3
Kansas	11.3	60.6	18.6	9.6	88.7	28.2	86.6
Kentucky	21.0	59.7	11.5	7.8	79.0	19.3	83.8
Louisiana	19.5	59.9	13.4	7.1	80.5	20.6	83.7
Maine	11.0	63.4	17.0	8.6	89.0	25.6	86.3
Maryland	13.0	52.5	19.3	15.2	87.0	34.5	89.9
Massachusetts	12.0	51.1	21.1	15.7	88.0	36.9	92.4
Michigan	13.0	62.4	15.1	9.5	87.0	24.7	89.5
Minnesota	9.1	60.2	21.0	9.7	90.9	30.7	86.1
Mississippi	21.5	59.8	12.2	6.5	78.5	18.7	82.6
Missouri	15.0	61.1	15.4	8.6	85.0	24.0	83.2
Montana	9.3	64.3	18.4	8.0	90.7	26.5	81.2
Nebraska	10.5	62.2	18.8	8.5	89.5	27.3	85.1
Nevada	17.2	62.1	14.0	6.6	82.8	20.6	81.0
New Hampshire	10.1	58.1	20.1	11.7	89.9	31.8	88.0
New Jersey	13.7	52.0	21.7	12.5	86.3	34.2	90.5
New Mexico	18.0	56.9	14.2	10.9	82.0	25.1	87.0
New York	15.7	53.1	17.9	13.4	84.3	31.3	90.1
North Carolina	17.7	57.2	17.1	8.0	82.3	25.1	87.5
North Dakota	11.8	62.7	18.7	6.7	88.2	25.5	84.6
Ohio	13.7	63.0	14.8	8.5	86.3	23.3	85.7
Oklahoma	15.7	62.0	15.2	7.2	84.3	22.4	83.2
Oregon	12.5	59.7	17.8	10.0	87.5	27.7	84.3
Pennsylvania	13.3	61.0	15.9	9.8	86.7	25.7	86.7
Rhode Island	16.5	54.2	17.9	11.5	83.5	29.3	91.6

GROUPING	TEACHERS WITH ADVANCED DEGREE (%) 2003–2004[8]	TEACHER SALARY ($, average) 2004–2005[9]	SAT SCORE (average score) 2007[10]	STUDENTS ELIGIBLE FOR SUBSIDIZED LUNCH (% in public elementary secondary) 2005–2006[11]	PRESCHOOL GROSS ENROLLMENT RATIO (%) 2005[12]	MAXIMUM INCOME FOR CHILD-CARE SUBSIDY ($ annually) 2002[13]	STATE SPENDING ON EDUCATION ($ per pupil) 2004–2005[14]
United States	48.1	49,568	1511	...	57.8	—	—
Female	...	...	1501	...	57.6	—	—
Male	...	...	1526	...	57.9	—	—
American Indian/Alaska Native	...	...	1454	...	50.7	—	—
Asian/Pacific Islander	...	...	1605	...	57.7	—	—
Black/African American	...	...	1277	...	59.5	—	—
Hispanic/Latino	...	...	1370	...	44.8	—	—
White	...	...	1579	...	61.7	—	—
Alabama	60.6	40,343	1673	51.7	54.8	18,048	7,066
Alaska	41.3	54,420	1527	34.2	57.3	44,328	10,830
Arizona	49.2	44,539	1546	47.3	44.6	22,908	6,261
Arkansas	38.4	42,037	1709	52.8	54.1	19,601	7,504
California	43.1	60,080	1513	48.8	53.4	33,852	8,067
Colorado	54.0	45,843	1674	33.1	54.8	25,668	7,730
Connecticut	74.2	60,923	1533	26.1	72.6	45,805	11,572
Delaware	53.4	52,806	1489	36.9	61.0	27,768	10,910
District of Columbia	51.3	60,682	1411	55.5	48.6	27,921	12,979
Florida	36.6	42,645	1472	45.8	61.3	20,820	7,207
Georgia	52.7	48,298	1472	49.8	65.8	24,278	8,028
Hawaii	55.5	45,959	1463	40.5	56.9	46,035	8,997
Idaho	27.0	43,726	1599	37.6	40.1	20,472	6,283
Illinois	53.5	57,748	1793	37.3	66.3	24,243	8,944
Indiana	61.9	48,635	1487	36.0	56.4	19,848	8,798
Iowa	34.3	41,884	1807	32.0	64.6	19,432	7,972
Kansas	44.5	40,682	1742	38.8	63.3	25,680	7,706
Kentucky	70.6	42,563	1685	52.2	54.3	22,208	7,118
Louisiana	33.9	40,361	1699	61.2	64.1	29,040	7,605
Maine	34.3	42,499	1388	33.7	54.7	34,303	10,106
Maryland	56.3	54,324	1498	31.4	60.6	22,463	9,815
Massachusetts	60.2	56,675	1546	27.9	69.3	27,312	11,267
Michigan	55.5	57,814	1700	35.8	56.9	26,064	9,329
Minnesota	50.2	48,692	1776	30.0	60.5	38,169	8,662
Mississippi	35.5	37,983	1677	69.5	62.4	27,999	6,575
Missouri	50.8	40,455	1775	39.2	59.6	17,784	7,717
Montana	33.6	39,951	1603	34.5	57.8	20,820	8,058
Nebraska	39.5	40,959	1726	34.7	59.7	25,260	8,282
Nevada	55.8	45,047	1486	41.3	32.1	33,576	6,722
New Hampshire	42.5	45,614	1554	17.1	61.1	26,376	9,448
New Jersey	42.2	58,755	1499	26.6	77.6	28,300	13,800
New Mexico	41.0	40,826	1641	56.1	53.8	28,300	7,580
New York	78.0	58,340	1478	44.2	61.6	28,644	14,119
North Carolina	31.7	44,962	1486	42.5	55.0	32,628	7,159
North Dakota	27.4	37,837	1742	29.6	52.0	29,340	8,159
Ohio	52.7	50,546	1600	32.5	58.0	25,680	9,260
Oklahoma	33.4	38,555	1708	54.5	54.2	29,040	6,613
Oregon	58.0	52,724	1550	43.2	50.8	25,680	8,115
Pennsylvania	50.3	54,707	1474	31.5	59.3	28,300	10,552
Rhode Island	51.6	55,509	1486	34.7	53.4	31,230	10,371

Access to Knowledge *continued*

GROUPING	LESS THAN HIGH SCHOOL (%) 2005[1]	HIGH SCHOOL GRADUATE (%) 2005[2]	BACHELOR'S DEGREE (%) 2005[3]	GRADUATE OR PROFESSIONAL DEGREE (%) 2005[4]	HIGH SCHOOL GRADUATE OR HIGHER (%) 2005[5]	BACHELOR'S DEGREE OR HIGHER (%) 2005[6]	COMBINED GROSS ENROLLMENT RATIO (%) 2005[7]
South Carolina	18.3	58.7	15.0	7.9	81.7	23.0	83.8
South Dakota	11.4	64.0	17.6	7.0	88.6	24.7	80.9
Tennessee	18.8	59.4	14.1	7.6	81.2	21.8	80.9
Texas	21.2	53.6	17.0	8.2	78.8	25.1	84.5
Utah	9.9	62.3	19.2	8.7	90.1	27.9	83.8
Vermont	10.5	57.0	20.2	12.3	89.5	32.5	87.9
Virginia	14.6	52.2	19.8	13.4	85.4	33.2	87.5
Washington	11.2	58.7	19.6	10.5	88.8	30.1	83.9
West Virginia	18.8	64.3	10.2	6.8	81.2	16.9	82.1
Wisconsin	11.2	63.8	16.8	8.1	88.8	25.0	86.6
Wyoming	8.7	68.2	15.5	7.7	91.3	23.2	81.7

1. Source: American Community Survey 2005. Percent of people 25 years and over with educational attainment less than a high school diploma.

2. Source: American Community Survey 2005. Percent of people 25 years and over with educational attainment of high school diploma.

3. Source: American Community Survey 2005. Percent of people 25 years and over with educational attainment of a bachelors' degree.

4. Source: American Community Survey, 2005. Percent of people 25 years and over with educational attainment of a professional or graduate degree.

5. Source: American Community Survey, 2005. Percent of people 25 years and over with educational attainment of a high school diploma or higher.

6. Source: American Community Survey, 2005. Percent of people 25 years and over with educational attainment of a bachelor's degree or higher.

7. Source: American Community Survey, 2005. Population of any age enrolled in school divided by population 3–24 years old.

GROUPING	TEACHERS WITH ADVANCED DEGREE (%) 2003–2004[8]	TEACHER SALARY ($, average) 2004–2005[9]	SAT SCORE (average score) 2007[10]	STUDENTS ELIGIBLE FOR SUBSIDIZED LUNCH (% in public elementary secondary) 2005–2006[11]	PRESCHOOL GROSS ENROLLMENT RATIO (%) 2005[12]	MAXIMUM INCOME FOR CHILD-CARE SUBSIDY ($ annually) 2002[13]	STATE SPENDING ON EDUCATION ($ per pupil) 2004–2005[14]
South Carolina	51.0	43,814	1459	51.6	54.2	17,350	7,555
South Dakota	26.2	35,336	1758	32.3	56.9	22,113	7,197
Tennessee	52.3	43,108	1711	47.0	49.8	24,324	6,729
Texas	27.2	42,571	1481	48.0	54.4	34,272	7,267
Utah	32.6	41,487	1658	32.5	51.2	23,928	5,257
Vermont	45.4	46,231	1542	26.5	58.8	31,032	11,835
Virginia	39.4	46,468	1520	31.1	60.4	26,172	8,891
Washington	56.3	47,453	1567	37.2	51.5	31,236	7,560
West Virginia	61.1	39,821	1528	49.1	46.3	20,820	9,005
Wisconsin	45.1	45,121	1760	29.3	51.0	25,680	9,744
Wyoming	37.2	41,930	1680	31.4	56.5	18,828	10,255

8. Source: Table 64. Highest degree earned, years of full-time teaching experience, and average class size for teachers in public elementary and secondary schools, by state: 2003–04, Digest of Education Statistics 2006, National Center for Education Statistics, Institute of Education Studies, U.S. Department of Education. http://nces.ed.gov/programs/digest/d06/tables/dt06_064.asp?referrer=list. Teachers with post baccalaureate degree (masters, education, or doctoral, %), 2003-2004.

9. Source: Table 76. Estimated average annual salary of teachers in public elementary and secondary schools, by state or jurisdiction (in constant 2005–2006 $). Digest of Education Statistics 2006, National Center for Education Statistics, U.S. Department of Education. http://nces.ed.gov/programs/digest/d06/tables/dt06_076.asp?referrer=list.

10. Source: Tables 1, 2, 8, College-Bound Seniors 2007, National Report, College Board. http://www.collegeboard.com/prod_downloads/about/news_info/cbsenior/yr2007/national-report.pdf; College-Bound Seniors 2007, State Profile Reports. http://www.collegeboard.com/about/news_info/cbsenior/yr2007/reports.html. Mean SAT score, total critical reading, mathematics and writing, 2007 high school graduates.

11. Source: Table 7. Number and percent of students in city, suburban, town, and rural public elementary and secondary schools with membership who are eligible for free or reduced-price lunch, by state or jurisdiction: School year 2005–06, U.S. Department of Education, National Center for Education Statistics, Common Core of Data (CCD), "Public Elementary/Secondary School Universe Survey," 2005–06, Version 1a. http://nces.ed.gov/pubs2007/pesschools06/tables/table_7.asp. % in public elementary and secondary schools, free- or reduced price lunch eligible.

12. Source: American Community Survey, 2005. Population of any age, enrolled in nursery school and pre-school as percentage of total population 3 and 4 years old.

13. Source: Table 3.1. Access to early childhood programs, by state: 2002. State Education Reforms, National Center for Education Statistics. http://nces.ed.gov/programs/statereform/res_tab1.asp. Maximum annual income for a family of three to qualify for child-care subsidy, in $.

14. Source: Table 8. Per Pupil Amounts for Current Spending of Public Elementary-Secondary School Systems by State, U.S. Census Bureau, "Public Education Finances, 2005."

A Decent Standard of Living

GROUPING	MEDIAN EARNINGS ($) 2005[1]	LABOR FORCE PARTICIPATION RATE (% 16 to 64) 2006[2]	PER CAPITA GDP BY STATE ($) 2005[3]	STATE MINIMUM WAGE ($ per hour) 2007[4]	INCOME RATIO (top 20% to bottom 20%)[5]	POVERTY (% of population below federal poverty threshold) 2006[6]
United States	27,299	74.5	36,842	—	7.3	13.3
GENDER						
Female	22,000	69.3	—	—	—	14.7
Male	32,850	79.7	—	—	—	11.9
RACE/ETHNICITY						
American Indian/Alaska Native	21,037	64.5	—	—	—	26.6
Asian/Pacific Islander	31,518	72.1	—	—	—	11.0
Black/African American	23,025	69.2	—	—	—	25.3
Hispanic/Latino	20,255	72.6	—	—	—	21.5
White	30,485	76.2	—	—	—	9.3
STATE						
Alabama	23,817	69.7	29,127	...	7.1	16.6
Alaska	30,388	76.8	43,893	7.25	5.8	10.9
Arizona	26,764	72.8	32,445	6.75	7.7	14.2
Arkansas	22,122	71.7	27,535	6.25	6.9	17.3
California	30,018	72.6	40,302	7.50	7.6	13.1
Colorado	29,438	77.8	40,630	6.85	6.8	12.0
Connecticut	35,387	77.9	49,114	7.65	6.9	8.3
Delaware	30,702	75.1	58,214	7.15	5.8	11.1
District of Columbia	36,948	74.9	119,354	7.00	12.4	19.6
Florida	25,951	73.7	32,930	6.67	7.6	12.6
Georgia	27,320	73.5	35,079	—	6.4	14.7
Hawaii	29,287	76.9	36,848	7.25	6.9	9.3
Idaho	21,888	75.2	29,521	—	5.6	12.6
Illinois	29,598	76.0	38,568	7.50	6.8	12.3
Indiana	26,442	76.1	33,653	—	6.4	12.7
Iowa	25,618	80.8	34,951	7.25	5.4	11.0
Kansas	25,038	79.4	33,298	—	6.5	12.4
Kentucky	24,435	70.4	29,421	—	7.6	17.0
Louisiana	23,467	69.8	30,798	—	7.6	19.0
Maine	24,844	76.6	29,822	6.75	6.5	12.9
Maryland	35,144	78.2	38,245	6.15	7.2	7.8
Massachusetts	33,544	77.7	45,423	7.50	7.3	9.9
Michigan	27,468	73.7	33,612	7.15	6.7	13.5
Minnesota	29,687	81.3	40,462	—	5.8	9.8
Mississippi	22,042	68.6	23,498	—	7.1	21.1
Missouri	25,422	75.9	32,858	6.50	6.0	13.6
Montana	21,472	76.0	26,989	—	5.9	13.6
Nebraska	24,865	81.8	35,849	—	5.6	11.5
Nevada	28,486	75.5	39,555	6.33	5.9	10.3
New Hampshire	31,054	79.7	37,424	—	6.0	8.0
New Jersey	35,468	76.1	43,720	7.15	7.5	8.7
New Mexico	22,131	71.8	30,561	—	7.2	18.5
New York	30,983	72.6	45,042	7.15	8.1	14.2
North Carolina	25,111	74.4	35,763	6.15	7.4	14.7
North Dakota	23,789	80.7	33,488	—	5.6	11.4
Ohio	26,706	75.8	34,250	6.85	6.4	13.3
Oklahoma	22,901	72.4	27,963	—	6.3	17.0
Oregon	24,825	75.0	36,456	7.80	6.3	13.3
Pennsylvania	27,395	74.3	34,343	6.25	7.0	12.1
Rhode Island	30,742	76.7	35,456	7.40	6.8	11.1

GROUPING	FEDERAL REVENUE TO EACH STATE ($) 2004[7]	EMPLOYMENT-POPULATION RATIO (%) 2006[8]	UNEMPLOYMENT RATE (% 16 and over) 2006[9]	UNION MEMBERSHIP TO EMPLOYED (%) 2006[10]	BELOW BASIC FAMILY BUDGET (% of persons)[11]	STATE EITC (% of federal)*[12]
United States	7,222	69.2	4.6	12.0	28.3	—
Female	—	64.5	4.6	10.9	...	—
Male	—	73.8	4.6	13.0	...	—
American Indian/Alaska Native	—	56.2	...	...	...	—
Asian/Pacific Islander	—	68.1	3.0	10.4	...	—
Black/African American	—	60.0	8.9	14.5	...	—
Hispanic/Latino	—	66.8	5.2	9.8	...	—
White	—	71.8	4.0	11.7	...	—
Alabama	8,619	64.5	3.6	8.8	33.8	—
Alaska	12,885	67.2	6.7	22.2	28.2	—
Arizona	7,309	68.7	4.1	7.6	33.5	—
Arkansas	7,080	66.2	5.3	5.1	26.8	—
California	6,474	67.3	4.9	15.7	33.7	—
Colorado	6,533	72.8	4.3	7.7	27.6	—
Connecticut	8,649	72.8	4.3	15.6	22.3	—
Delaware	6,326	70.3	3.6	10.8	23.4	20.0
District of Columbia	67,982	67.1	6.0	10.3	48.0	35.0
Florida	7,009	69.2	3.3	5.2	31.0	—
Georgia	6,247	67.4	4.6	4.4	25.6	—
Hawaii	9,651	69.2	2.4	24.7	37.2	—
Idaho	6,437	70.7	3.4	6.0	37.5	—
Illinois	6,043	70.2	4.5	16.4	22.0	22.0
Indiana	6,079	70.6	5.0	12.0	24.1	24.1
Iowa	6,505	76.7	3.7	11.3	20.5	20.5
Kansas	6,994	74.2	4.5	8.0	22.5	22.5
Kentucky	7,649	65.0	5.7	9.8	27.7	—
Louisiana	7,298	63.7	4.0	6.4	28.2	28.2
Maine	8,248	72.0	4.6	11.9	28.9	28.9
Maryland	11,645	73.4	3.9	13.1	20.2	20.2
Massachusetts	8,279	73.1	5.0	14.5	31.8	31.8
Michigan	5,982	66.5	6.9	19.6	22.6	22.6
Minnesota	5,644	76.9	4.0	16.0	18.3	18.3
Mississippi	7,695	61.8	6.8	5.6	29.6	—
Missouri	7,947	70.6	4.8	10.9	22.6	—
Montana	8,085	71.8	3.2	12.2	40.3	—
Nebraska	6,751	77.3	3.0	7.9	19.5	19.5
Nevada	5,469	71.1	4.2	14.8	32.0	—
New Hampshire	6,124	76.0	3.4	10.1	21.9	—
New Jersey	6,353	71.1	4.6	20.1	23.3	23.3
New Mexico	10,437	66.6	4.2	7.8	35.3	35.3
New York	7,484	67.6	4.5	24.4	35.3	35.3
North Carolina	6,467	68.2	4.8	3.3	32.7	32.7
North Dakota	9,513	76.7	3.2	6.8	26.2	—
Ohio	6,388	70.2	5.5	14.2	22.3	—
Oklahoma	7,562	67.4	4.0	6.4	34.9	34.9
Oregon	6,084	70.1	5.4	13.8	29.9	29.9
Pennsylvania	7,649	69.5	4.7	13.6	23.5	—
Rhode Island	7,630	71.9	5.1	15.3	28.9	28.9

A Decent Standard of Living *continued*

GROUPING	MEDIAN EARNINGS ($) 2005[1]	LABOR FORCE PARTICIPATION RATE (% 16 to 64) 2006[2]	PER CAPITA GDP BY STATE ($) 2005[3]	STATE MINIMUM WAGE ($ per hour) 2007[4]	INCOME RATIO (top 20% to bottom 20%)[5]	POVERTY (% of population below federal poverty threshold) 2006[6]
South Carolina	24,532	72.6	29,136	—	7.0	15.7
South Dakota	23,110	80.8	34,873	—	5.3	13.6
Tennessee	24,984	72.4	33,773	—	7.7	16.2
Texas	24,952	73.2	36,277	—	8.1	16.9
Utah	23,144	76.9	30,903	—	5.8	10.6
Vermont	26,260	79.0	33,629	7.53	6.0	10.3
Virginia	31,108	76.4	40,827	—	7.2	9.6
Washington	29,052	75.2	38,141	7.93	7.2	11.8
West Virginia	22,691	66.3	24,662	6.55	7.0	17.3
Wisconsin	27,387	80.2	34,945	6.50	5.5	11.0
Wyoming	23,752	79.4	38,744	—	5.2	9.4

1. Source: Tables B20017 Median Earnings by Sex by Work Experience for the Population 16 and older. Years with Earnings, B20017B, B20017C, B20017D, B20017H, and B20017I. American Community Survey, 2005. Earnings are defined as the sum of wage or salary income and net income from self-employment, and do not include interest, dividends, rental income, Social Security income, and public assistance income.

2. Source: Tables GCT2301. Percent of People 16 to 64 Years Who Are in the Labor Force (Including Armed Forces): http://factfinder.census .gov/servlet/GCTTable?_bm=y&- state=gct&-context=gct&-ds_ name=ACS_2006_EST_G00_&-_box_ head_nbr=GCT2301&-mt_name =&-tree_id=306&-redoLog=true&- _caller=geoselect&-geo_id=&- format=US-9&-_lang=en. Table B23001. Sex by Age by Employment Status for the Population 16 Years and Over, 2006; Table B23002C. Sex by Age by Employment Status for the Population 16 Years and Over (American Indian and Alaska Native Alone); Table B23002H. Sex by Age by Employment Status for the Population 16 Years and Over (White Alone, Not Hispanic or Latino); Table B23002B. Sex by Age by Employment Status for the Population 16 Years and Over (Black or African American Alone); Table B23002I. Sex by Age by Employment Status for the Population 16 Years and Over (Hispanic or Latino Alone); Table B23002D. Sex by Age by Employment Status for the Population 16 Years and Over (Asian Alone), http://factfinder.census.gov/ servlet/DatasetMainPageServlet?_ program=ACS&_submenuId=&_ lang=en&_ts=. All from 2006 American Community Survey, U.S. Census Bureau.

3. Source: Table 2. Per capita real GDP by state. Regional Economic Accounts, Bureau of Economic Analysis, U.S. Department of Commerce, 2005. http://www.bea.gov/newsreleases/ regional/gdp_state/gsp_newsrelease .htm.

4. Source: Minimum Wage Laws in the States—January 1, 2008, U.S. Department of Labor, Employment Standards Administration, Wage and Hour Division. http://www.dol .gov/esa/minwage/america.htm. State minimum wage (if greater than federal minimum wage).

5. Source: Table 2. Ratio of Incomes of top and bottom fifths of families 2001–2003 (2002 dollars). Pulling Apart: A State-By-State Analysis of Income Trends, by Jared Bernstein, Elizabeth McNichol, and Karen Lyons, Economic Policy Institute, January 2006. http://www.epinet.org/studies/ pullingapart/1-18-00sfp.pdf.

6. Source: Table GCT1701. Percent of People Below Poverty Level in the Past 12 Months (For Whom Poverty Status Is Determined): 2006. http://factfinder.census.gov/servlet/ GCTTable?_bm=y&-state=gct&- context=gct&-ds_name=ACS_ 2006_EST_G00_&-_box_head_ nbr=GCT1701&-mt_name=&-t ree_id=306&-_caller=geoselect&- geo_id=&-format=US-9&-_lang=en; Table 17001, Poverty Status in the Past 12 Months by Sex by Age; 17001C (American Indian or Alaska Native Alone). Table 17001D (Asian Alone); Table 17001B (Black or African American Alone); 17001I (Hispanic or Latino); Table 17001H (White Alone, Not Hispanic or Latino). 2006 American Community Survey, U.S. Census Bureau. http://factfinder.census.gov/ servlet/DatasetMainPageServlet?_ program=ACS&_submenuId=&_ lang=en&_ts=.

GROUPING	FEDERAL REVENUE TO EACH STATE ($) 2004[7]	EMPLOYMENT-POPULATION RATIO (%) 2006[8]	UNEMPLOYMENT RATE (% 16 and over) 2006[9]	UNION MEMBERSHIP TO EMPLOYED (%) 2006[10]	BELOW BASIC FAMILY BUDGET (% of persons)[11]	STATE EITC (% of federal)*[12]
South Carolina	7,158	66.2	6.5	3.3	25.2	—
South Dakota	8,564	76.7	3.2	5.9	14.9	—
Tennessee	7,701	66.7	5.2	6.0	25.8	—
Texas	6,308	67.5	4.9	4.9	35.0	—
Utah	5,728	73.2	2.9	5.4	26.9	—
Vermont	7,456	74.9	3.6	11.0	20.3	20.3
Virginia	12,150	70.8	3.0	4.0	23.4	23.4
Washington	7,228	69.4	5.0	19.8	26.9	—
West Virginia	8,364	61.5	4.9	14.2	38.1	—
Wisconsin	5,728	75.6	4.7	14.9	17.8	4 to 43
Wyoming	8,673	75.5	3.2	8.3	16.3	—

7. Source: Table 469. Federal Funds —Summary Distribution by State and Outlying Area: 2004, 2007 Statistical Abstract, U.S. Census Bureau, 2007. http://www.census.gov/compendia/statab/federal_govt_finances_employment/federal_budgetreceipts_outlays_and_debt/. Per capita federal funds outlays (dollars), 2004.

8. Source: Table GCT2303. Employment/Population Ratio for the Population 16 to 64 Years Old. http://factfinder.census.gov/servlet/GCTTable?_bm=y&-state=gct&-context=gct&-ds_name=ACS_2006_EST_G00_&-_box_head_nbr=GCT2303&-mt_name=&-tree_id=306&-redoLog=true&-_caller=geoselect&-geo_id=&-format=US-9&-_lang=en; Table B23001. Sex by Age by Employment Status for the Population 16 Years and Over; Table B23002C. Sex by Age by Employment Status for the Population 16 Years and Over (American Indian and Alaska Native Alone); Table B23002D (Asian Alone); Table B23002B (Black or African American Alone); Table B23002I (Hispanic or Latino Alone); Table B23002H (White Alone, Not Hispanic or Latino). 2006 American Community Survey, U.S. Census Bureau http://factfinder.census.gov/servlet/DatasetMainPageServlet?_program=ACS&_submenuId=&_lang=en&_ts=.

9. Source: Table 1 Employment status of the civilian noninstitutional population 16 years and over by region, division, and state, 2005–2006 annual averages. http://www.bls.gov/news.release/srgune.t01.htm. Table 2. Employment status of the civilian noninstitutional population 16 years and over by sex, 1971 to date. http://www.bls.gov/cps/cpsaat2.pdf. Table 3. Employment status of the civilian noninstitutional population by age, sex, and race. http://www.bls.gov/cps/cpsaat3.pdf. Table 4. Employment status of the Hispanic or Latino population by age and sex. http://www.bls.gov/cps/cpsaat4.pdf. All from Bureau of Labor Statistics, U.S. Department of Labor.

10. Source: Table 5. Union affiliation of employed wage and salary workers by state, 2006. http://www.bls.gov/news.release/union2.t05.htm; Table 40. By selected characteristics, Bureau of Labor Statistics, U.S. Department of Labor, 2006. http://www.bls.gov/cps/cpsaat40.pdf.

11. Source: Table 3. Percentage and number of persons in families with incomes less than family budgets (by state). Basic family budgets: Working families' incomes often fail to meet living expenses around the U.S., by Sylvia A. Allegretto, September 1, 2005. Economic Policy Institute. http://www.epinet.org/content.cfm/bp165.

12. Source: Table 1. State EITC based on Federal EITC. Tax Policy Center and Brookings Institution. http://www.taxpolicycenter.org/taxfacts/displayafact.cfm?Docid=293. * For Minnesota, EITC varies according to income. For Wisconsin, EITC is 4% with 1 child up to 43% with 3 children.

Preserving the Earth for Future Generations

STATE	CARBON DIOXIDE EMISSIONS (million metric tons)[1]	CARCINOGEN RELEASES (pounds)[2]	LEAD RELEASES (pounds)[3]	MERCURY RELEASES (pounds)[4]	DIOXIN RELEASES (grams)[5]	SUPERFUND SITES[6]	PROTECTED FOREST (acres)[7]	PROTECTED FARM AND RANCH LAND (acres)[8]	ENERGY CONSUMPTION (trillion BTUs per capita)[9]	WATER CONSUMPTION (gallons per day, per capita)[10]
United States	5,939	923,071,546	469,271,160	4,396,402	85,501	1,229	1,579,348	54,488	342,024	144,978
Alabama	141	14,908,199	4,502,233	299,527	408	13	10,127	1,309	479,024	224,641
Alaska	46	201,604,472	197,922,301	45,308	1	5	717	40	1,177,491	48,650
Arizona	96	9,665,758	6,528,155	4,715	16	8	...	0	250,089	131,173
Arkansas	64	3,705,107	674,936	2,576	79	10	...	0	414,124	407,721
California	394	12,488,237	4,377,542	64,415	210	94	11,584	2,015	234,158	151,159
Colorado	92	6,580,188	6,236,724	3,484	6	17	541	1,177	300,243	292,937
Connecticut	45	1,404,613	288,078	1,464	6	14	7,347	1,305	265,316	121,859
Delaware	17	850,277	122,208	2,040	17,719	14	1,684	280	368,262	168,453
District of Columbia	4	1,818	1,703	...	0	1	...	...	328,318	1,725
Florida	256	12,635,790	650,482	7,932	89	48	4,742	663	256,737	125,764
Georgia	174	9,412,478	728,426	7,167	602	15	13,790	176	352,087	79,400
Hawaii	22	153,247	46,192	211	0	3	37,055	200	257,939	52,908
Idaho	16	10,534,819	6,819,364	3,600	5	6	56,823	546	359,116	1,507,010
Illinois	236	10,104,241	2,227,172	26,792	30	43	493	313	312,341	110,312
Indiana	233	31,481,947	7,459,470	13,681	71	30	6,638	0	473,672	166,105
Iowa	80	3,491,305	696,914	4,846	367	11	1,339	0	409,300	114,820
Kansas	77	3,523,736	502,365	3,458	203	10	...	6,761	404,090	245,870
Kentucky	150	8,573,314	1,295,254	6,698	481	14	2,661	3,150	472,577	102,925
Louisiana	198	19,860,984	1,401,410	12,472	2,306	11	...	0	850,341	232,716
Maine	23	930,040	21,599	117	3,439	12	646,896	83	366,952	62,671
Maryland	81	1,835,911	278,890	5,718	14	17	1,247	1,116	275,676	149,344
Massachusetts	83	931,901	114,180	414	108	31	5,822	2,140	239,816	73,396
Michigan	187	8,003,832	1,038,615	5,313	12	65	360	463	308,768	100,619
Minnesota	100	2,965,437	417,987	2,188	10,070	25	6,241	322	359,110	78,667
Mississippi	65	4,097,910	366,985	1,998	12	4	...	0	420,630	104,055

1. Source: EPA. http://www.epa.gov/climatechange/emissions/downloads/CO2FFC_2004.pdf. State CO_ Emissions from fossil fuel combustion, 1990–2004.1. Source: EPA. http://www.epa.gov/climatechange/emissions/downloads/CO2FFC_2004.pdf. State CO_ Emissions from fossil fuel combustion, 1990–2004.

2. Source: Table B-22. TRI On- and Off-site Disposal or Other Releases, by State, 2005: Carcinogens. 2005 TRI Public Data Release eReport. EPA. http://www.epa.gov/tri/tridata/tri05/pdfs/eReport.pdf.

3. Source: Table B-25. TRI On- and Off-site Disposal or Other Releases, by State, 2005: Lead and Lead Compounds. EPA. http://www.epa.gov/tri/tridata/tri05/pdfs/eReport.pdf.

4. Source: Table B-28. TRI On- and Off-site Disposal or Other Releases, by State, 2005: Mercury and Mercury Compounds. Toxics Release Inventory (TRI) Program, EPA http://www.epa.gov/tri/tridata/tri05/pdfs/eReport.pdf.

5. Source: Table B-31. TRI On- and Off-site Disposal or Other Releases, by State, 2005: Dioxin and Dioxin-like Compounds. Toxics Release Inventory (TRI) Program, EPA. http://www.epa.gov/tri/tridata/tri05/pdfs/eReport.pdf.

U.S. INDICATOR TABLES

Preserving the Earth for Future Generations *continued*

STATE	CARBON DIOXIDE EMISSIONS (million metric tons)[1]	CARCINOGEN RELEASES (pounds)[2]	LEAD RELEASES (pounds)[3]	MERCURY RELEASES (pounds)[4]	DIOXIN RELEASES (grams)[5]	SUPERFUND SITES[6]	PROTECTED FOREST (acres)[7]	PROTECTED FARM AND RANCH LAND (acres)[8]	ENERGY CONSUMPTION (trillion BTUs per capita)[9]	WATER CONSUMPTION (gallons per day, per capita)[10]
Missouri	138	40,974,736	37,242,284	7,560	16,895	26	...	901	321,911	147,090
Montana	35	18,621,677	14,219,545	30,241	32	14	164,785	1,277	434,759	918,870
Nebraska	43	1,248,047	265,246	2,200	5	13	...	0	373,806	718,767
Nevada	47	260,779,472	86,480,206	3,573,565	6	1	...	579	297,730	140,623
New Hampshire	22	219,357	37,966	161	10	20	214,824	611	263,234	97,913
New Jersey	130	1,482,827	534,653	2,063	141	114	5,413	3,014	304,378	66,078
New Mexico	58	4,312,809	3,799,171	16,970	43	13	5,132	16	360,589	179,215
New York	216	6,309,217	3,621,596	2,403	14	86	44,669	1,444	220,890	63,763
North Carolina	150	8,869,196	1,129,392	6,548	41	31	6,515	761	318,046	141,627
North Dakota	47	1,389,901	136,938	2,776	118	0	...	0	631,739	177,515
Ohio	262	26,935,818	8,485,390	24,246	7	30	436	3,531	351,250	97,770
Oklahoma	99	3,203,072	592,898	6,012	427	10	...	0	422,545	58,540
Oregon	43	8,528,101	204,213	2,291	74	12	25	508	305,217	202,549
Pennsylvania	275	14,478,635	3,813,045	22,771	12	93	2,918	2,672	327,923	81,019
Rhode Island	11	161,202	7,484	3	352	12	1,690	339	211,025	40,923
South Carolina	89	8,092,559	749,067	3,391	47	25	32,251	814	408,789	178,713
South Dakota	14	1,258,578	1,056,592	308	2	2	...	0	340,512	69,948
Tennessee	125	18,730,002	6,330,570	12,541	4,652	13	38,243	125	388,646	189,831
Texas	688	39,700,702	2,638,803	41,426	20,813	42	...	250	533,133	141,954
Utah	64	54,021,423	44,525,125	76,954	5,202	15	53,928	234	304,504	222,554
Vermont	7	49,229	5,947	5,510	0	11	60,711	7,486	273,597	73,420
Virginia	127	3,895,354	779,322	4,487	26	29	5,770	428	342,737	124,744
Washington	85	9,248,810	6,434,678	1,356	99	48	14,795	419	323,884	90,090
West Virginia	112	5,567,848	833,348	9,779	68	9	...	1,625	455,110	284,791
Wisconsin	107	3,744,610	491,245	11,035	134	37	54,772	1,166	335,324	141,508
Wyoming	64	651,372	128,360	2,743	9	2	...	4,229	902,917	1,047,021

6. Source: Superfund National Priorities List Sites, U.S. EPA. http://www.epa.gov/superfund/sites/npl/npl.htm.

7. Source: Acres protected as of 2/1/06, Forest Service, USDA. http://www.fs.fed.us/spf/coop/programs/loa/flp_projects.shtml.

8. Source: Acres protected, FY 2007, Farm and Ranch Lands Protection Program, Natural Resources Conservation Service, USDA. http://www.nrcs.usda.gov/programs/frpp/2007_Easements/07FRPPAcres.pdf.

9. Source: Table S1. Energy Consumption Estimates by Source and End-Use Sector, 2004 (Trillion Btu). Energy Information Administration. http://www.eia.doe.gov/emeu/states/sep_sum/plain_html/sum_btu_1.html. For Population: Table 1: Annual Estimates of the U.S. Population for Regions and States: April 1, 2000, to July 1, 2007. U.S. Census Bureau. http://www.census.gov/popest/states/NST-ann-est.html.

10. Source: Table 2. Total water withdrawals by water-use category, 2000. U.S.Geological Survey. http://pubs.usgs.gov/circ/2004/circ1268/htdocs/table02.html. For Population: Table 1: Annual Estimates of the U.S. Population for Regions and States, April 1, 2000 to July 1, 2007. U.S. Census Bureau. http://www.census.gov/popest/states/NST-ann-est.html. Total water withdrawals per capita (gallons per day).

U.S. INDICATOR TABLES

Housing and Transportation

GROUPING	RENTERS SPENDING 30% OR MORE ON HOUSING [%] 2006[1]	OWNERS SPENDING 30% OR MORE ON HOUSING [percent] 2006[2]	OWNER-OCCUPIED HOUSING UNITS [as % of all housing] 2006[3]	OCCUPIED HOUSING UNITS WITH 1.01 OR MORE OCCUPANTS PER ROOM [%] 2006[4]	COMMUTE 60 MINUTES OR MORE [% of workers 16 and over] 2006[5]	HOMELESS [total number] 2007[6]	HOMELESS [% of population] 2007[7]	HOMELESS YOUTH ENROLLED IN SCHOOL/ AFTER-SCHOOL [total number] 2005–2006[8]
United States	46.0	36.9	67.3	3.0	7.9	744,313	0.30	...
GENDER								
Female	—	—	—	—	6.3	...	...	...
Male	—	—	—	—	9.4	...	...	...
RACE/ETHNICITY								
American Indian/Alaska Native	...	...	56.0	...	...	...	...	...
Asian/Pacific Islander	...	...	60.3	...	...	...	...	...
Black/African American	...	...	46.3	...	...	...	...	...
Hispanic/Latino	...	...	49.3	...	...	...	...	...
White	...	...	74.0	...	...	...	...	...
STATES								
Alabama	41.0	28.8	71.8	1.7	5.8	4,731	0.10	12,891
Alaska	37.8	34.2	64.5	7.0	3.8	2,749	0.41	3,217
Arizona	45.2	37.4	68.5	4.6	6.8	12,264	0.21	19,123
Arkansas	42.3	26.9	68.3	2.3	4.5	5,626	0.20	10,934
California	51.9	51.8	58.4	7.8	10.1	170,270	0.47	169,722
Colorado	47.1	38.5	68.7	2.2	6.0	21,730	0.47	12,689
Connecticut	47.6	39.6	69.5	1.6	6.9	5,357	0.15	2,031
Delaware	46.0	31.3	74.4	1.3	6.3	1,108	0.13	1,565
District of Columbia	45.3	37.8	45.8	2.8	8.8	5,518	1.00	...
Florida	52.0	44.9	70.3	2.5	7.5	60,867	0.34	28,934
Georgia	45.6	33.6	67.7	1.9	9.9	27,161	0.30	33,870
Hawaii	45.7	45.7	59.5	9.1	8.1	5,943	0.47	908
Idaho	38.7	33.9	71.3	2.7	4.6	5,424	0.38	1,849
Illinois	46.0	38.7	69.9	2.4	11.3	16,599	0.13	17,769
Indiana	44.5	26.7	72.1	1.5	5.3	9,857	0.16	7,547
Iowa	40.3	25.1	73.3	1.2	3.2	8,130	0.27	5,819
Kansas	40.8	25.8	69.9	1.6	3.1	5,278	0.19	3,064
Kentucky	40.0	27.7	70.7	1.4	5.3	4,934	0.12	17,058
Louisiana	42.5	28.7	68.5	3.1	7.8	5,476	0.12	118,351
Maine	42.2	33.4	72.8	1.1	5.5	2,775	0.21	1,220

1. Source: Table GCT2515. % of Renter-Occupied Units Spending 30% or More of Household Income on Rent and Utilities, 2006. http://factfinder.census.gov/servlet/GCTTable?_bm=y&-state=gct&-context=gct&-ds_name=ACS_2006_EST_G00_&-_box_head_nbr=GCT2515&-mt_name=&-tree_id=306&-_caller=geoselect&-geo_id=&-format=US-9&-_lang=en. ACS, 2006.

2. Source: Table GCT2513. % of Mortgaged Owners Spending 30% or More of Household Income on Selected Monthly Owner Costs. http://factfinder.census.gov/servlet/GCTTable?_bm=y&-state=gct&-context=gct&-ds_name=ACS_2006_EST_G00_&-_box_head_nbr=GCT2513&-mt_name=&-tree_id=306&-redoLog=true&-_caller=geoselect&-geo_id=&-format=US-9&-_lang=en. ACS, 2006.

3. Source: Owner-occupied housing units as percent of all housing units, 2006. Table B25003. Tenure; Table B25003C. Tenure (American Indian and Alaska Native Alone Householder); Table B25003I. Tenure (Asian Alone Householder); Table B25003B. Tenure (Black or African American Alone Householder); Table B25003H. Tenure (White Alone, Not Hispanic or Latino Householder); Table B25003H. Tenure (White Alone, Not Hispanic or Latino Householder) http://factfinder.census.gov/servlet/DatasetMainPageServlet?_program=ACS&_submenuId=&_lang=en&_ts=. ACS, 2006.

4. Source: Table GCT2509. % of Occupied Housing Units With 1.01 or More Occupants Per Room. http://factfinder.census.gov/servlet/GCTTable?_bm=y&-state=gct&-ds_name=ACS_2006_EST_G00_&-_box_head_nbr=GCT2509&-mt_name=&-redoLog=true&-_caller=geoselect&-geo_id=&-format=US-9&-_lang=en. ACS, 2006.

U.S. INDICATOR TABLES
Housing and Transportation *continued*

GROUPING	RENTERS SPENDING 30% OR MORE ON HOUSING [%] 2006[1]	OWNERS SPENDING 30% OR MORE ON HOUSING [percent] 2006[2]	OWNER-OCCUPIED HOUSING UNITS [as % of all housing] 2006[3]	OCCUPIED HOUSING UNITS WITH 1.01 OR MORE OCCUPANTS PER ROOM [%] 2006[4]	COMMUTE 60 MINUTES OR MORE [% of workers 16 and over] 2006[5]	HOMELESS [total number] 2007[6]	HOMELESS [% of population] 2007[7]	HOMELESS YOUTH ENROLLED IN SCHOOL/ AFTER-SCHOOL [total number] 2005–2006[8]
Maryland	43.7	35.0	69.4	1.6	13.1	7,995	0.14	7,430
Massachusetts	48.6	41.8	64.9	1.5	9.3	14,730	0.23	10,153
Michigan	47.8	35.2	75.2	1.6	5.6	26,124	0.26	13,234
Minnesota	44.6	33.9	76.3	1.6	4.6	7,313	0.14	7,297
Mississippi	42.7	33.1	70.7	3.3	6.4	1,652	0.06	6,555
Missouri	42.3	28.7	70.7	1.6	5.0	7,135	0.12	14,071
Montana	40.0	34.7	69.9	1.6	4.5	1,343	0.14	1,952
Nebraska	39.0	27.5	67.9	1.7	3.0	3,350	0.19	2,602
Nevada	48.1	45.4	62.0	3.7	5.8	16,402	0.68	6,052
New Hampshire	46.4	39.0	72.1	1.0	7.8	3,233	0.25	1,013
New Jersey	47.3	44.7	67.3	2.5	13.2	19,385	0.22	4,383
New Mexico	41.9	31.0	69.7	3.4	4.4	5,256	0.27	5,173
New York	48.1	40.9	55.6	4.3	16.1	61,094	0.32	26,213
North Carolina	42.7	31.3	68.1	2.0	5.4	10,765	0.12	10,786
North Dakota	36.0	23.0	66.7	0.9	3.0	655	0.10	685
Ohio	44.9	31.8	70.0	1.2	4.3	16,165	0.14	11,977
Oklahoma	41.4	26.8	68.6	2.4	3.9	4,869	0.14	3,452
Oregon	47.0	39.1	64.8	2.5	5.0	16,221	0.45	13,159
Pennsylvania	43.0	32.6	71.7	1.0	7.8	15,298	0.12	25,000
Rhode Island	44.9	43.5	63.0	1.6	5.1	6,866	0.64	462
South Carolina	40.3	31.8	70.3	1.6	4.9	7,958	0.19	6,538
South Dakota	34.0	26.8	69.2	2.1	2.7	1,029	0.13	896
Tennessee	42.3	31.5	69.9	1.6	5.1	8,066	0.14	9,619
Texas	44.4	33.3	65.2	4.8	7.1	43,630	0.19	195,521
Utah	42.1	33.1	72.0	3.8	4.3	3,104	0.13	10,087
Vermont	47.1	36.5	71.9	1.2	4.9	927	0.15	681
Virginia	42.1	34.2	69.9	1.4	9.3	10,346	0.14	10,564
Washington	44.9	39.8	65.5	2.4	7.8	23,970	0.38	13,942
West Virginia	39.3	24.5	74.7	0.9	9.4	1,522	0.08	2,779
Wisconsin	43.3	33.4	70.5	1.4	4.1	6,773	0.12	6,987
Wyoming	30.0	26.9	69.5	1.9	6.2	487	0.10	678

5. Source: Table B080121. Sex of workers by travel time to work. http://factfinder.census.gov/servlet/DatasetMainPageServlet?_program=ACS&_submenuId=&_lang=en&_ts=. ACS, 2006.

6 and **7.** Source: Table 2. Estimates of Homelessness by State. Homelessness Counts, by Mary Cunningham and Meghan Henry, Homelessness Research Institute, National Alliance to End Homelessness, January 2007. http://www.endhomelessness.org/content/article/detail/1440.

8. Source: Appendix 1. Total Homeless Children and Youth Enrolled in Local Education Agencies, 2003–2006. Title VII-B of the McKinney-Vento Homeless Assistance Act, National Center for Homeless Education, June 2007. http://www.ed.gov/programs/homeless/2003-2006feddatacomparisonrpt.pdf.

Protecting Personal and Community Security

GROUPING	VIOLENT CRIME RATE (per 100,000 inhabitants) 2006[1]	PROPERTY CRIME RATE (per 100,000 inhabitants) 2006[2]	HOMICIDE (per 100,000 inhabitants) 2002-2004[3]	HOMICIDE AND SUICIDE BY HANDGUN [%] 2005[4]	SUICIDE (average per 100,000 inhabitants) 2002-2004[5]	RAPE 2006[6]	RAPE (per 100,000 inhabitants) 2007[7]	STATE POLICE BUDGET ($ per resident) 2000[8]	PRISONERS, STATE OR FEDERAL JURISDICTION (total number) 2006[9]	PRISONERS (per 100,000 inhabitants) 2006[10]	CHILD MALTREATMENT RATE (per 1,000 children) 2005[11]
United States	474	3,335	6	…	11	92,455	31	—	1,570,861	526	12
GENDER											
Female	…	…	3	…	4	…	…	—	103,100	68	…
Male	…	…	10	…	18	…	…	—	1,399,100	951	…
RACE/ETHNICITY											
American Indian/Alaska Native	…	…	8	…	11	…	…	—	…	…	…
Asian/Pacific Islander	…	…	3	…	6	…	…	—	…	…	…
Black/African American	…	…	22	…	5	…	…	—	562,800	1536	…
Hispanic/Latino	…	…	8	…	6	…	…	—	308,000	699	…
White	…	…	3	…	13	…	…	—	527,100	265	…
STATES											
Alabama	425	3,936	9	68.4	12	1,649	36	20.00	28,241	615	8
Alaska	688	3,605	7	59.4	21	509	76	87.00	5,069	748	14
Arizona	501	4,628	9	76.1	16	1,941	32	24.00	35,892	582	4
Arkansas	552	3,968	7	68.4	14	1,308	47	22.00	13,729	489	12
California	533	3,171	7	73.8	9	9,212	25	3.00	175,512	484	10
Colorado	392	3,451	4	64.1	17	2,076	44	15.00	22,481	472	8
Connecticut	281	2,504	3	48.0	8	636	18	34.00	20,566	588	14
Delaware	682	3,418	4	62.2	11	400	47	87.00	7,206	845	10
District of Columbia	1,508	4,654	35	…	6	185	32	…	…	…	25
Florida	712	3,986	6	…	14	6,475	36	9.00	92,969	515	32
Georgia	471	3,889	8	71.7	11	2,173	23	14.00	52,792	565	20
Hawaii	281	4,230	2	10.0	10	355	28	…	5,967	467	9
Idaho	247	2,419	2	67.6	16	587	40	36.00	7,124	487	5
Illinois	542	3,020	8	75.7	8	4,078	32	30.00	45,106	353	9
Indiana	315	3,502	6	72.2	12	1,835	29	17.00	26,091	414	12
Iowa	284	2,803	2	55.3	11	828	28	12.00	8,875	299	21
Kansas	425	3,750	5	54.7	13	1,238	45	9.00	8,816	320	4
Kentucky	263	2,545	5	70.1	14	1,297	31	31.00	20,000	476	20
Louisiana	698	3,994	13	77.4	11	1,562	36	28.00	37,012	872	11
Maine	116	2,519	1	36.8	12	339	26	32.00	2,120	161	12

1. Source: Violent crime rate per 100,000 inhabitants, 2006. Table 5. Crime in the U.S. by State, 2006, FBI, U.S. Department of Justice, September 2007. http://www.fbi.gov/ucr/cius2006/data/table_05.html.

2. Source: Property crime rate per 100,000 inhabitants, 2006. Table 5. Crime in the U.S. by State, 2006, Criminal Justice Information Services Division, FBI, U.S. Department of Justice, September 2007. http://www.fbi.gov/ucr/cius2006/data/table_05.html.

3. Source: Homicide rate, average per 100,000 population, Injury Mortality: US/State, 2001–2004, Health Data for All Ages, NCHS, CDC, U.S. Department of Health and Human Services. http://www.cdc.gov/nchs/health_data_for_all_ages.htm.

4. Source: Bureau of Justice Statistics, Office of Justice Programs, U.S. Department of Justice. http://bjsdata.ojp.usdoj.gov/dataonline/Search/Homicide/State/StateHomicide.cfm.

5. Source: Injury Mortality: US/State, 2001–2004, Health Data for All Ages, NCHS, CDC, U.S. Department of Health and Human Services. http://www.cdc.gov/nchs/health_data_for_all_ages.htm. Average suicide rate per 100,000 population.

6. Source: Forcible rapes, 2006. Table 1. Crime in the U.S. by Volume and Rate per 100,000 Inhabitants, 1987-2006, Table 5. Crime in the U.S. by State, 2006, Criminal Justice Information Services Division, FBI, U.S. Department of Justice, September 2007. http://www.fbi.gov/ucr/cius2006/data/table_05.html.

U.S. INDICATOR TABLES
Protecting Personal and Community Security *continued*

GROUPING	VIOLENT CRIME RATE (per 100,000 inhabitants) 2006[1]	PROPERTY CRIME RATE (per 100,000 inhabitants) 2006[2]	HOMICIDE (per 100,000 inhabitants) 2002-2004[3]	HOMICIDE AND SUICIDE BY HANDGUN (%) 2005[4]	SUICIDE (average per 100,000 inhabitants) 2002-2004[5]	RAPE 2006[6]	RAPE (per 100,000 inhabitants) 2006[7]	STATE POLICE BUDGET ($ per resident) 2000[8]	PRISONERS, STATE OR FEDERAL JURISDICTION (total number) 2006[9]	PRISONERS (per 100,000 inhabitants) 2006[10]	CHILD MALTREATMENT RATE (per 1,000 children) 2005[11]
Maryland	679	3,481	10	75.9	9	1,178	21	47.00	22,945	410	10
Massachusetts	447	2,391	3	55.0	7	1,742	27	35.00	11,032	172	25
Michigan	562	3,213	7	68.7	11	5,269	52	27.00	51,577	511	10
Minnesota	312	3,080	3	63.5	10	1,645	32	12.00	9,108	177	7
Mississippi	299	3,209	10	69.6	12	1,000	34	17.00	21,068	727	8
Missouri	546	3,827	6	70.1	12	1,764	30	27.00	30,167	517	7
Montana	254	2,688	3	29.4	20	269	29	19.00	3,572	377	10
Nebraska	282	3,341	3	38.5	10	548	31	19.00	4,407	250	15
Nevada	742	4,089	8	60.2	19	1,079	43	26.00	12,901	518	8
New Hampshire	139	1,874	1	37.5	11	344	26	25.00	2,805	214	3
New Jersey	352	2,292	5	66.0	7	1,237	14	24.00	27,371	316	5
New Mexico	643	3,937	9	49.6	19	1,094	56	22.00	6,639	342	15
New York	435	2,053	5	57.6	6	3,169	16	21.00	63,315	328	16
North Carolina	476	4,121	7	62.4	12	2,495	28	17.00	37,460	422	16
North Dakota	128	2,000	2	14.3	13	193	30	19.00	1,363	214	11
Ohio	350	3,679	5	57.3	11	4,548	40	18.00	49,166	429	15
Oklahoma	497	3,604	6	69.0	14	1,488	42	25.00	26,243	734	16
Oregon	280	3,672	3	60.8	16	1,195	32	56.00	13,707	371	15
Pennsylvania	439	2,444	5	71.9	11	3,401	27	42.00	44,397	358	2
Rhode Island	228	2,587	3	47.1	8	285	27	36.00	3,996	376	14
South Carolina	766	4,242	8	69.4	11	1,762	41	14.00	23,616	545	11
South Dakota	171	1,620	3	42.9	13	336	43	18.00	3,359	426	8
Tennessee	760	4,128	8	70.5	13	2,142	36	25.00	25,745	424	13
Texas	516	4,082	7	67.1	11	8,372	36	17.00	172,116	735	10
Utah	224	3,516	2	49.1	15	869	34	16.00	6,430	249	18
Vermont	137	2,305	2	62.5	14	150	24	49.00	2,215	357	8
Virginia	282	2,478	6	69.5	11	1,792	23	28.00	36,688	480	4
Washington	346	4,480	4	61.5	13	2,746	43	27.00	17,561	276	5
West Virginia	280	2,622	5	55.6	15	389	21	41.00	5,733	317	25
Wisconsin	284	2,818	3	68.0	12	1,131	20	9.00	23,431	421	8
Wyoming	240	2,981	4	50.0	20	140	27	32.00	2,114	412	8

7. Source: Forcible rapes per 100,000 inhabitants. Table 1. Crime in the U.S. by Volume and Rate per 100,000 Inhabitants, 1987-2006, Table 5. Crime in the United States by State, 2006, Criminal Justice Information Services Division, FBI, U.S. Department of Justice, September 2007. http://www.fbi.gov/ucr/cius2006/data/table_05.html.

8. Source: Budget, state police, highway patrol, or similar agency, per resident. Budgets, 2000. Bureau of Justice Statistics. U.S. Department of Justice. http://bjsdata.ojp.usdoj.gov/dataonline/Search/Law/Law.cfm.

9 and **10.** Source: Table 1. Prisoners under the jurisdiction of State or Federal correctional authorities, 2006. Bureau of Justice Statistics December 2007 Bulletin, NCJ 219416. Data do not include local, juvenile or military inmates. For total population: Population Division, U.S. Census Bureau, Table 1: Annual Estimates of the Population for the United States, Regions, States, and Puerto Rico: April 1, 2000 to July 1, 2007 (NST-EST2007-01). Population Division, U.S. Census Bureau, Table 3: Annual Estimates of the Population by Sex, Race, and Hispanic Origin for the United States: April 1, 2000 to July 1, 2007 (NC-EST2007-03). Race/ethnicity data include only sentenced prisoners.

11. Source: Table 3–4. Child Maltreatment 2005. U.S. Department of Health and Human Services. http://www.acf.hhs.gov/programs/cb/pubs/cm05/cm05.pdf. Child maltreatment includes physical, sexual, psychological abuse, medical or other neglect and/or abandonment.

Protecting National Security

STATE	NUMBER OF ARMY RECRUITS 2006[1]	ARMY RECRUITS (per 1,000 youth) 2005[2]	ARMY RECRUITS (per 1,000 youth) 2006[3]	CHANGE from 2005–2006[4]
United States	68,556	1.57	1.63	3.78
Alabama	1,518	2.17	2.35	8.37
Alaska	238	2.10	2.13	1.28
Arizona	1,554	1.82	1.85	1.38
Arkansas	981	2.22	2.47	11.14
California	6,339	1.31	1.21	-7.33
Colorado	1,134	1.79	1.72	-3.89
Connecticut	386	0.81	0.83	1.89
Delaware	105	1.01	0.89	-11.44
District of Columbia	61	0.71	0.89	25.36
Florida	4,301	1.68	1.87	11.03
Georgia	2,525	1.72	1.92	11.76
Hawaii	346	1.48	1.94	31.00
Idaho	388	1.59	1.73	8.61
Illinois	2,534	1.37	1.41	2.58
Indiana	1,763	1.72	1.96	14.15
Iowa	663	1.55	1.53	-1.34
Kansas	863	1.84	2.07	12.67
Kentucky	990	1.66	1.71	3.29
Louisiana	921	1.61	1.32	-18.17
Maine	432	2.09	2.37	13.56
Maryland	1,135	1.37	1.45	5.99
Massachusetts	777	0.98	0.91	-6.80
Michigan	2,595	1.54	1.79	16.39
Minnesota	751	1.03	0.99	-3.72
Mississippi	582	1.36	1.31	-3.93
Missouri	1,676	1.89	2.00	5.80
Montana	335	2.52	2.39	-5.25
Nebraska	447	1.75	1.68	-4.16
Nevada	577	1.67	1.81	8.28
New Hampshire	293	1.46	1.61	10.07
New Jersey	936	0.90	0.83	-8.13
New Mexico	538	1.47	1.81	23.04
New York	3,219	1.13	1.23	8.71
North Carolina	2,533	1.92	2.13	10.93
North Dakota	103	1.44	1.02	-29.23
Ohio	2,615	1.56	1.62	3.82
Oklahoma	1,296	2.41	2.44	1.35
Oregon	943	1.67	1.87	12.07
Pennsylvania	2,058	1.24	1.20	-2.94
Rhode Island	144	0.85	0.95	11.27
South Carolina	1,298	1.92	2.13	11.00
South Dakota	183	1.97	1.52	-23.06
Tennessee	1,468	1.51	1.79	18.76
Texas	8,214	2.27	2.38	5.02
Utah	396	0.96	0.91	-4.91
Vermont	84	0.97	0.92	-4.84
Virginia	1,925	1.85	1.80	-2.88
Washington	1,414	1.58	1.55	-1.89
West Virginia	462	1.97	1.94	-1.30
Wisconsin	1,396	1.54	1.72	11.38
Wyoming	121	1.83	1.53	-16.17

1–4. National Priorities Project. http://www.nationalpriorities.org/ charts/Army-recruits-total-and-per-1000-youth-by-state-2005.html.

OECD INDICATOR TABLES
Demographics

COUNTRY	TOTAL POPULATION (in millions) 2006[1]	POPULATION UNDER AGE 15 (% of total population) 2006[2]	POPULATION AGE 65 AND OVER (% of total population) 2006[3]	AGING INDEX (population 65 and over per 100 youth under 15) 2006[4]
U.S. Rank	1	5	23	24
United States	299	20.6	12.4	60.2
Australia	21	19.3	12.8	66.3
Austria	8	15.2	17.0	111.8
Belgium	11	16.6	17.6	106.0
Canada	33	17.3	13.3	76.9
Czech Republic	10	14.3	14.4	100.7
Denmark	5	18.7	15.2	81.3
Finland	5	17.1	16.1	94.2
France	61	18.1	16.6	91.7
Germany	82	14.1	19.2	136.2
Greece	11	14.2	18.3	128.9
Hungary	10	15.5	15.4	99.4
Iceland	0	21.7	11.8	54.4
Ireland	4	20.1	10.9	54.2
Italy	59	14.0	20.2	144.3
Japan	128	13.9	20.2	145.3
Korea	48	18.1	9.8	54.1
Luxembourg	1	18.8	13.8	73.4
Mexico	104	30.4	5.5	18.1
Netherlands	16	18.1	14.2	78.5
New Zealand	4	21.0	12.4	59.1
Norway	5	19.4	15.0	77.3
Poland	38	15.9	13.0	81.8
Portugal	11	15.8	17.2	108.9
Slovak Republic	5	16.2	11.9	73.5
Spain	44	14.4	16.5	114.6
Sweden	9	17.2	17.4	101.2
Switzerland	7	16.2	16.3	100.6
Turkey	73	28.9	5.5	19.0
United Kingdom	60	17.7	16.0	90.4

1. Source: World Development Indicators Online Database. Total population counts all residents regardless of legal status or citizenship—except for refugees not permanently settled in the country of asylum. World Bank estimates from: census reports, United Nations Population Division's World Population Prospects, national statistical offices, household surveys conducted by national agencies, Macro International, 2007.

2. Source: World Development Indicators Online Database. Definition: Percentage of the total population in age group 0 to 14. World Bank estimates from: census reports, United Nations Population Division's World Population Prospects, national statistical offices, household surveys conducted by national agencies and Macro International, 2007.

3. World Development Indicators Online Database. Definition: Percentage of total population 65 or older. World Bank estimates from: census reports, the United Nations Population Division's World Population Prospects, national statistical offices, household surveys conducted by national agencies and Macro International, 2007.

4. Calculated from columns 2 and 3. Definition: Number of people age 65 and over per 100 youths under age 15.

A Long and Healthy Life

COUNTRY	LIFE EXPECTANCY AT BIRTH Male 2007[1]	LIFE EXPECTANCY AT BIRTH Female 2007[2]	INFANT MORTALITY RATE (per 1,000 live births) 2007[3]	TOTAL HEALTH EXPENDITURE (% of GDP) 2004–2005[4]	HEALTH EXPENDITURE PUBLIC (% of GDP) 2004[5]	HEALTH EXPENDITURE PRIVATE (% of GDP) 2004[6]	
U.S. Rank	23	23	25	1	11	1	
United States	75.1	80.5	7	15.3	6.9	8.5	
Australia	78.4	83.4	5	9.5	6.5	3.1	
Austria	76.8	82.4	4	10.2	7.8	2.5	
Belgium	76.4	82.6	4	10.3	6.9	2.8	
Canada	78.1	83.0	5	9.8	6.8	3.0	
Czech Republic	73.0	79.3	5	7.2	6.5	0.8	
Denmark	75.5	80.0	5	9.1	7.1	1.5	
Finland	75.9	82.3	4	7.5	5.7	1.7	
France	76.5	83.4	4	11.1	8.2	2.3	
Germany	76.3	82.1	4	10.7	8.2	2.5	
Greece	76.0	81.2	6	10.1	4.2	3.7	
Hungary	69.7	77.7	8	8.1	5.7	2.2	
Iceland	79.5	83.2	3	9.5	8.3	1.6	
Ireland	75.9	81.0	5	7.5	5.7	1.5	
Italy	77.4	83.5	5	8.9	6.5	2.2	
Japan	79.1	86.3	3	8.0	6.3	1.5	
Korea	74.4	81.8	3	6.0	2.9	2.7	
Luxembourg	75.8	82.1	5	8.3	7.2	0.8	
Mexico	73.6	78.5	17	6.4	3.0	3.5	
Netherlands	76.2	81.6	4	9.2	5.7	3.5	
New Zealand	77.6	81.9	5	9.0	6.5	1.9	
Norway	77.7	82.5	3	9.1	8.1	1.6	
Poland	71.1	79.0	8	6.2	4.3	2.0	
Portugal	76.4	81.1	5	10.2	7.0	2.8	
Slovak Republic	71.0	78.6	7	7.1	5.3	1.9	
Spain	76.5	83.7	4	8.2	5.7	2.4	
Sweden	78.6	82.9	2	9.1	7.7	1.4	
Switzerland	78.2	83.7	4	11.6	6.7	4.8	
Turkey	67.3	72.0	37	7.6	5.6	2.1	
United Kingdom	76.6	81.2	5	8.3	7.0	1.1	

1, 2, and **3.** Source: United Nations Population Fund, "State of the World Population 2007." http://www.unfpa.org/swp/2007/presskit/pdf/sowp2007_eng.pdf.

4. Source: OECD Health at a Glance, 2007. Data from most recent available year.

5 and **6.** Source: World Development Indicators Online Database, World Bank, 2007 from sources: World Health Organization, World Health Report and updates and OECD. Public health expenditure consists of recurrent and capital spending from government budgets, external borrowings and grants, and health insurance funds. Private health expenditure includes direct household (out-of-pocket) spending, private insurance, charitable donations, and direct service payments by private corporations.

COUNTRY	HEALTH EXPENDITURE (PPP US$ per capita) 2005[7]	NEW AIDS CASES (per million population) 2005[8]	TOBACCO CONSUMPTION (% of population smoking daily) 2005 or latest available year[9]	OBESITY (% of adult population) 2005 or latest available year[10]	SUICIDE (per 100,000 population) 2001–2004[11]	PRACTICING PHYSICIANS (per 1,000 inhabitants) 2005 or latest year available[12]
U.S. Rank	1	1	28	1	8	21
United States	6,401	137	16.9	32.2	10.2	2.4
Australia	3,128	13	17.7	21.7	10.2	2.7
Austria	3,519	12.5	...	9.1	14.5	3.5
Belgium	3,389	15.5	20.0	12.7	...	4.0
Canada	3,326	9.8	17.3	18.0	10.6	2.2
Czech Republic	1,479	1.1	24.3	17.0	13.0	3.6
Denmark	3,108	8.9	26.0	11.4	11.3	3.6
Finland	2,331	5.4	21.8	14.1	18.4	2.4
France	3,374	22	23.0	9.5	15.3	3.4
Germany	3,287	8.1	24.3	13.6	10.3	3.4
Greece	2,981	9.1	38.6	21.9	2.6	4.9
Hungary	1,337	3.3	30.4	18.8	22.6	3.0
Iceland	3,443	3.4	19.5	12.4	11.7	3.7
Ireland	2,926	11.2	27.0	13.0	10.0	2.8
Italy	2,532	25.4	22.3	9.9	5.6	3.8
Japan	2,358	2.9	29.2	3.0	19.1	2.0
Korea	1,318	1.4	25.3	3.5	24.2	1.6
Luxembourg	5,352	17.4	23.0	18.6	12.5	2.5
Mexico	675	45.3	26.4	30.2	...	1.8
Netherlands	3,094	12.1	31.0	10.7	7.9	3.7
New Zealand	2,343	8.3	22.5	20.9	13.0	2.2
Norway	4,364	8.5	25.0	9.0	10.9	3.7
Poland	867	4.3	26.3	12.5	14.0	2.1
Portugal	2,033	79.5	17.0	12.8	8.7	3.4
Slovak Republic	1,137	0.6	24.3	15.4	11.9	3.1
Spain	2,255	36	28.1	13.1	6.6	3.8
Sweden	2,918	5.1	15.9	10.7	11.4	3.4
Switzerland	4,177	37.1	26.8	7.7	14.0	3.8
Turkey	586	5	32.1	12.0	...	1.5
United Kingdom	2,724	13.3	24.0	23.0	6.3	2.4

7. Source: OECD Health at a Glance, 2007.

8. Source: OECD Health at a Glance, 2007. European data extracted from European Center for the Epidemiological Monitoring of AIDS. All data from 2005 except Norway and Mexico (2003) and France (2004).

9. Source: OECD Health at a Glance 2007: OECD Indicators.

10. Source: OECD Health at a Glance, 2007. Percentage of adult population with Body Mass Index over 30. Data from latest year available from 2002—2005 except Austria, Australia, and Portugal (1999).

11. Source: OECD Health at a Glance, 2007. Age-standardized suicide rates per 100,000 population.

12. Source: OECD Health at a Glance, 2007. Data for Spain include dentists and stomatologists. Ireland, the Netherlands, New Zealand and Portugal provide number of all physicians entitled to practice.

OECD INDICATOR TABLES

Access to Knowledge

COUNTRY	POPULATION LACKING FUNCTIONAL LITERACY SKILLS (% aged 16–65) 1994–2003[1]	PERFORMANCE IN SCIENCE LITERACY TEST (top score 1,000) 2006[2]	PERFORMANCE IN MATH LITERACY TEST (top score 1,000) 2006[3]	PUBLIC EXPENDITURE ON EDUCATION (% of GDP) 2004[4]	PUBLIC EXPENDITURE ON EDUCATION (% of government expenditure) 2004 or most recent year available[5]	INTERNET USERS (per 1,000 people) 2004–2005[6]	SPENDING ON RESEARCH AND DEVELOPMENT (% of GDP) 2003–2006[7]	SPENDING ON RESEARCH AND DEVELOPMENT (PPP$ per capita) 2003–2006[8]
U.S. Rank	4	21	25	9	6	10	7	3
United States	20.0	489	474	5.9	15.3	630	2.7	1058
Australia	17.0	527	520	4.8	13.3	698	1.8	542
Austria	...	511	505	5.5	10.8	486	2.4	868
Belgium	18.4	510	520	6.1	12.2	458	1.8	588
Canada	14.6	534	527	5.2	12.5	520	2.0	697
Czech Republic	...	513	510	4.4	10.0	270	1.4	291
Denmark	9.6	498	513	8.6	15.3	527	2.4	829
Finland	10.4	563	548	6.5	12.8	534	3.5	1169
France	...	495	496	5.9	10.9	430	2.1	651
Germany	14.4	516	504	4.6	9.8	455	2.5	737
Greece	...	473	459	4.3	8.5	180	0.6	143
Hungary	...	504	491	5.5	11.1	297	1.0	170
Iceland	...	491	506	8.1	16.6	869	2.8	963
Ireland	22.6	508	501	4.8	14.0	276	1.2	481
Italy	47.0	475	462	4.7	9.6	478	1.1	307
Japan	...	531	523	3.6	9.8	668	3.2	940
Korea	...	522	547	4.6	16.5	684	3.0	666
Luxembourg	...	486	490	...	8.5	690	1.6	924
Mexico	...	410	406	5.4	25.6	181	0.4	40
Netherlands	10.5	525	531	5.4	11.2	739	1.8	563
New Zealand	18.4	530	522	6.8	20.9	672	1.1	266
Norway	7.9	487	490	7.7	16.6	735	1.5	627
Poland	...	498	495	5.4	12.7	262	0.6	78
Portugal	...	474	466	5.7	11.5	279	0.8	166
Slovak Republic	...	488	492	4.3	10.8	464	0.5	83
Spain	...	488	480	4.3	11.0	348	1.1	306
Sweden	7.5	503	502	7.4	13.0	764	3.9	1252
Switzerland	15.9	512	530	6.0	13.0	498	2.9	1024
Turkey	...	424	424	4.0	12.4	222	0.7	51
United Kingdom	21.8	515	495	5.4	12.1	474	1.7	560

1. Source: UNDP, Human Development Report 2007/2008. http://hdrstats.undp.org/indicators/30.html. Percent of adults ages 16–65 lacking functional literacy using standardized literacy test—scoring at level 1 on the International Adult Literacy Survey. Data refer to most recent year available during period specified.

2 and **3.** Source: U.S. Department of Education, National Center of Education Statistics, 2007, http://nces.ed.gov/pubs2008/2008016.pdf. Program for International Student Assessment (PISA) 2006. Average performance of 15-year-old students in science and math literacy.

4 and **5.** Source: World Development Indicators Online Database, World Bank. From UNESCO Institute for Statistics. Public expenditure on education consists of current and capital public expenditure on education plus subsidies to private education at the primary, secondary, and tertiary levels. Data for Canada refer to 2003.

6. Source: World Development Indicators Online Database, World Bank, 2007. Internet users are people with access to the worldwide network. Data from International Telecommunication Union, World Telecommunication Development Report and database, and World Bank estimates.

7 and **8.** Source: UNESCO Institute for Statistics, 2007. "Science and Technology Reports." http://stats.uis.unesco.org/unesco/ReportFolders/reportFolders.aspx. Data refer to the most recent year available during the period specified. Contains some provisional data as per source.

OECD INDICATOR TABLES
A Decent Standard of Living

COUNTRY	GROSS DOMESTIC PRODUCT (PPP$ per capita) 2006[1]	GDP GROWTH RATE (annual %) 2006[2]	INCOME RATIO OF RICHEST 10% TO POOREST 10% 1994–2004[3]	POPULATION LIVING BELOW 50% OF MEDIAN INCOME (%) 2000–2004[4]	CHILD POVERTY RATE (%) around 2000[5]	UNEMPLOYMENT RATE (% 15 and over) 2005[6]	LONG-TERM UNEMPLOYMENT (% of total unemployment) 2005[7]	SAVINGS RATE (as % of household disposable income) 2004–2005[8]	MATERNITY LEAVE (weeks entitlement, paid or unpaid)[9]	STATUTORY MINIMUM PAID ANNUAL LEAVE (number of days)[10]
U.S. Rank	2	14	3	2	2	18	24	17	23	27
United States	44,155	3.3	15.9	17.0	21.6	5.1	11.8	-0.4	12	0
Australia	35,493	2.4	12.5	12.2	11.6	5.1	17.7	-3.7	...	20
Austria	35,560	3.1	6.9	7.7	13.3	5.2	25.3	9.1	16	25
Belgium	34,713	3.2	8.2	8.0	4.1	8.1	51.6	...	15	20
Canada	35,030	2.8	9.4	11.4	13.6	6.8	9.6	1.2	17	10 to 20
Czech Republic	22,791	6.1	5.2	4.9	7.2	7.9	53.6	0.5	28	20
Denmark	36,354	3.2	8.1	5.6	2.4	4.8	25.9	1.1	18	25
Finland	35,195	5.5	5.6	5.4	3.4	8.4	24.9	-0.1	18	20
France	33,408	2.0	9.1	7.3	7.3	9.8	42.5	11.5	16	25
Germany	31,744	2.8	6.9	8.4	12.8	11.1	54.0	10.7	14	20
Greece	25,076	4.3	10.2	14.3	12.5	9.6	53.7	-7.8	17	20
Hungary	19,585	3.9	5.5	6.7	13.1	7.2	46.1	...	24	20
Iceland	38,885	2.6	...	...	...	2.6	11.2	...	13	...
Ireland	41,925	6.0	9.4	16.2	15.7	4.3	34.3	...	26	20
Italy	30,654	1.9	11.6	12.7	15.7	7.7	52.2	11.6	21	20
Japan	32,385	2.2	4.5	11.8	14.3	4.4	33.3	3.2	14	10 to 20
Korea	23,800	5.0	7.8	...	...	3.7	0.8	4.4	12	8 to 20
Luxembourg	69,246	6.2	...	6.0	...	4.5	26.3	...	16	25
Mexico	11,532	4.8	24.6	20.2	24.8	3.5	2.4	...	12	....
Netherlands	36,219	2.9	9.2	7.3	9.0	5.2	40.1	7.1	16	20
New Zealand	26,736	1.7	12.5	...	14.6	3.7	9.4	...	12	20
Norway	43,579	2.9	6.1	6.4	3.6	4.6	9.5	...	26	21
Poland	15,444	5.8	8.8	8.6	9.9	17.7	52.2	2.4	16	20
Portugal	21,943	1.3	15.0	...	15.6	7.6	48.6	...	17	22
Slovak Republic	17,827	8.3	6.7	7.0	...	16.2	68.1	...	28	20
Spain	28,554	3.9	10.3	14.2	15.6	9.2	32.6	4.6	16	22
Sweden	35,162	4.4	6.2	6.5	3.6	7.7	18.9	8.7	15	25
Switzerland	37,919	2.7	9.0	7.6	6.8	4.4	38.8	9.1	16	20 to 25
Turkey	9,073	6.1	16.8	...	21.1	10.3	39.6	...	12	...
United Kingdom	34,983	2.8	13.8	12.5	16.2	4.6	22.4	-0.1	52	20

1. Source: World Development Indicators Online Database, World Bank, 2007. GDP Per Capita (PPP) is gross domestic product on a purchasing power parity (PPP) basis divided by population as of July 1 for the same year. Purchasing power parity is a rate of exchange that accounts for price differentials across countries, allowing for international comparison.

2. Source: World Development Indicators Online Database, World Bank, 2007. GDP Growth Rate is gross domestic product growth on an annual basis adjusted for inflation and expressed as a percent.

3. Source: UNDP, Human Development Report 2007–2008. Data refer to the most recent year available during the period specified.

4. Source: UNDP, Human Development Report 2007-2008. Data refer to the most recent year available during the period specified. For Czech Republic, Hungary, Netherlands, Poland, Slovak Republic, and United Kingdom data refer to a year between 1996 and 1999.

5. Source: OECD, 2007. Babies and Bosses—Reconciling Work and Family Life (Vol. 5). Table 1.1. http://www .oecd.org/document/45/0,3343,en_ 2649_34819_39651501_1_1_1,00 .html#Selection. Child poverty rate is the share of children with equivalized incomes less than 50% of the median for the entire population.

6 and 7. Source: International Labour Organization, Key Indicators of the Labour Market database (KILM), Fifth Edition, CD-ROM version.

Unemployment refers to the share of the labor force 15 and over without work but available for and seeking employment. Data for the Netherlands for total unemployment rate is from 2003. Long-term unemployment refers to number of people with continuous periods of unemployment extending for a year or longer, expressed as % of the total unemployed. Long-term unemployment data for Iceland and Sweden refer to 2004. Reference period: April.

8. Source: OECD Factbook 2007. http://oberon.sourceoecd. org/vl=2579969/cl=12/nw=1/rpsv/ factbook/02-02-02.htm. Saving rate is household net saving rate estimated by subtracting household consumption expenditure from household disposable income. Data refer to the most recent year available during the period specified.

9. OECD, 2007, Babies and Bosses; Reconciling Work and Family Life (Vol. 5): A Synthesis of Findings for OECD Countries.

10. OECD, 2007, Babies and Bosses— Reconciling Work and Family Life (Vol. 5): A Synthesis of Findings for OECD Countries, Table 7.1. http://www .oecd.org/document/45/0,3343,en_ 2649_34819_39651501_1_1_1,00 .html#Selection. In Canada, Japan, Korea, and Switzerland, leave entitlement increases with tenure. Maternity leave is employment-protected leave for employed women around childbirth (or adoption in some countries). All countries have guaranteed paid maternity leave except Australia, Korea, and the U.S.

Preserving the Earth for Future Generations

COUNTRY	ELECTRICITY CONSUMPTION (billion of kilowatt-hours) 2004[1]	GDP PER UNIT OF ENERGY USE (ratio of $ to kg oil equivalent in 2000 PPP$) 2004[2]	CARBON DIOXIDE EMISSIONS (% of world's total) 2004[3]	CARBON DIOXIDE EMISSIONS (tons per capita) 2004[4]	WATER CONSUMPTION (meters³ per capita) 2005 or latest available[5]
U.S. Rank	1	23	1	2	1
United States	4,185.0	4.6	21.6	20.4	1,730
Australia	239.5	4.8	1.38	19.0	930
Austria	67.2	7.3	0.28	9.4	470
Belgium	93.4	5.2	0.46	12.2	650
Canada	588.1	3.4	2.14	18.5	1420
Czech Republic	68.6	4.0	0.46	12.5	200
Denmark	37.6	7.9	0.20	10.2	120
Finland	90.7	3.8	0.25	13.2	450
France	510.2	5.9	1.50	6.9	560
Germany	614.2	6.2	3.19	10.7	430
Greece	62.2	7.4	0.40	10.0	830
Hungary	41.2	5.9	0.22	5.9	580
Iceland	8.6	2.5	0.01	7.8	570
Ireland	27.2	9.5	0.16	11.1	330
Italy	349.0	8.2	1.76	8.5	730
Japan	1,080.0	6.4	4.63	10.1	680
Korea	371.0	4.2	1.68	9.8	550
Luxembourg	7.5	6.1	0.04	26.5	140
Mexico	223.1	5.5	1.58	4.2	730
Netherlands	117.0	5.8	0.65	11.1	560
New Zealand	41.8	5.1	0.12	8.4	1410
Norway	122.0	5.9	0.16	9.6	750
Poland	144.9	5.1	1.14	8.3	300
Portugal	51.6	7.1	0.24	6.3	860
Slovak Republic	28.7	3.9	0.15	7.9	200
Spain	277.0	6.9	1.28	8.3	900
Sweden	149.6	4.5	0.20	6.2	300
Switzerland	64.6	8.3	0.16	6.1	350
Turkey	150.0	6.2	0.87	3.4	620
United Kingdom	403.3	7.3	2.03	9.4	250

1. Source: United Nations Department of Economic and Social Affairs, Statistics Division. Database. 2007, New York. http://unstats.un.org/unsd/default.htm. Electricity Consumption: total electricity generated annually plus imports and minus exports.

2. Source: The World Bank, "Little Green Data Book," Washington DC, 2007. http://siteresources.worldbank.org/INTDATASTA/64199955-1178226923002/21322619/LGDB2007.pdf. The ratio of energy use to GDP indicates total energy consumption from a range of production and consumption activities used to support economic and social activity.

3. Source: Calculated using data from United Nations Statistics Division Environment Indicators http://unstats.un.org/unsd/environment/air_co2_emissions.htm.

4. Source: United Nations Statistics Division Environment Indicators http://unstats.un.org/unsd/environment/air_co2_emissions.htm.

5. Source: OECD Factbook 2008. Water consumption is abstraction of freshwater from ground or surface water sources, permanently or temporarily, and conveyed to the place of use, measured in meters cubed per capita.

OECD INDICATOR TABLES
Protecting Personal and Community Security

COUNTRY	VICTIMIZED BY CRIME (% of total population) 2000–2004[1]	PROPERTY CRIME (% of population victimized) 2000–2004[2]	ROBBERY (% of population victimized) 2000–2004[3]	SEXUAL INCIDENTS (% of population victimized) 2000–2004[4]	MURDER (per 100,000 population) 2003[5]	PRISONERS (per 100,000 population) 2004[6]
U.S. Rank	4	8	17	16	2	1
United States	22.8	8.7	0.6	1.5	5.6	725
Australia	35.5	12.6	1.2	4.0	1.5	120
Austria	12.2	5.0	0.6	2.4	0.8	97
Belgium	17.8	9.0	1.2	1.1	1.8	88
Canada	26.5	9.1	0.9	2.1	1.7	107
Czech Republic	...	...	...	...	2.3	169
Denmark	19.3	9.3	1.0	3.8	1.2	70
Finland	12.7	3.9	0.3	1.7	2.0	66
France	12.0	6.6	0.8	0.4	1.6	91
Germany	13.1	4.4	0.4	3.2	1.0	96
Greece	12.3	5.6	1.4	2.1	0.8	82
Hungary	10.0	4.8	0.9	0.3	2.3	163
Iceland	...	...	...	...	1.4	39
Ireland	22.1	10.5	2.2	4.5	1.1	85
Italy	12.6	7.6	0.3	3.4	1.2	97
Japan	16.5	2.8	0.1	1.2	0.5	58
Korea	...	...	...	...	2.2	121
Luxembourg	12.7	7.8	0.7	0.6	0.9	121
Mexico	...	...	...	...	13.0	178
Netherlands	19.8	7.8	0.5	3.3	1.3	123
New Zealand	35.6	13.9	0.7	2.7	1.3	168
Norway	18.0	4.6	0.5	2.2	1.1	65
Poland	15.0	7.1	1.3	1.3	1.7	210
Portugal	10.4	8.7	1.0	0.8	2.6	129
Slovak Republic	...	...	...	...	2.7	165
Spain	9.0	4.9	1.3	0.7	1.3	138
Sweden	16.2	5.5	1.0	3.8	2.1	81
Switzerland	17.1	3.1	0.7	2.1	2.6	81
Turkey	...	...	...	...	3.8	100
United Kingdom	21.0	13.5	1.3	2.4	2.0	139

1–4. Source: United Nations Interregional Crime and Justice Research Institute (UNICRI), 2005. "Burden of Crime in the EU." International Crime and Victimization Surveys. Turin, Italy. http://www.unicri.it/wwd/analysis/icvs/pdf_files/EUICS%20-%20The%20Burden%20of%20Crime%20in%20the%20EU.pdf, and J.N. Van Kesteren, P. Mayhew, and P. Nieuwbeerta, P., "Criminal Victimisation in Seventeen Industrialised Countries: Key-findings from the 2000 International Crime Victims Survey," The Hague, Ministry of Justice, WODC, 2000. http://www.unicri.it/wwd/analysis/icvs/pdf_files/key2000i/index.htm. All data from 2000 or 2004 except New Zealand (1992) and Norway (1989).

5. Source: United Nations, Office on Drugs and Crime. Ninth United Nations Survey on Crime Trends and the Operations of Criminal Justice Systems, 2003-2004. Number of murders reported to police per 100,000.

6. Source: OECD.Stat. http://stats.oecd.org/wbos/Index.aspx?usercontent=sourceoecd.

Political Participation

COUNTRY	SEATS IN PARLIAMENT/CONGRESS HELD BY WOMEN [%] 2007[1]	REGISTERED VOTERS WHO VOTED IN LAST PARLIAMENTARY ELECTION [%] 2007 or most recent election[2]	REGISTERED VOTERS WHO VOTED IN LAST PRESIDENTIAL ELECTION [%] 2007 or most recent election[3]	VOTING AGE POPULATION* WHO VOTED IN LAST PARLIAMENTARY ELECTION [%] 2007 or most recent election[4]	VOTING AGE POPULATION* WHO VOTED IN LAST PRESIDENTIAL ELECTION [%] 2007 or most recent election[5]
U.S. Rank	22	30	6	29	10
United States	16.3	47.5	67.4	46.6	49.3
Australia	24.7	94.8	—	81.7	—
Austria	32.3	74.2	71.6	72.6	68.6
Belgium	34.7	86.6	—	83.2	—
Canada	20.8	64.9	64.7	54.6	—
Czech Republic	15.5	64.5	—	76.7	—
Denmark	36.9	87.2	86.6	83.1	—
Finland	38.0	66.7	74	65.2	76.8
France	12.2	60.3	79.7	59.9	72.3
Germany	31.6	77.7	—	98.4	—
Greece	13.0	74.1	93	89.0	—
Hungary	10.4	64.4	—	59.0	—
Iceland	33.3	83.6	62.9	86.2	86.2
Ireland	13.3	67.0	46.7	66.7	47.7
Italy	17.3	83.6	—	84.9	—
Japan	9.4	58.6	—	59.0	—
Korea	13.4	60.0	63.0	55.7	92.5
Luxembourg	23.3	91.7	—	56.9	—
Mexico	22.6	58.9	64	48.2	60
Netherlands	36.7	80.3	—	70.1	—
New Zealand	32.2	81.0	—	72.5	—
Norway	37.9	77.4	—	73.1	—
Poland	20.4	53.9	51	47.6	62.6
Portugal	21.3	64.3	61.5	69.3	57.2
Slovak Republic	20.0	54.7	43.5	78.9	79.2
Spain	36.0	77.2	—	73.8	—
Sweden	47.3	80.1	—	77.7	—
Switzerland	25.0	48.3	—	34.9	—
Turkey	4.4	84.2	—	80.4	—
United Kingdom	19.7	61.4	—	57.6	—

1. Source: UN Statistics Division. Database, United Nations, 2007. http://unstats.un.org/unsd/cdb/cdb_advanced_data_extract.asp.

2–5. Source: International Institute for Democracy and Electoral Assistance (IDEA) 2007. "Voter Turnout, A Global Survey." Stockholm. Reprinted by permission of International IDEA.

* Voting age population includes all citizens above the legal voting age.

OECD INDICATOR TABLES
Protecting National Security

COUNTRY	EXPENDITURE ON DEFENSE (PPP US$ per capita) 2006[1]	MILITARY EXPENDITURE (% of GDP) 2006[2]	ARMED FORCES PERSONNEL (thousands) 2006[3]
U.S. Rank	1	1	1
United States	1,825	4.15	1,498
Australia	640	1.80	51
Austria	306	0.85	40
Belgium	379	1.13	40
Canada	426	1.16	64
Czech Republic	380	1.72	26
Denmark	503	1.41	30
Finland	446	1.35	32
France	771	2.41	354
Germany	423	1.31	246
Greece	1,017	3.24	161
Hungary	214	1.17	44
Iceland	—	0.0	0
Ireland	213	0.53	10
Italy	482	1.66	440
Japan	304	0.95	252
Korea	621	2.70	692
Luxembourg	605	0.80	2
Mexico	46	0.38	280
Netherlands	548	1.50	46
New Zealand	255	1.00	9
Norway	751	1.50	16
Poland	292	1.97	148
Portugal	439	2.11	91
Slovak Republic	307	1.73	17
Spain	301	1.05	222
Sweden	482	1.41	25
Switzerland	335	0.90	23
Turkey	240	2.85	612
United Kingdom	857	2.59	181

1. Source: Calculated using 2005 GDP in PPP$, military expense as % of GDP (Column 2) and total 2005 population using World Development Indicators.

2. Source: World Development Indicators Online Database, World Bank, 2007. Reprinted with permission from Stockholm International Peace Research Institute (SIPRI), Yearbook: Armaments, Disarmament and International Security. SIPRI military expenditures data are derived from the NATO definition. See http://www.sipri.org/contents/milap/milex/mex_definition.html for full definition. Data for some countries are based on partial or uncertain data or rough estimates.

3. Source: World Development Indicators Online Database, World Bank, 2007. From International Institute for Strategic Studies, the Military Balance. Armed forces personnel are active duty military personnel, including paramilitary forces if the training, organization, equipment, and control suggest they may be used to support or replace regular military forces.

References

IN THIS SECTION:

Methodological Notes

The American Human Development Index

The modified American Human Development Index measures the same three basic dimensions as the standard HD Index, but it uses different data in order to better reflect the U.S. context and to maximize available data. All data come from official U.S. government sources. The most recent year for which data are available is 2005, owing to the typical lag time of two to three years.

In the American Human Development Index:

- **A long and healthy life** is measured using life expectancy at birth, calculated from mortality data from the Centers for Disease Control and Prevention, National Center for Health Statistics, and population data from the U.S. Census Bureau, 2005.

- **Access to knowledge** is measured using two indicators: school enrollment for the population age three and older, and educational degree attainment for the population twenty-five years and older. Both indicators are from the American Community Survey, U.S. Census Bureau, 2005.

- **Decent standard of living** is measured using median earnings from the American Community Survey, U.S. Census Bureau, 2005.

Before the HD Index itself is calculated, an index needs to be created for each of these dimensions. To calculate these indices—the health, education, and income indices—minimum and maximum values (goalposts) are chosen for each underlying indicator. Performance in each dimension is expressed as a value between 0 and 10 by applying the following general formula:

$$\text{Dimension Index} = \frac{\text{actual value} - \text{minimum value}}{\text{maximum value} - \text{minimum value}} \times 10$$

The HD Index is then calculated as a simple average of the dimension indices.

 Health Index

The Health Index measures the relative achievement in life expectancy at birth. Life expectancy is calculated by constructing a life table. Life tables are a series of columns of data; the only raw data needed are the population and the number of deaths. All other columns of data and the expectation of life are calculated from these.

Life tables in this report have been constructed using Chiang's method of abridged life tables. Abridged life tables aggregate deaths and population data into age groups, rather than using single year of age as do complete life tables. The age groups used were under 1, 1–4, 5–9, . . . , 80–84, and 85 and over. The Chiang method is well established and widely used internationally.[196]

Death data were obtained from the National Center for Health Statistics (NCHS). NCHS data record all deaths occurring in the United States, and include cause of death, county of residence, race, sex, and age. The public use mortality files made available by NCHS do not include county identifiers for deaths in counties with fewer than one hundred thousand people, for confidentiality reasons. We obtained county identifiers for all deaths through a special request to NCHS.[197]

Population data are the bridged-race population estimates of the July 1, 2005, population, produced by the U.S. Census Bureau in collaboration with NCHS.[198]

The Health Index is obtained by scaling the life expectancy at birth values using the minimum and maximum goalposts:

$$\text{Health Index}_i = \frac{LE_i - LE_{MIN}}{LE_{MAX} - LE_{MIN}} \times 10$$

where LE_i is the life expectancy at birth for unit i and LE_{MIN} and LE_{MAX} are the goalposts.

The observed ranges for life expectancy at birth were:

Grouping	Minimum	Maximum
States	73.8 (District of Columbia)	81.7 (Hawaii)
Race/Ethnicity	73.0 (African Americans)	86.3 (Asians)
Race/Ethnicity × Gender	69.4 (African American males)	88.8 (Asian females)
Congressional Districts	72.6 (5th CD, Kentucky)	82.9 (8th CD, Virginia)

The goalposts are determined based on the range of the indicator observed on all possible groupings and also taking into account possible increases and decreases in years to come, and adjusted in order to achieve a balance in the final index (see **Balancing the American HD Index Components**). The goalposts were set at 66 (minimum) and 90 (maximum).

 Education Index

The Education Index measures the relative achievement in both educational attainment and combined primary, secondary, and tertiary gross enrollment. An index for educational attainment and one for gross enrollment are calculated, and the two indices are combined to create the Education Index, with two-thirds weight given to educational attainment and one-third weight to gross enrollment.

EDUCATIONAL ATTAINMENT INDEX

The Educational Attainment Index measures the overall educational level of the adult population, and is based on a very simple premise—that more education is better. In addition to the obvious benefits of education for greater earnings potential for individuals, higher educational attainment is associated with many other benefits as well. These can include better health, increased civic participation, increased ability to adjust to change, clearer self-identity, and greater social capital passed on to their children. For society, a better-educated population is associated with reduced dependency on public support programs, lower crime rates, political stability, and environmental benefits.

The Educational Attainment Index utilizes three indicators: percentage of the population twenty-five years and older who have completed high school (a high school diploma or equivalent, such as GED), percentage of the population twenty-five years and older with a bachelor's degree (does not include community college and associate degree) and percentage of the population twenty-five years and older with a graduate degree (master's, professional, or doctoral degree). Each category represents the percentage of the population that has attained *at least* that educational level. Thus, the percentage of high school graduates includes those with a bachelor's degree or higher; and the percentage of the population with a bachelor's degree includes those with a graduate degree.

An Educational Attainment Score is computed by adding the three indicators. This way, those with a graduate degree are counted three times, because they also must have a bachelor's degree and a high school diploma; and those with a bachelor's degree are counted twice, because they must have a high school diploma. Thus, if two communities have the same percentage of high school graduates, but one has a higher percentage of persons with a bachelor's degree, the one with more bachelor's degrees will get a higher Educational Attainment Score. The minimum value for the Educational Attainment Score is 0 —100 percent of the adult population with less than a high school diploma—and the maximum value is 3 —100 percent with a graduate degree.

The data source is the American Community Survey, tables B15002 (Sex by Educational Attainment for the Population 25 Years and Over), B15002B, B15002C, B15002D, B15002H, and B15002I (same, for Black or African American Alone, American Indian and Alaska Native Alone, Asian Alone, White Non-Hispanic Alone, and Hispanic).

The Educational Attainment Index is obtained by scaling the Educational Attainment Score values using the minimum and maximum goalposts:

$$\text{Educational Attainment Index}_i = \frac{EAS_i - EAS_{MIN}}{EAS_{MAX} - EAS_{MIN}} \times 10$$

where EAS_i is the Educational Attainment Score for unit i and EAS_{MIN} and EAS_{MAX} are the goalposts.

The observed ranges for the Educational Attainment Score were:

Grouping	Minimum	Maximum
States	1.036 (Mississippi)	1.540 (District of Columbia)
Race/Ethnicity	0.755 (Latinos)	1.546 (Asians)
Race/Ethnicity × Gender	0.739 (Latino males)	1.656 (Asian males)
Congressional Districts	0.608 (20th CD, California)	1.804 (14th CD, New York)

The goalposts were set at 0.5 (minimum) and 2.0 (maximum).

ENROLLMENT INDEX

The Enrollment Index measures the relative achievement in combined primary, secondary, and tertiary gross enrollment. The indicator used is the combined gross enrollment ratio for primary, secondary, and tertiary levels. This is computed as the ratio of the number of students—of any age—enrolled at all three levels to the size of the population of the official age group corresponding to these levels. For the United States, the appropriate age group would be approximately five to twenty-four years of age. However, both the ACS and the decennial Censuses, when presenting enrollment data by race/ethnicity, combine nursery school, prekindergarten, and kindergarten together. Thus, the enrollment ratio has to take nursery school and prekindergarten into account, and the age group used to calculate the ratio is set as three to twenty-four years of age.

The enrollment ratio is a *flow* variable; it gives an indication of the future level of educational attainment for a given community, as opposed to the educational attainment indicator, which measures the present *stock* of education. Even though school attendance is mandatory in the primary and secondary levels, there is considerable variation in the enrollment ratio, due to high school dropout rates and enrollment in preschool and tertiary levels.

The data source is the American Community Survey, tables B14001 (School Enrollment by Level of School for the Population 3 Years and Over), B14001B, B14001C, B14001D, B14001H, and B14001I (same, for Black or African American Alone, American Indian and Alaska Native Alone, Asian Alone, White Non-Hispanic Alone, and Hispanic); table B14002 (Sex by School Enrollment by Type of School by Age for the Population 3 Years and Over); tables B01001 (Sex by Age), B01001B, B01001C, B01001D, B01001H, and B01001I (same, for Black or African American Alone, American Indian and Alaska Native Alone, Asian Alone, White Non-Hispanic Alone, and Hispanic).

The Gross Enrollment Ratio is given by:

$$\text{Gross Enrollment Ratio}_i = \frac{ENR_i}{P3TO24_i}$$

where ENR_i is the population (of any age) enrolled in school, at all levels, and $P3TO24_i$ is the population from three to twenty-four years of age. The Enrollment Index is then obtained by scaling the gross enrollment ratio using the minimum and maximum goalposts:

$$\text{Enrollment Index}_i = \frac{GER_i - GER_{MIN}}{GER_{MAX} - GER_{MIN}} \times 10$$

where GER_i is the Educational Attainment Score for unit i and GER_{MIN} and GER_{MAX} are the goalposts.

The observed ranges for the Gross Enrollment Ratios in the 2005 ACS were:

Grouping	Minimum	Maximum
States	80.2% (Idaho)	99.8% (District of Columbia)
Race/Ethnicity	78.8% (Latinos)	102.3% (Asians)
Race/Ethnicity × Gender	76.1% (Latino males)	106.0% (Asian females)
Congressional Districts	70.5% (4th CD, Arizona)	111.6% (8th CD, California)

The goalposts were set at 70 percent (minimum) and 100 percent (maximum). Since these are gross enrollment ratios, and use the population of *any age* enrolled in school, it is possible to obtain ratios greater than 100 percent, due to over-age enrollment. When this happens, the value is capped at 100 percent, so the Enrollment Index is never greater than 10.

The Educational Attainment and the Enrollment Indices are combined to form the Education Index, with two-thirds weight to Educational Attainment and one-third to Enrollment:

$$\text{Education Index}_i = \frac{2}{3} EAI_i + \frac{1}{3} EI_i$$

where EAI_i is Educational Attainment Index, and EI_i is Enrollment Index.

 # Income Index

In the HD Index, income serves as a surrogate for all the dimensions of human development not reflected in a long and healthy life and access to knowledge. Following the standard UNDP methodology, a logarithmic transformation is applied to the income indicator, to reflect a decreasing returns to scale assumption—an income increase at lower income levels has a greater impact on the overall level of material well-being than the same increase at higher income levels. Once a high enough income threshold is reached, additional income increases will have very little impact on material well-being.

Given the tremendous gaps in wealth and assets in the United States, which are much larger than the income gaps, especially across racial lines, a wealth indicator would be a worthy addition to the income index. Wealth is one of the key drivers of the intergenerational transmission of advantage, and an asset cushion is often what separates those who can remain middle class from those who experience periods of poverty in the case of a shock such as short-term unemployment or a serious illness. Unfortunately, wealth data are scarce and not available at the subnational level, and had to be left out.

The ACS offers several income measures; median earnings of the population sixteen years and older was chosen because it is the only income measure that is available for all the groupings used in this report (gender, race/ethnicity, gender by race/ethnicity, regions, states, congressional districts). Earnings are defined as the sum of wage or salary income and net income from self-employment, and do not include interest, dividends, rental income, Social Security income, and public assistance income. Only individuals with earnings are included in the computation of the median; "zero earners" are excluded.

The data source is the American Community Survey, tables B20017 (Median Earnings by Sex by Work Experience for the Population 16+ Yrs with Earnings), B20017B, B20017C, B20017D, B20017H, and B20017I (same, for Black or African American Alone, American Indian and Alaska Native Alone, Asian Alone, White Non-Hispanic Alone, and Hispanic).

The Income Index is obtained by scaling the median earnings values using the minimum and maximum goalposts:

$$\text{Income Index}_i = \frac{\log(y_i) - \log(y_{MIN})}{\log(y_{MAX}) - \log(y_{MIN})} \times 10$$

where y_i is the Median Earnings for unit i and y_{MIN} and y_{MAX} are the goalposts.

The observed ranges in the 2005 ACS were:

Grouping	Minimum	Maximum
States	$21,472 (Montana)	$36,948 (District of Columbia)
Race/Ethnicity	$20,255 (Latinos)	$31,518 (Asians)
Race/Ethnicity × Gender	$16,147 (Latina Females)	$37,269 (White Males)
Congressional Districts	$16,767 (20th CD, California)	$51,139 (14th CD, New York)

The goalposts were set at $13,000 (minimum) and $55,000 (maximum).

Calculating the Human Development Index

The HD Index is obtained by the simple average of the health, education, and income indices:

$$\text{HD Index}_i = \frac{\text{Health Index}_i + \text{Education Index}_i + \text{Income Index}_i}{3}$$

Since all three components range from 0 to 10, the HD Index itself also varies from 0 to 10, with 10 representing the highest level of human development.

EXAMPLE:

Calculating the HD Index for the United States

1. HEALTH Index

The life expectancy at birth for the U.S. was 78.0 years in 2005. The Health Index is given by

$$\text{Health Index} = \frac{78 - 66}{90 - 66} \times 10 = \textbf{5.00}$$

2. EDUCATION Index

In 2005, 84.2 percent of U.S. residents had at least a high school diploma, 27.2 percent had at least a bachelor's degree, and 10.0 percent had a graduate degree. Then, the Educational Attainment Score is 0.842 + 0.272 + 0.100 = 1.214. The Educational Attainment Index is then

$$\text{Educational Attainment Index} = \frac{1.214 - 0.5}{2.0 - 0.5} \times 10 = 4.76$$

The combined gross enrollment ratio was 86.8 percent, and the Enrollment Index is then

$$\text{Enrollment Index} = \frac{86.8 - 70}{100 - 70} \times 10 = 5.61$$

The Educational Attainment Index and the Enrollment Index are then combined to obtain the Education Index:

$$\text{Education Index} = \frac{2}{3} 4.76 + \frac{1}{3} 5.61 = 5.04$$

3. INCOME Index

Median earnings in 2005 were $27,299. The Income Index is then

$$\text{Income Index} = \frac{\log(27,299) - \log(13,000)}{\log(55,000) - \log(13,000)} \times 10 = \textbf{5.14}$$

4. HUMAN DEVELOPMENT Index

Once the dimension indices have been calculated, the HD Index is obtained by a simple average of the three indices:

$$\text{HD Index} = \frac{5.00 + 5.04 + 5.14}{3} = 5.06$$

Differences between the American HD Index and the Standard HD Index

The standard HD Index, created by UNDP and published in the annual Human Development Reports, was developed to measure human development in all countries of the world, ranging from very-low-income countries in sub-Saharan Africa to high-income OECD countries. Thus, some of the indicators used (and the goalposts for each indicator) are not very well suited to measure human development in a high-income country like the United States, since they have to accommodate a very wide range.

The American HD Index follows the same principles of the standard HD Index, and measures the same three basic dimensions of human development—health, access to knowledge, and standard of living—but has been modified in order to better reflect the context of a developed country.

The table below lists the indicators used in the American HD Index and the standard HD Index:

Dimension	Indicator	
	AMERICAN HD Index	STANDARD HD Index
Health	Life expectancy at birth	Life expectancy at birth
Knowledge	Educational attainment Gross enrollment ratio	Adult literacy rate Gross enrollment ratio
Standard of living	Median earnings	GDP per capita

In the health dimension, the same indicator is used (life expectancy at birth), but the goalposts are changed. The standard HD Index uses goalposts of twenty-five years (minimum) and eighty-five years (maximum), to accommodate the enormous gap in life expectancy around the world. For the American HD Index, the goalposts were set at sixty-six years and ninety years, a range that accommodates the variations across all groupings used in the Report. Since life expectancies in the United States are higher than in most countries, and do not go anywhere near the lower limit of twenty-five years set in the standard

HD Index, using the standard HD Index goalposts would cluster all Health Index values around the maximum value of 10, providing very little differentiation among states, congressional districts, and so on.

In the knowledge dimension, adult literacy rate was replaced by the educational attainment index. Adult literacy is a relevant indicator in a global context, where low-income countries still have very high illiteracy levels, but is largely irrelevant for developed nations, where most of the adult population has basic reading and writing skills and the labor market demands increasingly sophisticated skills. Functional literacy (the ability to read, write, and speak in English, and compute and solve problems at levels of proficiency necessary to function on the job and in society, achieve one's goals, and develop one's knowledge and potential) would be a good indicator, but suffers from severe data availability problems. Thus, the educational attainment index was used. It captures the overall educational level of the population, and is a good indicator of how well any given population is prepared to satisfy an increasingly demanding labor market.

The other knowledge indicator, combined gross enrollment ratio, is the same in both the American HD Index and the standard HD Index, but with a slight modification—the enrollment in the American HD Index includes nursery school and prekindergarten, and the age group used in the denominator of the enrollment ratio has been adjusted to accommodate this. The goalposts were also changed, from 0 to 100 percent in the standard HD Index to 70 to 100 percent in the American HD Index, in order to reflect the ranges observed on all American HD Index groupings.

In the standard of living dimension, GDP per capita was replaced by median earnings. For relatively closed economies, such as countries, GDP per capita is a good indicator of the income appropriated by the local population. However, for smaller geographical areas within a country, such as states and congressional districts, which are much more open economies, substantial portions of the income generated within the community are used to remunerate production factors owned by persons who do not reside in that community (e.g., profits from a large manufacturing plant located in the community), and thus do not adequately represent the income available to local residents.

As a result of these modifications, *the American HD Index and the standard HD Index are not comparable.* In order to reduce comparisons, the American HD Index varies from 0 to 10 instead of from 0 to 1, as does the standard HD Index.

Balancing the American HD Index Components

Ideally, the components of a composite index should be balanced; that is, on average, each component should contribute equally to the final index (assuming an equal weights system). The HD Index uses equal weights for the components, but this is not enough to warrant a balanced index. If the distributions of the components are not similar, some of the components may end up contributing to the final index more than others—in effect, making the *implicit weights* not equal. For instance, if one of the components has a range of 7 to 9, with the values clustered around 8, and the others have an average value of 5, the component with higher values will have a higher implicit weight, even though all components should have equal weights.

One way to ensure that no single component has a disproportionate implicit weight is to examine the distributions of the components and adjust the goalposts, so that the ranges and the distributions are similar.

The goalposts for each component of the American HD Index were carefully adjusted in order to accommodate the ranges of the observed values, allow for growth in future years, and create a balanced final index.

The resulting indices have median values close to 5, and well-balanced ranges and distributions, as shown by the box-and-whisker plots (the plots are for the congressional district indices; the state indices

Box and Whisker Plot

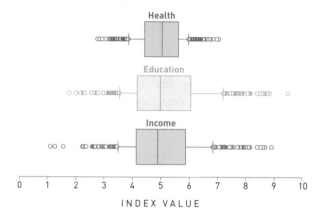

show a very similar pattern).

The Health Index has a slightly more compressed range, because the goalposts have to accommodate the values for life expectancy by gender and race/ethnicity, which have a wider range than the ranges observed for states and congressional districts.

The average values and average contributions of each component, both for states and congressional districts, show a well-balanced index, with each component contributing equally, on average, to the final index.

American HD Index Components

by STATE

Component	Average Value	Average Contribution
Health	4.92	33.1%
Education	4.97	33.4%
Income	5.01	33.5%

by CONGRESSIONAL DISTRICT

Component	Average Value	Average Contribution
Health	5.02	33.5%
Education	5.03	32.7%
Income	5.20	33.8%

Estimation of Life Expectancy at Birth for Congressional Districts

The Multiple Cause of Death data used in the calculation of life expectancy at birth does not contain congressional district identifiers, so it is not possible to compute life expectancies directly for the congressional districts; they have to be estimated.

A procedure was created to build abridged life tables for each congressional district based on county level data. Congressional district boundaries do not conform to county boundaries; some congressional districts lie entirely within a single county, while others comprise parts of several different counties. The procedure generates a "geographic correspondence file" between congressional districts and counties, indicating what proportion of the congressional district's population lives in each county. This is done using Census blocks, the smallest geographic unit utilized by the Census Bureau. Then the death counts and population totals for each county are allocated to congressional districts, based on the allocation factors from the correspondence file. This creates the life tables for each congressional district, which allow the estimation of the life expectancies.

The figure below illustrates this process. It shows the Thirteenth Congressional District in Illinois, comprising parts of Cook, DuPage, and Will counties. The proportion of each county's population that lives in the congressional district is computed, based on the Census block populations, and those proportions are then used to allocate death counts and population totals for the congressional district.

The Thirteenth Congressional District, Illinois

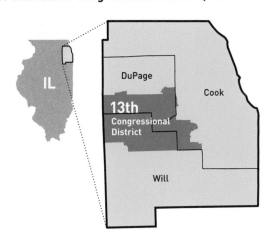

For this example, we have:

County	Population	Share	Deaths, < 1 year	Population, < 1 year
Cook IL	84,393	0.016	150	81,598
DuPage IL	375,163	0.402	70	12,431
Will IL	271,606	0.406	50	9,434

Population is the county's population residing in the congressional district; *share* is percentage of the county's total population residing in the congressional district; *deaths* is the number of deaths of county residents in the age bracket (those are fictional numbers used for illustration purposes only, since the actual data are protected by a nondisclosure agreement); and *population* is each county's population in the age bracket. Thus, 1.6 percent of Cook County's residents, 40.2 percent of DuPage County's residents, and 40.6 percent of Will County's residents live in the Thirteenth Congressional District. The procedure then allocates 1.6 percent of the death counts in Cook County, 40.2 percent of the death counts in DuPage County, and 40.6 percent of the death counts in Will County to the target congressional district. The number of deaths in the < 1 year age bracket for the congressional district is given by

$$(0.016 \times 150) + (0.402 \times 70) + (0.406 \times 50) = 50.84$$

and the population in the same age bracket is given by

$$(0.016 \times 81,598) + (0.402 \times 12,431) + (0.406 \times 9,434) = 10,133$$

This procedure is repeated for all the age brackets, resulting in an abridged life table for the congressional district, which is then used to compute the life expectancy at birth.

In some instances, several congressional districts are entirely contained inside a single county; when this happens, the county's life expectancy at birth is assigned to all the congressional districts.

The Geographic Correspondence File was generated by the MABLE/Geocorr application, developed by John Blodgett, from the University of Missouri St. Louis, and jointly owned by Blodgett and CIESIN (Consortium for International Earth Science Information Network, at Columbia University), whom we gratefully acknowledge.

American HD Index Historical Trends

The American HD Index for 1960, 1970, 1980, 1990, and 2000 uses different data sources, listed below.

INCOME

1960–2000:
U.S. Census Bureau,
Current Population Survey

Historical Income Data, Table P-43.
Workers, (Both Sexes Combined—All),
Median and Mean Earnings: 1974 to 2005
http://www.census.gov/hhes/www/
income/histinc/p43ar.html

The income definitions on the American
Community Survey (used in the current
American HD Index) and the Current
Population Survey are slightly different,
and thus their income measures are not
strictly comparable. Median earnings
reported in the CPS, used in the historical
American HD Index, were proportionally
adjusted, based on the ratio observed
between the 2005 ACS median earnings
and the 2005 CPS median earnings, in
order to minimize discontinuity problems
between the historical series and the
current HD Index values.

LIFE EXPECTANCY AT BIRTH

1960–2000:
National Center for Health Statistics

Health, United States, 2007, Hyattsville,
MD: 2007, Table 27. Life expectancy at
birth, at 65 years of age, and at 75 years
of age, by race and sex: United States,
selected years 1900–2004

EDUCATIONAL ATTAINMENT

1960–1980
U.S. Census Bureau

A Half-Century of Learning: Historical
Census Statistics on Educational
Attainment in the United States, 1940 to
2000, Table 1. Percent of the Population
25 Years and Over with a High School
Diploma or Higher by Sex and Age, for the
United States: 1940 to 2000
http://www.census.gov/population/
socdemo/education/phct41/table1.xls
Table 2. Percent of the Population 25
Years and Over with a Bachelor's Degree
or Higher by Sex and Age, for the United
States: 1940 to 2000
http://www.census.gov/population/
socdemo/education/phct41/table2.xls

1990:
U.S. Census Bureau

1990 Summary Tape File 3 (STF 3) -
Sample data, DP-2. Social
Characteristics: 1990

2000:
U.S. Census Bureau

Census 2000 Summary File 3 (SF 3)
- Sample Data, QT-P20. Educational
Attainment by Sex: 2000

SCHOOL ENROLLMENT

1960:

Population 5 to 24 years old
Enrollment 5 to 34 years old
U.S. Census Bureau,
Current Population Survey, October 1960

School Enrollment and Education of
Young Adults and Their Fathers: October
1960 (P20-110), Table 3—Fall School
Enrollment of the Civilian Noninstitutional
Population 5 to 34 Years Old, By Age,
Color, and Sex, For the United States:
October 1960, http://www.census
.gov/population/socdemo/education/p20-
110/tab-03-04.pdf

1970:

Population 3 to 24 years old
Enrollment 3 to 34 years old
U.S. Census Bureau,
Current Population Survey, October 1970

School Enrollment: October 1970
(P20-222), Table 1—Enrollment Status
of the Population 3 to 34 Years Old, by
Age, Race, Sex, and Selected Educational
Characteristics, for the United States:
October 1970, http://www.census
.gov/population/socdemo/school/p20-
222/tab01.pdf

1980:

Population 3 to 24 years old
Enrollment 3 to 34 years old
U.S. Census Bureau,
Current Population Survey, October 1980

School Enrollment—Social and Economic
Characteristics of Students: October
1980 (Advance Report) (P20-362), Table
6—Enrollment Status, for Persons 3 to 34
Years Old, by Age, Sex, Race, and Spanish
Origin: October 1980, http://www.census
.gov/population/socdemo/school/p20-
362/tab06.pdf

1990:

Population 3 to 24 years old
Enrollment 3 years and older
U.S. Census Bureau,
Current Population Survey, October 1990

School Enrollment—Social and Economic
Characteristics of Students: October 1990
(P20-460), Table 1—Enrollment Status
of the Population 3 Years Old and Over,
by Age, Sex, Race, Hispanic Origin, and
Selected Educational Characteristics:
October 1990, http://www.census
.gov/population/socdemo/school/p20-
460/tab01.pdf

2000:

Population 3 to 24 years old
Enrollment 3 years and older
U.S. Census Bureau,
Current Population Survey, October 2000

School Enrollment—Social and Economic
Characteristics of Students: October 2000
(PPL-148), Table 1—Enrollment Status of
the Population 3 Years Old and Over, by
Age, Sex, Race, Hispanic Origin, Nativity,
and Selected Educational Characteristics:
October 2000, http://www.census
.gov/population/socdemo/school/ppl-
148/tab01.xls, Internet Release date:
June 1, 2001

Notes

PART 1

Understanding Human Development

[1] United Nations Statistics Division, Millennium Development Goals Indicators.

[2] United Nations Children's Fund. *Report Card 7, Child Poverty in Perspective: An Overview of Child Well-Being in Rich Countries* 2007.

[3] Stonecash, *Inequality and the American Public.*

[4] Fletcher, "Middle-Class Dream Eludes African American Families."

[5] Becker and Tomes, "Human Capital and the Rise and Fall of Families."

[6] Bradbury and Katz, "Are Lifetime Incomes Growing More Unequal?"

[7] Mazmuder and Levine, "Growing Importance of Family and Community."

[8] Corak, *Do Poor Children Become Poor Adults?*

[9] Roemer, "Equal Opportunity and Intergenerational Mobility."

[10] Sawhill and Morton, "Economic Mobility."

[11] Nord, Andrews, and Carlson, *Household Food Security in the United States.*

[12] Alesina and La Ferrara, "Participation in Heterogeneous Communities"; Wilkinson, *Unhealthy Societies*; Marmot, *Status Syndrome.*

[13] California Department of Transportation, "Seismic Retrofit Program, Fact Sheet."

[14] United States Geological Survey, "Earthquake Hazards Program."

[15] United States Department of Health and Human Services, "Summary Child Maltreatment 2005."

[16] United Nations Development Programme. *Human Development Report 2002.*

PART 2

What the American Human Development Index Reveals

[17] The income measure used in this report is personal earnings. Because household earnings are pooled within a family or household, it is impossible to disaggregate the data by gender. While in some circumstances this may lead to an underestimation of women's standards of living—for instance, a woman working part-time as a nursery school teacher and married to a corporate CEO surely has a material standard of living well beyond what her income alone would allow—it is the only way to capture the gender disparities in earned income and control over economic resources. Research supports the view that a less-moneyed spouse has fewer options, less social standing, and greater vulnerability if the relationship breaks down.

[18] Using data from the 2007/2008 *Human Development Report*, a regression of the log of GDP per capita and life expectancy for 181 countries yields an r^2 of 0.65, meaning that 65 percent of the variance in life expectancy is explained by the variance in income.

[19] Preston, "Changing Relation between Mortality and Level of Development."

[20] Deaton, "Global Patterns of Income and Health."

PART 3

The Building Blocks of the HD Index

A Long and Healthy Life

[21] Committee on the Consequences of Uninsurance, *Insuring America's Health.*

[22] Kaiser Family Foundation, "Statehealthfacts.org, Total State Government Health Expenditures as Percent of the Gross State Product, 2003."

[23] Levine et al., "Black-White Inequalities in Mortality and Life Expectancy."

[24] National Academies, Division of Behavioral and Social Sciences and Education, "Multiple Origins, Uncertain Destinies."

[25] United Nations Children's Fund (UNICEF), *State of the World's Children 2007.*

[26] Lleras-Muney, "Relationship between Education and Adult Mortality in the United States."

[27] Turnock, *Public Health.*

[28] Institute of Medicine, Committee on Assuring the Health of the Public in the 21st Century, *Future of the Public's Health in the 21st Century.*

[29] Kaiser Family Foundation, "Racial/Ethnic Differences in Cardiac Care."

[30] Siantz, "Understanding Health Disparities."

[31] National Academy of Sciences, *Cancer Care for the Whole Patient.*

[32] Kaiser Family Foundation, *The Uninsured: A Primer, October 2007.*

[33] Jaspin, Elliot, "State Paying More to Treat Late-Stage Breast Cancer."

[34] Frazer, "County Looks to Add Free Colonoscopies for Residents."

[35] Hao et al., "U.S. Congressional District Cancer Death Rates."

[36] National Center for Health Statistics, *Health, United States, 2006.*

[37] Disaster Center, "US States Crime 2004–2005."

[38] U.S. Department of Justice, Bureau of Justice Statistics, "Homicide Trends in the U.S. by Region."

[39] U.S. Department of Justice, Federal Bureau of Investigation, "2006 Crime in the United States, Expanded Homicide Data Table 6."

[40] Miller et al., "Rates of Household Firearm Ownership and Homicide across US Region and States."

[41] U.S. Department of Justice, Federal Bureau of Investigation, "2006 Crime in the United States, by Community Type."

[42] Centers for Disease Control and Prevention, "Understanding Intimate Partner Violence."

[43] U.S. Department of Justice, Bureau of Justice Statistics, "Homicide Trends in the U.S. by Region, Intimate Homicide."

[44] Ibid.

[45] Ibid.

[46] Center for Disease Control and Prevention, *HIV/AIDS Surveillance Report.*

[47] Kaiser Family Foundation, *AIDS at 25.*

[48] Ibid.

[49] Collins, *Improving Outcomes.*

[50] Carmona, "Obesity, Individual Responsibility, and Public Policy."

[51] World Health Organization, "Obesity and Overweight."

[52] National Academies, Division of Behavioral and Social Sciences and Education, "Multiple Origins, Uncertain Destinies."

[53] Centers for Disease Control and Prevention, "Disease Still a Major Problem."

[54] Southern Environmental Law Center, "Healthy Air."

[55] Akinbami, "State of Childhood Asthma."

[56] Davis, "Planning the Next Wave of SCHIP Research."

[57] Centers for Disease Control and Prevention, "Tested and Confirmed Elevated Blood Lead Levels by State."

[58] National Institute of Mental Health, "Suicide in the U.S."

[59] National Institute of Mental Health, "The Numbers Count."

[60] Frank and Glied, *Better but Not Well.*

[61] U.S. Department of Health and Human Services, "New Freedom Commission on Mental Health. 2003."

[62] Herman et al., "Homelessness among Individuals with Psychotic Disorders Hospitalized for the First Time."

[63] Susser, Lin, and Conover, "Risk Factors for Homelessness."

[64] McAlpine and Mechanic, "Utilization of specialty mental health care among persons with severe mental illness."

[65] Benavides, "The State of Mental Health Care in the United States."

[66] U.S. General Accounting Office, *Child Welfare and Juvenile Justice.*

[67] Anderson, "Supportive Housing Research FAQs."

[68] Perlman and Parvensky, *Denver Housing First Collaborative Cost Benefit Analysis and Program Outcomes Report.*

[69] Culhane, Metraux, and Hadley, "Public Service Reductions Associated with Placement of Homeless Persons with Severe Mental Illness in Supportive Housing."

[70] Corporation for Supportive Housing, "Is Supportive Housing Cost-Effective?"

[71] U.S. Government Accountability Office, "Nursing Homes."

[72] These programs only consider direct costs, and do not include emergency room care for those without coverage and other indirect costs.

[73] Sheils and Haught, "The Cost of Tax-Exempt Health Benefits in 2004."

[74] Centers for Medicare and Medicaid Services, "National Health Expenditure Data."

[75] U.S. Census Bureau, "Health Insurance Coverage: 2006."

[76] Centers for Medicare and Medicaid Services, "National Health Expenditure Data."

[77] Holahan, Cohen, and Rousseau, *Why Did Medicaid Spending Decline in 2006?*

[78] U.S. Department of Health and Human Services, Centers for Medicare and Medicaid Services, "State Children's Health Insurance (SCHIP)."

[79] Kaiser Family Foundation, "Statehealthfacts.org, Total SCHIP Expenditures."

[80] Kaiser Family Foundation, "Statehealthfacts.org, Monthly SCHIP Enrollment, June 2006."

[81] U.S. Government Accountability Office, *Military Health Care.*

[82] Committee on the Consequences of Uninsurance, *Hidden Costs, Value Lost.*

[83] Kaiser Family Foundation, *Uninsured.*

[84] Himmelstein, Thorne, Warren, and Woolhandler, "Illness and Injury as Contributors to Bankruptcy."

[85] Committee on the Consequences of Uninsurance, *Hidden Costs, Value Lost.*

[86] Ibid.

[87] Davis, "Uninsured in America."

[88] Committee on the Consequences of Uninsurance, *Hidden Costs, Value Lost.*

[89] Cutler et al., "Value of Antihypertensive Drugs."

[90] Olson, Tang, and Newacheck, "Children in the United States with Discontinuous Health Insurance Coverage."

[91] Centers for Medicare and Medicaid Services, "National Health Expenditure Data."

[92] Institute of Medicine. *The Future of the Public's Health in the 21st Century.*

[93] United Nations Children's Fund (UNICEF), *Report Card 7, Child Poverty in Perspective.*

[94] U.S. Department of Justice, Federal Bureau of Investigation, "2006 Crime in the United States, Expanded Homicide Data Table 6."

[95] Small Arms Survey, "Small Arms Survey 2007."

[96] Miller, "Firearm Availability and Unintentional Firearm Deaths."

Access to Knowledge

[97] US Department of Education, National Center for Educational Statistics. "Literacy in Everyday Life."

[98] Heckman and Krueger, *Inequality in America.*

[99] US Department of Education, National Center for Education Statistics, "Fast Facts."

[100] Annie E. Casey Foundation, Kids Count Data Center, "Indicators."

[101] Kozol, "Still Separate, Still Unequal."

[102] U.S. Department of Education, National Center for Education Statistics, "The Condition of Education 2006."

[103] Gross enrollment rates measure the population of any age enrolled in school; when "overage" students, those age twenty-five and older, are enrolled in school—for instance, in graduate programs or adult GED programs—the value can be greater than 100 percent. When this happens, the value is capped at 100 percent, so the Enrollment Index is never greater than 10.

[104] In the popular imagination, people living in low-income communities enjoy strong social support networks. While some surely do, in general, people living in poverty are also socially impoverished compared to wealthier Americans. See Edin and Kefalas, *Promises I Can Keep.*

[105] Conley, "The Effect of Birth Weight on Literal (and Figurative) Life Chances."

[106] Steven, "Growing Evidence for a Divorce Divide."

[107] Dye and Johnson, "Child's Day."

[108] Campaign for Educational Equity, "Facts and Figures."

[109] U.S. Department of Education, National Center for Educational Statistics, "The Condition of Education."

[110] Hsin, "Mothers' Time with Children and the Social Reproduction of Cognitive Skills."

[111] Hart and Risley, *Meaningful Differences in the Everyday Experience of Young American Children.*

[112] Bianchi el al., "Inequality in Parental Investment in Childrearing."

[113] US Department of Education, National Center for Educational Statistics, "The Condition of Education."

[114] Bendar et al., "An Education Strategy to Promote Opportunity, Prosperity, and Growth".

[115] Coalition for Evidence-Based Policy, "Perry Preschool Project."

[116] Coalition for Evidence-Based Policy, "Abecedarian Project."

[117] Gormley and Phillips, "Effects of Universal Pre-K in Oklahoma."

[118] U.S. Department of Education, Education Finance Statistics Center, "Financial Information on Public Elementary/Secondary Education, 2007."

[119] Barbanel and Fessenden, "6-Figure Salaries?"

[120] Dillon, "With Turnover High, Schools Fight for Teachers.

[121] U.S. Department of Education, National Center for Education Statistics, "The Condition of Education."

[122] Harry and Anderson, "The Disproportionate Placement of African American Males in Special Education Programs."

[123] Dye and Johnson, "Child's Day."

[124] Laureau et al., "Social Class and Children's Time Use."

[125] Dye and Johnson, "Child's Day."

[126] Meyer et al., "Elementary and Secondary Education."

[127] U.S. Department of Education, National Center for Education Statistics, "America's Charter Schools."

[128] Ibid.

[129] Campaign for Educational Equity, "Facts and Figures."

[130] TIMSS and PIRLS International Study Center, "Trends in International Mathematics and Science Study."

[131] U.S. Department of Education National Center for Education Statistics, "State Comparisons, National Assessment of Educational Progress, 2007."

[132] U.S. Department of Education, Office of Special Education Programs, "Participation in Education."

[133] U.S. Department of Education, National Center for Education Statistics, "The Condition of Education."

[134] Western, "Mass Imprisonment and Economic Inequality."

[135] U.S. Department of Education, National Center for Education Statistics, "Condition of Education 2007."

[136] U.S. Department of Education, National Center for Education Statistics, "Trends in Undergraduate Persistence and Completion 2007."

[137] Haycock and Gerald, "Engines of Inequality."

[138] Karabel, "New College Try."

[139] Ibid.

[140] U.S. Department of Education, Institute of Education Sciences, National Center for Education Statistics, "Student Effort and Educational Progress."

[141] Haycock and Gerald, "Engines of Inequality," endnotes. All income and grant figures come from a special analysis of the *National Postsecondary Student Aid Study* (2003–04), conducted by Jerry Davis for the Education Trust.

[142] U.S. Department of Education, National Center for Education Statistics, "Digest of Education Statistics 2005."

[143] Conley, "Capital for College."

[144] Carneiro and Heckman, "Human Capital Policy."

[145] Deil-Aman, "To Teach or Not to Teach Social Skills."

[146] Dowd, "Community Colleges as Gateways and Gatekeepers."

[147] For current purposes, "immigrant" includes all people born abroad; "second-generation immigrant" includes all people born in the United States with one or more immigrant parent. The source of the data is the U.S. Bureau of the Census, Current Population Survey, Basic Monthly March 2003, 2005, and 2007 files.

[148] Holzer, "What Employers Want: Job Prospects for Less Educated Workers."

[149] U.S. Census Bureau, "The Big Payoff."

[150] Grossman, "Human Capital Model in Handbook of Health Economics."

A Decent Standard of Living

[151] Cohen, Consumers' Republic.

[152] Professor Diana Pearse created the original self-sufficiency budget in 1996 for Wider Opportunities for Women (WOW) with initial funding from the Ford Foundation. In 2000, the Economic Policy Institute developed "basic family budgets." Their online calculator is available at http://www.epi.org/content .cfm/issueguides_poverty_poverty.

[153] Inflation-adjusted mean income of men jumped from $19,381 to $44,850, and the mean income of women almost tripled from $9,368 to $26,261 (U.S. Census Bureau, Current Population Survey, Annual Social and Economic Supplements, Table P-3. Race and Hispanic Origin of People by Mean Income and Sex: 1947 to 2005).

[154] Woo et al. "Subsidies for Assets."

[155] It is important to note that the households in each percentile are not necessarily the same because they are classified by income and by wealth separately.

[156] Child Trust Fund, "Key Facts about the Child Trust Fund"; Loke and Sherraden, "Building Assets from Birth"; Sodha, "Lessons from across the Atlantic."

[157] U.S. Department of Health and Human Services, "About the Assets for Independence Act"; Mills, Patterson, Orr, and DeMarco, "Evaluation of the American Dream Demonstration."

[158] Mohn, "Building Employees' Nest Eggs."

[159] U.S. Census Bureau, Current Population Survey, "Annual Social and Economic Supplements, Mean Income Received by Each Fifth and Top 5 Percent of Families, All Races."

[160] Ibid.

[161] See Wolfe, "New Politics of Inequality"; Wolfe, Wal-Mart's Pay Gap.

[162] John J. Heldrich Center for Workforce Development, "Making Career Connections."

[163] See, for example, Blinder, "How Many U.S. Jobs Might Be Offshorable?"

[164] Zabin, Dube, and Jacobs, "Hidden Public Costs of Low-Wage Jobs in California."

[165] Mishel, Bernstein, and Allegretto, "State of Working America, 2006–2007."

[166] Krueger, "Economic Scene."

[167] Berube and Katz, "Katrina's Window: Confronting Concentrated Poverty Across America."

[168] Author's calculations from: Harrison and Beck, "Bureau of Justice Statistics Bulletin"; Walmsley, "World Prison Population List (seventh edition)"; U.S. Census Bureau (population).

[169] Blumstein, "Roots of Punitiveness in a Democracy."

[170] Blumstein and Beck, "Population Growth in U.S. Prisons."

[171] Bonczar, Bureau of Justice Statistics.

[172] Western, "Mass Imprisonment and Economic Inequality"

[173] Landsburg, "Ready to Have a Baby?"

[174] See, for example, McCrate, "Working Mothers in a Double Bind."

[175] Crittendon, Price of Motherhood.

[176] Budig and England, "Wage Penalty for Motherhood."

[177] Reanalysis of National Longitudinal Survey of Youth data by Heymann in England and Folbre, "Who Should Pay for the Kids?"

[178] Widener, "Family-Friendly Policy."

[179] Cutler, Katz, Card, and Hall, "Macroeconomic Performance and the Disadvantaged."

[180] Mishel et al., The State of Working America 2006/2007.

[181] See, for example, the following studies that constitute a large literature on this subject. Alesina and Perotti, "Income Distribution, Political Instability, and Investment"; Alesina and Rodrik, "Distributive Politics and Economic Growth"; Benabou, "Inequality and Growth"; Benhabib and Rusticini, "Social Conflict, Growth and Income Distribution"; Bertola, "Market Structure and Income Distribution in Endogenous Growth Models."

[182] See, for example, Reich, "Living Wage Ordinances in California."

[183] Pollin and Luce, "Intended vs. Unintended Consequences"; Luce and Pollin, "Can U.S. Cities Afford Living Wage Programs?"

[184] In a study of the effects of Baltimore's living wage ordinance, such positive effects were observed more often within larger firms, where workers' hours and income were higher and employee turnover was less than among similar, smaller-scale entities. Niedt, Ruiters, Wise, and Schoenberger, "Effects of the Living Wage in Baltimore."

[185] Woo et al., "Subsidies for Assets."

PART 4
8-Point Human
Development Agenda

[186] U.S. Department of Education, National Center for Education Statistics, "Fast Facts."

[187] Greene and Winters, "Leaving Boys Behind."

[188] Heckman, "Catch 'em Young."

[189] Cohany and Sok, "Trends in Labor Force Participation of Married Mothers of Infants."

[190] Bevan et al., "Family-Friendly Employment."

[191] Widener, "Family-Friendly Policy."

[192] Boston College, Sloan Work and Family Research Network, "Conversations with the Experts."

[193] U.S. Census Bureau, "Wealth and Asset Ownership."

[194] Misra and Ganzini. "Medical Care for Patients with Severe and Persistent Mental Illness."

[195] Thanks to Neva Goodwin for her work on "people-holding institutions."

Methodological Notes

[196] For details, see Chiang, *Life Table and Its Applications*; Fitzpatrick, *Calculating Life Expectancy and Infant Mortality Rates*; and Toson and Baker, *Life Expectancy at Birth*.

[197] National Center for Health Statistics, *Multiple Cause of Death Files for 2005 with All Counties Coded by NCHS Identified*.

[198] National Center for Health Statistics, *Bridged-Race Population Estimates*.

Glossary

Agency: People's ability to act, individually and collectively, to further goals that matter to them. Autonomy, control, empowerment, and the exercise of free choice are critical aspects of agency.

Agricultural subsidies: Federal monetary assistance given by the government to individuals or groups, such as farmers or commercial agriculture, to support production of farm products.

Capabilities: The personal and societal assets that enable people to fulfill their potential.

Chronic disease: Diseases that can often be prevented or controlled but not cured.

Combined gross enrollment ratio: The number of students enrolled in primary, secondary, and tertiary levels of education, regardless of age, as a percentage of the population of theoretical school age for these three levels of education.

Congressional district: A geographic area whose residents are represented in the House of Representatives. Every ten years the number of congressional districts within each state may change in order to make the population of every congressional district in the country as close to equal as possible, presently with approximately 650,000 residents per district.

Correlation: An association between two variables such that when one changes in magnitude, the other also changes. A correlation may be positive or negative. If positive, as one variable increases so does the other.

If negative, as one variable increases the other decreases. A statistically significant correlation does not necessarily imply a cause-and-effect relationship.

Correlation coefficient: A measurement of the strength of a correlation between two variables. The values of the coefficient run from +1 (perfect positive correlation) through 0 (no correlation) to –1 (perfect negative correlation).

Earned Income Tax Credit (EITC): A refundable federal income tax credit for low-income working individuals and families, administered by the Internal Revenue Service. Over half of U.S. states with an income tax have developed state EITCs, which are generally calculated as a percentage of the federal credit.

Earnings: The sum of wage or salary income and net income from self-employment received in exchange for labor. Earnings represent the amount of income received regularly for people sixteen years old and over before deductions for personal income taxes, Social Security, bond purchases, union dues, Medicare deductions, etc. An earner has either wage/salary income or self-employment income, or both.

Error margin: A range between which there is a high probability that the data are accurate.

Family budget: The amount that a basic family can be expected to pay for necessary living costs in housing, child care, health care, food, transportation, and taxes in an average year. This basic budget does not include expenses such as funds for savings, vacations, or insurance.

Gross domestic product (GDP): GDP is one way to measure the size of a country's economy. It is the sum of value-added by all resident producers in the economy plus any taxes and less any subsidies not included in the valuation of output.

Gross enrollment ratio: The total number of students of any age enrolled at a given education level, expressed as a percentage of the population of the official age group corresponding to those levels. Gross enrollment ratios in excess of 100 percent indicate that there are pupils or students outside the theoretical age group who are enrolled in that level of education.

Human development: A process of enlarging people's opportunities and freedoms and improving their well-being, enabling them to lead long, healthy lives; to have access to knowledge; to enjoy a decent standard of living; and to participate in the decisions that affect them.

Human Development Index (HDI): A composite index measuring average achievement in three basic dimensions—a long and healthy life, access to knowledge, and a decent standard of living—which can be used to objectively compare regions as well as monitor advances and declines over time.

Human poverty: The lack of basic human capabilities and opportunities for living a tolerable life.

Human security: Protection of the vital core of human lives from critical threats; it includes safety from chronic threats, such as discrimination or unemployment; freedom from violence; and protection from sudden crises, such as a severe economic downturn, an environmental disaster, or the outbreak of epidemic.

Income poverty: The assessment of poverty on the basis of income.

International development: Long-term, sustainable strategies for people to generate secure livelihoods and improve their quality of life. It differs from humanitarian aid, which is aimed at short-term solutions to specific crises.

Intimate partner violence: Violence between two people who share intimate lives.

Life expectancy at birth: The number of years a newborn infant would live if prevailing patterns of age-specific mortality rates at the time of birth were to remain unchanged during the child's life, often used as a summary health measure.

Mean earnings: The sum of the amount of earnings received prior to any tax deductions of the entire population of those sixteen years or older, divided by the number of individuals sixteen years or older.

Median earnings: The median divides the earnings distribution into two equal parts: one-half of the cases falling below the median and one-half above the median. Median earnings is restricted to individuals sixteen years old and over with earnings and is computed on the basis of a standard distribution. In 2005 median earnings in the United States were $27,299 (see Earnings).

Net worth: See wealth.

OECD: The Organisation for Economic Co-Operation and Development comprises thirty "affluent" or "industrialized" countries, including Australia, Austria, Belgium, Canada, Czech Republic, Denmark, Finland, France, Germany, Greece, Hungary, Iceland, Ireland, Italy, Japan, Korea, Luxembourg, Mexico, the Netherlands, New Zealand, Norway, Poland, Portugal, Slovak Republic, Spain, Sweden, Switzerland, Turkey, the United Kingdom, and the United States.

Poverty measure: The primary statistic for measuring the extent of poverty in the United States. A set of poverty thresholds are determined by the Census Bureau, and poverty guidelines issued by the Department of Health and Human Services, are used to determine eligibility for many government programs. Those considered "poor" live in families with incomes below the poverty threshold for their family type (based on family size and number of children in the family). The official government poverty threshold is based on the cost of food. The 2007 poverty threshold for a family of four (two adults and two children) is an income of $21,027 before taxes.

Preston Curve: A graph of the correlation between income and life expectancy across various countries, named after its creator Samuel Preston.

Public health: The science and art of disease prevention, prolonging life, and promoting health and well-being through organized community effort (C. E. A. Winslow definition).

Sampling error: The difference between an estimate based on a sample and the corresponding value that would be obtained if the estimate were based on the entire population.

Self-sufficiency budget: A policymaking tool being developed by organizations in every state to provide a better means to determine whether a family can afford a decent standard of living than the current poverty measure.

Statistical significance: The likelihood that a finding or a result is caused by something other than just chance. Usually, this is set at less than 5 percent probability, meaning that the result is at least 95 percent likely to be accurate (or that this result would be produced by chance no more than 5 percent of the time).

Supportive housing: Affordable housing linked to health, mental health, and other support services for special-needs populations, such as those with chronic mental illness, the physically or developmentally disabled, victims of domestic violence, and others, to allow residents to live as independently as possible.

Unemployment rate: The number of those above sixteen years of age who are without work and are actively seeking work, divided by the civilian labor force.

Wealth: The amount possessed by an individual, including physical and financial assets, minus debt. Also referred to as net worth.

Bibliography

PART 1

Understanding
Human Development

Adams, James Truslow. *Epic of America*. Boston: Little Brown and Co., 1931.

Alesina, Alberto F., and Eliana La Ferrara. "Participation in Heterogeneous Communities." *Quarterly Journal of Economics* 115, no. 3 (2000): 847–904.

Alkire, Sabina. "Concepts and Measures of Agency." January 2008 OPHI Working Paper 9 (unpublished). http://www .ophi.org.uk/pubs/Alkire_Agency_WP9 .pdf. (accessed April 1, 2008)

——."Conceptual Framework for Human Security." http://www.humansecurity -chs.org/activities/outreach/frame.pdf.

——."Dimensions of Human Development." *World Development* 30, no. 2 (2002): 181-205.

Basu Ray, Deepayan. "A Human Security Assessment of the United States." Background paper commissioned for *American Human Development Report 2008-2009*.

Becker, Gary S., and Nigel Tomes. "Human Capital and the Rise and Fall of Families." *Journal of Labor Economics* 4, no. 3 (1984): S1–S39.

Bradbury, Katherine, and Jane Katz. "Are Lifetime Incomes Growing More Unequal? Looking at New Evidence on Family Income Mobility." *Federal Reserve Bank of Boston Regional Review* (Fourth Quarter 2002). http://www.bos.frb.org/economic/ nerr/rr2002/q4/index.htm (accessed October 8, 2007).

California Department of Transportation. "Seismic Retrofit Program, Fact Sheet." http://www.dot.ca.gov/hq/ paffairs/about/retrofit.htm (February 1, 2008).

Corak, Miles. *Do Poor Children Become Poor Adults? Lessons from a Cross Country Comparison of Generational Earnings Mobility*. Bonn, Germany: Institute for the Study of Labor and Statistics Canada, 2006. http://ftp.iza .org/dp1993.pdf (accessed November 28, 2008).

Fletcher, Michael A. "Middle-Class Dream Eludes African American Families." *Washington Post*, November 13, 2007, sec. 1.

Foundation for Child Development. "What Is the FCD Child Well-Being Index?" http://www.fcd-us.org/issues_more/ issues_more_list.htm?cat_id=1604 (accessed September 2, 2007).

Heyman, Jody, Alison Earle, and Jeffrey Hayes. "The Work, Family and Equity Index: How Does the United States Measure Up?" Montreal, Canada: Institute for Health and Social Policy and Project on Global Working Families, 2007. http://www.mcgill .ca/files/ihsp/WFEI2007.pdf (accessed September 2, 2007).

Institute for Innovation in Social Policy. "The Index of Social Health." http:// iisp.vassar.edu/ish.html (accessed September 2, 2007).

Khandelwal, Namrita. "Political, Media and Civil Society Representation in the United States." Background paper commissioned for American Human Development Report 2008–09.

Mazmuder, Bhashkar, and David I. Levine. "The Growing Importance of Family and Community: An Analysis of Changes in the Sibling Correlation in Men's Earnings." http://www .chicagofed.org/publications/ workingpapers/papers/wp2003-24.pdf (accessed October 8, 2007).

Marmot, Michael. *The Status Syndrome: How Social Standing Affects Our Health and Longevity*. New York: Times Books, 2004.

National Priorities Project. "Where Do Your Tax Dollars Go? Notes and Sources (2007)." http://www.nationalpriorities .org/tax_dollars_notes (accessed February 25, 2008).

National Urban League. "The State of Black America." http://www.nul .org/thestateofblackamerica.html (accessed September 2, 2007).

Nord, Mark, Margaret Andrews, and Steven Carlson. *Household Food Security in the United States, 2005, Economic Research Report No. 29*. Washington, DC: United States Department of Agriculture, Economic Research Service, 2006.

Redefining Progress. "Genuine Progress Indicator." http://www.progress.org/ sustainability_indicators/genuine_ progress_indicator.htm (accessed September 27, 2007).

Roemer, John E. "Equal Opportunity and Intergenerational Mobility: Going Beyond Intergenerational Income Transition Matrices." In *Generational Income Mobility in North America and Europe*, ed. Miles Corak, 48–57. Cambridge: Cambridge University Press, 2004.

Sawhill, Isabel, and John E. Morton. "Economic Mobility: Is the American Dream Alive and Well?" Washington, DC: Pew Charitable Trusts Economic Mobility Project, 2007. http://www.economicmobility.org/assets/pdfs/EMP%20American%20Dream%20Report.pdf (accessed November 29, 2007).

Sen, Amartya. "A Decade of Human Development." *Journal of Human Development* 1, no. 1 (2000): 17-23.

———. "Capability and Well-Being." *In The Quality of Life*, eds. Martha Nussbaum and Amartya Sen, 31–51. Oxford: Clarendon Press, 1993.

———. *Development as Freedom*. New York: Alfred A. Knopf, 1999.

———. *Inequality Reexamined*. Oxford: Oxford University Press, 1992.

Stonecash, Jeffrey M. *Inequality and the American Public: Results of the Fourth Annual Maxwell School Survey*. Syracuse, NY: Campbell Public Affairs Institute, 2007.

United Nations Children's Fund. *Report Card 7, Child Poverty in Perspective: An Overview of Child Well-Being in Rich Countries*. Florence, Italy: UNICEF Innocenti Research Centre, 2007.

United Nations Development Programme. *Human Development Report 2002*. New York: Oxford University Press, 2002.

———. *Human Development Report 2007/2008*. New York: Palgrave MacMillan, 2007.

United Nations Statistics Division. Millennium Development Goals Indicators. "Indicator 4.2 Infant Mortality Rate." http://mdgs.un.org/unsd/mdg/SeriesDetail.aspx?srid=562 (accessed August 15, 2007).

United States Census Bureau. "American Religious Identification Survey. Table 74. Self-Described Religious Identification of Adult Population: 1990 and 2001." http://www.census.gov/compendia/statab/tables/08s0074.pdf (accessed February 25, 2008).

———. "Fact Sheet 2006 American Community Survey Data Profile Highlights." http://factfinder.census.gov/servlet/ACSSAFFFacts?_event=&geo_id=01000US&_geoContext=01000US&_street=&_county=&_cityTown=&_state=&_zip=&_lang=en&_sse=on&ActiveGeoDiv=&_useEV=&pctxt=fph&pgsl=010&_submenuld=factsheet_1&ds_name=null&_ci_nbr=null&qr_name=null&reg=null%3Anull&_keyword=&_industry= (accessed February 11, 2008).

United States Department of Health and Human Services. "Summary Child Maltreatment 2005." http://www.acf.hhs.gov/programs/cb/pubs/cm05/summary.htm (accessed September 27, 2007).

United States Geological Survey. "Earthquake Hazards Program." http://earthquake.usgs.gov/ (accessed September 27, 2007).

University of Pennsylvania School of Social Policy and Practice. "Richard Estes Research." http://www.sp2.upenn.edu/people/faculty/estes/10.html (accessed September 2, 2007).

Wilkinson, Richard G. *Unhealthy Societies: The Afflictions of Inequality*. London: Routledge, 1996.

World Bank. "GNI Per Capita 2006, Atlas Method and PPP." http://siteresources.worldbank.org/DATASTATISTICS/Resources/GNIPC.pdf (accessed August 20, 2007).

PART 2

What the American Human Development Index Reveals

Deaton, Angus. "Global Patterns of Income and Health: Facts, Interpretations and Policies" WIDER Annual Lecture delivered in Helsinki, Finland, September 29, 2006.

Preston, Samuel H. "The Changing Relation between Mortality and Level of Development." *Population Studies* 29, no. 2 (1975): 239–48.

PART 3

The Building Blocks of the HD Index

A Long and Healthy Life

Agarwal, Bina, and P. Panda. "Toward Freedom from Domestic Violence: The Neglected Obvious." *Journal of Human Development* 8, no. 3 (2007): 359–88.

Akinbami, Lara J. "State of Childhood Asthma, United States 1980–2005." Advanced Data from Vital and Health Statistics No. 381. Hyattsville, MD: National Center for Health Statistics, 2006. http://www.cdc.gov/nchs/data/ad/ad381.pdf (accessed December 8, 2007).

Alaska Bureau of Vital Statistics, Alaska Department of Health and Social Services. "Top 10 Leading Causes of Death for Alaska, 2005." http://www.hss.state.ak.us/DPH/bvs/death_statistics/Leading_Causes_Census/body.html (accessed November 15, 2007).

Alaska Health Care Strategies Planning Council. "Final Report: Summary and Recommendations." Juneau: Alaska Department of Health and Social Services, 2007. http://www.hss.state.ak.us/hspc/ (accessed November 18, 2007).

Alexander, Mary Jane, and Kim Hopper. "Capabilities and Psychiatric Disability: Rethinking Public Mental Health." Paper presented to Human Development and Capability Association Annual Conference, New School, New York, September 2007.

Anderson, Jacquelyn. "Supportive Housing Research FAQs: Is Supportive Housing Cost Effective?" Corporation for Supportive Housing. http://documents.csh.org/documents/policy/FAQs/CostEffectivenessFAQFINAL.pdf (accessed January 12, 2008).

Ariana, Proochista. "Health Inequalities in America." Background paper commissioned for *American Human Development Report 2008–2009*.

Bantle, John P., Susan K. Raatz, William Thomas, and Angeliki Georgopoulos. "Effects of Dietary Fructose on Plasma Lipids in Healthy Subjects." *American Journal of Clinical Nutrition* 72, no. 5 (November 2000): 1128–34.

Benavides, Blaire. 2007. "The State of Mental Health Care in the United States." Background paper commissioned for *American Human Development Report 2008–2009*.

Brown, E. R., V. D. Ojeda, R. Wyn, and R. Levan. *Racial and Ethnic Disparities in Access to Health Insurance and Health Care*. Menlo Park, CA: UCLA Center for Health Policy Research and Kaiser Family Foundation, 2000.

Burt, Martha, Laundan Y. Aron, and Edgar Lee with Jesse Valente. *Helping America's Homeless: Emergency Shelter or Affordable Housing?* Washington, DC: Urban Institute Press, 2001.

Carmona, Richard H. "Obesity, Individual Responsibility, and Public Policy." Presentation at American Enterprise Institute for Public Policy Research Conference on Obesity and Public Policy, Washington, DC, June 10, 2003.

Castor, M. L., M. S. Smyser, M. M. Taualii, A. N. Park, S. H. Lawson, and R. A. Forquera. "A Nationwide Population-Based Study Identifying Health Disparities between American Indians/Alaska Natives and the General Populations Living in Select Urban Counties." *American Journal of Public Health* 6, no. 8 (2006): 1478–84.

Catlin, Aarol, C. Cowan, M. Hartman, S. Heffler, and National Health Expenditure Accounts Team. "National Health Spending in 2006: A Year of Change for Prescription Drugs." *Health Affairs* 29, no. 1 (2008): 14–29.

Centers for Disease Control and Prevention. *The Burden of Chronic Diseases and Their Risk Factors: National and State Perspectives*. Atlanta: Centers for Disease Control and Prevention, 2004. http://www.cdc.gov/nccdphp/burdenbook2004/pdf/burden_book2004.pdf accessed December 10, 2007)

———. "Deaths: Final Data for 2004." *National Vital Statistics Reports* 55, no. 19 (August 21, 2007): 1–120. http://www.cdc.gov/nchs/data/nvsr/nvsr55/nvsr55_19.pdf (accessed November 15, 2007).

———. *HIV/AIDS Surveillance Report*. Vol. 17. Rev. ed. Atlanta: Center for Disease Control and Prevention, 2007. http://www.cdc.gov/hiv/topics/surveillance/resources/reports/2005report/default.htm (accessed December 8, 2007].

———. "Understanding Intimate Partner Violence, Fact Sheet 2006." http://www.cdc.gov/ncipc/dvp/ipv_factsheet.pdf (accessed February 25, 2008].

Centers for Disease Control and Prevention, National Center for Chronic Disease Prevention and Health Promotion. "Behavioral Risk Factor Surveillance System. Prevalence Data: Alaska—2006." http://apps.nccd.cdc.gov/brfss/page.asp?cat=XX&yr=2006&state=AK#XX (accessed November 15, 2007].

———. "Results of Behavioral Risk Factor Surveillance System." http://apps.nccd.cdc.gov/brfss/Trends/trendfigure_c.asp?state_c=US&state=MN&qkey=10020&SUBMIT1=Go (accessed January 15, 2008].

Centers for Disease Control and Prevention, National Center for Environmental Health. "Tested and Confirmed Elevated Blood Lead Levels by State, Year and Blood Level Group for Children < 72 Months, National Data 1997–2006." http://www.cdc.gov/nceh/lead/surv/stats.htm (accessed September 4, 2007].

Centers for Disease Control and Prevention, National Center for Health Statistics. "Compressed Mortality File 1999–2004." Centers for Disease Control and Prevention Wonder Online Database. http://wonder.cdc.gov/ (accessed October 2, 2007].

———. "Disease Still a Major Problem." http://www.cdc.gov/nchs/pressroom/06facts/obesity03_04.htm (accessed November 17, 2007].

———. *Leading Causes of Death, 1900–1998*. Hyattsville, MD: National Center for Health Statistics, 2007. http://www.cdc.gov/nchs/data/dvs/lead1900_98.pdf (accessed November 6, 2007].

Centers for Disease Control and Prevention, National Center for Injury Prevention and Control. "Suicide, Facts at a Glance Summer 2007." http://www.cdc.gov/ncipc/dvp/suicide/SuicideDataSheet.pdf (accessed October 9, 2007].

———. "WISQARS Leading Causes of Death Reports, 1999–2005." http://webappa.cdc.gov/sasweb/ncipc/leadcaus10.html#Advanced%20Options (accessed December 1, 2007].

Centers for Medicare and Medicaid Services. "National Health Expenditure Data." http://www.cms.hhs.gov/NationalHealthExpendData/02_NationalHealthAccountsHistorical.asp#TopOfPag (accessed December 11, 2007].

Cohen, Alan. "Smart Cards, Smarter Health Care." *PC magazine*, October 1, 2003. http://www.pcmag.com/article2/0,4149,1265440,00.asp (accessed September 15, 2007].

Collins, Chris. *Improving Outcomes: Blueprint for a National AIDS Plan for the United States*. New York: Open Society Institute, 2007.

Committee on the Consequences of Uninsurance. *Hidden Costs, Value Lost: Uninsurance in America*. Washington, DC: National Academies Press, 2003.

———. *Insuring America's Health: Principles and Recommendations*. Washington, DC: National Academies Press, 2004.

Conely, Dalton and Rebecca Glauber. "Gender, Body Mass, and Economic Status." NBER Working Paper No. 11343, April 2005. http://papers.nber.org/papers/w11343.pdf (accessed November 2007].

Corporation for Supportive Housing. "Is Supportive Housing Cost-Effective?" http://documents.csh.org/documents/policy/FAQs/CostEffectivenessFAQFINAL.pdf (accessed February 25, 2008].

———. "Supportive Housing Works to End Homelessness." http://www.csh.org/index.cfm?fuseaction=Page.viewPage&pageID=344 (accessed October 22, 2007].

Culhane, Dennis P., Stephen Metraux, and Trevor Hadley. "Public Service Reductions Associated with Placement of Homeless Persons with Severe Mental Illness in Supportive Housing." *Housing Policy Debate* 14, no. 1 (2002): 107–63.

Cutler, David M., G. Long, E. R. Berndt, J. Royer et al. "The Value of Antihypertensive Drugs: A Perspective on Medical Innovation." *Health Affairs* 26, no. 1 (January/February 2007): 97.

Davis, Karen. "Danish Health System through an American Lens." *Health Policy* 59, no. 2 (2002): 119–32.

———. "Uninsured in America: Problems and Possible Solutions." *British Medical Journal* 334 (2007): 346–48.

Davis, Matthew M. "Planning the Next Wave of SCHIP Research." *Pediatrics* 115 (2005): 492–94.

Deegan, Patricia. "CommonGround." http://www.changemakers.net/en-us/node/839 (accessed October 13, 2007).

DeNavas-Walt, Carmen, B. D. Proctor, and J. Smith. "Current Population Reports, P60-233, Income, Poverty, and Health Insurance Coverage in the United States: 2006." Washington, DC: U.S. Government Printing Office, 2007. http://www.census.gov/prod/2007pubs/p60-233.pdf (accessed January 15, 2008).

Disaster Center. "US States Crime 2004–2005, Crimes per 100,000 and Ranking." http://www.disastercenter.com/crime/US_States_Rate_Ranking.html (accessed February 25, 2008).

Duhigg, Charles. "At Many Homes, More Profit and Less Nursing." *New York Times*, September 23, 2007, business sec.

Eaton, Susan C. "Eldercare in the United States: Inadequate, Inequitable, but Not a Lost Cause," *Feminist Economics* 11, no. 2 (2005): 37–51.

Environmental Working Group. "Farm Subsidy Database." http://farm.ewg.org/farm/ (accessed December 5, 2007).

European Commission. "Eurobarometer: Health and Food, November 2006." http://ec.europa.eu/health/ph_publication/eb_food_en.pdf (accessed September 15, 2007).

Frank, Richard G., and Sherry A. Glied. *Better but Not Well: Mental Health Policy in the United States since 1950.* Baltimore: Johns Hopkins University Press, 2006.

Frazer, Jennifer. "County Looks to Add Free Colonoscopies for Residents." *Wyoming Tribune-Eagle*, September 4, 2007, A3.

Fronstin, Paul. *Issue Brief No. 310: Sources of Health Insurance and Characteristics of the Uninsured: Analysis of the March 2007 Current Population Survey.* Washington, DC: Employer Benefit Research Institute, 2007.

Fukawa, Tetsuo, and Nobuyuki Izumida. "Japanese Healthcare Expenditures in a Comparative Context." *Japanese Journal of Social Security Policy* 3, no. 2 (2004): 51–61.

Grossman, D. C., J. W. Krieger, J. R. Sugarman, and R. A. Forguera. "Health Status of Urban American Indians and Alaska Natives: A Population-Based Survey." *Journal of the American Medical Association* 271, no. 11 (2003): 845–50.

Grunbaum, J. A., et al. "Youth Risk Behavior Surveillance System, 2003." Centers for Disease Control and Prevention. MMWR Surveillance Summary Centers for Disease Control and Prevention (2004): 1–96.

Hajj, Jennifer. "Substance Abuse in the United States." Background paper commissioned for *American Human Development Report 2008–2009.*

Hao, Yongping, Elizabeth M. Ward, Ahmedin Jemal, Linda W. Pickle, and Michael J. Thun. "U.S. Congressional District Cancer Death Rates." *International Journal of Health Geographics* 5 (2006): 28.

Harper, Sam, J. Lynch, S. Burris, and G. Davey Smith. "Trends in the Black-White Life Expectancy Gap in the United States, 1983–2003." *Journal of the American Medical Association* 297 (2007): 1224–32.

Havel, Peter J., S. S. Elliott, N. L. Keim, J. S. Stern, and K. Teff. "Fructose, Weight Gain, and the Insulin Resistance Syndrome." *American Journal of Clinical Nutrition* 76, no. 5 (2002): 911.

Herman, D. B., E. S. Susser, L. Jandorf, J. Lavelle, and E. J. Bromet. "Homelessness among Individuals with Psychotic Disorders Hospitalized for the First Time: Findings from the Suffolk County Mental Health Project." *American Journal of Psychiatry* 155, no. 1 (1998): 109–13.

Himmelstein, David U., Deborah Thorne, Elizabeth Warren, and Steffie Woolhandler. "Illness and Injury as Contributors to Bankruptcy." Market Watch, Health Affairs. http://content.healthaffairs.org/cgi/reprint/hlthaff.w5.63v1 (accessed August 19, 2007).

Holahan, John, Mindy Cohen, and David Rousseau. *Why Did Medicaid Spending Decline in 2006?* Washington, DC: Kaiser Commission on Medicaid and the Uninsured, 2007.

Hughes, Dana, and Lisa Simpson. "Role of Social Change in Preventing Low Birth Weight." *Low Birth Weight* 5, no. 1 (Spring 1995). http://www.futureofchildren.org/pubs-info2825/pubs-info_show.htm?doc_id=79872 (accessed October 28, 2007).

Institute of Medicine, Committee on Assuring the Health of the Public in the 21st Century. *The Future of the Public's Health in the 21st Century.* Washington, DC: National Academy Press, 2002.

Institute of Medicine, Committee on Crossing the Quality Chasm: Adaptation to Mental Health and Addictive Disorders. *Improving the Quality of Health Care for Mental and Substance-Use Conditions.* Washington, DC: National Academy Press, 2006.

Jaspin, Elliot. "State Paying More to Treat Late-Stage Breast Cancer: Insurance Gaps Leave Many Women with No Access to Mammograms." *Houston Chronicle*, June 17, 2007, 2-star ed., sec. B.

Kaiser Family Foundation. *AIDS at 25: An Overview of Major Trends in the U.S. Epidemic.* Menlo Park, CA: Kaiser Family Foundation, 2006. http://www.kff.org/hivaids/upload/7525.pdf (accessed October 23, 2007).

———. "Alaska at-a-glance." http://www.statehealthfacts.org/profileglance.jsp?rgn=3 (accessed November 13, 2007).

——. "Racial/Ethnic Differences in Cardiac Care: The Weight of Evidence" (October 2002). http://www.kff .org/uninsured/loader.cfm?url=/ commonspot/security/getfile. cfm&PageID=14168 (accessed January 15, 2008).

——. "Statehealthfacts.org, Medicaid and SCHIP." http://www.statehealthfacts .org/comparecat.jsp?cat=4 (accessed November 3, 2007).

——. "Statehealthfacts.org, Monthly SCHIP Enrollment, June 2006." http://www .statehealthfacts.org/comparetable .jsp?ind=236&cat=4&yr=34&typ=1&sor t=a&o=a (accessed February 25, 2008).

——. "Statehealthfacts.org, Total SCHIP Expenditures, FY2007." http://www .statehealthfacts.org/comparetable .jsp?cat=4&ind=235 (accessed February 25, 2008).

——. "Statehealthfacts.org, Total State Government Health Expenditures as Percent of the Gross State Product, 2003." http://www.statehealthfacts .org/comparemaptable.jsp?ind= 284&cat=5 (accessed February 25, 2008).

——. The Uninsured: A Primer, October 2007. Menlo Park, CA: Kaiser Family Foundation, 2007.

Kawachi, Ichiro. "Income Inequality and Health." In Social Epidemiology, ed. L. F. Berkman and I. Kawachi. New York: Oxford University Press, 2000.

Levine, Robert S., et al. "Black-White Inequalities in Mortality and Life Expectancy, 1933–1999: Implications for Healthy People 2010." Public Health Reports 116, no. 5 (September–October 2001): 474–84.

Lillie-Blanton, M., Osula Evadne Rushing, and Sonia Ruiz. Key Facts: Race, Ethnicity and Medical Care. Menlo Park, CA: Kaiser Family Foundation, 2003. http://www.kff.org/minorityhealth/ upload/Key-Facts-Race-Ethnicity-Medical-Care-Figurebook.pdf (accessed October 2, 2007).

Lleras-Muney, Adriana. "The Relationship between Education and Adult Mortality in the United States." Review of Economic Studies 189, no. 215 (2005).

Matthews T. J., and M. F. MacDorman. "Infant Mortality Statistics from 2003." National Vital Statistics Reports 54, no. 16. Hyattsville, MD: National Center for Health Statistics, 2006. http://wwwtest.cdc.gov/nchs/data/ nvsr/nvsr54/nvsr54_16.pdf (accessed October 28, 2007).

——. "Infant Mortality Statistics from the 2004 Period Linked Birth/Infant Death Data Set." National Vital Statistics Reports 55, no. 15. Hyattsville, MD: National Center for Health Statistics, 2007. http://www.cdc.gov/nchs/data/ nvsr/nvsr55/nvsr55_14.pdf.6 (accessed January 15, 2008).

McAlpine, DD., and D. Mechanic. "Utilization of specialty mental health care among persons with severe mental illness: The roles of demographics, need, insurance, and risk." Health Services Research 35 (1 Pt 2): 277–92.

Miller, M., D. Azrael, and D. Hemenway. "Rates of Household Firearm Ownership and Homicide across US Region and States, 1988–1997." American Journal of Public Health 92, no. 12 (2002): 1988–93.

Miller, M., et al. "The Association between Changes in Household Firearm Ownership and Rates of Suicide in the United States, 1981–2002." Injury Prevention 12 (2006): 78–182.

——. "Firearm Availability and Unintentional Firearm Deaths, Suicide, and Homicide among 5–14 Year Olds." Journal of Trauma Injury, Infection and Critical Care 52 (2002): 267–75.

National Academies, Division of Behavioral and Social Sciences and Education. "Multiple Origins, Uncertain Destinies: Hispanics and the American Future, Health Status and Access to Care." http://www7.nationalacademies .org/cpop/HealthStatus.pdf (accessed December 14, 2007).

National Academy of Sciences. Cancer Care for the Whole Patient: Meeting Psychosocial Health Needs. Washington, DC: National Academies Press, 2007.

——. Multiple Origins, Uncertain Destinies: Hispanics and the American Future. Edited by Faith Mitchell and Marta Tienda. Washington, DC: National Academies Press, 2006.

National Association of State Budget Officers. "Per Capita Health Spending" (2003 data). Cited in United Health Foundation, America's Health Rankings. http://www.unitedhealthfoundation .com/shr2005/components/ healthexpend.html (accessed January 15, 2008).

National Center for Health Statistics. Health, United States, 2006: With Figurebook on Trends in the Health of Americans. Hyattsville, MD: National Center for Health Statistics, 2006. http://www.cdc.gov/nchs/data/hus/ hus06.pdf (accessed November 13, 2007).

——. Health, United States, 2007: With Figurebook on Trends in the Health of Americans. Hyattsville, MD: National Center for Health Statistics, 2007. http://www.cdc.gov/nchs/data/hus/ hus07.pdf (accessed November 13, 2007).

National Institute of Mental Health. "The Numbers Count: Mental Disorders in America." http://www.nimh.nih .gov/health/publications/the-numbers-count-mental-disorders-in-america.shtml (accessed June 27, 2007).

——. "Suicide in the U.S.: Statistics and Prevention." http://www.nimh.nih.gov/ health/publications/suicide-in-the-us-statistics-and-prevention.shtml (accessed December 10, 2007).

Olson, Lynn M., Suk-fong S. Tang, and Paul W. Newacheck. "Children in the United States with Discontinuous Health Insurance Coverage." New England Journal of Medicine 353 (2005): 382–91.

Organisation for Economic Co-Operation and Development. Health at a Glance, OECD Indicators 2005. Paris: OECD Publishing, 2005.

——. Health at a Glance, OECD Indicators 2007. Paris: OECD Publishing, 2007

Perlman, J., and J. Parvensky. Denver Housing First Collaborative Cost Benefit Analysis and Program Outcomes Report. Denver: Colorado Coalition for the Homeless, 2006.

Sheils, John, and Randall Haught. "The Cost of Tax-Exempt Health Benefits in 2004." *Health Affairs Web Exclusive*, February 25, 2004. http://content.healthaffairs.org/cgi/content/full/hlthaff.w4.106v1/DC1 (accessed January 15, 2008).

Siantz, Mary Lou de Leon. "Understanding Health Disparities: The Hispanic Experience." Presentation at Health Disparities in the United States conference, Woodrow Wilson Center Global Health Initiative, Washington, DC, April 4, 2006.

Small Arms Survey. "Small Arms Survey 2007: Chapter 2 Summary, Completing the Count—Civilian Firearms." http://www.smallarmssurvey.org/files/sas/publications/year_b_pdf/2007/2007SAS_English_press_kit/2007SASCh2_summary_en.pdf (accessed February 25, 2008).

Southern Environmental Law Center. "Healthy Air." http://www.southernenvironment.org/air (accessed December 8, 2007).

Squires, Sally. "Sweet but Not So Innocent?" *Washington Post*, March 11, 2003, health sec.

Susser, E., S. P. Lin, and S. A. Conover. "Risk Factors for Homelessness." *American Journal of Epidemiology* 15, no. 2 (1991): 546–56.

Turnock, Bernard J. *Public Health: What It Is and How It Works*. 3rd ed. Sudbury, MA: Jones and Bartlett Publishers, 2004.

United Nations Children's Fund (UNICEF). *Report Card 7, Child Poverty in Perspective: An Overview of Child Well-Being in Rich Countries*. Florence, Italy: UNICEF Innocenti Research Centre, 2007.

———. *State of the World's Children 2007: Women and Children, the Double Dividend of Gender Equity*. New York: Gist and Herlin Press, 2006. http://www.unicef.org/sowc07/docs/sowc07.pdf (accessed October 28, 2007).

U.S. Census Bureau. "A Child's Day: 2004, Selected Indicators of Childhood Well-Being." http://www.census.gov/population/www/socdemo/2004_detailedtables.html (accessed November 5, 2007).

———. "Health Insurance Coverage: 2006." http://www.census.gov/hhes/www/hlthins/hlthin06/hlth06asc.html (accessed January 15, 2008).

———. "2005 American Community Survey." http://spreadsheets.google.com/pub?key=pPDUv4FF5xvincigt7-oxDQ&gid=5 (accessed January 15, 2008).

U.S. Department of Commerce, Economics and Statistics Administration. "Income, Poverty and Health Insurance Coverage in the United States: 2006."

http://www.census.gov/prod/2007pubs/p60-233.pdf (accessed August 28, 2007).

U.S. Department of Health and Human Services, Centers for Medicare and Medicaid Services. "State Children's Health Insurance (SCHIP): State Children's Health Insurance Program Summary." http://www.cms.hhs.gov/MedicaidGenInfo/05_SCHIP%20Information.asp (accessed February 25, 2008).

———. New Freedom Commission on Mental Health. 2003. *Achieving the Promise: Transforming MentalHealth Care in America. Final Report*. No: SMA-03-3832. Rockville, MD: USDHHS.

U.S. Department of Justice, Bureau of Justice Statistics. "Homicide Trends in the U.S. by Region." http://www.ojp.usdoj.gov/bjs/homicide/region.htm (accessed September 29, 2007).

———. "Homicide Trends in the U.S. by Region, Intimate Homicide." http://www.ojp.usdoj.gov/bjs/homicide/intimates.htm (accessed February 25, 2008).

U.S. Department of Justice, Federal Bureau of Investigation. "2006 Crime in the United States." http://www.fbi.gov/ucr/cius2006/offenses/violent_crime/index.html (accessed October 18, 2007).

———. "2006 Crime in the United States, by Community Type." http://www.fbi.gov/ucr/cius2006/data/table_02.html (accessed February 25, 2008).

———. "2006 Crime in the United States, Expanded Homicide Data Table 6." http://www.fbi.gov/ucr/cius2006/offenses/violent_crime/index.html (accessed February 25, 2008).

U.S. General Accounting Office. *Child Welfare and Juvenile Justice: Federal Agencies Could Play a Stronger Role in Helping States Reduce the Number of Children Placed Solely to Obtain Mental Health Services*. Washington, DC: U.S. General Accounting Office, 2003.

U.S. Government Accountability Office. *Military Health Care: Tricare Cost-Sharing Proposals Would Help Offset Increasing Health Care Spending, but Projected Savings Are Likely Overestimated*. Washington, DC: U.S. Government Accountability Office, 2007.

———. *Nursing Homes: Despite Increased Oversight, Challenges Remain in Ensuring High-Quality Care and Resident Safety*. Washington, DC: U.S. General Accounting Office, 2005.

World Health Organization, Europe. *Highlights on Health in Denmark, 2004*. Copenhagen: WHO Regional Office for Europe, 2006.

World Health Organization, Global Strategy on Diet Physical Education and Health. "Obesity and Overweight." http://www.who.int/dietphysicalactivity/media/en/gsfs_obesity.pdf (accessed October 8, 2007).

Zeratsky, Katherine. "Ask a Food and Nutrition Specialist: High-Fructose Corn Syrup: Why Is It So Bad for Me?" Mayo Clinic. http://www.mayoclinic.com/health/high-fructose-corn-syrup/AN01588 (accessed December 5, 2007).

Access to Knowledge

Alliance for Catholic Education. "Teacher Formation Program." 2007. http://ace.nd.edu/academic-programs/teacherprogram (accessed September 2007).

Annie E. Casey Foundation, Kids Count Data Center. "Indicators." http://www.aecf.org/MajorInitiatives/KIDSCOUNT.aspx (accessed September 18, 2007).

Barbanel, Josh, and Ford Fessenden. "6-Figure Salaries? To Many Teachers, a Matter of Course." *New York Times*, June 5, 2005.

Baum, Sandy, and Kathleen Payea. *Trends in Student Aid 2006*. Washington, DC: The College Board, 2006

Bendor, Joshua, Jason Bordoff, and Jason Furman. "An Education Strategy to Promote Opportunity, Prosperity, and Growth." Hamilton Project Strategy Paper, February 2007. www3.brookings.edu/views/papers/200702education.pdf (accessed September 22, 2007).

Bianchi, Suzanne, Philip Cohen, Sara Raley, and Kei Nomaguchi. "Inequality in Parental Investment in Childrearing: Time, Expenditures and Health." Russell Sage Foundation, February 2003. http://www.russellsage.org/programs/main/inequality/050516.323700/ (accessed November 2007).

Bowen, William G, Martin A. Kurzweil, and Eugene M. Tobin. *Equity and Excellence in American Higher Education*. Charlottesville: University of Virginia Press, 2005.

Bowles, Samuels, Herbert Gintis, and Melissa Osborne Groves, eds. *Unequal Chances: Family Background and Economic Success*. Princeton, NJ: Princeton University Press, 2005

Brantlinger, Ellen A. *Dividing Classes: How the Middle Class Negotiates and Justifies School Advantage*. London: Falmer Press, 2003.

Brint, Steven, and Jerome Karabel. *The Diverted Dream: Community Colleges and the Promise of Educational Opportunity in America, 1900–1985*. New York: Oxford University Press, 1989.

Campaign for Educational Equity, Teachers College, Columbia University. "Facts and Figures." http://www.tc.edu/equitycampaign/detail.asp?Id=The+Equity+Gap&Info=Facts+and+Figures (accessed February 2008).

Carneiro, Pedro, and James Heckman. "Human Capital Policy." National Bureau of Economic Research, February 2003. http://www.ecdgroup.com/pdfs/heckman_article-20_05_2003-17_59_04.pdf (accessed February 2008).

Chernoff et al. "Preschool: First Findings for the Third Follow-Up of the Early Childhood Longitudinal Study, Birth Cohonort (ECLS-B)." Washington, D.C.: U.S. Department of Education, National Center for Education Statistics, 2007.

Coalition for Evidence Based Policy. "Abecedarian Project (High-Quality Child Care/Preschool for Children from Disadvantaged Backgrounds." http://www.evidencebasedprograms.org/Default.aspx?tabid=33 (accessed September 18, 2007).

———. "Perry Preschool Project (High-Quality Preschool for Children from Disadvantaged Backgrounds)." http://www.evidencebasedprograms.org/Default.aspx?tabid=32 (accessed September 18, 2007).

Conley, D. "Capital for College: Parental Assets and Educational Attainment." *Sociology of Education* 74 (2001): 59–73.

———. "Decomposing the Black-White Wealth Gap: The Role of Parental Resources, Inheritance, and Investment Dynamics." *Sociological Inquiry* 71 (2001): 39–66.

———. "The Effect of Birth Weight on Literal (and Figurative) Life Chances." National Bureau of Economic Research, 2004.

———. *Pecking Order: A Bold New Look at How Family and Society Determine Who We Become*. Vintage, 2005.

———, ed. *Wealth and Poverty in America*. Malden, MA: Blackwell Publishing, 2002

Conley, Dalton, and N. Bennett. "Outcomes in Young Adulthood for Very-Low-Birth-Weight-Infants." *New England Journal of Medicine* 347, no. 2 (2002): 141.

Conley, Dalton, and Jean W. Yeung. "The Black-White Achievement Gap and Family Wealth." National Poverty Center, Gerald R. Ford School of Public Policy, University of Michigan, Working Paper, 2004. http://npc.umich.edu/publications/u/working_paper07-02.pdf (accessed September 2007).

Corcoran et al. "The Changing Distribution of Education Finance: 1972–1997." Russell Sage Foundation, January 2003. http://www.russellsage.org/programs/main/inequality/050516.172581/ (accessed November 2007).

Danziger, Sheldon H., and Cecilia Elena Rouse. *The Price of Independence: The Economics of Early Adulthood*. New York: Russell Sage Foundation, 2007.

Decker, Paul T, Daniel P. Mayer, and Steven Glazerman. "The Effects of Teach for America on Students: Findings from a National Evaluation." Mathematica Policy Research Inc., 2004. http://www.mathematica-mpr.com/publications/PDFs/teach.pdf (accessed September 2007).

Deil-Amen, Regina. "To Teach or Not to Teach 'Social' Skills: Comparing Community Colleges and Private Occupational Colleges." *Teachers College Record* 108, no. 3 (2006): 397–421. http://www.tcrecord.org (accessed February 2008).

Dillon, Sam. "With Turnover High, Schools Fight for Teachers." *New York Times*, August 27, 2007.

DiMaggio, Paul, Eszter Hargittai, Coral Celeste, and Steven Shafer. "From Unequal Access to Differentiated Use: A Literature Review and Agenda for Research on Digital Inequality." Report prepared for the Russell Sage Foundation (2001). http://www.russellsage.org/programs/main/inequality/050516.338001/ (accessed November 2007).

Dowd, Alicia C. "Community Colleges as Gateways and Gatekeepers: Moving beyond the Access 'Saga' toward Outcome Equity." *Harvard Educational Review* (Winter 2007).

Dye, Jane Lawler, and Johnson Tallese. "A Child's Day: 2003." U.S. Census Bureau, January 2007. http://www.census.gov/prod/2007pubs/p70-109.pdf (accessed October 2007).

Eaton, Susan. *The Children in Room E4: American Education on Trial*. Chapel Hill, NC: Algonquin Books of Chapel Hill, 2007.

Edin, Kathryn, and Maria Kefalas. *Promises I Can Keep: Why Poor Women Put Motherhood Before Marriage* Berkeley: University of California Press, 2005.

Ellwood, David T., and Christopher Jencks. "The Growing Differences in Family Structure: What Do We Know? Where Do We Look for Answers?" New Inequality Program, Russell Sage Foundation, August 2001. http://www .russellsage.org/programs/main/ inequality/050221.100862/.

———. "The Uneven Spread of Single-Parent Families: What Do We Know? Where Do We Look for Answers?" in Social Inequality, ed. Kathryn Neckerman New York: Russell Sage, 2004

Fairfield, Hannah, "Masters Degrees Abound as Universities and Students See a Windfall." New York Times, September 12, 2007.

Fligstein, Neil, and Taek-Jin Shin. "The Shareholder Value Society: A Review of the Changes in Working Conditions and Inequality in the U.S., 1976–2000." Russell Sage Foundation, March 2003. http://www.russellsage.org/programs/ main/inequality/050516.492242/ (accessed November 2007).

Furstenberg, Frank. "Diverging Development: The Not-So-Invisible Hand of Social Class in the United States." Paper presented at the biennial meetings of the Society for Research on Adolescence, San Francisco, CA, March 23–26, 2006.

Gillers, Gillian. "Learning Curve." Current Magazine, MSNBC, April 10, 2006. http://www.msnbc.msn.com/ id/12206029/site/newsweek (accessed September 2007).

Gormley, William T., Jr., and Deborah Phillips. "The Effects of Universal Pre-K in Oklahoma: Research Highlights and Policy Implications." Policy Studies Journal 33, no. 1 (2005): 65–82.

Grossman, Michael. "Human Capital Model in Handbook of Health Economics." NBER Working Paper 7078 (1999).

Harry, Beth, and Mary G. Anderson. "The Disproportionate Placement of African American Males in Special Education Programs: A Critique of the Process." Journal of Negro Education 63, no. 4 (1994)

Hart, Betty, and Todd R. Risley. Meaningful Differences in the Everyday Experience of Young American Children. Baltimore: Brookes Publishing, 1995.

Hauser, Robert M. "Progress in Schooling: A Review." Russell Sage Foundation, June 2002. http://www.russellsage .org/programs/main/ inequality/050516.322671/ (accessed November 2007).

———, Devah I. Pager, and Solon J. Simmons. "Race-Ethnicity, Social Background, and Grade Retention." Center for Demography and Ecology, University of Wisconsin–Madison, July 2000. http://www.ssc.wisc.edu/ cde/cdewp/2000-08.pdf (accessed September 2007).

Haveman, Robert, Gary Sandefur, Barbara Wolfe, and Andrea Voyer. "Inequality of Family and Community Characteristics in Relation to Children's Attainments: A Review of Trends in Levels of and Inequality in Characteristics and Attainments, and Estimated Relationships between Them." Russell Sage Foundation, December 2001. http://www.russellsage.org/programs/ main/inequality/050516.264100/ (accessed November 2007).

Haycock, Kati, and Danette Gerald. "Engines of Inequality: Diminishing Equity in the Nations Premier Public Universities." The Education Trust, 2006. http://www2.edtrust.org/NR/ rdonlyres/F755E80E-9431-45AF-B28E-653C612D503D/0/EnginesofInequality. pdf (accessed January 2008).

Hayden, Dolores. Building Suburbia Green Fields and Urban Growth, 1820–2000. New York: Pantheon, 2003.

Heckman, James, and Alan Krueger. Inequality in America: What Role for Human Capital Policies? Cambridge, MA: MIT Press, 2004.

Heckman, James J. "Catch 'em Young." Wall Street Journal, January 10, 2006. http://online.wsj.com/article/ SB113686119611542381.html (accessed February 2008).

Hochschild, Jennifer. Facing Up to the American Dream. Princeton, NJ: Princeton University Press, 1995.

———, and Nathan Scovronick. The American Dream and the Public Schools. New York: Oxford University Press, 2003.

Holzer, Harry H. "What Employers Want: Job Prospects for Less Educated Workers," American Journal of Sociology 102, no. 5 (March 1997): 1462–64.

Hsin, Amy. "Mothers' Time with Children and the Social Reproduction of Cognitive Skills." PhD diss., University of California, Los Angeles, 2006.

Jencks, Christopher, and Ellwood, David T. "The Spread of Single Parent Families in the United States since 1960," October 2002.

Johnson, Heather Beth. The American Dream and the Power of Wealth: Choosing Schools and Inheriting Inequality in the Land of Opportunity. New York: Routledge, 2006.

Kane, Thomas J. "College-Going and Inequality: A Literature Review." Russell Sage Foundation, June 2001. http://www.russellsage.org/programs/ main/inequality/050516.322671/ (accessed November 2007).

Karabel, Jerome. The Chosen: The Hidden History of Admission and Exclusion at Harvard, Yale, and Princeton. Boston: Houghton Mifflin, 2005.

———. "The New College Try." New York Times, September 24, 2007. http:// www.nytimes.com/2007/09/24/opinion/ 24karabel.html (accessed February 2008).

Karman, John R., III. "Program Lures Quality Teachers to State." Business First of Louisville, June 17, 2005. http:// louisville.bizjournals.com/louisville/ stories/2005/06/20/story2.html (accessed September 2007).

Karoly, Lynn A., Rebecca M. Kilburn, and Jill S. Cannon. "Early Childhood Intervention: Proven Results, Future Promise." RAND Corporation, 2005. http://www.rand.org/pubs/ monographs/2005/RAND_MG341.pdf (accessed September 2007).

Knowledge Is Power Program, 2007. www .kipp.org (accessed September 2007).

Kozol, Jonathan. "Still Separate, Still Unequal: America's Educational Apartheid." *Harper's Magazine* 311, no. 1864 (September 1, 2005).

La Comisión Económica para América Latina (CEPAL). "Panorama Social de America Latina." 2006. http://www.eclac.cl/cgi-bin/getProd.asp?xml=/publicaciones/xml/0/27480/P27480.xml&xsl=/dds/tpl/p9f.xsl&base=/tpl/top-bottom.xsl (accessed September 18, 2007).

Landsburg, Steven E. "The Price of Motherhood: Ready to Have a Baby? You'll Earn 10 Percent More If You Wait a Year." http://www.slate.com/id/2131645/ (accessed February 25, 2008).

Laureau, Annette. *Unequal Childhoods: Class, Race, and Family Life.* Berkeley: University of California Press, 2003

Laureau, Annette, Elliot B. Weininger, Dalton Conley, Melissa J. Velez. "Social Class and Children's Time Use." July 2006, unpublished working paper.

Leinbach, Timothy. "Studying Students Moving into Higher Education . . . to a Community College?!" *Teachers College Record*, August 19, 2005.

Levin, Henry M. "Social Costs of Inadequate Education," Summary of the first annual Teachers College Symposium on Educational Equity, New York, NY, October 24–26, 2005. http://www.tc.columbia.edu/i/a/3082_socialcostsofinadequateEducation.pdf (accessed September 18, 2007).

Lundquist, Susan Clampet, Kathryn Edin, Jeffrey R. Kling, and Greg J. Duncan. "Moving At-Risk Teenagers Out of High Risk Neighborhoods: Why Girls Fare Better Than Boys." Princeton University, March 2006.

Martin, Steven P. "Delayed Marriage and Childbearing: Implications and Measurement of Diverging Trends in Family Timing." Russell Sage Foundation, October 2002. http://www.russellsage.org/programs/main/inequality/050516.122912/ (accessed February 24, 2008).

Matthews, Jay. "Inside the KIPP School Summit." *Washington Post*, August 7. 2007.

mikebloomberg.com. "Mayor Bloomberg Releases Incentives Schedule for Opportunity NYC." http://www.mikebloomberg.com/en/issues/reducing_poverty/mayor_bloomberg_releases_incentives_schedule_for_opportunity_nyc (accessed September 18, 2007).

———. "Mayor Michael Bloomberg and Delegation Visit Mexico's 'Oportunidades' Program." http://www.mikebloomberg.com/en/issues/reducing_poverty/mayor_michael_bloomberg_and_delegation_visit_mexicos_oportunidades_program (accessed September 18, 2007).

Meyer, David, Daniel Princiotta, and Lawrence Lanahan. "Elementary and Secondary Education, The Summer After Kindergarten: Children's Activities and Library Use by Household Socioeconomic Status." *Education Statistics Quarterly*, 6, no. 3 (2005).

Meyers, Marcia, Dan Rosenbaum, Christopher Ruhm, and Jane Waldfogel. "Inequality in Early Childhood Education and Care: What Do We Know?" Russell Sage Foundation, May 2003. http://www.russellsage.org/programs/main/inequality/050516.725723 (accessed November 2007).

Miller, Amalia R. "The Effects of Motherhood Timing on Career Path." Department of Economics, University of Virginia, July 2005. http://www.virginia.edu/economics/papers/miller/fertilitytiming-miller.pdf (accessed January 16, 2008).

Neckerman, Kathryn M., ed. *Social Inequality.* New York: Russell Sage Foundation, 2004.

Nurse-Family Partnership. "Early History and Growth." http://www.nursefamilypartnership.org/content/index.cfm?fuseaction=showContent&contentID=8&navID=8 (accessed September 19, 2007).

NYC Teaching Fellows. "New York City Teaching Fellows." http://www.nycteachingfellows.org (accessed September 2007).

Partnership for 21st Century Skills. "Learning for the 21st Century." http://www.21stcenturyskills.org/images/stories/otherdocs/p21up_Report.pdf (accessed November 1, 2007).

Pebley, Anne R., and Narayan Sastry. "Neighborhoods, Poverty and Children's Well-being: A Review." Russell Sage Foundation, February 2001. http://www.russellsage.org/programs/main/inequality/050516.975023 (accessed February 24, 2008).

Phillips, Meredith, and Tiffani Chin. "School Inequality: What Do We Know?" Russell Sage Foundation, July 2003. http://www.russellsage.org/programs/main/inequality/050516.461131 (accessed November 2007).

Planty, Michael, and Jill Devoe. "An Examination of the Condition of School Facilities Attended by 10th-Grade Students in 2002." U.S. Department of Education, National Center for Education Statistics, October 2005. http://nces.ed.gov/pubsearch/pubsinfo.asp?pubid=2006302 (accessed November 1, 2007).

Rockefeller Foundation. "Opportunity NYC." http://www.rockfound.org/efforts/nycof/opportunity_nyc.shtml (accessed September 18, 2007).

Rosenbaum, James E., Regina Deil-Amen, and Ann E. Person. "After Admission: From College Access to College Success." Russell Sage Foundation, November 2006, chap. 1. http://www.russellsage.org/publications/books/060712.604907/chapter1_pdf, (accessed February 2008).

Rothstein, Richard. *Class and Schools: Using Social, Economic, and Educational Reform to Close the Black–White Achievement Gap.* Washington, DC: Economic Policy Institute, 2004.

Sen, Amartya. "The importance of basic education." Speech to the Commonwealth Education Conference, Edinburgh, October 28, 2003. http://people.cis.ksu.edu/~ab/Miscellany/basiced.html (accessed May 2007).

Soman, Leena, E. Katsiaouni, S. Mistry, V. Kabakchieva, and Z. Sanghani. "Inequality in American Policies and Institutions." School of International and Public Affairs, Columbia University Workshop in Economic and Political Development. Background paper commissioned for *American Human Development Report 2008–2009*.

Soufias, Emmanuel. "The PROGRESA/Oportunidades Program of Mexico and Its Impact Evaluation (I)." World Bank. siteresources.worldbank.org/PGLP/Resources/EmmanuelOportunidades.pdf (accessed September 18, 2007).

Steven, Martins P. "Growing Evidence for a Divorce Divide: Education and Marital Dissolution Rates in the US since the 1970s." Russell Sage Foundation Working Papers: Series on Social Dimensions of Inequality, 2004.

Teach for America. www.teachforamerica.org (accessed September 2007).

Tilly, Chris. "The Good, The Bad, and The Ugly: Good and Bad Jobs in the United States at the Millennium." Russell Sage Foundation, June 1996. http://www.russellsage.org/publications/workingpapers/The%20Good%2C%20the%20Bad%2C%20and%20the%20Ugly/document (accessed February 24, 2008).

TIMSS & PIRLS International Study Center, Lynch School of Education, Boston College. "Trends in International Mathematics and Science Study." http://timss.bc.edu/PDF/t03_download/T03_M_ExecSum.pdf (accessed February 24, 2008).

UNICEF Innocenti Research Center. "Child Poverty in Perspective: An Overview of Child Well-being in Developed Countries." http://www.unicef-irc.org/publications/pdf/rc7_eng.pdf (accessed September 2007).

U.S. Census Bureau. "The Big Payoff: Educational Attainment and Synthetic Estimates of Work-Life Earnings," July 2002. http://www.census.gov/prod/2002pubs/p23-210.pdf (accessed February 2008)

———. "Educational Attainment in the United States," 2006a.

U.S. Department of Education, Education Finance Statistics Center. "Financial Information on Public Elementary/Secondary Education, 2007." http://nces.ed.gov/edfin/ (accessed November 2007).

———. "America's Charter Schools: Results from the 2003 NEAP Pilot Study," 2005. http://nces.ed.gov/nationsreportcard/studies/charter/2005456.asp (accessed September 2007).

U.S. Department of Education, National Center for Education Statistics. "Comparative Indicators of Education in the United States and Other G-8 Countries: 2006," August 2007. http://nces.ed.gov/pubsearch/pubsinfo.asp?pubid=2007006 (accessed September 2008).

———. "The Condition of Education 2006." Indicator 36, http://nces.ed.gov/fastfacts/display.asp?id=6 (accessed September 18, 2007).

———. "The Condition of Education 2007." http://nces.ed.gov/fastfacts/display.asp?id=51 (accessed January 2008).

———. "The Condition of Education: Special Analysis 2007, High School Course-taking." http://nces.ed.gov/programs/coe/2007/analysis/sa_table.asp?tableID=853 (accessed September 2007).

———. "Digest of Education Statistics 2005." June 2006. http://nces.ed.gov/programs/digest/d05/tables/dt05_312.asp?referrer=report (accessed February 2008).

———. "Fast Facts." 2007. http://nces.ed.gov/fastfacts/display.asp?id=372 (accessed November 7, 2007).

———. "Highlights from PISA 2006: Performance of U.S. 15-Year-Old Students in Science and Mathematics Literacy in an International Context," December 2007. http://nces.ed.gov/PUBSEARCH/pubsinfo.asp?pubid=2008016 (accessed November 1, 2007).

———. "Literacy in Everyday Life—Results from the 2003 National Assessment of Adult Literacy." NCES 2007-480, April 2007. http://nces.ed.gov/fastfacts/display.asp?id=6 (accessed September 18, 2007).

———. "Participation in Education," 2007. http://nces.ed.gov/programs/coe/2007/section1/table.asp?tableID=668 (accessed September 18, 2007).

———. "State Comparisons, National Assessment of Educational Progress 2007."

———. "Trends in Undergraduate Persistence and Completion 2007." http://nces.ed.gov/programs/coe/2004/section3/indicator19.asp (accessed January 2008).

Wagner, Mary, Lynn Newman, Renée Cameto, and Phyllis Levine. "National Longitudinal Study 2: Changes over Time in the Early Post-School Outcomes of Youth with Disabilities." Office for Special Education Programs, U.S. Department of Education, 2005. http://www.nlts2.org/reports/2005_06/nlts2_report_2005_06_complete.pdf (accessed September 2007).

Western, Bruce. "Mass Imprisonment and Economic Inequality." *Social Research* 74, no. 2 (Summer 2007).

World Bank. "Mexico's Oportunidades Program." Case Study, Shanghai Poverty Conference, 2003–04. info.worldbank.org/etools/docs/reducingpoverty/case/119/summary/Mexico-Oportunidades%20Summary.pdf (accessed September 18, 2007).

A Decent Standard of Living

Adams, Scott, and David Neumark. "When Do Living Wages Bite?" National Bureau of Economic Research Working Paper Series, Working Paper no. 10561, June 2004. http://www.nber.org/papers/w10561.pdf.

———. "The Economic Effects of Living Wage Laws: A Provisional Review." National Bureau of Economic Research Working Paper Series, Working Paper no. 10562 (June 2004). http://www.nber.org/papers/w10562 (accessed February 9, 2005).

Alesina, A., and R. Perotti. "Income Distribution, Political Instability, and Investment." *European Economic Review* 40 (1996): 1203–28.

Alesina, A., and D. Rodrik. "Distributive Politics and Economic Growth." *Quarterly Journal of Economics* 109 (1994): 465–90.

Benabou, Roland. "Inequality and Growth." *National Bureau of Economic Research Macroeconomics Annual* 11 (1996): 11–74.

Benhabib, J., and A. Rustichini. "Social Conflict, Growth and Income Distribution." *Journal of Economic Growth* 1 (1996): 125–42.

Bertola, G. "Market Structure and Income Distribution in Endogenous Growth Models." *American Economic Review* 83 (1993): 1184–99.

Bernstein, Jared, Chauna Brocht, and Maggie Spade-Aguilar. "How Much Is Enough? Basic Family Budgets for Working Families." Washington, DC: Economic Policy Institute, May 2000. http://www.epinet.org/content.cfm/books_howmuch (accessed February 13, 2005).

Berube, Alan, and Bruce Katz. "Katrina's Window: Confronting Concentrated Poverty Across America." Washington, DC: The Brookings Institution, 2005.

Blinder, Alan. "How Many U.S. Jobs Might Be Offshorable?" CEPS Working Paper #142, March 2007.

Blumstein, Alfred. "The Roots of Punitiveness in a Democracy." *Journal of Scandinavian Studies in Criminology and Crime Prevention* 8 (2007): 2.

———, and Allen Beck, 1999. "Population Growth in U.S. Prisons, 1980–1996," in M. Tonry and J. Petersilia, eds., 17–61, *Prisons: Crime and Justice—A Review of Research*, Vol. 26. University of Chicago Press.

Bonczar, Thomas P. *Bureau of Justice Statistics, Special Report: Prevalence of Imprisonment in the U.S. Population, 1974–2001.* U.S. Department of Justice, Bureau of Justice Statistics. 2003. http://faculty.wvwc.edu/mei-tal/Prevalence%20of%20Imprisonment.pdf (accessed November 20, 2007).

Bouman, John, Marcia Henry, and Wendy Pollack. "Health Care for All, Make Work Pay and Redemptive Opportunities for People with Criminal Records." Sargent Shriver National Center on Poverty Law. Background paper commissioned for *American Human Development Report 2008–2009*.

Boushey, Heather, Chauna Brocht, Bethney Gundersen, and Jared Bernstein. "Hardships in America: The Real Story of Working Families." Economic Policy Institute, 2001. http://www.epinet.org/books/hardships.pdf (accessed December 3, 2007).

Bucks, Brian K., A. B. Kennickell, and K. B. Moore. "Recent Changes in U.S. Family Finances: Evidence from the 2001 and 2004 Survey of Consumer Finances." *Federal Reserve Bulletin* 92 (February 2006): A1–A38. U.S. Census Bureau.

Budig, Michelle, and Paula England. "The Wage Penalty for Motherhood." *American Sociological Review* 66 (2001): 204–25.

Burtless, Gary. "Growing American Inequality: Sources and Remedies." Brookings Institution, 1999. http://www.brookings.edu/articles/1999/winter_useconomics_burtless.aspx (accessed January 7, 2008).

Child Trust Fund. "Key Facts about the Child Trust Fund." http://www.childtrustfund.gov.uk/templates/Page____1177.aspx (accessed February 25, 2008).

Crittendon, Ann. *The Price of Motherhood: Why the Most Important Job in the World Is Still the Least Valued.* New York: Macmillan, 2002.

Cutler, David M., Lawrence F. Katz, David Card, and Robert E. Hall. "Macroeconomic Performance and the Disadvantaged." *Brookings Papers on Economic Activity* 1991, no. 2, 1–74.

Economic Policy Institute [EPI] Web site. "Living Wage: Facts at a Glance, 2002." http://www.epinet.org (accessed February 9, 2005).

———. "Living Wage Frequently Asked Questions." http://www.epinet.org (accessed January 22, 2005).

Employment Policies Institute. "Living Wage Movement FAQs." http://www.epionline.org/lw_faq_who.cfm (accessed February 11, 2005).

England, Paula, and Nancy Folbre. "Who Should Pay for the Kids?" *Annals of the American Academy of Political and Social Sciences* 563 (1999): 194–209.

Galor, O., and I. Zeira. "Income Distribution and Macroeconomics." *Review of Economic Studies* 60, no. 1 (1993): 35–52.

Greenstein, R. "The Earned Income Tax Credit: Boosting Employment, Aiding the Working Poor." Center on Budget and Policy Priorities, August 17, 2005. http://www.cbpp.org/7-19-05eic.htm (accessed December 12, 2007).

Harrison, Paige M., and Allen J. Beck. "Bureau of Justice Statistics Bulletin, Prisoners in 2005." NCJ 2006 215092. www.ojp.usdoj.gov/bjs/pub/pdf/p05.pdf; International Centre for Prison Studies, www.prisonstudies.org.

Health and Human Services. The 2005 HHS Poverty Guidelines: One Version of the US Federal Poverty Measure. http://aspe.hhs.gov/poverty/05poverty.shtml.

John J. Heldrich Center for Workforce Development. "Making Career Connections: How to Prepare Students for Professional Success," 2007. http://www.heldrich.rutgers.edu/uploadedFiles/Publications/Stoller_NJEA.pdf (accessed January 7, 2008).

Kammerman, Sheila B. "Parental Leave Policies: An Essential Ingredient in Early Childhood Education and Care Policies." *Social Policy Report* 14, no. 2 (2000).

Krueger, Alan. 2002. "Economic Scene: Sticks and Stones Can Break Bones, but the Wrong Name Can Make a Job Hard to Find." *New York Times*, December 12, 2002.

Landsburg, Steven E. "Ready to Have a Baby? You'll Earn 10 Percent More If You Wait a Year." slate.com, December 9, 2005. http://www.slate.com/id/2131645/.

Loke, V., and M. Sherraden. "Building Assets from Birth: A Comparison of the Policies and Proposals on Children Savings Accounts in Singapore, the United Kingdom, Canada, Korea and the United States." St. Louis: Center for Social Development, Working paper #06-14. http://gbweb.wustl.edu/csd/Publications/2006/WP06-14.pdf.

Lowe, Jeffrey S., T. C. Shaw, and C. Woods. "Developing a Reconstruction Plan for the Gulf Cost Region." Background paper commissioned for *American Human Development Report 2008–2009*.

Luce, Stephanie, and Robert Pollin. "Can U.S. Cities Afford Living Wage Programs? An Examination of Alternatives." *Review of Radical Political Economics* 31, no. 1 (1999): 16–53.

Mahoney, Melissa. "Retirement Security System in the United States." Background paper commissioned for *American Human Development Report 2008–2009*.

Mayer, Susan E.. "How Did the Increase in Economic Inequality between 1970 and 1990 Affect Children's Educational Attainment?." *American Journal of Sociology* 107 (2001): 1–32.

——. "How Economic Segregation Affects Children's Educational Attainment." *Social Forces* 81 (2002): 153–76.

McCrate, Elaine. "Working Mothers in a Double Bind: Working Moms, Minorities Have the Most Rigid Schedules, and Are Paid Less for the Sacrifice." Economic Policy Institute (EPI) Briefing Paper no. 124, May 2002.

Mills, G., R. Patterson, L. Orr, and D. DeMarco. "Evaluation of the American Dream Demonstration: Final Evaluation Report." Cambridge, MA: Abt Associates Inc., 2004 http://gwbweb.wustl.edu/csd/Publications/2004/ADDFinalReport.pdf.

Mishel, Lawrence, Jared Bernstein, and Sylvia Allegretto. "The State of Working America, 2006–2007." Economic Policy Institute and Cornell University Press, 2006.

Mohn, S. L. "Building Employees' Nest Eggs: A Great Return on Investment." *Chicago Business*, September 3, 2007.

Mutari, Ellen, and Deborah Figart. *Living Wage Movements: Global Perspective*. Advances in Social Economics. London: Routledge, 2004.

Pearce, Diana, and Jennifer Brooks. "The Real Cost of Living in 2002: The Self-Sufficiency Standard for New Jersey." *Legal Services of New Jersey Poverty Research Institute* 1 (2002): 1–50.

Pew Charitable Trusts. "Public Safety, Public Spending: Forecasting America's Prison Population 2007–2011." Citing Bureau of Justice Statistics, Key Facts at a Glance. www.ojp.usdoj.gov/bjs/glance/tables/exptyptab.htm.

Pollin, Robert. "What Is a Living Wage? Considerations from Santa Monica." *Review of Radical Political Economics* 34 (2002): 267–73.

——, Mark Brenner, and Stephanie Luce. "Intended vs. Unintended Consequences: Evaluating the New Orleans Living Wage Proposal." *Journal of Economic Issues* 36 (2002): 843–75.

Puri, Jyotsna. "Measuring Poverty in the US: The Economics of Deprivation, Need and Exclusion." Background paper commissioned for *American Human Development Report 2008–2009*.

Schmacher, Rachel, Danielle Ewen, Katherine Hart, and Joan Lombardi. "All Together Now: State Experienced in Using Community-Based Child Care to Provide Pre-Kindergarten." Center for Law and Social Policy. http://www.clasp.org/publications/all_together_now.pdf (accessed February 1, 2008).

Schulman, Karen, and Helen Blank. "Child Care Assistance Policies 2001–2004: Families Struggling to Move Forward, States Going Backward." National Women's Law Center. www.nwlc.org/pdf/childcaresubsidyfinalreport.pdf (accessed February 1, 2008).

Sodha, S. "Lessons from across the Atlantic: Asset-Building in the UK." Paper presented at the 2006 Assets Learning Conference, Phoenix, AZ, September 19-21, 2006. www.frbsf.org/community/research/assets/LessonsfromAcrosstheAtlantic.pdf.

Stanton, Elizabeth. "The Human Development Index: A History." *Political Economy Research Institute* (2007): 1. *Working Paper #127. University of Massachusetts, Amherst.*

——. "United States Specific Human Development Index.". Background paper commissioned for *American Human Development Report 2008–2009*.

U.S. Census Bureau, Current Population Reports. "Income, Poverty, and Health Insurance Coverage in the United States." http://www.census.gov/prod/2007pubs/p60-233.pdf (accessed August 28th, 2007).

——. Current Population Survey. "Annual Social and Economic Supplements, Mean Income Received by Each Fifth and Top 5 Percent of Families, All Races: 1966 to 2005." http://www.census.gov/hhes/www/income/histinc/f03ar.html (accessed February 26, 2008).

——. "Share of Aggregate Income Received by Each Fifth and Top 5 Percent of Families, All Races: 1947 to 2005." Annual Social and Economic Supplements. http://www.census.gov/hhes/www/income/histinc/f02ar.html (accessed December 15, 2007).

U.S. Department of Health and Human Services. "About the Assets for Independence Act." Washington, DC, 2008. http://www.acf.hhs.gov/programs/ocs/afi/assets.html.

Van Horn, Carl E., and Herbert A. Schaffner. *Work in America: An Encyclopedia of History, Policy and Society*. Vols. 1 and 2. Denver: ABC-CLIO, 2003.

Walmsley, Roy. "World Prison Population List (seventh edition), 2007." http://www.prisonstudies.org/ (accessed June 15, 2007).

Wheary, Jennifer, T. M. Shapiro, and T. Draut. "By a Thread: The New Experience of America's Middle Class." http://www.demos.org/pubs/BaT112807.pdf (accessed February 25, 2008).

Widener, Anmarie J. "Family-Friendly Policy: Lessons from Europe—Part II." *Public Manager* 36, no. 4 (Winter 2007/2008) 44.

Wolff, Edward. "Changes in Household Wealth in the 1980s and 1990s in the U.S." Levy Institute Working Paper No. 407, 2004.

——. "Recent Trends in Household Wealth in the United States: Rising Debt and the Middle-Class Squeeze," The Levy Economics Institute of Bard College. Working Paper No. 502, 2007.

Woo, Lillian, and David Bucholz. "Subsidies for Assets: A New Look at the Federal Budget." Report prepared for the Federal Reserve System, 2006. http://www.cfed.org/focus.m?parentid=31&siteid=2434&id=2434.

Zabin, Carol, Arindrajit Dube, and Ken Jacobs. "The Hidden Public Costs of Low-Wage Jobs in California." University of California Institute for Labor and Employment. The State of California Labor. 2004, no. 1 (2004): 3–44. http://repositories.cdlib.org/ile/scl2004/01 (accessed January 12, 2008).

PART 4
8-Point Human Development Agenda

Bevan, S., S. Dench, P. Tamkin, and J. Cummings. "Family-Friendly Employment: The Business Case." Department for Education and Employment (U.K.) Research Report 136, October 1999. http://www.employment-studies.co.uk/summary/summary.php?id=fambus (accessed February 25, 2008).

Boston College, Sloan Work and Family Research Network. "Conversations with the Experts: The California Paid Leave Program." http://wfnetwork.bc.edu/The_Network_News/17/The_Network_News_Interview17.pdf (accessed February 25, 2008).

Cohany, Sharon R., and Emy Sok. "Trends in Labor Force Participation of Married Mothers of Infants." *Monthly Labor Review* (February 2007). http://www.bls.gov/opub/mlr/2007/02/art2full.pdf (accessed February 4, 2008).

Greene, Jay P., and Marcus A. Winters. "Leaving Boys Behind: Public High School Graduation Rates." Civic Report No. 48 (April 2006). http://www.manhattan-institute.org/html/cr_48.htm (accessed February 25, 2008).

Heckman, James J. "Catch 'em Young." *Wall Street Journal*, January 10, 2006. http://online.wsj.com/article/SB113686119611542381.html (accessed February 2008).

Misra, Sahana, and Linda Ganzini. "Medical Care for Patients with Severe and Persistent Mental Illness." *Journal of General Internal Medicine* 21, no. 11 (November 2006): 1207–8.

Pandya, Sheel. "Caregiving in the United States." AARP Public Policy Institute Research Paper, April 2005. http://www.aarp.org/research/housingmobility/caregiving/fs111_caregiving.html (accessed February 22, 2008).

pbs.org. *Secret History of the Credit Card*. http://www.pbs.org/wgbh/pages/frontline/shows/credit/view/ (accessed February 25, 2008).

U.S. Census Bureau. "Wealth and Asset Ownership: Asset Ownership of Households, 2000, Table 1. Median Value of Assets for Households, by Type of Asset Owned and Selected Characteristics: 2000." http://www.census.gov/hhes/www/wealth/1998_2000/wlth00-1.html (accessed February 25, 2008).

U.S. Department of Education, Institute of Education Sciences, National Center for Education Statistics. "Student Effort and Educational Progress: Transition to College." http://nces.ed.gov/programs/coe/2007/section3/indicator25.asp (accessed February 25, 2008).

U.S. Department of Education, National Center for Education Statistics. "Fast Facts." 2007. http://nces.ed.gov/fastfacts/display.asp?id=372 (accessed November 7, 2007).

Widener, Anmarie J. "Family-Friendly Policy: Lessons from Europe—Part II." *Public Manager* 36, no. 4 (Winter 2007/2008): 44.

Methodological Notes

Chiang, C. L. *The Life Table and Its Applications*. Malabar, FL: Krieger, 1984.

Fitzpatrick, Justine. *Calculating Life Expectancy and Infant Mortality Rates*. Mapping Health Inequalities across London: Technical Supplement. London: London Health Observatory, 2001.

Manship, Karen. "The American Human Development Index Research Summary: Nonfinancial Returns to Education." Background paper commissioned for *American Human Development Report 2008–2009*.

National Center for Health Statistics. *Bridged-Race Population Estimates, United States*. July 1st Resident Population by State, County, Age, Sex, Bridged-race, and Hispanic Origin, 2006. On CDC WONDER Online Database, Vintage 2005.

——. *Multiple Cause of Death Files for 2005 with All Counties Coded by NCHS Identified*, 2008 (received by agreement with the NCHS).

Toson, Barbara, and Alan Baker. *Life Expectancy at Birth: Methodological Options for Small Populations*. National Statistics Methodological Series No. 33. London: Office for National Statistics, 2003.

Index to Indicators

Maps At-A-Glance

AMERICAN HUMAN DEVELOPMENT INDEX 2005
by STATE

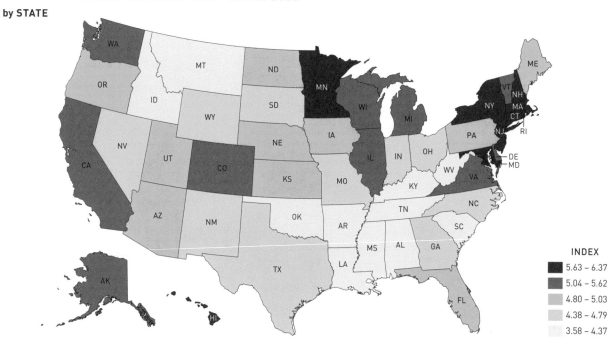

INDEX

- 5.63 – 6.37
- 5.04 – 5.62
- 4.80 – 5.03
- 4.38 – 4.79
- 3.58 – 4.37

HEALTH INDEX 2005: Life Expectancy at Birth
by STATE

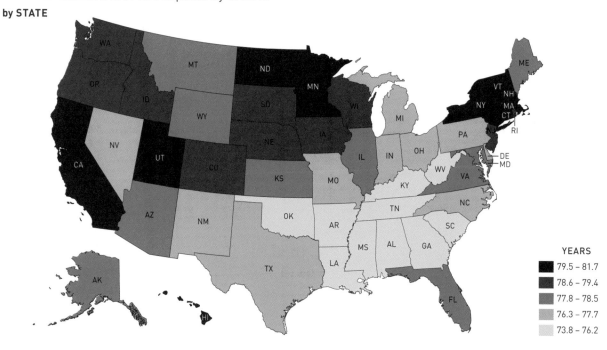

YEARS

- 79.5 – 81.7
- 78.6 – 79.4
- 77.8 – 78.5
- 76.3 – 77.7
- 73.8 – 76.2

EDUCATION INDEX 2005: Educational Attainment and School Enrollment
by STATE

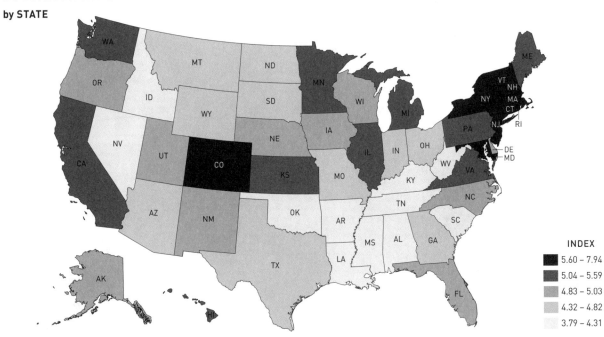

INDEX

- 5.60 – 7.94
- 5.04 – 5.59
- 4.83 – 5.03
- 4.32 – 4.82
- 3.79 – 4.31

INCOME INDEX 2005: Median Earnings for the Population 16 and Older
by STATE

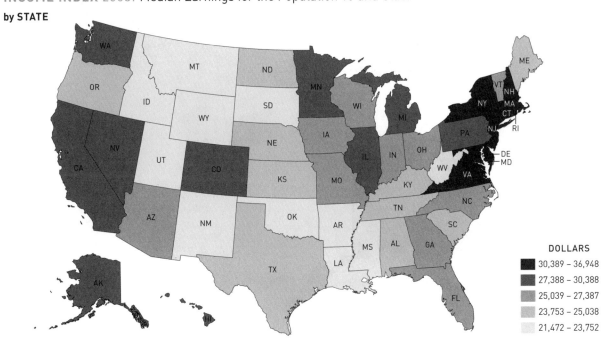

DOLLARS

- 30,389 – 36,948
- 27,388 – 30,388
- 25,039 – 27,387
- 23,753 – 25,038
- 21,472 – 23,752

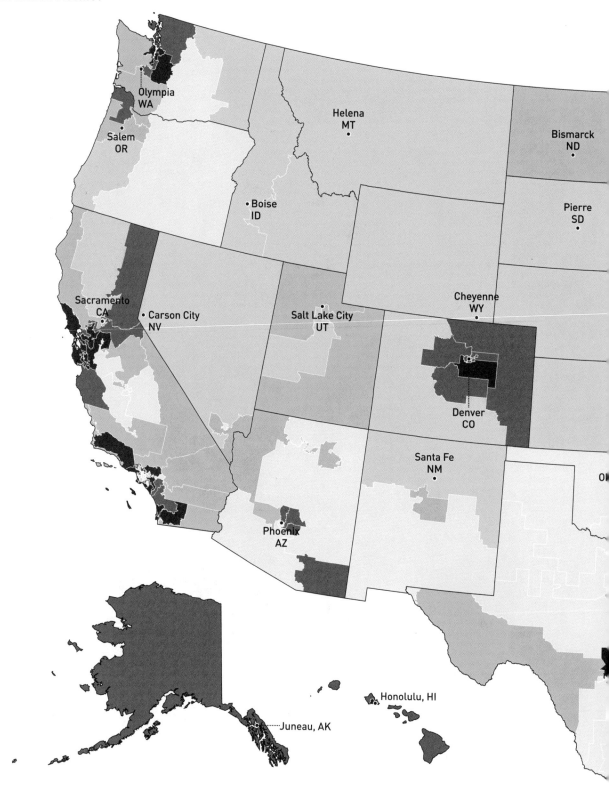

Olympia
WA

Salem
OR

Helena
MT

Bismarck
ND

Boise
ID

Pierre
SD

Sacramento
CA

Carson City
NV

Salt Lake City
UT

Cheyenne
WY

Santa Fe
NM

Denver
CO

Phoenix
AZ

Honolulu, HI

Juneau, AK

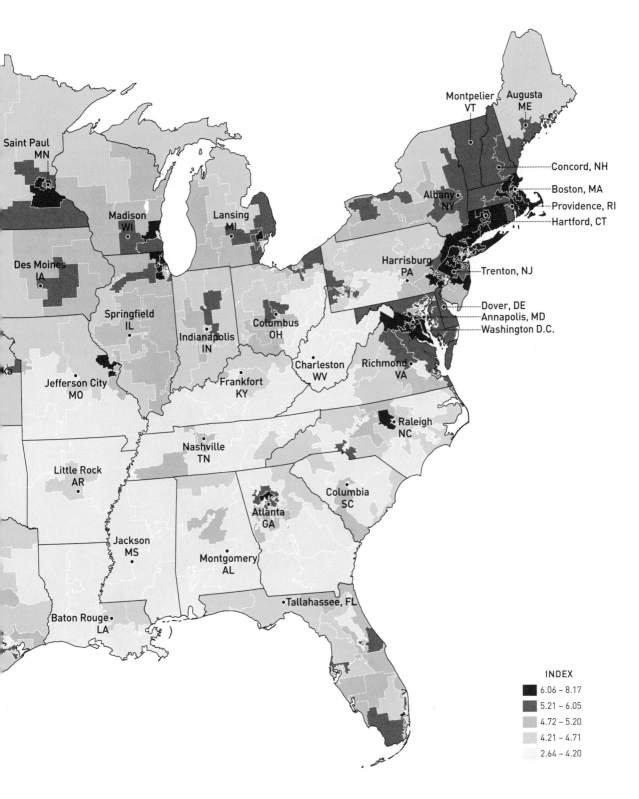

INDEX

■	6.06 – 8.17
■	5.21 – 6.05
■	4.72 – 5.20
■	4.21 – 4.71
■	2.64 – 4.20

THE MEASURE OF AMERICA

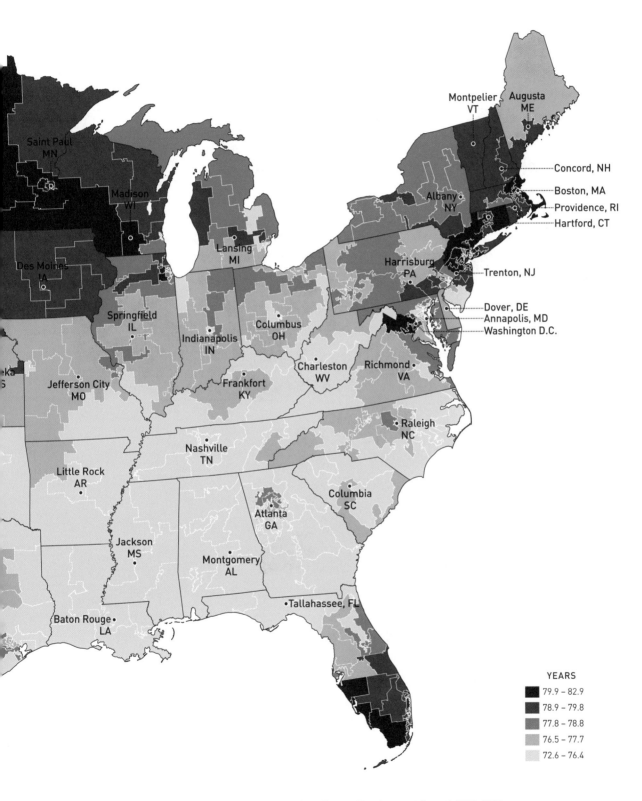

Montpelier
VT

Augusta
ME

Concord, NH

Boston, MA

Providence, RI

Hartford, CT

Albany
NY

Saint Paul
MN

Madison
WI

Lansing
MI

Harrisburg
PA

Trenton, NJ

Dover, DE

Annapolis, MD

Washington D.C.

Des Moines
IA

Springfield
IL

Indianapolis
IN

Columbus
OH

Charleston
WV

Richmond
VA

Jefferson City
MO

Frankfort
KY

Raleigh
NC

Nashville
TN

Little Rock
AR

Columbia
SC

Atlanta
GA

Jackson
MS

Montgomery
AL

Tallahassee, FL

Baton Rouge
LA

YEARS

■	79.9 – 82.9
■	78.9 – 79.8
■	77.8 – 78.8
■	76.5 – 77.7
■	72.6 – 76.4

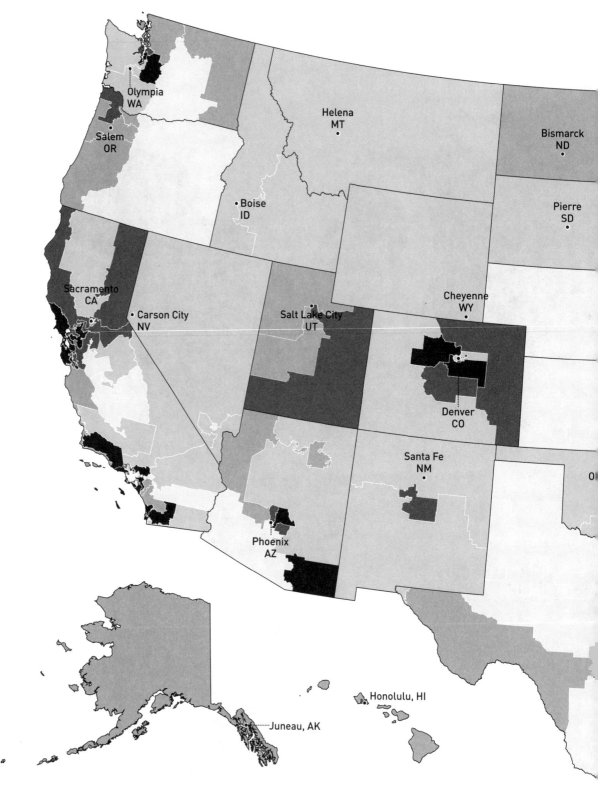

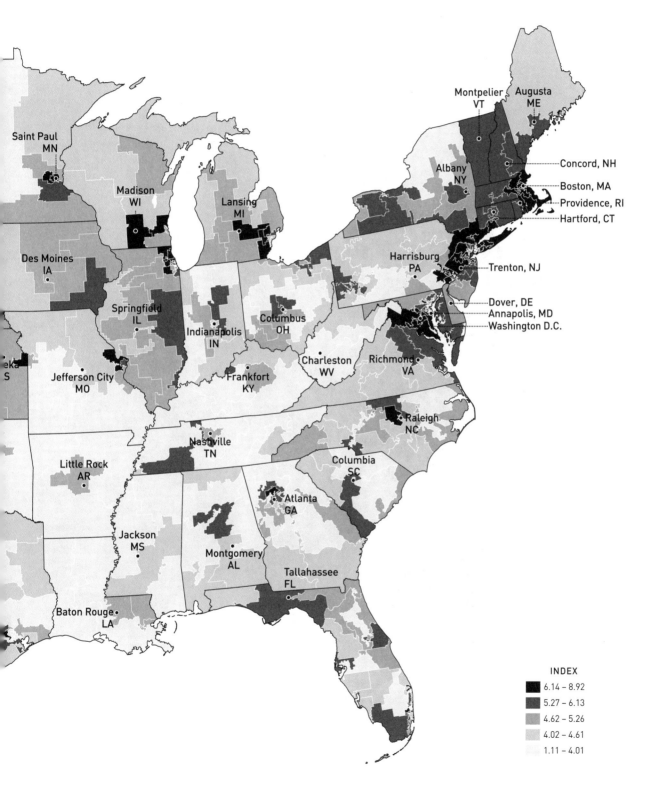

INDEX

■	6.14 – 8.92
■	5.27 – 6.13
■	4.62 – 5.26
■	4.02 – 4.61
□	1.11 – 4.01

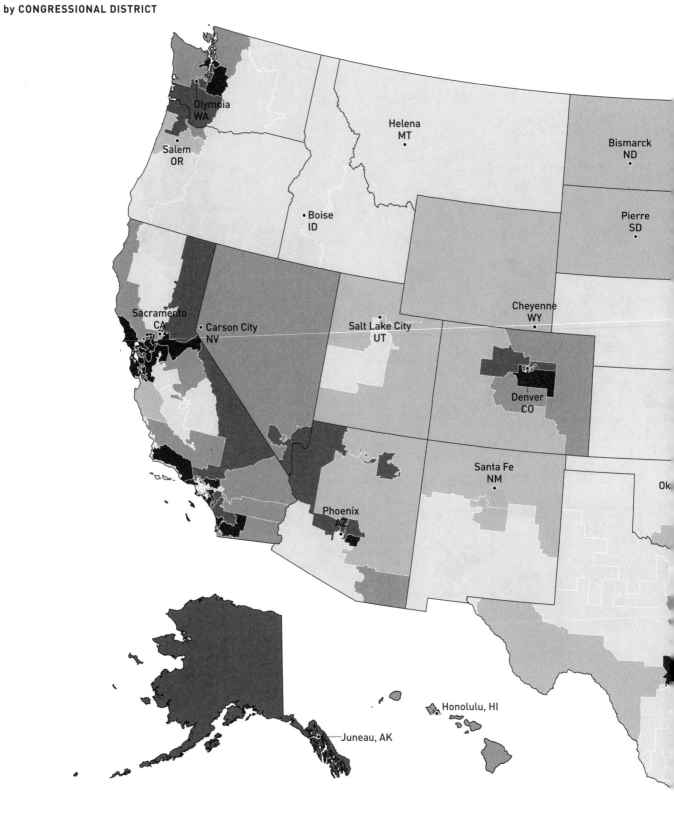

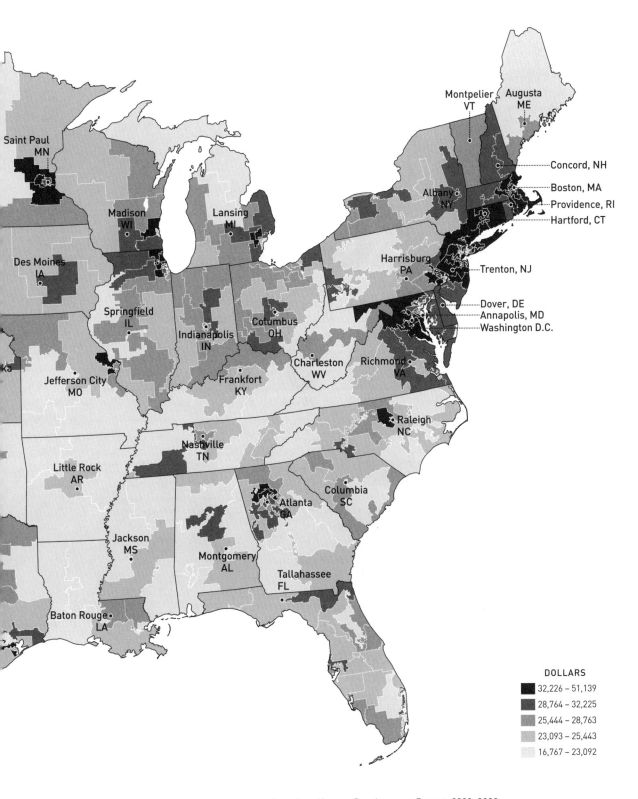

Montpelier
VT

Augusta
ME

Saint Paul
MN

----Concord, NH

Albany
NY

----Boston, MA
----Providence, RI
----Hartford, CT

Madison
WI

Lansing
MI

Des Moines
IA

Harrisburg
PA

----Trenton, NJ

Springfield
IL

Columbus
OH

----Dover, DE
----Annapolis, MD
----Washington D.C.

Indianapolis
IN

Charleston
WV

Richmond
VA

Jefferson City
MO

Frankfort
KY

Raleigh
NC

Nashville
TN

Little Rock
AR

Columbia
SC

Atlanta
GA

Jackson
MS

Montgomery
AL

Tallahassee
FL

Baton Rouge
LA

DOLLARS

■	32,226 – 51,139
■	28,764 – 32,225
■	25,444 – 28,763
■	23,093 – 25,443
■	16,767 – 23,092

WHO ARE WE?

KEY FACTS ABOUT THE U.S. POPULATION

Two hundred ninety-nine million, three hundred ninety-eight thousand, four hundred eighty-five **people**

The **U.S. population** in 2006 was
299,398,485

80.3 people
PER SQUARE MILE

GENDER

51% **Female** 49% **Male**

URBAN | RURAL

79% **Urban** 21% **Rural**

BIRTHPLACE

87% **Native born** 13% **Foreign born**

HOME OWNERSHIP

67% **Own** 33% **Rent**

AGE

27% 0-19
35% 20-44
25% 45-64
11% 65-85
2% 85+

RACE / ETHNICITY

White 66.2%

Latino 14.8%

African American 12.2%

Asian 4.3%

2+ Races 1.5%

Native American & Alaska Native 0.7%

Other 0.4%

RELIGION

Protestant 53%

Catholic 25%

No Preference 9%

Other 8%

Jewish 2%

Mormon 2%

Orthodox 1%

EMPLOYMENT

Education, Health Care, Social Assistance 21%

Manufacturing, Construction 20%

Trade 15%

Other 11%

Services (professional, scientific, administrative) 10%

Entertainment, Arts, Recreation, Accomodation 9%

Finance, Insurance, Real Estate 7%

Public Administration 5%

Agriculture, Forestry, Fishing, Hunting, Mining 2%

All data are from 2006, except religious preference data from 2001 and urban/rural data from Census 2000. Percentages may exceed 100 due to rounding.
Sources: Census Bureau, "Fact Sheet, 2006 American Community Survey Data Profile Highlights;" Census Bureau, "Census 2000 Summary File 1, Matrix P1;" Census Bureau, "American Religious Identification Survey."